Riverside

Volume One

**From Turkey Farm to Race Track to Shopping Mall
In Thirty Hot, Cold and Dusty Years**

Bob Schilling said:

"The track had been owned by a playboy, some car dealers, an oil man, a schemer and dreamer and finally, a real estate developer. We knew how it would turn out".

**Compiled By Dave Wolin
With An Introduction by Doug Stokes**

**Printed in the U.S.A.
Racing History Project
Box 5578
Bakersfield CA 93388
www.racinghistoryproject.com**

Table of Contents

A Brief Note About How To Use This Book

In order to not have a 1000 page book, we split this into two volumes and cropped many the newspaper and magazine articles. You can read the full text of the articles and clippings shown in this book plus many others on the attached DVD. All the photos and videos are on the DVD also.

About the Compiler: Long time racer, performance and racing industry marketer and promoter Dave Wolin has a unique background which assisted in writing this book. As he says, "like Forrest Gump, I was fortunate to be in a lot of the right places at the right time." Today he operates the non profit Racing History Project (www.racinghistoryproject.com), writes a few books and magazine articles, does some racing and driver coaching and builds a new hot rod every couple of years. He says; *"Thanks to my wife, Jane, for tolerating all the time I've put into this and the invaluable help from all those who have written about Riverside, taken photos, raced and worked on cars of the era."*

Dave (with help from many others) put on a number of racing history events from the "Legends of Riverside" to the "Tribute to the USRRC" and "Riverside Revisited". Each of these events generated a lot of e-mail questions and facebook posts; i.e "Who is that Scooter Patrick guy ?", "Who is Skip Hudson", "Who built Riverside" and so on, ad infiniteum.

  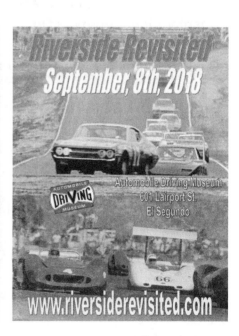

So we decided to answer those questions and more. There has been a lot of misinformation and outright fallacies about Riverside Raceway; its beginning and end. So, with help from all our friends and acquaintances, Dave Wolin became the compiler (a more accurate term than author for a guy who collected photos, magazine articles, clippings and quotes). In this book you get a partial history of everything that happened at Riverside, some interesting stories not previously heard, possibly some facts you readers didn't know and some never before seen photos. All should interest anyone who wondered how Riverside Raceway got started and what happened to it. This ended up at 1000 pages; through some sophisticated culling it's now almost 500; sorry if you were "left on the cutting room floor".

Dave Wolin: *"I'm calling myself the compiler as someone has to take the blame, Our other colleagues who helped wished to remain anonymous, (we don't blame them) since this is really a compilation - so all facts, alternative facts, opinions and remembrances are the responsibility of whoever gave them to us. Please don't complain if you disagree with the opinions or statements herein."*

To quote Mark Twain, "Persons attempting to find a motive in this narrative will be prosecuted; persons attempting to find a moral in it will be banished; persons attempting to find a plot in it will be shot."

Introduction By Doug Stokes

Riverside, for me, even after all these years, still figures in many of my conversations about classic racetracks and long gone venues that I really miss. Honestly I should be over it by now even if I was one of the last people to lap that joint and one of the first (civilians anyway) to see the incredible sweep and scope of the place. Thirty three years after its demise, every top professional that I've talked to who had raced there confirms the oft-stated axiom that: if you could go fast at RIR, you could go fast just about anywhere.

I crewed there far more often than I ever raced there, but I did "win" a race there once ... it was really a dead heat between myself and Pete Lyons driving Jim Russell School Van Diemens in a Media / Celebrity Event, but Pete pointed at me when we stopped on the pit apron and they gave me the flag to drive around with.

It's a pretty fair chance here that readers already know that Riverside was one the universally acknowledged great American road racing courses, fully ranking alongside Road America, Watkins Glen, and Sebring. And, as you'll read here, it was home to a wonderfully wide range of racing events from Karts to Formula One Cars to 1,000 horsepower Can Am bolides and sleek Formula 5000 open-wheelers. Bellowing NASCAR stockers roared there too, as did the straight line racers of the NHRA (with half-mile long drag races being run South to North on the long back straight. Then there was off road, motorcycles and topping it off; the best of the best drivers in the world all raced identical cars in the fabled IROC Series at Riverside to see who was best. The course had it all: a mile long straight, a snaking set of turns ("the esses") that led into the tough and unforgiving, dirt embankment-walled 180 degree Turn Six where spectators were drawn en masse, a blind-uphill entrance into Turn Seven, and easy looking Turn One just past the pits that could (with proper breath control) be taken flat out. Riverside could be blistering hot or bone-numbingly cold (and sometimes on the same race weekend!) but it was a real race track and that was all that really mattered.

There were a lot of people who had a great time at Riverside, I was one of them. As I hope you'll understand after reading Dave's saga of the place, a bit of the excitement that was such a part of this track. Riverside was one damn special joint. Compiler's Note - Stokes has been the Director of the International Kart Federation, the PR guy for Mickey Thompson, Gale Banks, Perris and Irwindale and is a Chapman Award Winner and recipient of the Motor Press Guild's Lifetime Achievement Award.

From 1957 to 1989, Riverside was the home of racing in Southern California. World class sportscars, stock cars, Indy cars, motorcycles, go karts, drag racing, off road and numerous advertising photo shoots, movies and commercials, vehicle testing, driver training; it all happened here.

This book is based on the stories told at the "Legends of Riverside", a series of events held at the now defunct Riverside International Automotive Museum. Many of the photos, provided by the late Doug Magnon, come from the background slide shows at the "Legends of Riverside events. Over 5000 more came from those who responded to my Facebook requests for information. So, sorry, no attribution is possible but we appreciate your contribution. My guess - many of the photos came from Will Edgar, Pete Lyons, Frank Sheffield, Tam McPartland, Dave Friedman, Getty Images, Bob D'Olivo, Brent Martin, Martin Hill, Pat Brollier, Bob Tronolone, Woodland Auto Display, Albert Wong, Henry Ford Museum, IMMRC, Michael Keyser and Don Hodgdon among others, so thanks.

Starting out as a story of the competitors in the first pro race at Riverside, the 1958 Times Grand Prix, celebrated at the first "Legends of Riverside" event, this book has evolved into a mini history of Riverside. As we said, rather than produce a 1000 page book, we will be producing it in two volumes, a much more manageable size, accompanied by a DVD with, photos, magazine and newspaper articles, programs, posters, films and videos along with a selection of photos from Allan Kuhn and Kurt Oblinger. In this first volume, we cover the beginnings of the track, early pro sportscar racing, the U.S. Road Racing Championship and the Can Am, both the "real" Can Am and the later single seat series, IMSA, Open wheel cars from midgets to go karts to Formula 5000 and Indy car, some other non racing events no one had heard of previously, some stories of crooks and criminals and photos from the "Legends of Riverside" events.

While we are relating some of Riverside history, this is by no means more than an incomplete account. For historical purposes we recommend the existing well written books such as Pete Lyon's Riverside International Raceway and Dick Wallen's Palace of Speed

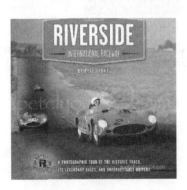 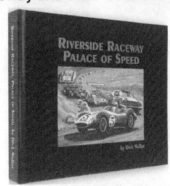

What's on the DVD ?

Never Before Seen Interviews

Dan Gurney, Phil Hill, Carroll Shelby, Dick Guldstrand, Sam Hanks, Warren Olsen, Bill Pollack, Bruce Kessler, Davey Jordan, John Morton, Joe Playan. Bill Watkins, Jack McAfee, Bill Murphy, Ruth Levy and Cy Yedor.

Racing Videos

1957 Sports Car Races, 1960 Lap of Riverside, 1962 Grand Prix for Sportscars, 1963 Times Grand Prix, 1964 Champion Spark Plug Commercial, 1964 Times Grand Prix,1965 Can Am, 1966 - on Compilation, 1968 Rex Mays 300, 1971 David Hobbs Can Am, 1983 Cart Budweiser 500, 1984 - 85 - 86 IMSA Times Grand Prix and 1988 Riverside History.

Racing Films
Bruce Kessler's "Sound of Speed" - James Garner's "The Racing Scene"

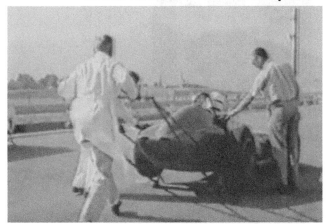 

Plus All the Magazine Articles, Newspaper Clippings, Photos and More

Note: If your book did not come with a DVD, please contact us. It's free with print book purchase, $12.95 for Kindle users. Order it at www.racinghistoryproject.com/amazon.htm

Chapter One - How It All Began

In 2008, Dave Wolin, with some past expertise in putting on racing history events, conspired with Doug Magnon, owner of the Riverside Raceway Museum, to develop some events about Riverside history. They put together a team, among them Davey and Norma Jordan, Doug Stokes, Dusty Brandel and a few others. The first meeting, at a now extinct Marie Callenders in Newhall, produced a few optional plans. Following meetings, at George Petersen's restaurant (Giovanni's - now sold) in West Covina (the racing connection, his wife is Chuck Parson's daughter) determined the format of events, potential guests and so on.

The first event, unparalleled in the collection of racing personalities in attendance, provided a benchmark, hard to follow. Fully half the field of the 1958 Times Grand Prix and numerous others, in some cases unseen for years, turned up to discuss their role in Riverside racing history. Following is some information, the balance of photos in Chapter Fifteen. Nick Hunzicker designed a poster, signed by all the luminaries

Check on the Racing History Project website - there may still be a few posters left
www.racinghistoryproject.com

Riverside had some racing history in the past. In 1905, a 3.8 mile hillclimb, using the then dirt Box Springs Grade Road, now the intersection of I-215 and U.S. 60, was held on Thanksgiving Day, attracted ten entries and was won by L.A. car dealer George Bradbeerin a Premier. In 1906, the event expanded to a number of different classes with 67 entries and despite rain and freezing weather, local driver Tommy Pillow won in a Stevens Duryea. In 1907, the winner was a Stoddard Dayton with a reported illegal carburetor. In 1908 a Stanley Steamer set fastest time on a new shortened course, the last time the event was held. The Stanley Steamer was described as sounding like a barking terrier and left a white trail of steam in its wake. Later March Field, adjacent to riverside, held sports car races in the 50's.

MOTOR MEN GET BUSY FOR BIG HILL CLIMB.

FROM now on until the day officially set for the gathering of the automobile clans on our own Eagle Rock road, or the Riverside Box Springs grade—or perchance the Elysian Park testing ground for all local demonstrators—not much will be doing in the motoring field but hill climb.

Plans for the biggest event the local dealers have ever put through, are being formulated. The character of the contest is such that each agent will conclude he has a show in some class or other, and there is every prospect that the event will be anything but an empty honor for the car that wins it. Motor men sometimes contend that victories in these endurance runs, hill

left Syracuse, N. Y., yesterday consigned to Ralph C. Hamlin, the agent in this city. The model B will be viewed with considerable interest by the motoring public, as it is already a much-talked-about machine.

The 1906 Packard arrived last Monday, and Bert Dingley, the Western Motor Car Company's demonstrator, has been kept busy running it over the hills ever since.

The wagon is rated at twenty-four-horse-power, and performs equal to some makes that are listed at forty. It is one of the handsomest machines ever shown here; is splendidly finished and embodies a number of radical departures from past practice that seem likely to establish themselves with the mo-

STEVENS-DURYEA WINS RIVERSIDE HILL CLIMB.

Establishes New Record for Box Springs Grade—Tourist Car Takes the Free-for-All Runabout Event. Course in Perfect Condition.

RIVERSIDE had a successful series of hill-climbing races yesterday in spite of the weather. Wednesday the weather moderated at the Orange City and all things betokened a grand day for Thanksgiving and automobile racing. When the last motor-car enthusiast retired

and finished third in the $2500 class against the four-cylinder cars, beating the Rambler forty-horse-power, the thirty-five-horse-power Elmore and the thirty-horse-power Mitchell. He also came through the free-for-all runabout battle with considerable glory. Lynch drove like a veteran and attracted general attention by his con-

tevens-Duryea car which won hill-climbing contest on Box Spring grade at Riverside yesterday—Tom Pillow, drive

The most dangerous curve in the road

SECOND ANNUAL ORANGE EMPIRE
NATIONAL SPORTS CAR RACES
50¢

SOUVENIR PROGRAM
NOVEMBER 7, 1954

12266

30

MARCH AIR FORCE BASE, CALIFORNIA

March Field

Here are some of the poster signing photos

Bruce Kessler, Tommy Meehan, Ralph Ormsbee, Dave Friedman and Bill Pollack

Scooter Patrick, Doug Hooper, Jerry Grant, Eric Haga and Davey Jordan
And a brief view of some of the racing legends In attendance - More can be seen in the Legends of Riverside - Chapter Fifteen.

Phil Henny and Davey Jordan

Doug Stokes and Chuck Jones

Gayle and Peter Brock, EFR and Tony A2Z

Albert Wong and Dave Friedman

Parnelli Jones and Dan Gurney

Fitzpatrick, Grant and Follmer

Don't know who some of these people are ? Read on and you'll learn about the part they played in Riverside Raceway history.

Chapter Two - The Creation of the Track

A lot of road racing happened in Southern California after World War II, Motorsports events proliferated; ranging from hillclimbs like Sandberg and Palos Verdes; road racing on airport and parking lot circuits like March Field, Palm Springs, Santa Barbara and Pomona and even a couple of purpose built race tracks; Paramount Ranch and Willow Springs. A couple of visionaries, contractor James Peterson and restauranteur Rudy Cleye saw the need for a professional road racing circuit, found a 600 acre turkey ranch, acquired some financing from race team owner John Edgar, fortuitous in that Edgar had just received a large inheritance, and went to work with expediency. The track opened in 1957 with two SCCA National events and a USAC Stock Car race.

Stuart Forbes Robinson: *"My dad was hands on in the building of the track. I was ten, my brother Ellott was fourteen and we'd get to ride along in the dirt looking at the course layout. it was really a long course in those days."*Compiler's Note – Stuart's father Elliot Forbes Robinson Sr. was long time force in Southern California racing. Stuart had a successful racing career as did his brother, best known as EFR.

—Lester Nehamkin

DUE TO BECOME one of the top road racing courses in America is the new Riverside (Calif.) International Motor Raceway, where work is being rushed in hopes of a race within two months. Paving of the 3.77-mile circuit is complete. This shot shows a pack of sportsters coming out of the 1-mile straight into the banked turn 1 at a recent testing preview. Top 4 lap averages were Pearce Woods, D-Jaguar, 96.77 mph; Ken Miles, RS Porsche Spyder, 94.14; Jim Peterson, SS Jaguar, 90.81, and Jack Bates, Mercedes-Benz 300SL, 90.27. Fastest through the traps: Woods, 153.58; Peterson, 143.08; Bates, 130.81; Miles, 125.52.

INTERNATIONAL MOTOR RACEWAY   RIVERSIDE, CALIFORNIA   ● WILLIAM L DUQUETTE   ● DONALD V KENDALL   ● ROBERT M ERIKSSON   ● JAMES E PETERSON
WEST COAST AUTOMOTIVE TESTING INCORPORTED   ASSOCIATE MEMBER · PASADENA CHAPTER · AMERICAN INSTITUTE OF ARCHITECTS   STRUCTURAL ENGINEER   LANDSCAPE ARCHITECT   GENERAL CONTRACTOR

Artist's rendering of the original track plan

—Vignolle & Powell

ANOTHER SPREAD of heavy machinery began pushing work last week at the 5.2-mile 3-in-1 International Motor Raceway near Riverside. Left: Rudy Cleye, head of the venture, shows course plans to C. E. Ingram, electrical contractor. Center: Heavy equipment—scrapers, caterpillars and water truck (right)— arrives at Edgemont-Sunnymead area. Right: Jim Peterson, in charge of engineering, points out a distant hillock to Cleye, behind wheel of jeep. Rough grading is now under way. They start laying the paving in a month. A two-lane underpass for autos into the infield and parking and viewing area is planned.

Charley Budenz: *"I grew up near U.C. Riverside, bicycle riding distance to the new racetrack under construction at the former turkey ranch - Hwy 395 and Hwy. 60. Our neighbors included track manager Roy Hord and a guy who owned a warehouse where Dan Gurney worked. My brothers and I would ride the nine miles uphill to the future track, watch the bulldozers at work and coast home downhill all the way "*

Riverside International Raceway Opens Saturday With Road Race

Southern California's newest and most extravagant speedway opens tomorrow, undoubtedly igniting a new era in automobile racing for the West Coast.

The course is the $800,000 Riverside International Motor Raceway, a tricky 3.3 mile paved layout with a daring 1.1 mile straight-away. The event is the California Sports Car Club's two-day race program which includes 14 races field, limiting it to experience drivers. They also announce grandstand seating for 5,000 h been erected at key vantage poin on the course.

The speedway is located ju six miles east of Riverside at tl junction of highways 60 and 39

MOTOR SPORTS
New Riverside Motor Raceway Making Plans for First Race

By PAUL WALLACE

Plans are well along for the first race at the new Riverside International Motor Raceway, certainly the most promising road race course to be built in the West and perhaps even in the U.S.

The inaugural contest at the ambitious new plant near March Field will be a California Sports Car Club event Sept. 21-22.

A national Sports Car Club of America meet may be held there in November. This is not when completed, it will have three road circuits ranging down from 5 miles. It also will include a circular track and an oval track suitable for sprint cars.

The course now has the medium road circuit, 3.3 miles, black-topped and completely finished.

The 3.3 route includes a long straightaway, 1.3 miles, and two miles of winding road including three shorter straights.

Two tunnels go to the infield. Temporary stands will be erect pers Motorcycle Club will have a scrambles race going today at Nall Flats in San Pedro.

The rugged course is located just west of the San Pedro Drive-In Theater on N. Gaffey St.

Small-bore cycles will compete in the morning with heat races for the big machines in the afternoon. Racing will run through most of the day, probably winding up around 4:30 p.m.

These races are free to the public and are amateur events

Doug Stokes: *"I guess I was 14, a sophomore at Covina High in 1957 but already a full-on racing nutjob and had heard about a new race track that was going to be built out in Riverside. Somehow I talked my stepfather, Milt Bramstedt, into taking me out to Riverside, a long ride in those days, to have a look at the track I had read about in Road and Track magazine. On a weekend, we drove in through what must have been the truck entrance and drove around the as yet unpaved track. What we saw was the perfectly laid out first configuration of the track completely graded, staked, and ready for the base layer to go in. After watching races on airport courses with cones and hay bales arbitrarily laid out to mark the course on an expanse of paving, here was a real road course that had fast bends, tight kinks, and a long, narrow-looking straight. It was Riverside in the raw and I'll never forget my first look"*

Ron Cummings: *"My high school buddies, already sports car racing fans, and I drove out to the track before it opened. We climbed the fence, walked around the already paved track, marveled at the size of the place"*

18

Chapter Three - Racing Begins

—Lester Nehamkin

NEW COURSE OPENS—One of America's finest road racing circuits, the 3.3-mile Riverside International Motor Raceway, stages its inaugural with a two-day program of races Saturday and Sunday, Sept. 21-22. Here, part of the field is seen during a press review session which was held last week at course near Los Angeles.

Dusty Brandel: *"I covered the first race for the Hollywood Citizen News (I also sold classified ads, writing about racing didn't pay much !!). We got to drive around the track, kind of in a parade but I got the loaner Rolls Royce up to about 100 mph entering turn nine. The salesman riding with us wasn't happy, no one else seemed to mind."* Compiler's Note - Dusty was the first woman allowed in the garage area at Indianapolis (in 1971), the first woman to get a NASCAR garage pass and is the long time president of the American Auto Racers and Broadcasters association as well as a member of the NASCAR Hall of Fame.

William Edgar: *"What a wonderful circuit and racing facility Riverside Raceway was. I was there when the bulldozers first came to dig the turns and that long back straight, the construction then in the spring of 1957 being financed by my father, John Edgar. And there, too, for the ribbon cutting in September '57 for the first race weekend when Richie Ginther won the inaugural main in the John Edgar Ferrari 410 Sport."* Compiler's Note - William

Edgar, son of racing pioneer and Riverside financier John Edgar, has had a long career in film and has written books and magazine articles covering motorsport.

Grand Opening 1957 - Track Manager Elliot Forbes Robinson and Lt. Gov. Harold Powers

Charley Budenz: *"I became the high school volunteer ticket taker (plus I was emptying trash*

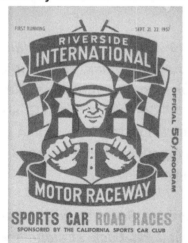

cans and painted red and white stripes on the turn nine wall). There were two gates off Day Street, the Main Gate and the Press Gate. I soon learned that the Press Gate, next to the track office and press building was the place to be, as all the drivers and celebrities came through there. So I sort of met Phil Hill, Dan Gurney, Steve McQueen, James Garner, Dan Blocker and a variety of movie stars. Pretty exciting for a high school kid" Compiler's Note - Charley raced a Fiat 124, retired from the Navy and now owns two Guldstrand GS90's

The opening race in September, an SCCA National, round fifteen of the Pacific Coast Championship, drew 20,000 fans who saw Richie Ginther win the over 1500 cc race in John Edgar's Ferrari, followed by Bill Murphy in a Kurtis Buick and Bill Pollack in a Maserati. Other notables at this event included Dan Gurney, sixth in a Corvette and Bob Bondurant, tenth in a TR-2. Chuck Daigh and Mickey Thompson were scored as DNF, Carroll Shelby did not start after a practice crash. In the under 1500cc category, 15 year old Ricardo Rodriguez won in a Porsche 550 RS, followed by Jean Pierre Kunstle and Joe Playan, also in Porsche 550's. Fifteen year old Ricardo Rodriguez won the under 1500cc class, after race director Elliott Forbes - Robinson obtained permission from the highway patrol for him to compete. Porsche Speedster driver Lou Bracker won the production car race. The race was marred by the death of driver John Lawrence and spectator, Donald Billie, who fell off his motorcycle. Note that the Valley Times reported that "the press accommodations were the worst ever with the facility taken over by women and children wearing assorted passes. In spite of the inconveniences, we predict great things for the future of the raceway as its well situated geographically"

Riverside Raceway Driver Meets Death

The opening of the Riverside International Motor Raceway was marred yesterday by the death of 36-year-old John Lawrence of Pasadena, whose car flipped over twice and crushed him during the main event finals.

Lawrence died last evening while undergoing surgery at Riverside Community hospital. He suffered severe facial, chest and spinal injuries in yesterday's finals at the new $800,000 raceway.

Saturday, Carroll Shelby had to be taken to Riverside Community hospital for treatment of facial cuts received when his car piled up.

Also, Donald Billie, 21, of Ontario, was taken to Community hospital with "critical" injuries received when he fell off his motorcycle while attempting to round the fast track's first turn.

20,000 Fans

Lawrence's death was a tragic note to the otherwise exciting two-day event which saw little Ritchie Ginther, driving a 4.9 liter Ferrari, capture the one-hour main event before an estimated 20,000 fans yesterday.

Ginther virtually won the big race by elimination as the lead changed 11 times during the hour-long event, with challengers dropping out as quickly as they grabbed the lead.

In his Italian car, Ginther hit 150 miles per hour down the 1.1 mile straightaway at the spanking new $800,000 Riverside track.

Ginther held third place early in the race as Pete Woods, in his Jaguar, and Chuck Daigh, in a Ford-powered Trautman Barnes Special, swapped the lead nine times.

Jag Blows Up

with only seven minutes to go.

Ginther took the lead, holding a slight edge on Bob Drake, also in a 4.9 liter Ferrari. Drake lost out on a turn, skidding on turn one and winding up in the sand.

Ginther roared across first, followed soon after by Daigh, who recovered in time for a second-place. Jerry Austin in a D Jaguar finished third.

Earlier in the day, 15-year-old Ricardo Rodriguez of Mexico, tooled his Porsche RS Spyder to victory over J. P. Kunstle and Joe Playan, both in Spyders.

Bill Love captured first place with an overall victory in the race for under 2000 cc production cars.

Love, driving his AC Bristol, won his sixth race in as many starts with the AC, beating out Al Cadrobbi in a Porsche Carrera coupe and Gordon Crowder, also in an AC Bristol.

Dan Garney in a Corvette took first in the over 2,000 cc. production car main event, with Etiwanda's John Colombero placing second in his Mercedes Benz 300 SL.

von Kaesborg Fifth

Redlands' Lek von Kaesborg, driving his 300 SL, rolled away with fifth place in the production car main event and captured a seventh-place in the overall category.

The ladies race was won by Ruth Levy in a Porsche Spyder, followed by Mary Davis in an Aston Martin and Linda Scott, of Los Angeles, in Bill Love's Bristol.

Saturday, Chuck Daigh and the youthful Mexican, Rodriguez, captured the inaugural main events.

Carroll Shelby, the national driving champion, was forced out of competition early when his 4.5 Maserati cracked up on the north turn during one of his practice rounds.

Daigh edged out Woods and Drake in the qualifying rounds.

Carroll Shelby crashed in practice

24

Doug Stokes: *"I saw Shelby auger that 4.5 Maserati into the bank on the outside of turn six. He got banged up pretty good that day, but it wasn't until years later that I heard the story of what happened at the hospital. As it turned out Shelby's face was very badly cut up in the wreck (seat belts were optional and for sissies anyway). The ER doctors brought in a plastic surgeon to reconstruct Shelby's face and he was presented with a head shot from the team's press folder and told that was what Carroll Shelby had looked like earlier in the day."*

Joe Scalzo on Ricardo – *"Ricardo's big and hot summer weekend of 1957. A lot went on. Nothing, however, topped the shock of the under 1,500cc main event: a silver Porsche RS with "Mexico" emblazoned across its flanks had led all opponent Lotus, Cooper-Climaxes and rival Porsches on such a merry dash that not only had it won, but lapped everything except second, third and fourth. And, jumping out its cockpit had come Ricardo, still some four months shy of his sixteenth birthday and looking younger still."*

Ovation for Mexican Boy Wonder

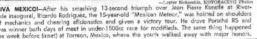

—Lester Nehamkin, MOTORACING Photos

VIVA MEXICO!—After his smashing 13-second triumph over Jean Pierre Kunstle at Riverside inaugural, Ricardo Rodriguez, the 15-year-old "Mexican Meteor," was hoisted on shoulders of mechanics and cheering aficionados and given a victory tour. He drove Porsche RS and was winner both days of meet in under-1500cc race for modifieds. The same thing happened the week before (inset) at Torreon, Mexico, where the youth walked away with major honors.

15-YEAR-OLD MEXICAN SPORTS CAR 'NATURAL'

BY PAT RAY
Mirror-News Sports Writer

Young Ricardo Rodriguez, the 15-year-old Mexican sports car driving sensation, can't miss being a world champion by the time... land, it was the way that he did it.

When he is not racing, Ricardo is a normal fun-loving, prank-playing teen-ager, but when he gets behind the...

His fastest lap was 2m. 17.5s. and the slowest was 2m. 22s. despite the fact that this was only his third ride in the Porsche.

On top of all his natural ability Ricardo is further blessed...

He was the unrestricted motorcycle champ of Mexico in 1956, when he "retired" from the two-wheel competition after a four year career.

He made his sports car debut in 1955, driving...

the first time.

He finished second to Ken Miles.

His next race was at Torreon on Sept. 15 and it was here that he became a national hero. He won while...

Ritchie Ginther Wins Thrilling Riverside Race

By JIM REINHOLD

A little man with a big foot on his 4.9 liter Ferrari throttle, Ritchie Ginther, captured the grueling one hour main event yesterday in thrilling competition that officially opened the Riverside International Motor Raceway.

Ginther of Hollywood shot down the 1.1 mile straightaway topping 150 miles an hour during the rocket-fast race in which the lead shifted 11 times.

Here's how nearly 20,000 sunburned fans peered through dust clouds over the 3.3 mile course to see the race:

Pete Woods shot to an early lead in his mighty D Jaguar. He dueled back and forth for the lead with Chuck Daigh in the Ford powered Trautman Barnes Special, Saturday's winner.

JAG BLOWS UP

After these two speedsters changed the lead nine times as Ginther laid in third spot, the D

DAIGH, RODRIGUEZ CAPTURE RIVERSIDE RACEWAY EVENTS

Freckle - faced Chuck Daigh in a Ford powered Special and the sensational 15-year - old Mexico City wonder Ricardo Rodriguez scored main event wins yesterday in initial road races over the fabulous International Motor Raceway near Riverside.

Youthful appearing Daigh from North Hollywood was followed closely by Pete Woods in a D Jaguar and Bob Drake in a 4.9 Ferrari during the short qualifying main event before 8,000 dust covered spectators.

Blackness struck early in the day — first racing meet to be held over the 3.3 high speed road course — when Carroll Shelby, national driving champion from Dallas piled up John Edgar's 4.5 Maserati on the north turn during first laps of practice. He was hospitalized for facial cuts. The tall Texan is not expected to be back for today's racing card, which gets under way at noon.

Another injury also marred opening-day festivities, when Donald Billie, 21, of 1354 Chaffey Ct., Ontario, fell off his motorcycle while attempting to round the first turn.

Billie also was taken to Community Hospital where attendants said he was in critical condition with head injuries.

San Bernardino County was well represented with local drivers nabbing three trophy winning positions.

Rocketing to an impressive overall win on the track which brings speeds topping 150 miles an hour was Bill Love in his high-powered AC Bristol.

This is the fifth win in as many starts for the startling two-liter English racer and equally startling driving by Love.

In the third race, John Colombero of Etiwanda whipped around the nine-turn course to capture a first in class and a third overall in his potent Mercedes Benz 300 SL. He was followed seconds later by Lek von Keasborg, prominent racing attorney who will receive a second in class award for his smooth ride in his silver No. 10 300 SL.

Other winners yesterday included an Alfa Romeo, Rod Bowers, Hermosa Beach and a Porsche Carrera Speedster, Lou Bracker, Hollywood. A Grand Prix motorcycle race will be repeated today.

In November 1957, 30,000 people saw Carroll Shelby win the big bore modified race in John Edgar's Ferrari on a chilly day, followed by 26 year old Dan Gurney, who stunned the crowd with his performance in only his tenth race in Frank Arciero's 4.9 Ferrari. Masten Gregory, after starting on the pole by virtue of winning the five lap qualifying race, finished third in Temple Buell's similar car, Fourth was Walt Hansgen in Briggs Cunningham's's D Jag and Richie Ginther in another John Edgar car, a Ferrari 410. Jack McAfee won the small bore modified race in Stan Sugarman's Porsche 550, followed by Pat Pigott in a Lotus 11 and Skip Conklin in another Lotus 11.

Shelby in John Edgar's 450 S Maserati Leading Walt Hansgen in the Cunningham D Jag

SHELBY POSTS RIVERSIDE VICTORY; GURNEY'S SECOND PROVES STUNNER!

See Page 1

—W. R. C. Shedenhelm

BOOMING AROUND the 1st lap of feature National SCCA Riverside Raceway classic is Masten Gregory, heading the pack here in 4.7 Maserati. Following is Carroll Shelby, 4.5 Maserati, eventual victor, and, lost in cloud of dust, are Walt Hansgen, D-Jaguar, and Dan Gurney, 4.9 Ferrari. Shelby won over Gurney by 5 seconds and averaged 81.8mph.

Hansgen, Gregory and Shelby Top Riverside Race Entries

By MAURY POWELL
MOTORACING Staff Correspondent

CARROLL SHELBY AND JAN HARRISON
After Spa Victory . . . Riverside This Weekend

WALTER HANSGEN NO. 1 D-JAG DRIVER IN U.S.
He's Entered In Big National Race at Riverside

RIVERSIDE, Nov. 13—SCCA's triple-header West Coast National Championship series comes to a frothing finale here at Riverside International Motor Raceway's 3.2-mile course Nov. 16-17, with everything pointing to this being the "gasser" of them all.

Race Co-ordinator George Cary, Jr., who got the frigid finger from Fate at Palm Springs earlier this month when chill weather set in and cut down the crowd, announces two big names for this one.

He hit the jackpot with Walt Hansgen, Westfield, N.J., who has been giving everybody the "Mark of Zorro" treatment with Briggs Cunningham's white 3-8 D-Jag throughout the East; and Masten Gregory, Kansas City, one of the few Americans to cut the mustard with a European factory team.

L. W. Stephenson, team manager for Temple Buell of Denver, Colo., phoned Cary from Miami today that Gregory's 4.7 Maser would be flown to Los Angeles

flipped the car during the Carocas meet.

HANSGEN BIG ATTRACTION

Hansgen comes here fresh from a string of wins over the East's finest, his latest being recorded at the new Virginia International Raceway, Danville, Va., several weeks ago.

Another Atlantic Seaboard ace is smooth-driving Paul O'Shea, Port Chester, N.Y., a mean man with the new Mercedes-Benz 300SL. He was third behind Pete Lovely and John von Neumann at Pebble but should go better on this course.

Carroll Shelby, peerless at Palm, cannot be counted out despite a fourth at Pebble. His tire combination on the 3-liter Maser wasn't right, according to Chief Mechanic Joe Landaker, but the Dallas, Tex., ace will be in the thick here with John Edgar's 4.5 Maser.

Johnny von Neumann heads up the Ferrari fire brigade with his silvery 25 Testa Rossa. He's augmented

RIVERSIDE RACEWAY THREAT—Porsche Spyder champion Jack McAfee will compete in National Sports Car Races this weekend over the three-mile International Mo-

John Dixon*: "The supporting race to the Kiwanis Grand Prix was a big bore productionr ace - I was there helping Bob Bondurant. Jim Jeffords protested our recapped tires.. We protested his illegal motor. The tech guys took one look at Jeffords Corvette and said they cancel each other out and let it go."*

Jim Gessner: *"The supporting race was also an "east vs: west" Corvette battle. National Champ Jim Jeffords and his "Purple People Eater" Corvette, sponsored by Nickey Chevrolet and crew chiefed by Corvette ace Ronnie Kaplan, against guys like Bondurant. The race was shortened due to a bad crash; Jeffords passed Bondurant under the yellow; the stewards spotted it and gave Bondurant the win. Jeffords and his sponsor, Nickey Chevrolet, protested. In September 1959, then SCCA exec John Bishop wrote a letter denying the protest and upholding the Bondurant win"* Compiler's Note - At the 2009 Legends of Riverside Event Jim Jeffords told Bondurant that you beat me, no question about it. The fact that they remembered it was impressive !!

RIVERSIDE ROAD RACE CONTENDER

This is Skip Conklin of Long Beach and his Lotus Lemans MKXI which will be a top class G entry Nov. 16-17 in the First National Riverside Championship Road Races on the Riverside Raceway.

Qualifying is at 2:30 p.m. Saturday. Sunday's races start at 12 noon. Entries include Phil Hill, Carroll Shelby, Walt Hansgen, Paul O'Shea, Pete Lovely, John Von Neumann and Masten Gregorey.

PICTURE OF CONCENTRATION—Ginny Simms, a laboratory technician, wheels Triumph TR-3 roadster into Turn 6 at the new Riverside Raceway. Miss Simms, winning onetime in a famous amateur run, is one of the Southland's leading amateur sports car race drivers, can be found driving on most week-ends.

RIVERSIDE INTERNATIONAL MOTOR RACEWAY

AMERICA'S BID FOR GRAND PRIX RACING

THIS IS THE WAY IT'S GOING TO BE WHEN FINISHED

Joe Playan in his Porsche 550; Bob Drake and Jack McAfee behind him

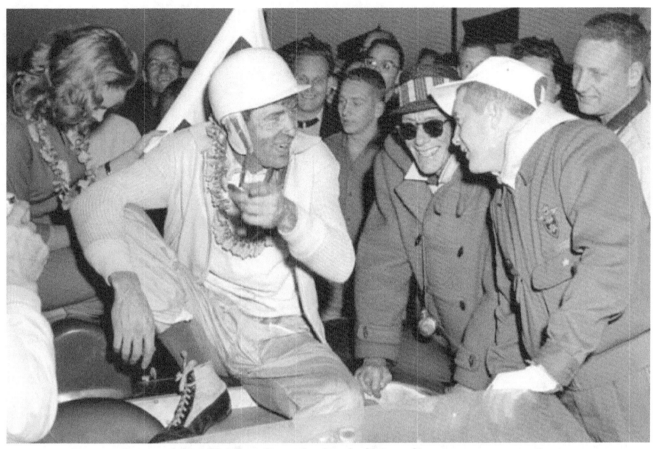

Shelby after winning in November

NEXT TO Carroll Shelby's big win at Riverside in point of interest was the spectacular ride turned in by 26-year-old Dan Gurney, of Riverside, in Frank Arciero's 4.9 Ferrari. Comparative newcomer was a great 2nd in his first race for big bores.

Lew Bracker*: "I won the Production race in a Carrera Speedster. What a great track !! I was accustomed to airports and other makeshift circuits. This was such a pleasure to drive a track built for racing. And it was ideal for my Porsche Carrera"* **Compiler's Note - Lew retired from racing long ago but continued his involvement by writing a book about his friend James Dean, "Jimmy and Me", available on Amazon and at Autobooks in Burbank.**

Bill Pollack's Dean Van Lines Lister Chevrolet

Race winner Richie Ginther

Chapter Four - Pro Racing Arrives

The Grand Prix For Sportscars; 1958 - 1965

SCCA didn't allow prize money, claiming they were an organization for amateurs. The SCCA National Championship was the top category in U.S road racing. Some pro races were put on in the Bahamas, the Bahamas Speed Week becoming a popular winter event with prize money, running from 1954 to 1966. Other U.S. competitors found themselves banned from SCCA after accepting prize money. So when USAC put together a professional series in 1958, many racers jumped on board.

Riverside became the site of the U.S. Grand Prix for Sportscars, the final round of the USAC Road Racing Championship, sponsored by the Times Mirror organization, publisher of the Los Angeles Times. 70,000 attended the event, won by pole qualifier Chuck Daigh in a Scarab after a battle with Phil Hill, who dropped out with vapor lock problems, followed by Dan Gurney in Frank Arciero's Ferrari 375MM in second and Bill Krause in a D- Jaguar in third. A lap behind in fourth was Jean Behra in a Porsche RSK, the under two liter winner. Winner Daigh collected $5000. A very hot day, newspapers reported dusty conditions and heavy traffic getting in and out of the track.

Daigh and Scarab Pull Upset At USAC-Riverside Opener

Hill's Retirement in 4.1 Ferrari Paves Way for Californian's Victory

By KEN MILES

To the immense delight of some 70,000 Californians who attended the first open car race to be held in the West, the race was won by a local driver in a car designed and prepared in California. To the vast majority of the enormous crowd, Chuck Daig tory in the Scarab could not have been more popular.

Total entries for the "U.S. Grand Prix" numbered 52, of which 42 event reached the starting grid, practice, politics and mechanical difficulties taking thei We were all very disappointed when Stirling Moss could not be present, but pe under the circumstances it was as well, since the car that he was to have driven p quite unreliable.

Hill Sets New Record

This was one race for which nobody could justifiably complain of lack of practice, the course being open on the Sat-

ing in some very cre times though he was short of steam down the The Reventlow organ in the meantime, was

Daigh Hot at Riverside

TRACKSIDE TEMPERATURES at Riverside Raceway were over 100 deg. last Sunday for the U.S. Grand Prix. Yes, it really was a hot Daigh as Chuck Daigh of Long Beach won the 200-mile sports car race in Lance Reventlow's Chevy-pow- ered Scarab. He won handily after an early duel with Phil Hill, 4.1 Ferrari, who later was forced out. Here, Daigh leads Hill through Turn 6. All photos by W. R. C. Sheden- helm, George Woods and Gus V. Vignolle of MOTORACING.

Phil Hill leading Richie Ginther

Winner Chuck Daigh in the Scarab leading Phil Hill in the Ferrari 412. Chuck Porter's Mercedes SLS is parked in the background.

Bobby Unser in the Kurtis Olds, followed by Floyd Burt in a Buick Special

Joe Scalzo: *"Reventlow and his Scarabs had eight wins in thirteen starts and the Ferraris were ducking for cover. By far the most prestigious win occurred in Reventlow Automotive's home, southern California, at Riverside Raceway, host to the first professional Grand Prix in the history of American sports car racing, the 200-mile Times Mirror meet, which attracted a record 70,000 spectators. Heavy pride had been on the line. Taking no chances that his stable of caterwauling, overhead cam, prancing stallions would lay down to some Egyptian beetle that really was little more than hot rod with push rods, Ferrari's L.A. distributor and erratic racing driver, a German - all his Ferraris were painted Teutonic silver - named Johnny von Neuman spared no expense. Von Neuman already owned a Ferrari quartet - his own 4.1, which had just won Vacaville, a pair of Testa Rossa three liters for Richie Ginther, and a third Testa Rossa for his racing stepdaughter, Josie. So von Neuman had had the factory import to Riverside the fastest, most fearsome, engine it had going - 4.1 liters of power with a dubious history.*

Bringing out a fifth Ferrari - this one red; to house the 4.1. von Neuman named future World Champion Phil Hill his pistolero. But it was a scorching day at Riverside and, just as had happened to the late Musso at Monza, the 4.1 overheated, and the Grand Prix was won in a runaway by Chuck Daigh's first-string Scarab, which itself was threatening to overheat. Richie Ginther's Testa Rossa had Daigh's Scarab almost lap it twice; von Neuman's 4.1 didn't complete a lap; didn't even make around the first corner. Bearing down on Reventlow's hated Scarab just ahead of him, von Neuman became overexcited, mistook the throttle for the brake, and took a big bite out of Reventlow's rear end, mortally wounding both the Scarab and himself. Reventlow, his fuel lank squashed and gushing fuel, threw a temper tantrum when he was blackflagged and kicked out of the Times - Mirror Grand Prix. And that was the short, Ferrari-bashing, 1958 season of Reventlow Automotive and its brilliant Scarabs".

George Keck: *"We convoyed down from Seattle; Pete Lovely with his Lotus on a Thames van converted into a car carrier; Ralph Ormsbee with his HWM, Tommy Meehan with his Maserati and I; all with open two wheel trailers. Pre I-5, old Highway 99 went through every*

little town, stoplights, speed traps and all. A non stop 1000 mile ride with my crew man, Joachim. We stopped in Sausalito to pick up my rebodied Porsche 550 from Nade Borgeault in Sausalito who accompanied us to Riverside. This was to be the first outing for my RS Keck as we called it; was built out of a wrecked 550 with a 12 gallon fuel tank; we were the only ones who had to stop for fuel during the race but finished 21st anyway. Had to leave right after we got our prize money, $75, in order to get to work on Monday morning. This was the first time I'd ever gotten money to race and SCCA later wanted to ban us for accepting money. That sort of fell by the wayside."

Nade Bourgeault and George Keck at Riverside

Ray Crawford; Kurtis Chevrolet

Ralph Ormsbee; HWM Chevrolet

41

Bobby Unser practiced in Ak Miller's Devin

Left to right, Bill Pollack, Lister-Chevrolet, Bill Kraus, D-Jaguar and Richie Ginther, Ferrari leaving a corner at the recent Riverside Grand Prix, Krause, Ginther and Pollack finished the 203 mile event third, fifth and eight respectively.

Photo—Robitschek

Jerry Unser in Mickey Thompson's Kurtis leads Troy Ruttman in the Bill Murphy Kurtis

Jerry Unser – Mickey Thompson in wheelchair

Ron Cummings: *"Mickey Thompson was injured when Ak Miller t-boned him at turn five. Mickey had run out of gas causing the car to turn ninety degrees. Ak came around the blind corner in his own 500SX El Caballo II and t-boned Thompson's Kurtis. Thompson had mounted a small flat plate on his dashboard. That plate split open Thompson's knee. So Jerry Unser stepped in to drive the car in the race"*

Riverside management found that the only events making money were sports car races, hence the addition to the USAC Road Racing Championship in 1959, the July Kiwanis Grand Prix, and the October Grand Prix for Sportscars, both big bore sportscar showdowns. The weekends included some regional supporting races and a vintage exhibition. A crowd of 20,000 saw pole qualifier Richie Ginther win the Kiwanis event in John Von Neumann's Ferrari 412 on a hundred degree day, followed by Sam Weiss and Ken Miles. both in a Porsche RSK's. Chuck Daigh led for awhile then dropped out with overheating problems. Ginther picked up $2450 for the win

With L.A Times promotion, 75,000 turned up to watch Phil Hill win $7750 for first place in the October Grand Prix For Sportscars driving Eleanor Von Neumann's Ferrari TR, followed by Lloyd Ruby in a Maserati 450S and Ken Miles in a Porsche RSK.

Ginther Riverside Winner

Ferrari, Then 4 Porsches

BY GUS V. VIGNOLLE
MOTORACING Staff Writer
RIVERSIDE, Calif., July 19 --- Richie Ginther, slight 28-year old driver from Granada Hills, Calif., was contemplating entering a Northern Calif. pro race following his smashing victory here today in the 150-mile "Kiwanis Grand Prix" for $10,000.
He drove Eleanor von Neumann's 4.1-liter Ferrari to victory at an average speed of 88.75 mph, three-quarters of a lap ahead of Sam Weiss, Sacra-

44

Ginther leads Moss

Andy Porterfield; Devin

THE QUEEN SELLS A TICKET

Gale Storm of Encino, queen of the $10,000 Kiwanis Grand Prix for sports cars at Riverside International Raceway, July 19, sells the first ticket to Lt. Gov. Rickard G. Norlander as a start toward raising money for underprivileged and crippled children. Reserved tickets will be sold only through Kiwanis clubs.

HILL WINS BLOODY RIVERSIDE GRAND PRIX

(Continued From B—3)

the dusty road course watching early race pace setters Stirling Moss from England and Richie Ginther of Granada Hills retire

Jack Graham of San Jose slammed his Chevrolet powered Aston Martin into the rear of Gurney's car, spilling gasoline, oil and debris onto the course. Rodger Ward, winner of this

Charley Budenz: *"I met Briggs Cunningham as he was attempting to push his broken Birdcage Maserati onto a single axle trailer, pulled by a non descript pickup truck. We high school hangers on jumped in to help. He was a regular guy, thanked us and drove off. It was hard to picture him as the Americas Cup winner and exceptionally wealthy car owner."*

Jack McAfee with Vasek Polak's Porsche RS – 60

USAC To Sanction Road Racing

INDIANAPOLIS (AP)— The United States Auto Club announced last night it will add professional closed-circuit road racing to the classes of races it sanctions.

The USAC already has sanctioned the championship circuit for specially built big race cars, including the Indianapolis 500-mile event; sprints, midgets and stock cars.

Duane Carter, director of competition for the club, said it hopes to have the new division operating by late summer. Tracks involved include Lime Rock Park, Lime Park, Conn.; Virginia International Raceway, Danville, Va.; Marlboro Motor Raceway, Marlboro, Md., and Riverside International Raceway, Riverside, Calif.

Carter said USAC will apply to the International Automobile Federation for approval of the American professional sports car races so there can be a greater interchange of cars and drivers between the U.S. and the rest of the world.

Joe Scalzo's take on Dan Gurney and the Arciero 4.9 Ferrari – *"At Riverside, the seemingly-jinxed 4.9 involved itself instill another massive starting line wreck. After stalling, it took a hurtling, hybrid Pontiac-powered Aston-Martin raced by a San Jose plumber straight up its tailpipe. The impact split open the 4.9's huge fuel tank, allowing hundred of gallons of high-test to gush everywhere, but there was no fire. As for Dan, the impact whiplashed his helmet against the roll-over bar, severely rang his bell and knocked him unconscious, and he was forced to do time in the crash house recovering from concussion and shock.*

Hollywood Driver Von Neumann Win

VACAVILLE (AP)—John von Neumann of Hollywood drove a Ferrari with a bashed-in rear end to beat out Jack McAfee by two seconds in the feature national sports car race at the Vaca Valley Speedway yesterday.

At the start the race was between Von Neumann and Lance Reventlow, Barbara Hutton's son. He was driving a Scarab and both were clocked at over 138 miles an hour, leaving the field behind. Reventlow piled up his Scarab on a hay bale after spinning on an oil slick in the 34th lap. Von Neumann caved in the rear end of his car on a hay bale on the 29th lap and fell behind McAfee in a Porsche-Spyder. Von Neumann caught up four laps from the end.

McAFEE OPENS NEW LOCATION

John von Neumann, Southern California, Arizona and Southern Nevada Volkswagen distributor, left, congratulates Jack McAfee, prominent VW - Porsche dealer and sports car race driver, on the opening of his new headquarters, 1108 Hollywood Way, Burbank. While Sam Weill Jr., second from left, sales manager for Competition Motors, and Lindley Bothwell, 1959 regional executive of the Sports Car Club of America's Los Angeles Region, looks on.—Photo by Les Nehamkin.

Earl Gandel: *"Riverside connected stories - My first job, after college and the army; I went to work for John Von Neumann in January 1960. He had already stopped racing at the request of VW, because he was by then too valuable to lose, had divorced Eleanor, who got the Ferrari distributorship in settlement, winch was then run by Richie Ginther. Got rid of his race cars to people like Otto Zipper, John Edgar and Tony Parravano and wasn't sponsoring anyone anymore. VW and Porsche were totally separate parent companies then, Competition Motors was VW only, Porsche Car Distributors for Porsche only, although both in the same building in Culver City with the same cast of characters. Vasek Polak was the only "Porsche only" dealer in SoCal, Nevada and Arizona, and in the US, I believe. 16 of the 40 some VW dealers here also paired with Porsche, most of them John's buddies, like Otto, Chick Iverson, Dick Morgensen and D.D. Michelmore. Strangely, it took years for Jack McAfee, then a VW dealer in Burbank, to get Porsche, even though he was the closest thing to a factory race driver here. I ran into him in the 90's and asked if he still had any of his old race cars. He said no, he had no interest in old race cars. He said, "They're like old ballerinas." Long before Lotus, Bob Challman was sales manager for Vasek Polak. Porsches were on six month back order at retail, you had to pay a premium to get one on the west coast. Challman got on a plane and went around the country, picking up cars from distributors who didn't have that problem. When John saw registrations that year and saw that Vasek was selling more cars than von Neumann's own store in Hollywood, he was greatly pissed off because all of Vasek's cars were supposed to come from the distributor. Nothing illegal, just dirty pool. Part of racing !!"*

In 1960 there were again two Riverside USAC events, in April, the Los Angeles Examiner Grand Prix and, in October, the Times Grand Prix for Sports Cars. Fourth place qualifier Carroll Shelby won in the Camoradi Tipo 61 Birdcage Maserati, picking up $6200. He was followed by Ken Miles in the RSK and Pete Lovely, driving Jack Nethercutt's Ferrari Testa Rossa. Pole qualifier Bob Drake had ignition problems and third place qualifier Dan Gurney, in the Balchowsky Buick Special, blew the motor. The supporting Formula Junior race was won by Jim Hall in an Elva DKW. In October, a crowd of 80,000 at the Times race saw Bill Krause win in a Birdcage Tipo 61 Maserati, followed by Bob Drake in 'Ol Yeller II and Augie Pabst in the Meister Brauser Scarab. Krause's win netted him $8550. Moss dropped out with transmission problems; Gurney with a blown head gasket. A close scrape for Krause; he ran out of gas on the cool down lap and had to be towed to victory circle.

JIM HALL, in Chevy-powered Troutman-Barnes Chaparral, leads Dan Gurney, Lotus, at lower end of turn 7 in Riverside sports car Grand Prix. Hall took 3rd, and it was the best effort by an American car. (MOTOR-ACING photo by Bill Norcross)

By 1961, the failing USAC championship had only four races scheduled, including Riverside's Grand Prix for Sportscars in October. 70,600 people turned out in near 100 degree weather to see an international field with pole qualifier Jack Brabham winning $6925, driving a Climax powered Cooper Monaco, followed by Bruce McLaren in a similar car. Third was Jim Hall in the first of his Chaparral's, built by Troutman Barnes. Oliver Gendebien won the under two liter category in a Lotus 19 Monte Carlo.

BILL KRAUSE gets checkered flag as he wins 3rd annual LA Times-Mirror 200-mi. Grand Prix for sports cars at Riverside Intl. Raceway. He averaged a record 91.5mph.

Fred Knoop's Huffaker Chrysler DNF'd as Daigh passes in the Scarab

Augie Pabst in the Scarab leading Carroll Sheby

Another View of Shelby and the Birdcage Tipo 61 Maserati

Miles, McAfee Enter Grand Prix

BY BOB THOMAS

This country's 1-2 punch among the small-bore sports car drivers—Ken Miles and Jack McAfee—provided the icing yesterday for a flurry of interesting entries for the Times-Mirror-sponsored United States Grand Prix for sports cars Oct. 10-11 at Riverside International Raceway.

"This is war," so the saying goes, when Miles and McAfee take off from the same grid. For the first time they square off against each other in the world's most popular and explosive small road race missile — the Porsche RSK Spyder.

Miles' Sponsors

Miles has been entered for the $20,000, 200-mile classic by Otto Zipper and Bob Estes of Precision Motors in Beverly Hills.

McAfee's name was tossed in by another big figure in West Coast road racing, John von Neumann, whose RSK made its debut last July at Riverside when Easterner Bob Holbert drove it to fourth place over-all, a notch behind Miles.

The lean Britisher, Miles, now a U.S. citizen and inhabitant of the Hollywood Hills, made a shambles of the big cars at Santa Barbara last Sunday, winning

won the last two times they've tangled. In each case the loser ran second.

They're hard to pry apart at the wire. But, despite this feud, they were Porsche teammates this year at Sebring, finishing eighth overall.

Miles just loves to beat the big boys and will be shooting for the top prize as well as first in his class. He won the works last March in the International Grand Prix at Pomona in a Porsche RS.

Other Entries

Three other important entries were filed yesterday—Jean Pierre Kunstle, Eric Hauser and Johnny Mantz.

Kunstle of Carmel, drives the first European entry, a 2-liter Lotus Ferrari XV, put into the race by the Swiss racing team, Écurie les Mordus.

Hauser will drive the West's most famous special, Old Yeller, for its sponsor, Dean Van Lines. Repainted—white, this time—it is a 5,800-cc. Chevrolet powerhouse.

Mantz, an Indianapolis veteran and local hero in the Gilmore Stadium midget days, was entered with the C & B Manufacturing Special, a Mercedes - Corvette formerly owned by Chuck Porter. Angeleno Dick Becker now owns the car.

ACE DRIVER—Jack McAfee will drive in Times Grand Prix at Riverside.
Times photo

Cycle Stars Return

Standouts Sammy Tanner, Al Gunter, Johnny Gibson, Johnny Muckenthaler and Bob SirKegian return from the Midwest to compete in tonight's 12-event motorcycle racing chase at Ascot Stadium.

Augie Pabst to Be at Wheel of Scarab Mark III in Grand Prix

BY BOB THOMAS

Augie (What'll you have?) Pabst. 25-year-old scion of the Milwaukee brewing family, and one of those potent Lance Reventlow Scarabs will head up an important three-car midwestern entry in the $20,000 Times-Mirror United States Grand Prix for sports cars at Riverside Oct. 10-11.

This was assured yesterday when Henry P. Heuer, owner of the Peter Hand Brewery Co. of Chicago, filed entries for young Pabst and his son, Harry J. Heuer.

The three cars involved are the powerful Scarab Mark III, recently purchased from Reventlow; the Bocar XP-5, celebrated special of the nation's beer belt, and a 2.5-liter Ferrari.

Young Heuer owns the Scarab and Bocar and will drive the latter in the rich 200-miler at Riverside International Raceway. He entered the cars as the Meister Brausers I and III.

Pabst to Pilot Scarab

Pabst, national point leader of the United States Auto Club's road racing division for sports cars, will handle the Scarab, a twin to last year's U.S. Grand Prix winning car which Chuck Daigh drove. The third car of the team is owned by Pabst and may be held in reserve for the boys, although another driver may be named later.

Pabst and the Scarab ate up a star-studded field at

GRAND PRIX ENTRY—Augie Pabst will drive the Scarab Mark III in Times Grand Prix Oct. 10-11.

winning the featured 164-mile Formula Libre race over a 3.27-mile course very similar to the Riverside layout. Augie also won the all-sports car prelude in his Ferrari.

On the local scene, the Scuderia Excelsior team of Pasadena filed an entry yesterday for Joe Playan. The Inglewood road racer will handle a 4,500-cc. Corvette-powered OSCA.

Another addition to the

Fresno where George Harm, owner of radio station KARM, entered driver Chuck Cornett and a 2-liter Ferrari.

Over-the-counter sale of Grand Prix tickets opens today at the Southern California Music Co., 737 S Hill St., and at the lobby of The Times. Mail orders will continue.

Proceeds from the second annual event will go to

BRABHAM AT RIVERSIDE

Champion due to Drive E-Jaguar

By GUS V. VIGNOLLE
Editor of MOTORACING

Soft-spoken, unobtrusive Jack Brabham of Australia, who won the Formula 1 world's driving championship for Cooper-Climax in 1959 and again this year, will compete in the USAC $20,000-plus Grand Prix for sports cars at Riverside Raceway Oct. 16.

He will drive an E-type Jaguar owned by Connecticut sportsman Briggs Cunningham. Brabham, along with Stirling Moss of Great Britain (2.5-liter Lotus) and Phil Hill, Santa Monica, Calif. (3-liter Ferrari), ranks as the outstanding attraction.

The 200-mile race over the 3.2-mile course already has lured one of the greatest fields ever gathered for one race in this country.

DRAKE IN OLD YELLER

Other late developments:

Bob Drake will drive Max Balchowsky's famed Old Yeller II Buick Spl.

Roy Salvadori of England goes in a 2.5 Cooper Monaco, and Paul O'Shea in a 3.8 D-Jag, both for famed Ecurie Ecosse.

Chuck Daigh, Long Beach, Calif., who won the 1st running of this LA Times-Mirror race in 1958 in one of Lance Reventlow's Chevy Scarabs, will pilot the same car again for the 1960 race.

The other Scarab will be driven by personable Augie Pabst of Milwaukee, who now must be recognized as one of the best sports car pilots in the country. The 2 Scarabs now race under the brewery banner of the Meister Brausers, and were sold by Reventlow to Harry Heuer, Chicago beer titan. Heuer has been driving one of the Scarabs, and his progress during the last 6 months has been sensational. This observer saw him go more than a year ago at Vacaville, where he was just

TWO OF THE biggest attractions at the $70,000-plus USAC sports car race at Riverside Oct. 16 will be Stirling Moss of Great Britain, left, and world champion Jack Brabham of Australia. Moss will drive a 2.5-liter Lotus, and Brabham an E-type Jaguar owned by Briggs Cunningham. (MOTORACING photo by Gus V. Vignolle)

fair; but since then he has been right up there among the front ranks.

DAIGH IN SCARAB

Heuer has relinquished his car to Daigh, naturally a more experienced pilot.

Answering a number of queries as to whose "Birdcage" Maserati Carroll Shelby, winner at Le Mans last year with Roy Salvadori, will drive, the answer is: J. Frank Harrison's car. This Chattanooga, Tenn., sportsman, who now has one of the top sports car racing stables in the country, owns two 4.5 Maseratis, two "Birdcage" Masers and has 2 new "Birdcages" coming to the US from Italy.

DRIVERS LISTED

Following are other drivers all set for the Riverside classic, although some are questionable at this writing: Dan Gurney, Joakim Bonnier, Olivier Gendebien, Lloyd Ruby, Roger Penske, Eddie Crawford, Walt Hansgen, Briggs Cunningham, Bill Krause, Richie Ginther, George Constantine, Bob Holbert, Ken Miles, Loyal Katskee.

Most of this same field competes Oct. 22-23 at Laguna Seca near Del Monte on the Monterey Peninsula. Amateur races, featuring the Cal Club and LA SCCA, will be held Oct. 15 at Riverside, the day before the big race.

TOP DRIVERS AT GRAND PRIX PARTY

The Grand Prix Restaurant, co-owned by Bob Drake and Mary Davis, will hold its 3rd annual pre-GP party Wednesday night, Oct. 12, to give drivers, owners, race officials, members and sports car fans a chance to

Pabst Captures Race in Scarab

WATKINS GLEN, N.Y., Sept. 24 —Milwaukee's Augie Pabst smashed the race record in an American-made Chevy Scarab today in winning the 101-mile annual Grand

RIVERSIDE RACE LURES TOP FIELD

Some of America's leading drivers are included in a record breaking field of 180 entered for the amateur-pro sports car racing carnival at Riverside International Raceway Saturday and Sunday, July 18-19, headlined by Sunday's USAC-Sanctioned $9300 150-mile Kiwanis Grand Prix.

The Grand Prix is being held

D-Jaguar. Bruce's entry is conditional, depending on how the car responds in practice.

Kessler's mount, owned by Max Gordon of San Diego, will be tested

Chuck Daigh's Troutman Barnes Special

VETERAN—Duane Carter will race in Kiwanis Grand Prix at Riverside raceway.

Riverside Gets Duane Carter for Grand Prix

Ginther Snares Kiwanis Grand Prix Feature

RIVERSIDE, Cal. (AP)—Ritchie Ginther of Granada Hills, Cal., Sunday won the 150-mile $10,000 Kiwanis Grand Prix at the Riverside International Raceway.

Ginther, driving a Ferrari covered the distance in 1:44:5.6. He averaged 88.75 miles per hour for the 47 laps.

Sam Weiss of Sacramento, Cal., three quarters of a lap back, was second, followed by Ken Miles of Hollywood, Bob Halbut of Philadelphia, Ricardo Rodriguez of Mexico City and Chuck Daigh of Long Beach, Cal. All drove Porsches.

It's Ginther at Riverside

CAMERA OF Bill Novaross catches a fine closeup of Richie Ginther on his way to victory in Riverside USAC pro race, July 19. He drove Eleanor von Neumann's 4.1 Ferrari, averaged 88.75mph for the 150 miles. Additional photos—pages 1, 4 and 5.

Bob Oker

Bill Stroppe; Mercury

Art Bunker - Porsche RSK

Lloyd Ruby; Maserati 450S

Chuck Daigh

Ricardo Rodriguez

Skip Hudson

Bob Holbert

Jack Flaherty's Lister Jag ended up in top of the turn six guardrail

Skip Hudson leading

GRAND PRIX THRILLS RECORD CROWD OF 80,000

RECORD TURNOUT—Here is panoramic view showing part of record crowd of 80,000 on hand yesterday at Riverside Raceway for third annual Times-Mirror Grand Prix. Bill Krause won the 202.25 mile feature.

Ken Miles in the Otto Zipper / Bob Estes Porsche RSK

Leading Drivers in Auto Classic

STIRLING MOSS — Although he never actually has won world driving title in Formula I Grand Prix racing, Moss is regarded in international circles as the greatest road-racing driver currently active. He enters U.S. Grand Prix driving at the peak of his 13-year-old career, having won three consecutive Formula I events as well as cinching the world factory title for England's Aston Martin in a sports car competition at Goodwood, Eng., last month. After early mechanical woes, which cost him what appeared to be certain Grand Prix victories in Holland and Monte Carlo, he won handily in the Italian Grand Prix at Monza and the Portuguese Grand Prix at Lisbon. The slightly balding 30-year-old Englishman is married and maintains homes in Nassau and London. He'll drive a powerful 4.2-liter Aston Martin, which was specially prepared and sent to California for this race.

DAN GURNEY — Dan surprised many of the fans by finishing second last year, but his performances this year as a freshman member of the Ferrari factory team have been even more outstanding. Despite only four Grand Prix races, the handsome 28-year-old Riverside driver ranks fourth in

world standing. Gurney again will drive the 4.9 Ferrari entered by Frank Arciero. Dan makes his homes in Riverside and Modena, Italy. He is married with two children, Johnny, 4, and Lyndee, 2.

RODGER WARD — Since his record victory at Indianapolis, Rodger has been the hottest American driver. In addition to the 500 - miler, Rodger has chalked up enough victories already to cinch the 1959 U.S. racing championship. Although his road-racing experience is limited, Ward is a quick learner and should fare well tomorrow. The 38-year-old makes his home in Speedway, Ind., with wife Jo. Ward began his racing career here in midgets after the war and moved through the ranks in American racing to the top position.

JOSIE VON NEUMANN — Third Ferrari entry of her mother, Eleanor von Neumann and only woman driver to get approval of USAC to compete in Riverside Grand Prix. She made her professional road-racing debut against men drivers in Kiwanis Grand Prix at Riverside. She completed 150-mile race in 14th position among more than 50 starters. Several men were unable to go route in the heat. She drives a 3-liter Ferrari. Josie entered and won first ladies' race ever held on the West Coast at Torrey Pines in 1951.

JACK McAFEE — A real American veteran of sports car racing. He was the 1956 National Sports Car Club of America under-1,500cc champion in a Porsche 550 Spyder. Recognized as one of the country's top small-car road race pilots, he'll drive a late-model Porsche RSK Spyder for John von Neumann in U.S. Grand Prix. A San Fernando Valley foreign car dealer, Jack always carries a letter from Dr. Porsche wishing him luck when racing. A big man, he fills his German Porsche with a solid 200 pounds on a 6-ft. frame.

RICHIE GINTHER — Ferrari's No. 1 representative on the West Coast. A close buddy of Hill, Richie may be the driver to beat today. He drives Eleanor von Neumann's powerful 4.1 Ferrari, the same machine which he drove to a 150 - mile "homefree" victory in the Kiwanis Grand Prix at Riverside last July. The 29-year-old tinymite, he weighs only 125 pounds, is married and lives in Granada Hills. He has been driving since 1951 when Phil Hill introduced him to the sport at Pebble Beach. Ginther is manager of Ferrari Representatives of California.

CHUCK DAIGH — Defending champion who became toast of American road racing last year by winning first Times - Mirror U S Grand Prix in Scarab Mark II, covering 203 miles in 2h. 17m. 15s. Chuck set Riverside qualifying record of 2:04.3 which rivals will be shooting at tomorrow. This time he drives 5,700cc Maserati for John Edgar of Encino. A master mechanic, Daigh played major role in development of Lance Reventlow Scarabs and now is chief testing engineer for Formula I Scarab which Reventlow is building for European Grand Prix racing. Daigh is married and father of two children. The 35-year-old driver - mechanic lives in Long Beach.

MICKEY THOMPSON — Unquestionably, the 30-year-old Mickey Thompson is the king of America's hot-rodders. He has been tinkering with automobiles since he

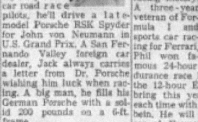

also manages a local drag-racing strip. He's married and makes his home in El Monte.

PHIL HILL — This 32-year-old member of Ferrari factory racing team from Santa Monica is the No. 1 American in European Grand Prix racing history. A three-year veteran of Formula I and sports car racing for Ferrari, Phil won famous LeMans 24-hour endurance race last year and the 12-hour Enduro at Sebring this year, co-driving each time with Oliver Gendebein. He will drive hottest car of Ferrari sports car team, a 3-liter Ferrari, which has been flown to the United States for U.S. Grand Prix and its new owner, Eleanor von Neumann. Hill set Monza lap record of 127.8 m.p.h. in Italian Grand Prix last month, finishing second to the great Stirling Moss.

MAX BALCHOWSKY — The 35-year-old Hollywood garage mechanic is one of the most popular figures in West Coast racing. Max, who gained his fame by consistently defeating the fancy imported cars with his home - built specials, debuts his latest creation today. Naturally, it's powered by a Buick engine and is dubbed Old Yeller No. 2. Chief assistant in developing the new car is wife, Ina, who blueprinted the chassis and has done a good share of the wrench work. Max was seventh here last year in the original "Old Yeller" and hopes to improve that finish with the new car.

AUGIE PABST — This 25-year-old scion of the Milwaukee brewing family has skyrocketed to prominence in U.S. road racing. And he drives one of the West Coast's favorite cars, the "All American" Scarab, purchased from builder Lance Reventlow. Pabst is current national USAC road-racing point leader. In his last two races he drove Scarab Mark III to victories at Meadowvale, Ill., and Vacaville, Cal. Augie also

won Meadowvale prelude in 2.5 Ferrari, which he owns and has brought to Riverside. Pabst entered U.S. Grand Prix as part of Peter Hand Brewery team along with young Harry Heuer, son of the owner of the Chicago beer company. Heuer drives a Bocar Special.

BILL KRAUSE — Bill comes by his racing ability naturally as both his father Arnold and uncle Bert were top-notch midget car owners during the heyday of that type racing locally. Bill was a surprise third in last year's race in his D-Jaguar. He will drive the Jag again this time but the original engine has been replaced with a red-hot Chevrolet. Krause has been racing since 1953. In fact, he won the first sports car race he ever entered at Bakersfield. He also has raced midgets and sprint cars and hopes to compete at Indianapolis. Married, the 26 - year - old Krause makes his home in Long Beach.

PEDRO RODRIGUEZ — Older of the two racing brothers makes his second appearance at Riverside in a Ferrari. Last July he drove like a veteran in a 3-liter Ferrari for Eleanor von Neumann. He was running second behind eventual winner Richie Ginther until mechanical difficulty put him out of the race. Young Pedro has driven in important races all over the world, including LeMans and Nurburgring in Germany. Pedro Rodriguez Sr., Senora Rodriguez and sister Conchita also are on the scene.

Prize Money Mark

Prize money for the Grand Prix establishes a new record for road racing in the United States. Drivers will be competing for a $20,000 purse and $5,000 in accessory money.

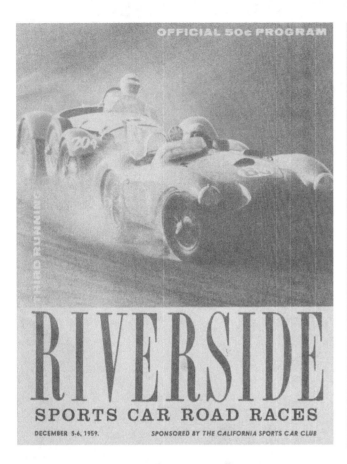

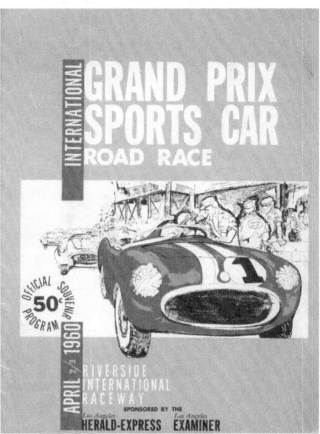

Phil Hill leading Moss

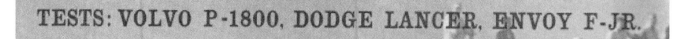

TESTS: VOLVO P-1800, DODGE LANCER, ENVOY F-JR.

ROAD & TRACK

February 1961
Fifty Cents

THE MOTOR ENTHUSIASTS' MAGAZINE

Competition: Pacific GP - Laguna Seca, U. S. Grand Prix - Riverside
How to measure your car's drag • The London and Turin Auto Shows

ACTION AT RIVERSIDE RACEWAY

Jo Bonnier

Bill Krause; D Jag Chevy

Stirling Moss; Aston Martin

Augie Pabst; Scarab

Clem Proctor; Aston Martin

Ak Miller; Devin Olds

Joe Playan; Osca

Jeff Kline: *"I moved to California in September, 1961 and this was the first race I had ever attended. I was so stoked by all the famous drivers and exciting cars, amazed by the size of the crowd. Prompted me to learn more and become a racer myself"* Compiler's Note – Jeff was a successful competitor in IMSA, 1987 Camel Light champ and still can be found driving some vintage cars pretty quickly,

Eric Hauser; Ol Yeller

67

Big changes in 1960 as investor Edgar expected more return on his investment

Riverside Raceway Changes Owners

Special to Competition Press

RIVERSIDE, Calif. — Nearly completed is a transaction which will give Dean Mears, Pacific Coast Class C Production racing champion, title to Riverside International Raceway, a 3.275-mile course near here.

Estimated price for the multi-purpose plant (it has been used for drag, stock car and motorcycle racing, too) is "around $250,000," although more than a half million has been poured into it since its inception.

THE LARGEST crowds drawn to the course were for the 1958 and '59 Los Angeles Times Grand Prix, both in the neighborhood of 70,000. Scheduled for April 2-3 is the Los Angeles Examiner GP, another race of internatioanl standing.

Mears is said to be planning improvements and changes in the layout of the course and its facilities, along with a financial program that would put it into a paying basis.

As a part of the deal with John Edgar, Rudy Cleye and Steve Mason, Mears will receive Edgar's 5.7 Maserati and a Lister. Mears drove a Mercedes-Benz 300SL roadster to the Pacific championship last season.

1960 winner Bill Krause; Birdcage Maserati

Krause Threat in Grand Prix Driving New Maserati Birdcage

BY DICK HYLAND

Long Beach's Billy Krause will drive a new Maserati Birdcage in the $20,000 Times-Mirror Grand Prix for Sports Cars Oct. 16 at Riverside Raceway.

That is most significant news.

In the glory days of California tennis, internationally famed stars were licked in the Pacific Southwest Championships by unheralded local players.

Krause Great Prospect

Next month, in the Times-Mirror classic at Riverside, this same feat could be accomplished by Billy Krause. He could defeat Phil Hill, Carroll Shelby, Walt Hansgen, Sterling Moss, Briggs Cunningham, Richie Ginther, Dan Gurney — the entire field of world famed road racing drivers entered. This time unheralded Krause will have the iron, a machine equal to those

LATEST ENTRY—Billy Krause, Long Beach, has entered Times-Mirror Grand Prix. Riverside Oct. 16.

Bill Krause Wins Grand Prix

By PAUL WALLACE
To P-T Staff Writer

RIVERSIDE—Long Beach's Bill Krause, perennial hard luck guy on the pro sports car racing circuit, brought home a winner here Sunday in the 3rd annual Times-Mirror Grand Prix.

The 27-year-old father of three ran away with the 200-mile chase in his first ride in a new 2.8 litre Birdcage Maserati after early competition from Dan Gurney and Stirling Moss collapsed.

Both Gurney and Moss in the spectacularly fast new Lotus 19s dropped out in the early stages with mechanical ills.

Bob Drake in Max Balchowsky's popular homebuilt special, the Buick powered Old Yeller II, wound up second closely pursued by beer scion Augie Fabst in a Chevrolet-engined Scarab.

New Jersey's Walt Hansgen completed the sweep for Maserati by wheeling Briggs Cunningham's 2 litre Type 60 Maserati to first place in the Under 2000 cc class ahead of old pro Ken Miles in a Porsche RS-60.

Hansgen's Maserati is identical to Krause's mount except for a smaller engine.

Thompson 11th in the Chevy-engined Stingray and Bob Bondurant, 12th in a Maserati-powered Ferrari.

MILES WAS 13th overall with the first Porsche in followed by Pete Ryan in another Porsche RS-60. Bob Holbert was 4th in the small car class and Jack McAfee 5th. Both drove Porches.

Both Indianapolis winner Rodger Ward in a Porsche and Daigh driving an outgunned Lister-Jag for Cunningham couldn't get up enough speed to qualify.

George Constantine in a Lister-Chevy and Jo Bonnier in a Porsche suffered mechanical failure after running second in their classes to near the halfway point.

Krause, of 20 Barclay St., picked up about $8,800 prize money for his win, achieved in front of an estimated 80,000 spectators.

The day's only casualty was Don Hulette. He escaped with cuts, minor burns and possible fractured ribs when his car cartwheeled off the course.

The two consolation races were won by Hulette and Alan Connell in a Lister-Corvette and Birdcage Maser respectively.

Moore Scores 4 TDs as Colts Tumble Rams

(Continued From Page C-1)

several runs while rookie Dick Bass provided a few thrills with twisting excursions in the final quarter. Here is scoring in detail:

First Quarter: Ram Defense Sparkles

A scoreless first period was highlighted by tenacious Ram defense that didn't allow the Colts a first down in three offensive series. Particularly brilliant was a red-dog by Les Richter that caught Alan Ameche behind the line of scrimmage on a third-and-inches situation.

Sparked by Arnett's 51yard end run, the Rams travelled from their own 27 to the Colts 22 the first time they had the ball. Danny Villanueva missed a field goal from the 35.

Second Quarter: Moore Takes Charge

Rams 3, Colts 0—Lou Michaels, playing before his Kentucky homefolks, stunned the crowd with a 51-yard field goal that barely made it across the cross bar. It broke his own club record of 50 yards set against the 49ers this year.

Colts 7, Rams 3—The Colts wasted no time striking back. From his own 43, Moore shot up the middle and sped downfield on a line into the end zone. The play came on an audible signal by Unitas when Richter jumped offsides attempting to shoot the gap. Before Richter had recovered the gap was shut by Moore.

Steve Myhra converted the first of four extra points.

BILL KRAUSE WINS RACE IN MASERATI

69

Spectacular Field Goes in Riverside Sports Car Classic

Facts & Figures For Road Races

WHAT: Two-day sports car race meeting Oct. 15-16.

Saturday, Oct. 15 — So. Calif. Amateur Sports Car Races.

Sunday, Oct. 16 — 200-Mile Grand Prix for sports cars.

WHERE: Riverside Intl. Raceway, 5 miles east of Riverside at the junction of U.S. Highways 60 and 395.

SPONSOR and SANCTION: Grand Prix for sports cars is sponsored by the Los Angeles Times-Mirror Co. on behalf of Times

Stirling Moss; Lotus 19

Jim Jeffords: Maserati

George Constantine; Lister

Dick Guldstrand: "Riverside has all the elements to test both man and machine; a real high speed straight; a real high speed high banked turn nine; a real gutsy turn one. That was a turn that separated the men from the boys. You either did it flat out or you weren't competitive. An incredibly good racetrack"

Bob Drake; 'Ol Yeller

Don Hulette crashed and destroyed his car. He was uninjured

Grand Prix For Sports Cars Due Sunday At Riverside

The deep-throated reverberations of chained horsepower will fill the smoky blue air at Riverside International Raceway Sunday when the Fourth Annual Grand Prix for Sports Cars gets started at 2 p.m.

The Grand Prix will cap three days of raceway activities when the grinding of gears and the muted roar of revved-up engines will attract thousands to the Los Angeles Times sponsored benefit.

Race fans who have the time can enjoy three days of racing activities which begin at 10 a.m. Friday.

The Friday events will consist of racing cars from all over the world competing for choice spots in the Sunday lineup for the big event.

Only six cars will be selected Saturday there will be several events including motorcycle races, a three-hour production car endurance affair, and amateur car racing.

The Grand Prix will consist of 62 laps around the oval shaped battleground for many of the nation's top race drivers.

Information received here is that the tickets can be obtained at the gate each day. The Chamber of Commerce office at Riverside reportedly has advance tickets for the three-day event.

Reserve seats cost $2 more than the price of general admission.

General admission for the Sunday event costs $2.

JIM HALL, in Chevy-powered Troutman-Barnes Chaparral, leads Dan Gurney, Lotus, at lower end of turn 7 in Riverside sports car Grand Prix. Hall took 3rd, and it was the best effort by an American car. (MOTOR-ACING photo by Bill Norcross)

Hometown Boy Enters Race At Riverside

gave him his chance. Last year he again took over as driver for the Montebello, Calif., building contractor who by then had acquired a Lotus Monte Carlo. In that car, Gurney set a course record for sports cars as the fastest qualifier with a time of 2:00.94 minutes for the nine-turn, 3.275-mile course.

Gurney refuses to pick a fa-

'Best Sports Car Field Ever,' Says Gurney

BY DICK HYLAND

Dan Gurney is a 31-year-old Southern Californian, raised in Riverside, who went abroad and made good. He is the top driver for the Porsche factory team.

Via the point system in vogue for various nationals' Grand Prix races in Europe, North and South America, Gurney is presently the fourth ranking sports car driver in the world.

Has 13 Points

Ahead of him are Santa

Asked to pick a favorite for the Times-Mirror classic excluding himself, Gurney backed off before leaving Riverside for Watkins Glen.

"I couldn't," the crew cut blonde who looks like a college halfback said. "There are at least a dozen cars with a chance to win at Riverside. I honestly feel it is the most competitive field I've seen anywhere, good cars as well as good drivers.

Bill Krause leading Jack Brabham and Walt Hansgen

Krause and Miles

Carroll Shelby

Phil Hill

Dick Thompson; Stingray

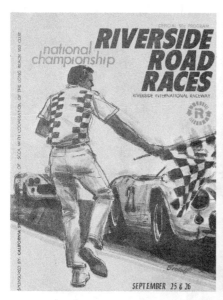

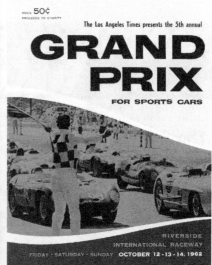

A crowd of 70,600 saw Jack Brabham win $11,000 and a Pontiac Grand Prix in 1961 driving a Cooper Monaco followed by Bruce McLaren in a similar car. Jim Hall, in the Troutman Barnes Chaparral was third.

70,600 SEE BRABHAM CAPTURE GRAND PRIX

WATCHING CARS WHIZZ BY—Part of huge crowd of 70,600 watches Turn Six as Jack Brabham, shown in front, duels with Bruce McLaren on Riverside Raceway in fourth annual Times Mirror Grand Prix

MOTOR RACING
and ECONOMY CAR NEWS

7th Year— NO. 1—Los Angeles, Calif.   OCT. 27-NOV. 3, 1961
(Published bi-weekly except last issue of calendar year)   25¢

The Winners--Brabham and Moss

ON SUCCESSIVE Sundays, crowds totalling 133,100 spectators turned out for sports car races at Riverside, Calif., and Laguna Seco (near Monterey, Calif.). They saw Jack Brabham, left, of Australia, 1959-60 world's road racing champion, win in a Cooper at Riverside and Stirling Moss of England, biggest attraction in the racing world, triumph at Laguna Seco. He won both here in a Lotus. Complete charts, stories and photos on inside pages. (MOTORACING photos by Gus V. Vignolle)

HOMECOMING — Riverside's Dan Gurney, No. 1 member of the European Porsche factory team, returns home to drive Frank Arciero's Lotus 19 Monte Carlo in fourth annual Grand Prix for Sports Cars at Riverside International Raceway, Sunday. H. set lap record last year (2:00.93).

Judith Selby: *"That was a great race. After the race, I had a brief driving seminar with Ken Miles in my 1960 Austin Healy Sprite. Back in the times of no roll bar, no seat belts etc. My mother, Penny Brady (wife of Jack) was clerking for Ken. He was standing up on turn six.. At the drivers meeting, he kind of grinned down that nose and said, "You just can't go fast enough for me to tell if you know what you're doing or not!! That fun little car was topped out at 85 mph on the straight, even downhill - I twiddled my thumbs for the rest of the straight. A couple of years later he came to Scooter Patrick's and my wedding."*

Two Cooper Monacos; Bruce McLaren leading Jack Brabham

Bob Harris; Campbell Special

Dan Gurney; Lotus 19

Fred Knoop Ferrari 412's

Skip Hudson

PAST WINNERS — It was Chuck Daigh (top) the 1st year (1958) in a Chev.-Scarab, and last year it was Phil Hill (bottom) in a 3-liter Ferrari. Who will it be Sunday, Oct. 16, in the 3rd annual LA Times-Mirror $20,000-plus, 200-mile sports car classic at Riverside Raceway? Both go again, plus such international aces as Brabham and Moss. Complete entry list on Page 5; other photos, stories and selections on inside pages. — (MOTORACING photos by Gus V. Vignolle and W. R. C. Shedenhelm)

Jim Hall; Chaparral

With finances not improving a new group purchased the track. Ed Pauley (of Pauley Pavillion fame), Fred Levy, and Roy Lewis; recognizable names; took over the debt ridden track and brought in Les Richter as manager. Richter brought NASCAR to the track, became the best spokesperson they ever had and almost achieved solvency.

Pauley, Levy Buy Into Riverside Raceway

EDWIN PAULEY

ROY LEWIS

FRED LEVY

Edwin Pauley, wealthy independent oil producer and Democratic party chieftain, and Fred Levy, Jr., have purchased a substantial interest in Riverside Int'l Raceway and have become stockholders and directors, it was announced by Roy G. Lewis, Riverside president.

No figure was announced, but it is believed they have invested "at least $1 million."

This bids fair to make Riverside one of the biggest and outstanding road racing courses in the world.

Both Pauley and Levy are part owners of the LA Rams pro football

team with Dan Reeves, Bob Hope and Hal Seley.

Pauley was associated years ago with Paul Schissler, Riverside general manager, in ownership of the old Hollywood Bears pro football team that played at Gilmore Stadium.

Les Richter

1962 was the last year for the USAC series; a crowd of 76,400 saw Roger Penske win in the Zerex Special, followed by Jim Hall in a Chaparral and Masten Gregory in a Lotus 19. Penske's win paid $9200 and a new Pontiac, The race was marred by the death of Pat Pigott, considered an up and coming young star. The GT race, a three hour event, was won by Doug Hooper in a Mickey Thompson owned Corvette after the Cobras broke.

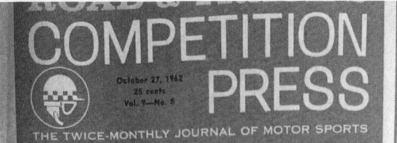

Penske Wins Big Ones in West

NEW SPECIAL BEST FIELD AT RIVERSIDE

By JAMES T. CROW

RIVERSIDE, Calif.—So Roger Penske, that nice young man from Gladwyne, Pa., won himself a bit more than $12,000 in money and goods by coming in first at the end of the 5th Times Grand Prix at Riverside on Oct. 14th.

Penske's win also puts him back into the lead for the North American Championship, his victory moving Dan Gurney back to 2nd place and tightening the contest for the three races that remain to be counted in the final standings.

Second, 3rd and 4th behind Penske at the finish were Jim Hall's Chaparral, Masten Gregory's 2.5 UDT-Rosebud Lotus 19, and Bruce McLaren's 2.7 Cooper Monaco, the only contestants still on the same lap as the winner at the end of the 77-lap, 200.2-mi race.

Fifth overall, and winner of the under-2-liter division, was Innes

TWO 2nds ADD UP TO 1st AT LAGUNA SECA

By JAMES T. CROW

LAGUNA SECA, Calif. — Dan Gurney won the 1st heat, Lloyd Ruby the 2nd, but when the results were added up for the 2-heat 200-mi Pacific GP at Laguna Seca on Oct. 21, it was Roger Penske who carried off the overall prize.

Penske, driving the same barely disguised F-1 Cooper Spl in which he won at Riverside, finished 2nd in both heats, added another $500 to the loot he's earned in the past two weekends and extended his lead for the North American championship. Roger's two 2nds beat out USAC-driver Ruby's 4th and 1st. Gurney didn't finish the 2nd heat.

Bruce McLaren finished 3rd in the 1st heat, 4th in the 2nd. Bruce got off to two bad starts, spinning in Heat I, starting from the back with an in-gear battery-start in Heat II because of an inoperative

MERRILL LOWELL has announced that the PALM SPRINGS GP, first planned as an international F-1 race, then as a $10,000 FIA National Open, has been cancelled for the present. However, there will be, according to Lowell, an amateur club race at the Thermal Airport location as soon as arrangements can be made with the Cal Club.

SCRAMP, sponsors at Laguna Seca, has signed with SCCA for the sanction at next year's PACIFIC GRAND PRIX. May be battled out in ACCUS-FIA meeting next month. USAC had the sanction in the past and is sure to object to the switch.

MARLBORO'S always-popular "Refrigerator Bowl" races are all set for January. More details later . . . EDDIE SACHS, the Indy driver, talked to at the Detroit Auto Show, says that JIM CLARK'S demonstration at Indy (see page 8) shows clearly that rear-engined Indy cars are on their way. "Give 'em two years," Eddie says . . . MEXICAN GP, now finally set for Nov. 4 at the Autodromo in Mexico City, is shaping up as a truly international event . . . From there it's PUERTO RICO, then NASSAU, then the championship deciding SOUTH AFRICAN GP on Dec. 29th . . .

Roger Penske of Gladwyne, Pa., is greeted by officials, newsmen and well wishers as he drives his Climax into the winner's circle with the Grand Prix Trophy in the rear.

Chuck Daigh - Maserati

Innes Ireland - Lotus 19

Masten Gregory

Storm Over Penske's Car

MOTORACING Photo by Don Schoenfeld

Winner Penske and Controversial Car

Don Hulette and Jerry Grant; following the field

MOTOR and Economy Car News
RACING

7th Year-No. 24-Culver City, Calif.
(Published bi-weekly except last issue of calendar year)

Oct. 19-26, 1962
25¢

MOTORACING photo by Gus V. Vignolle

HERE'S PART of the massive crowd of 76,400 which turned out to Riverside Intl. Raceway Oct. 14 for the 5th annual L.A. Times Grand Prix for Sports Cars. The action here is at turn 6, and the car booming through is the

Climax-powered Cooper Monaco of Bruce McLaren, of New Zealand. McLaren was 4th behind Roger Penske, Jim Hall and Masten Gregory. The race was marred by the death of Pat Pigott.

John Cannon practiced in the Dailu but didn't start

Augie Pabst and Harry Heuer discuss the woes of motor racing. Augie's Type 63 Maserati caught fire on the first lap; Harry's Scarab had clutch problems that prevented him from a higher-placed finish.

Augie Pabst: *"I bought this 2.5 liter Testa Rossa for $5000, took it out to Riverside and blew it up. Neglected to change from the warm up plugs and burned a piston !! Left it there with Richie Ginther who rebuilt the engine for me. Wonderful guy, great driver and mechanic. Then in 1961, my Maserati caught fire on the third lap"*

Augie Pabst in the Cunningham 151 Maserati

Frank Monise following Chuck Daigh

STINGRAY WINS 3-HR RACE

STINGRAY CORVETTE of Dave MacDonald, hotly pursued by AC Cobra of Bill Krause. Krause caught this Corvette, later went out with broken axle. Doug Hooper, driving another 'Ray, won 3-hr amateur race.

On Saturday before the Times Grand Prix, there was the 3-hr Times Invitational for amateur drivers and it was in this race that the 1963 Corvette Stingray made its successful competition debut as Doug Hooper kept his machine together to come in a winner.

It wasn't all that easy, however, as four of the thundering coupes (Dave MacDonald, Bob Bondurant, Jerry Grant and Hooper) started the race, filling four of the first 5 places after the race settled down. Interfering with the all-Corvette front-runners was another "XP" American-engined car, Carroll Shelby's AC Cobra driven by Bill Krause.

Krause went out after front-runner Dave MacDonald's Stingray and brooked no nonsense from the fiberglass monster, thundering along glued on its fastback for 8 laps. Krause took over in the 9th lap, bringing cheers from some fans, boos from others.

The Krause display of the Cobra was impressive, snorting and snuffing away from the privately-owned but factory-helped Corvettes at a great rate, assisted by a monstrous MacDonald spin.

The Cobra wasn't to last long, however, breaking an axle on the 15th lap, turning the lead back to MacDonald. Dave stayed in front another 10 laps, then pitted for tires, handing the lead over to Ed Mackey's Lotus-Alfa.

Mackey's hybrid lasted till the 1 hr 15 min mark, then retired with a seized engine and the sole surviving Stingray, Hooper's, moved into the lead.

But Hooper's victory still wasn't assured. Jay Hills, taking over Clyde Freeman's old 1500 RS, starting a min and a half behind the Corvette, moved up and up and up, from 4th to 2nd, poking at the lead by the 2½-hr mark, then was suddenly out of the race with clutch trouble.

Safe then, finally, Hooper cruised on to the finish to win by over a lap ahead of the smoothly-driven Carrera of Bob Kirby/Alan Johnson and another lap in front of Lew Spencer's Morgan SS.

As there were no Ferrari Berlinettas on hand it may not have proved much but it sure was fun.

—J. G. Anthony

G-H PROD, H MOD (20 laps)—1. Serge May (Lotus 7), 2. John English (Alfa), 3. Doc Doyle (Alfa). Class wins—GP, May; HP, Larry Nelson (Sprite); HM, Paul Grubl (Crosley Spl). Av spd —75.6 mph
3-HR RACE—1. Doug Hooper ('63 Corvette), 2. Bob Kirby/Alan Johnson (Carrera), 3. Lew Spencer (Morgan SS), 4. Art Snyder/Red Faris (BMC Genie), 5. Dave Jordan (Porsche N), 6. Ken Miles (Alpine), 7. Ray Pickering (Alpine), 8. Terry Hall (Porsche S-90), 10. E. Valsecchi (TR-4). Class wins—XP, Hooper; BP, Kirby/Johnson; CP, Spencer; DP, Bill Nickel (Porsche S); EP, Valsecchi; FP, Jordan; GM, Snyder/Faris. Distance—252.2 miles (97 laps); Av Speed—84.06 mph

Sting Ray Debut Big Success
Hooper Captures 3-Hr. Enduro

Editor's Note---The following story was omitted from the last issue of MOTORACING because of lack of space.

RIVERSIDE, Calif., Oct. 13 --- Doug Hooper, La Crescenta, Calif., who has been driving for Hansen's Chev., today switched and drove a new Corvette Sting Ray for Mickey Thompson, the fastest man on wheels.

And what he did was unusual---win in a new production car in its first out. It was the 3hr. enduro prelude to the LA Times GP for sports cars. He averaged 84.06mph, covering 97 laps, or 252.2mi.

Hooper finished more than a lap ahead of a Porsche Carrera driven by Bob Kirby and Alan Johnson. Lew Spencer was 3rd in his Morgan Plus 4. The Snyder/Faris duo, in Art's BMC Genie, was 4th, and Dave Jordan, Porsche 1600, was 5th.

There was terrific interest in the face because of the clash between the Sting Ray and another

production job making its local debut---Carroll Shelby's Ford-powered AC Cobra.

Bill Krause drove the Cobra and was actually leading the race when it was sidelined about a half-hour after the start with a broken axle. Said Shelby: "It was a tough break, but at least a consolation to know we were in front when the axle broke."

Hooper also had the fastest lap (No. 75), turning 1:43.1.

Dave MacDonald, also driving a String Ray, led the Cobra early in the going. He lost the lead to Krause when he was out due to a coil wire coming loose. MacDonald returned to regain the lead when the Cobra became a DNF. Wheel trouble later forced MacDonald out for good.

Hooper took charge at the half-way mark, and his biggest threat was Jay Hills, Porsche star. Hills was about to nail him when his clutch went out.

Class winner: Bp, Kirby/Johnson: Cp, Spender: Dp, W. Nickel, Porsche 1600; Ep, E. Valsecchi. TR4: Fp, Jordan: Xp, Hooper; Dm, John Masterson, Mercedes; Em, T. Piedrabuena, MG Spl; Gm, Snyder/Faris.

Although victorious, Hooper had trouble on turn 7, spinning there on three consecutive laps.

Ed Leslie of Monterey, Calif., won the Sunday $1600 Form. Jr. race in a Lotus 22. Then came: 2 Augie Pabst, Brabham-Ford; 3, Pete Lovely, Lotus 20; 4. Rob Nethercutt, Lotus 22; 5. Walt Hansgen, Cooper.

Lovely led for the first six laps, then Pabst through lap 12. From the 13th to the finish (25 laps) it was Leslie, one of the most improved drivers in the country.

RACE WINNER—Driver Doug Hooper of Los Angeles, left, talks to Mickey Thompson, car owner, after winning the three hour Enduro in Riverside.
AP Wirephoto

In 1962, Carroll Shelby started a driving school at Riverside, possibly the first race driving school ever. Pete Brock was the instructor and the car used was a Cobra. More about Driving Schools in Chapter Fourteen.

Carroll Shelby School of Racing

Here's that chance you've been looking for. Let Carroll Shelby teach you on world-famous Riverside Raceway. If you are already racing, sign up and take seconds off your lap times.

Your Car or Ours • • • Go Quickly Safely

Carroll Shelby is a former Le Mans 24-Hr. race winner (with Roy Salvadori),-Nat'l. SCCA champion & 1960 USAC Road Racing King.

WRITE FOR DETAILS
Carroll Shelby — 12812 Biola, La Mirada, Calif.

John Morton: *In 1962, I drove out from Waukegan, Illinois to attend Shelby's school. The school car was CSX2000, the first Cobra built. Got there a week early; Pete Brock, the instructor, said, "What are you doing here, stick around ?" What a week !! Reventlow was testing a rear engine Scarab, went to lunch with him and Brock. Shelby came out to test a Cobra with Bill Krause. Asked him for a job - then worked at Shelby's for three years !!*

The Times Grand Prix, part of what was becoming the "Fall Pro Series" with Laguna Seca, Mosport and St. Jovite drew a crowd 82,000 in October 1963, said to be largest crowd in sports car racing history in North America. Dave MacDonald won $14,340 and a new Pontiac, driving Carroll Shelby's King Cobra, followed by Roger Penske in the Zerex Special and Pedro Rodriguez in the Genie Mark 8. Cobras swept the 100 mile GT supporting race - first was Bob Bondurant, followed by Allen Grant, Lew Spencer and Dan Gurney.

MacDonald's Helpers Had Fingers Crossed

BY CHARLIE PARK
Times Staff Representative

RIVERSIDE — Carroll Shelby, wearing a floppy, black cowboy hat, paced in front of Dave MacDonald's pit at Riverside Raceway Sunday. The ex-driver who is the genius behind the Cooper Fords and Ford Cobras, had a stop watch in his right hand.

He rushed to the rail as MacDonald's blue No. 98 flashed past, then returned to the pits to call out the time to a trio of girls operating the computing boards — Diane Bell, Pam Blackwell and Natalie Rice.

fruitful day in which Shelby's entries scored a sweep — Bob Bondurant earlier had driven a Cobra to victory in the one-hour Gran Turismo.

Other behind-the-scenes events were not so pleasurable during the afternoon.

When Dan Gurney's Genie Ford went out after overheating, the Californian grabbed one of the rubber balls they stuff in the carburetor stacks during repairs and angrily threw it back over the wire fence.

Taken in Stride

The buffs called his car the "Calliope" because of the way the eight exhaust

fence at turn 6A but it was only a minor disturbance.

There were almost as many autos as people. They were parked as far as the eye could see. "Tightwad Hill," above the back straight, was jammed. Some of the smarties parked miles away and put-putted up on motorcycles they had toted along.

Station Wagons

Best view of the race was enjoyed by the crew of the raceway's decorators truck, which had one of those extension ladders like a fire wagon. They parked near the finish line.

came in those van-like station wagons, then raised awnings and picnicked it up.

The large number of women, both in the audience and the pits, was astounding. Equally so were the tight capri pants that seemed to be the uniform of the day.

The Fords even won the

"old-timers" race, with ancient "Black Widow" chugging in first.

MacDonald leads Penske and Holbert

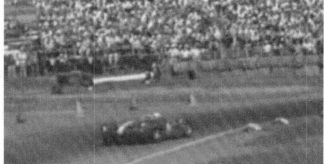

1963 Times Grand Prix Video - Watch it on the attached DVD

Rodriguez to Drive Genie in Grand Prix

BY BOB THOMAS

A quiet young Mexican lad, who drives an automobile with the bubbling emotion of the Latin that he is, widens and brightens the international flavor of the West's top sports car event—The Times Grand Prix at Riverside Raceway.

Pedro Rodriguez, a youngster, an international competitor despite his 23 years, Tuesday became an official entry in the $55,000 benefit 200-mile race which will be run Sunday, Oct. 13.

Ford Engine

The Mexico City racer, well known to local fans who have seen him and his late brother, Ricardo, many times at Riverside Raceway, will be wheeling "something special" over the 2.6-mile road course against such drivers as defending champion Roger Penske, Indianapolis winner Parnelli Jones and Ferrari ace John Surtees.

It's the latest creation of San Francisco auto sportsman Kjell Qvale and Joe Huffaker. It is dubbed the...

...would never again be a partner of auto racing.

But soft-spoken Pedro, who found expression on the race track, didn't stay away long.

He pursued his career in fact, with such determination that he very nearly qualified for a spot in the Indianapolis 500 earlier this year, and on the final day was bumped from a starting spot on the final day by a young driver who had concentrated on sports cars.

Rodriguez began the racing year impressively by winning the three-hour Daytona Continental, putting a Ferrari to a record triumph over the demanding road course of the Daytona Beach Speedway in February.

Pedro averaged 102.074 m.p.h. in a 12-cylinder Ferrari GTO, overcoming a record of 99.914 m.p.h. posted by British ace Stirling Moss in 1961.

Finished Third

His brother, 23-year-old endure the following month, was killed last fall during practice runs for the world-champion Graham Hill...

...of San Francisco, was second at Kent.

Interestingly enough, these two Genie creations—the Chevy and Olds powered cars—have been entered in the sixth annual Times Grand Prix.

Paul Reinhart, well known for his Corvette driving talents will pilot the Genie-Chevy while Bike Saint will be in the Genie-Olds.

Pedro, incidentally, is warming up to his Riverside test. He ran second in the Bridgehampton 500-miler.

ADVERTISEMENT

Treat Your Shoes To
STOP ATHLETE'S FOOT!

If you've tried all kinds of remedies and liquids to stop Athlete's Foot without success, then we give you four-five are successfully being re-infected by the fungus spores in your shoes. Buy now you can lick this problem with Caswell-Pascaquin Powder, because it works (the way): (1) kills the fungus spores in your shoes, (2) inhibits growth in your shoes, (3) makes fungus growth between your toes. So invest Athlete's Foot successfully, sprinkle Caswell-Pascaquin Powder between your toes and in your shoes.

FOLLOW! THE RAMS!
See Hi-Lites of
RAMS vs **DETROIT LIONS**
TONIGHT - 9:30
KCOP-CH. 13

Wins Grand Prix

MacDonald Surprises

RIVERSIDE, Calif. (AP) — Young Dave MacDonald proved one thing at Riverside Raceway —the big names don't always win the big races.

MacDonald, tabbed as an up and coming driver in the road race circuit, beat out racing greats like Rodger Ward, Dan Gurney, A. J. Foyt, Jimmy Clark, John Surtees, Augie Pabst and Graham Hill Sunday and won the 200-mile Grand Prix for sports cars.

He led the field of 31 cars after the first three laps and set a course record in his Cooper Ford. MacDonald toured the twisting 2.6-mile track for an average speed of 96.273 miles per hour. The winning time was...

Ward, Foyt, Gurney, Jim Hall and Richie Ginther were forced out by mechanical trouble.

Parnelli Jones, 1963 Indianapolis 500 winner, had trouble with his original mount and did not get a replacement ride.

MacDonald won $14,340 of the $35,000 purse.

Pedro Rodriguez, Mexico City, driving a Genie Ford, came in third, more than two laps behind the winner. Britisher John Surtees, competing in a Ferrari three liter despite a painful foot injury suffered in the U.S. Grand Prix, finished fourth.

Current World Grand Prix champion Clark finished fifth, but was first among the drivers of small-bore, or two-liter cars.

Dave MacDonald in the King Cobra wins the 1963 LA Times Grand Prix.

Marilyn Halder: *"I was Marilyn Fox then. Doing commercials and assorted photo shoots, I was hired by the Powerine Oil Company to appear at gas station openings and general publicity functions. Turned out we were soon to be a gasoline sponsor at the relatively new Riverside Raceway. I got so involved and became Miss Powerine, waving flags with the starter, kissing winners (after I asked their wives if it was OK) and as it turned out, marrying a race car driver, Lothar Motschenbacher."*

Bob Harris   **Roger Penske**

93

Jim Clark in the Bob Challman Lotus 23

Parnelli Jones and Jim Clark

Carroll Shelby and Dave MacDonald

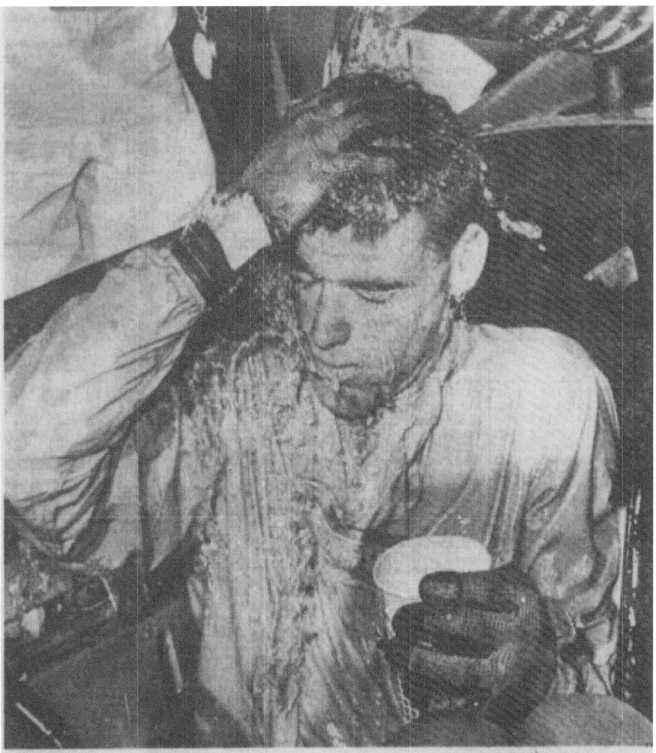

THE WATER'S JUST RIGHT—Dave MacDonald of El Monte, who lapped the field in winning the Times Grand Prix at Riverside Sunday, cools off after the race as crewmen dump ice cold water on him.

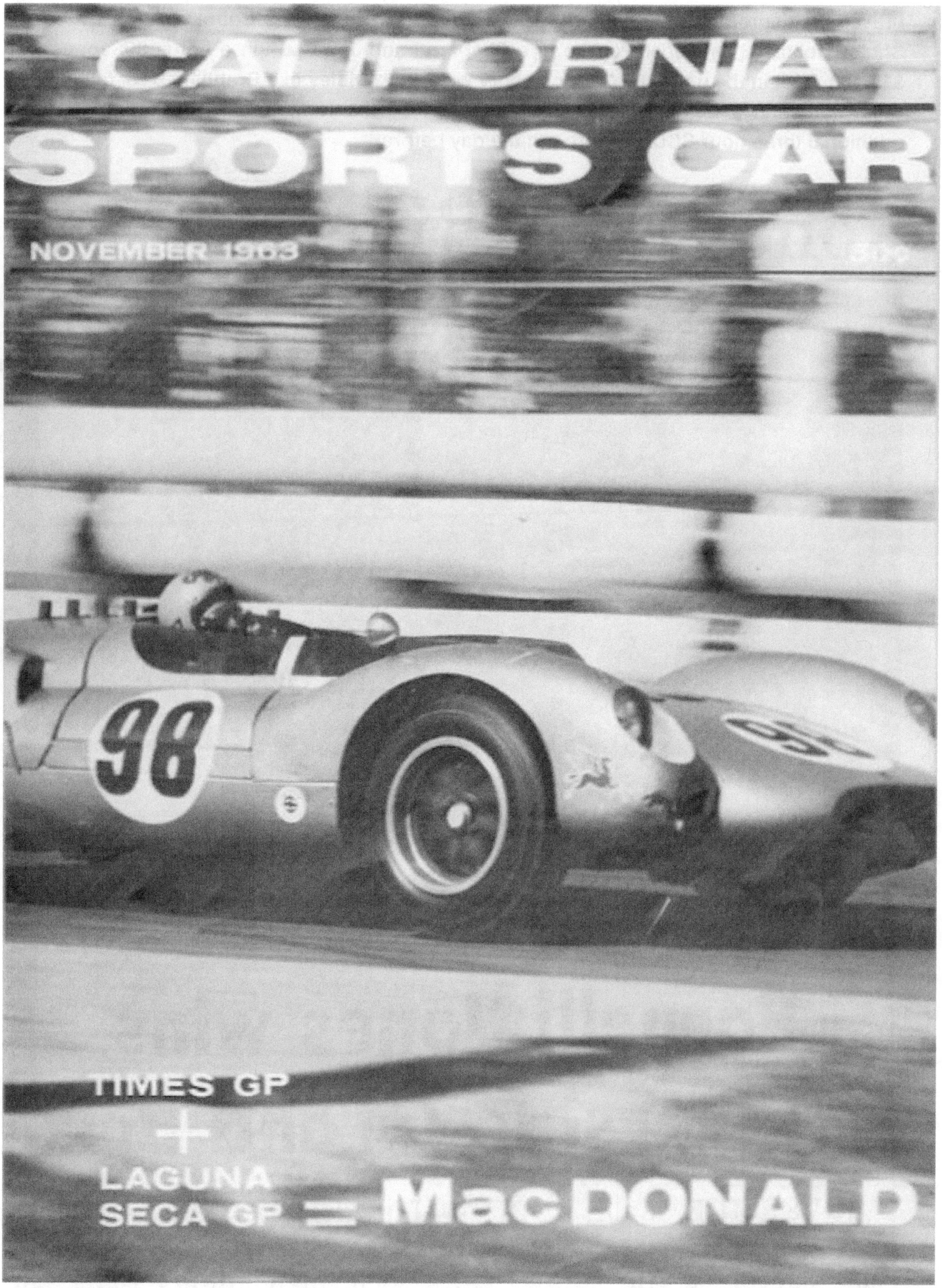
CALIFORNIA
SPORTS CAR
NOVEMBER 1963
98
TIMES GP
+
LAGUNA
SECA GP = MacDONALD

The Times Grand Prix, as part of the "Fall Pro Series" that included Mosport and Kent, came back in October,1964 but the USRRC was taking its place in the future. A crowd of 83,330 braved 93 degree weather to see Parnelli Jones win in a King Cobra entered by Carroll Shelby, followed by Roger Penske in a Chaparral and Jim Clark in a Lotus 30. Jones won $14,450. First in the under two liter category was Hugh Dibley in a Brabham BT8, followed by Rick Muther in a Lotus 23. Rick Muther also won the formula car supporting race. An additional three hour SCCA enduro ran the day before.

SPORTS Independent (Pasadena) —15
Monday, Oct. 12, 1964

Jones Cops Riverside Prix

83,330 watch race

Parnelli Jones wins Riverside Grand Prix

RIVERSIDE, Calif. (UPI) — Parnelli Jones—not content with his successes in stock car.

Philadelphia, who drove a Chaparral Chevrolet.

Scotsman Jimmy Clark, driv-

RECORD CROWD SEES RECORD GRAND PRIX RACE

THRILL SEEKERS—Part of the record crowd of 83,330 fans at Times Grand Prix Sunday at Riverside Raceway, crowd near famed 7.5 turn to watch sports cars in 77 lap, 200 mile feature event.

Bobby Unser in the Arciero Lotus 19 ahead of the Dave Ridenour Genie

Rocky Moran: *"Riverside was my first ever race; I must have been 14 or 15; got me hooked on racing. Read Road & Track and Car & Driver with the results a month late (until I discovered National Speed Sport News !!) Got into go karts and went from there."* Complier's Note – Rocky was not only successful in go karts, he went on to compete in 24 Indy car races including three Indy 500's, won the 1993 Daytona 24 hour and had a continuing ride in the AAR GTP Toyota.

OUT OF THE MAINSTREAM—His Lotus 19 spewing dust, Jerry Grant spins off the track at turn No. 2 Saturday during a Times Grand Prix trial run. Grant returned to the track and continued the race.

Times photo

100

Allen Grant; Cheetah

Jim Clark; Lotus

Bruce McLaren; McLaren

Roger Penske; Chaparral

Brabham leading Challman and Ridenour

Dan Gurney; Lotus 19

Hap Sharp; Chaparral

George Wintersteen; Cooper Monaco

Richie Ginther; Cooper Ford

Tommy Hitchcock; Brabham BT8

Al Unser; Lotus 19

Rick Muther; Lotus 23

A.J. Foyt; Hussein 1

Rick Muther; Lotus 23 dicing with Charles Cox; Cooper Ford

Shelby Team – Parneli Jones and Bob Bondurant

George Wintersteen leading Chares Cox

Augie Pabst,, Bobby Unser, Ronnie Bucknum, Parnelli Jones and Jim Clark

Ted Sutton: *"The day after the race we tested the coupe. After a test session, Ken Miles had me put the car up on jackstands and remove the diff cover. He got under the car and counted the teeth on the ring gear so he could calculate the top speed. I asked him what it was but he said; privileged information"*

Compiler's Note: Ted Sutton was part of the original Shelby team, now building replica GT350R's

Another record crowd of 84,478 saw Hap Sharp win the 1965 Times Grand Prix For Sports Cars in a Chaparral, followed by Jim Clark in a Lotus 40 and Bruce McLaren in his own Mclaren Olds. George Follmer won the under two liter category in a Lotus 23 Porsche. A consolation race for those who didn't qualify was won by Roger McCluskey. In 1966 the Times Grand Prix became a Can Am.

Hap Survives Times GP Roulette

By Charles Fox
News Editor

RIVERSIDE, Calif., Oct. 31 — Hap Sharp pushed his Chaparral 2A around the 2.6-mi. Riverside course while an international field crumbled before him and world champion Jim Clark fought a bucking Lotus 40 be-

hind, to inherit a win worth over $14,000 before a crowd of 88,000.

But the moral victor in this race of kings was the reticent 28-year-old New Zealand constructor/driver, Bruce McLaren in his London-built McLaren-Olds. Finishing third behind Clark, McLaren ran

over a piece of glass when lying second in the opening laps and was forced to pit for :01.25 with a flat right rear tire.

He rejoined the race over a lap down and proceeded to unlap himself and get to within 22 secs. of Sharp before the end.

The lead changed three times be-

COMPETITION PRESS &
AUTOWEEK

NOVEMBER 27, 1965

25 CENTS

Chaparral Wins Riverside:
SHARP TOPS CLARK

Hap Sharp, winner of the 200-mile 1965 Los Angeles Times Grand Prix at Riverside International Raceway, set a new track record of 102.989 mph using Royal 76 gasoline in his Chaparral II.

Hap Sharp wins the Grand Prix at Riverside with Royal 76 gasoline

...the same chemical tune-up premium you get at any Union Oil service station

Many racing fuels are special blends — but not the gasoline that Hap Sharp used in his record-shattering win at Riverside.

He powered his Chaparral II with Royal 76 — **the exact same premium gasoline you get from your neighborhood Union Oil dealer!**

Royal 76: the West's most powerful premium. The gasoline that proved itself where the name of the game is **power.**

Why not prove it to yourself . . . in your car? See how Royal 76 puts back the POW in power . . . gives your engine a chemical tune-up every mile you drive.

Stop in at the Sign of the 76 and fill up with Royal 76. It's **the same gasoline** that won at Riverside.

And only Union Oil has it!

UNION OIL COMPANY OF CALIFORNIA

HAP TOO SHARP FOR GRAND PRIX RIVALS

BY BOB THOMAS
Times Auto Editor

RIVERSIDE — An oil drilling contractor turned race driver . . . a piece of glass . . . a record crowd . . . and a broken speed barrier.

These were all chapters in a fast-moving auto-racing drama that was written Sunday at Riverside International Raceway.

The story was really James (Hap) Sharp of Midland, Tex., the oilman.

After, all, he beat the world's best collection of race drivers by driving a home-built sports car, a Chaparral, to a record breaking victory in the 8th annual Times Grand Prix for Sports Cars.

Clark Finishes Second

And 37-year-old Sharp did it efficiently, quickly and quite calmly despite the fact that he drove much of the way with the world champion, Jimmy Clark of Scotland, licking his heels.

Clark finished second under sunny skies before 84,478 witnesses, largest turnout in the history of the charity classic. His Lotus 40-Ford was not quite fast enough to cope with the 102.989 m.p.h. average posted by Sharp.

Sharp covered the 200 miles — 77 laps around the 2.6 mile, 9-turn road circuit—in one hour, 56 min-

utes, 28 seconds; the first man to break both the two hour and 100 m.p.h. barriers. Last year's winner, Parnelli Jones, averaged 99.245 m.p.h.

Gentleman racer Sharp, who has been digging oil wells for years and years

but racing only since 1958, cut his way to something of a California gusher — $14,640 of a $49,000 purse, including a 1966 Pontiac Grand Prix automobile.

But for a piece of glass the story might have had a different ending.

HAP AS IN HAPPY—Hap Sharp has a grin as big as his home state of Texas following his win Sunday in the $49,000 Times Grand Prix at Riverside.

The fragment of glass spoiled the victory chances of the favorite, Bruce McLaren of New Zealand, who managed to finish third, 22 seconds behind Sharp despite a flat tire early in the race which set him back more than a lap. There was little doubt that the young Kiwi had the fastest car on the track, an Oldsmobile - powered McLaren, built in his own shop in England.

Clark, who had worked within three seconds of the winner late in the race, relaxed a futile chase in the final laps to finish six seconds back. The run was worth $4,900 to the 1965 world champion and Indianapolis 500 winner.

Stars Fall Out

So torrid was the pace of the race, however, that most of the "hot shot" entries weren't around at the end. Attrition collected such notables as defending champion Jones, Walt Hansgen, Graham Hill, Dan Gurney, Richie Ginther and Jerry Grant.

And some of the top stars never did get to the line, so tough was the competition during the three days of trials. Among them were Jim Hall, Sharp's Chaparral racing partner who had shared early favoritism with McLaren; Jackie Stewart of Scotland;

Please Turn to Pg. 4, Col. 3

NEW LEADER—Hap Sharp (65) takes over lead in Times Grand Prix Sunday at Riverside as previous pacesetter Bob Bondurant (11) hits wall in Turn 6 after brakes locked on his Lola 70. Bondurant was uninjured and Sharp, once in front, never looked back as he took top money in 200-mile race classic.

Earl Gandel: *"From 1959 to 1964, I was the advertising and p.r. manager for Competition Motors, VW & Porsche distributors for the Southwest. Huschke von Hanstein of Porsche was visiting at the time, and I had the job of showing him around so I took him out to Riverside. We were met by Glen Davis, then General Manager of the track, who drove us up to the ticket gate. He said "wait a minute", and got out of the car, walked up to the car in front of us, and tapped on the trunk. Two kids promptly got out. I asked how he knew? He said, "hand prints in the dust on the trunk door". Incidentally, Glen Davis was my hero when I was 10 or 11. He and "Doc" Blanchard were Mr. Inside and Mr. Outside, playing football for West Point in the forties, and were national heroes. Davis won the Heisman Trophy, twice, I think. It was a memorable honor just to meet him. While walking around the pits, von Hanstein spotted and stopped to talk with Zora Arkus Duntov, who was there with Chevrolet. He described the details of the Dick Thompson car, the one with the torpedo headrest. As he walked away, von Hanstein said quietly, "Thank God it's only experimental."*

Riverside Lineup Called Best Ever

LOS ANGELES—Jimmy Clark will head the largest lineup of international drivers ever assembled at the eighth annual $40,000 GP for sports cars at Riverside International Raceway Saturday and Sunday Oct. 30-31. The race is open

and Bruce McLaren of New Zealand. Brabham is the only foreig ever to win the event.

The date marks a slight depart for the race, which previously held earlier in October. "The cha of date will add the advantage

Bruce Wins Times Warm Up

By Charles Fox
News Editor

RIVERSIDE, Calif., Oct. 30 — Bruce McLaren, the 28-year-old New Zealand driver-constructor who lives and works in London, survived one of Riverside's notoriously bad starts and swept to a convincing win in his McLaren-Olds ahead of Jim Hall's 2c Chaparral and Jerry Grant's Lotus-Chev., in the 20-lap L.A. Times Grand Prix qualifying race.

After a last minute announcement to the big bore drivers that a rolling start in two-two grid formation would be held on the back straight going into turn nine, the entire field was kept waiting while Dan Gurney arrived with his McLaren-Ford.

Gurney's crew was unloading his car on the pit road as the field moved off behing Indy veteran Sam Hanks in the pace car and Gurney set off in pursuit as the pack moved into the back straight.

Gurney had blown his engine during qualifying for the qualifying race on Friday, and his crew had taken the car back to Costa Mesa and worked all night putting in an experimental 289 Ford with Gurney-Weslake heads.

As the flag dropped all hell broke loose.

Mike Goth in a McLaren-Olds ran into USAC champ Mario Andretti's Lola-Chev and both spun. Goth continued, but Andretti, driving a Lola team car, was put out of contention for the weekend with front end damage.

Charlie Hayes, in the Nickey McLaren-Chev, ran into Bob Bondurant in the Pacesetter Homes Lola-Chev when the left front disc locked up on the McLaren, but both cars continued.

As the field swept past at the end of the first lap, McLaren led Hall and Grant (in the Alan Green Harris Lotus-Chev) with Parnelli Jones and Walt Hansgen in the two Mecom Lola-Chevys.

Hayes pulled into the pits to check handling problems and set off again as Hap Sharp pulled his Chaparral 2 in, to have his gas tank cap secured.

Meanwhile McLaren was setting a blistering pace and pulled out a two second lead over Hall, who had Grant and Jones chewing at his heels, while Hansgen fell back, running some five seconds ahead of Sharp.

Behind Sharp, Graham Hill, in the Coombs McLaren Elva-Olds led Jim Clark and Richie Ginther in the team Lotus 40s, with Hill gradually pulling away.

By the halfway mark, Clark had taken Ginther and Hill caught Sharp. At the head of the pack McLaren continued to build his lead to the end and Jones and Grant fought for third.

Jones took Grant on lap 15 but could not hold on and Grant squeezed by into third spot just before the final whistle.

TIMES GRAND PRIX OVER-2-LITER QUALIFYING RACE, RIVERSIDE, CALIF., OCT. 30.

TOP TEN: 1 - McLaren; 2 - Jim Hall, Chaparral 2C; 3 - Jerry Grant, Lotus-Chev; 4 - Parnelli Jones, Lola-Ford; 5 - Walt Hansgen, Lola-Ford; 6 - Cannon; 7 - Graham Hill, McLaren-Olds; 8 - Sharp; 9 - Bob Bondurant, Lola-Chev; 10 - Clark.

Bruce Ward: "My dad, Joe Ward. went down to Bob Challman's Lotus store in Manhatton Beach on the Wednesday before the race to pick up his new Elan. It came over from England on a cargo flight along with other cars for the Times Grand Prix on the next Sunday. He took it to Riverside Thursday, practiced, the clutch broke, they went back to Challman's, did an all nighter , qualified close to last at Friday, and raced it on Saturday. finishing 17th overall and third under two liters, beaten in class by George Follmer and Doug Revson, both in Lotus 23's "

Ken Miles tailed by Joe Ward in the Elan

111

David Hobbs: *"This was my first race there. My Lola T-70 car owner, Harold Young, under funded (and an alcoholic) had us struggling all through the fall season, St. Jovite, Mosport and by Riverside the car was pretty well done. We qualified 18th, next to my friend Hugh Dibley and well behind polesitter Bruce McLaren. The race was a standing start; my clutch was failing and and the car was trying to creep along. The starter was obviously not used to a standing start and kept us all hanging out. Meanwhile my clutch is about fried and but we managed to hang on for 64 laps. Incredibly disappointing; long way from UK for that to happen. Chris Economaki was on hand and interviewed me, my first appearance on U.S. TV;, little did I think then that would be my career for 41 years!! Being very young, mad as hell and frustrated with our whole enterprise I think I dropped the F- word more that once giving old Chris a bit of a shock !! We became very good friends many years later; working on ESPN broadcasts."*

Chris Amon

Jim Clark

Gerry Bruihl / George Follmer; Lotus 23's

Bruce McLaren

Augie Pabst

Charlie Hayes

Jim Hall; Chaparral

Skip Scott; GT40

Franz Weis driving Hap Sharp's Chaparral to the pits. Wesley Sweet holding the flag.

Driver Parade

Dan Gurney in his new McLaren-Ford, Bruce McLaren in the Olds-powered version, and Jackie Stewart in the Surtees Lola-Chev head the field at Riverside Oct. 31.

Times GP Boasts Finest Field in Racing

RIVERSIDE, Calif. — America's greatest road racing field — the best of Europe and the U.S.A. — has taken shape for the eighth running of the $40,000 Times GP for sports cars at Riverside International Raceway, Oct. 31.

Drivers from all parts of the world began assembling as early as last Monday at the 2.6-mi track for the 77-lap, 200-mi charity classic.

Defending champion Parnelli Jones, the '63 Indianapolis 500 winner, faces no less a challenge than that of '65 world and 500 champion Jimmy Clark of Scotland.

In addition, there is record depth of top cars and drivers for the race which annually draws more than 80,000 spectators.

From the grand prix circuits come former world champion Graham Hill of England, as well as Jackie Stewart of Scotland, Jack Brabham of Australia, Bruce McLaren of New Zealand and Americans Dan Gurney and Ronnie Bucknum.

This country's most prominent driver, four-time national champion and two-time Indianapolis 500 winner A. J. Foyt, headed South from his second place Sacramento finish for early week tests of his new Lotus 40-Ford.

Third place Sacramento finisher and new USAC champion Mario Andretti will drive for the Lola factory entry (Surtees) teaming with Stewart.

But the man to beat is still America's number one sports car figure — Jim Hall of Texas with his Chaparral-Chevy backed up by teammate Hap Sharp, also of Midland. Last May Hall established a new Riverside one-lap record average speed of 106.263 mph.

En route from England are Hugh P. K. Dibley, David Hobbs and New Zealander Chris Amon who will drive the interesting new Ford GTX-1.

Jones and his Mecom Lola 70 teammate, Walt Hansgen who won the Monterey Grand Prix Oct. 17., will renew a duel of Texans (Mecom vs. Hall) at Riverside.

Riverside Raceway is located 50 mi. east of Los Angeles at the junction of highways 395 and 60.

Times GP Crowd Big and Unruly

RIVERSIDE, Calif., Oct. 31 — The largest crowd ever to attend the Grand Prix, 84,000 plus, was treated to better parking facilities, more and permanent concession stands with adequate supplies of drinks to help combat the high temperature, permanent sanitation buildings, and larger and better-placed grandstands to go with one of the highest car attrition rates in the history of the event.

The parking areas were filling up rapidly by 9am and by 10 the grandstands at turn 5, the favorite viewing area, were filled.

The newly leveled-off infield at turn 6 was well set up for spectators, and cars were parked about 50 yards back from the turn with lots of area available for standing room spectators.

The crowd was graced by the usual number of teen age drunks who remained under control as long as police patrolled. After the race when all visible police had left to direct traffic, the parking lot became a raceway for motorcycles and a battling ground for beer bottle throwers.

It was at this point that first aid areas saw more action than they had all day when suddenly they were beseiged with bottle wounds and scraped knees and elbows.

Eldon Builds Slot Track at Riverside

RIVERSIDE, CALIF., OCT. 31 — An automobile raceway has opened within a famous raceway.

The formal unveiling of an elaborate and permanent slot car facility, the Eldon Model Car Racing Center, in the heart of Riverside International Raceway took place before the eighth running of the Times GP for sports cars here.

Situated in the infield area of the raceway, the four-lane slot car track is housed within an air-conditioned 20 by 40 foot A-frame building.

 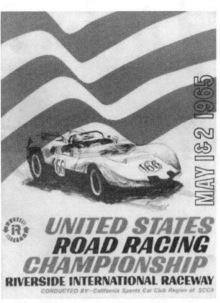 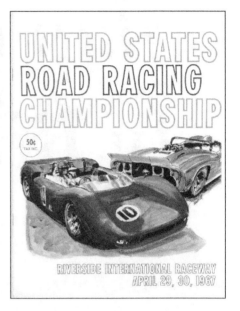

Giving up the battle (also losing it) against racing for money, in 1962, SCCA, headed by future IMSA owner John Bishop, created the U.S. Road Racing Championship. Originally for both sports racers and GT cars, over and under two liters, it lasted through 1968 but couldn't compete with the stars of the Can Am which began in 1965. In 1963 it consisted of eight races, none of which were at Riverside. Riverside got on board in the ten race 1964 season again with a USRRC race in April, billed as the richest race of its kind in the world. Skip Hudson won the over two liter class in a Cooper Chevy over Chuck Daigh in a Lotus 19. Bobby Unser won under two liters in a Lotus 23. In a separate GT category race, Ken Miles won the over two liter category in a Cobra and Scooter Patrick won under two liters in a Porsche 904.

Front Row - L to R - Dave MacDonald. Skip Hudson and Jerry Titus

Skip Hudson First In Riverside Race

By JERRY DIAMOND
Examiner Sports Car Writer

RIVERSIDE — Veteran race driver Skip Hudson finally made good in national competition and picked his home town track to turn the trick.

Driving a Cooper Chevy owned by Nickey Chevrolet of Chicago, Hudson boomed

Lotus 19 and Bobby Unser of Albuquerque, N. M., who who finished first in the under 2-litre division in a Lotus.

Ken Miles of Hollywood turned in an iron man performance as he finished

(Continued on Page 52, Col 1)

Hudson Wins at Riverside

IN TWO ACTS

U.S. Road Racing Title Drama Unfolds Today at Riverside

BY BOB THOMAS
Times Auto Editor

RIVERSIDE — A two-act adventure in auto racing will be staged today at Riverside Raceway. If it were baseball, it would be billed as a doubleheader.

Actually, it's the first Riverside running of a United States Road Racing Championship event — a dual-pronged affair that features a 182-mile (that's 70 laps) sports car race at 2:15 p.m., preceded by a 125-mile (48 laps) race for Grand Touring (GT) machines which are somewhat loosely classified as production sports cars.

Up for grabs is $11,000 in purse and accessory money.

Prominent in both races is Shelby-American which puts the favored team in each category with three Cooper-Ford sports cars in one and Cobra-Ford production cars in the other.

Most prominent name of 26-year-old Dave MacDonald of El Monte, making his first sports car appearance at the Raceway since he sped to a brilliant victory in the Times Grand Prix last fall.

Pole Winner

MacDonald won the pole with a qualifying lap of 100.8 m.p.h. around the 2.6-mi. course.

This was no surprise but there were several other surprises in the first two rows. Skip Hudson of Arlington, driving the Cooper Chevy he rode to a second place finish behind Mac-Donald last week at Phoenix, earned a front row berth with a qualifying time of 99.97 m.p.h.

Also on the front row was Jerry Titus, magazine editor, in the Cheetah Corvette.

Oilman Jim Hall of Midland, Tex., had a fast time early in the day, but retired to rebuild the engine of his Chaparral, which was throwing oil. The car will be

Defending USRRC champion Bob Holbert of Warrington, Pa., clocked an identical time with Hall and sits on the second row.

MacDonald's Cobra teammate, Ken Miles of Hollywood, set a new record for Grand Touring cars with a 1:38.4 qualifying lap in his Ford Cobra.

Miles and Ed Leslie were the only two Cobra drivers who attempted to qualify, and Leslie also made the front row for the 125-mile manufacturers' point race, which will be flagged off at noon.

Next in qualifying times came a pair of new Porsche 904 GTs driven by Scooter Patrick of Manhattan Beach and Don Wester of Monterey.

GRAND TOURING RACE
First Row — Ken Miles, Ford Cobra, 1:38.4; Ed Leslie, Ford Cobra, 1:40.0; Scooter Patrick, Porsche 904 GT, 1:40.4.
Second Row—Don Wester, Porsche 904, 1:40.4; Dick Goldstrand, Stingray, 1:41.6.
Third Row—Kurt Neumann, Porsche 904 GT, 1:42.2; Bill Krause, Stingray, 1:42.5; Dennis Harrison, Porsche 165.

Jerry Titus; Cheetah

Jim Hall; Chaparral

119

Dave MacDonald; Lang Cooper

Ken Miles; Cobra

The Arciero whirly-bird lays an egg at start-finish, to the consternation of officials at the Times Grand Prix at Riverside. Pilot Bill Scott and passenger Phil Arciero escaped injury in the crash, which took place while the copter was attempting to dust the track. Note the hat suspended in mid-air in the photo.　　　(Cam Warren photo)

'Copters Wow Customers With Riverside Sideshow

By Joyce Uphoff

RIVERSDIE, Calif. — Saturday was what we, in the trade, call a slow slalom day — so I decided to catch the action at Riverside raceway.

A few of the Grand Prix circuit boys and lots of the local sporty car drivers were gathering to run a 3 hour enduro and a snappy GP race for grid positions for the L.A. Times Hootnanny on Sunday.

Having secured a couple of passes from What's His Name of the Times — and this is a real

"Man from U.N.C.L.E." type feat — I settled down on the start finish tower to enjoy the local color.

Color! Such color you have never seen! Lined up on the grid are the world's greatest GP drivers, to say nothing of several million dollars worth of machinery, all waiting to battle for the honor of Sunday's pole.

With lap chart in hand, I watched them roar off the start and into turn 1, banging and steaming all

(Continued on page W-3)

Hollywood Dramatics Add To All-Star Cast at GP

By Cam Warren

RIVERSIDE, Calif. — Sophia Loren was missing, and likewise Anthony Quinn, although acceptable standins for either could have been found without going any farther than the paddock.

Otherwise all the ingredients for a Cinamascope spectacular were present here, including the cast of thousands.

It was hot and dusty, and quite a crowd was present around the water hole.

There was even a row of cars parked along the crest of a hill on the horizon, looking for the world like those Apaches about to attack the defenseless wagon train.

More than 80,000 fans were on hand, and each must have brought his own automobile.

They started lining up at the gates at daybreak, and by 9:30 the parking areas were nearly full, and the grandstand began to bloom with all the colors of the rainbow.

Two robins, a little mixed up about the season, picked straw out of a haybale to build themselves a nest in some far-off tree.

Riverside raceway — which might be described as a grassless Road America — was about to be the scene of one of the world's greatest sports car races, and judging from the lineup of cars and drivers in the program, the claim to fame was not exaggerated.

In spite of the international flavor, there was a certain Southern California stamp on the whole affair. The weather, for instance. It was cold in the wee hours. Then the sun came up, and it got very hot indeed.

A breeze came up, and dropped

the temperature a little, but also blew the smog in from Los Angeles. Then we had a strong wind which blew the smog away but made the dust fly.

Meanwhile, back on the track, Augie Pabst stormed into turn 6 discovered the throttle on the Mecom Lola coupe was stuck open and stuffed the car under a guard rail.

The car was pretty well totaled but Augie climbed out shoeless and unhurt, picking shreds of fibre glass out of his coveralls.

Another car spun toward a turn marshal, who managed to escape serious injury only by deftly hurdling it.

Then there was The Great Helicopter Crash. This unscheduled show-stopper occurred Saturday between qualifying races. It all began when the Chaparral driven by Hap Sharp sprung an oil leak just at the start of the over 2 liter event.

Before he could be flagged off there was an oil slick clear around the course, which caused Bob Bondurant to spin his Cobra in turn 1 effectively blocking the track.

The rest of the cars were red-flagged, while crews got busy spreading cement on the oil. Although there was a street-sweeper on hand, the operator couldn't be found, so a couple of whirlybirds were called in to blow off the excess cement dust.

This seemed to be working satisfactorily, and the officials were just about to restart the race when one of the choppers got its tail caught in some overhead wires.

Down it came with a great crash right in the middle of the track

120

In the May 1965 race, 15,379 people saw Jim Hall win in a Chaparral in the over two liter category with his teammate Hap Sharp second in another Chaparral. Don Wester was third in a Genie Ford. George Follmer's Lotus Porsche ran fourth overall, won under two liters and was to be the series champion, the only time an under two liter car was able to do that. In the accompanying GT race, Ken Miles again won the over two liter GT class in a Cobra as did Scooter Patrick in under two liters in a Porsche 904, followed by Bob Johnson in another Cobra and Davey Jordan in another Porsche 904.

121

Hall Smashes Records in Win

By BRUCE GRANT
Sun-Telegram Auto Editor

RIVERSIDE — Texan Jim Hall automatically ran away from the field yesterday for a record-routing U.S. Road Racing Championship triumph at Riverside International Raceway.

The lean, millionaire oilman from Midland, Tex., driving a Chaparral, with

one hour, 48 minutes and 49.4 seconds to cover 70 laps on the 2.6-mile course.

It was a record, to be sure. Hall's average speed was 100.346 miles per hour — fastest for any sports car here.

Indianapolis 500 veteran Parnelli Jones held the old record of 99.182 mph, which he set in

ral and its automatic transmission. The 29-year-old graduate of Cal Tech said he had "no problems at all."

Hap Sharp, Hall's Chaparral partner from Midland, finished 16 seconds behind the winner in a twin to the victory car.

lone San Bernardino County entry, finished 12th overall in his Lotus Elan. He was seventh in his class, two spots behind former Ontario resident Tony Settember, who drove a Lotus 23.

Veteran Ken Miles recovered from two spinouts to overtake Scooter Patrick and repeat as

CHAPARRAL WINS—Jim Hall drives his Chevrolet powered Chaparral around the turn enroute to a record win at the Riverside International Raceway.

Hall Sets Track Speed Mark In Winning Riverside Road Race

RIVERSIDE — AP — If Jim Hall had not changed his college major from geology to mechanical engineering, who knows?

He probably would not hold the Riverside International Raceway's speed record for distance automobile racing and be the proud owner of

for stock cars, won by Ken Miles of Hollywood.

Miles averaged 93.60 miles an hour in a Cobra, taking $1,200 in prize money and

Jeff Macpherson: *"Riverside – Where I learned to race !! The LA Times Grand Prix was the annual event that while sunburnt and dehydrated in the turn six grandstands, I learned the names of my lifelong heroes, Dan Gurney and Jim Clark. All I wanted to do was be like them!. I was fortunate to race in Formula Atlantic and Super Vee and a few other categories, liked the Off Road part most. Plus it was possible to run a dual wheel truck through the tunnels at 85mph...but only with the proper lubricant!"*

Skip Scott – GT40

Riverside Raceway Twin Bill Boasts Twin Queens, Too

Sports car racing's double-header USRRC event at Riverside International Raceway May 2 calls for a delightfully different twin bill of fare — two identical race queens.

They are Nancy and Susan Robbins, 21-year-old twins from Manhattan Beach. Nancy, who'll be "Miss GT" in honor of the 125-mile race for grand touring cars, and Susan, "Miss Sports Car," who will reign over the 182-mile sports car event that day, are American Airlines stewardesses.

The twin beauties will be witnessing their first sports car race, although they are avid devotees of water skiing, golf, tennis and other sports.

The Riverside USRRC event will be the second on an 11-race national pro circuit that will determine national sports car manufacturing and driving championships.

The 1964 driving champ, Jim Hall of Midland, Tex., and the '65 point leader, George Foll-

Grant Joins Field for Riverside 182-Miler

Veteran race driver Jerry Grant who, with co-driver Dan Gurney, dominated most of the 12-hour endurance race at Sebring, Fla., last month, is an official entrant for the 182-mile U.S. Road Racing Championship race at Riverside International Raceway May 1.

The 31-year-old driver, formerly of Kent, Wash., but now residing in Costa Mesa will pilot a brand-new English Lola sports car in the $15,000 classic, second in a nine-race series across the nation to decide the coveted U.S. Road Racing Championship for drivers.

The car was entered by Gurney's All-American Racers Inc., of Santa Ana, and is powered by a 289-cubic-inch Gurney-Westlake Ford engine. It is the same mount Grant used for recent tire tests at Riverside, where he set an unofficial lap record of 1:26.4 or 108.333 miles an hour.

"I feel certain we can get that down to a flat 1:25," the Indianapolis 500 veteran Grant said after the test. "The car is new yet and this has been our first time out with it. We have a few more things to do before it will be completely ready for racing."

The existing one-lap record at Riverside is 106.489 mph, set last October by Bruce McLaren. Grant and the more than 40 other expected competitors will have a chance to better that officially April 29, when the 2.6-mile course opens for practice and qualifying.

Two other events will serve as companion features to the May 1 USRRC at Riverside.

A 30-minute event for A-B-C-D production sports cars will start the day's activity beginning at 10:45 a.m. and will be followed by the Mission Bell Trophy race, a 100-mile event for sedans of both European and American manufacture.

The featured USRRC will be flagged off at 2:30 p.m.

Sanctioned by the Sports Car Club of America (SCCA), the USRRC circuit this year will get underway at Las Vegas, Nev., on April 24.

Following the Riverside event on May 1, the circuit will move to Laguna Seca, Calif., and then on to Bridgehampton and Watkins Glen, N.Y. Competitors in the series will be racing for points and more than $150,000 in prize money.

100 Golfers Tee Off in CYO Match

Approximately 120 "cham-

124

Walt Hansgen; Scarab

Charley Hayes in the Lang Cooper leads Don Wester and Jim Hall

Huge Crowd

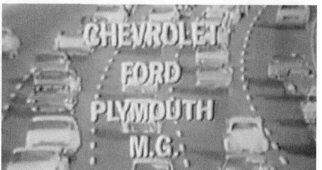

View this 1964 Champion Spark Plug Ad on the attached DVD

Bruce Ward: *"My dad ran his Elan in the USRRC GT race, finishing seventh overall and fourth under two liters. Ahead of him were guys like Ken Miles, Scooter Patrick and Davey Jordan. Not bad for a Riverside veterinarian. He also ran the main event in the under two liter category, finishing 13th overall and seventh under two liters."*

127

Read the 1965 Raceway Magazine USRRC article on the attached DVD

THE FASTEST CAR WE'VE EVER TESTED

ROAD&TRACK

JULY 1966   3/6 IN ENGLAND   SIXTY CENTS

CHARLIE HAYES' McLAREN ELVA CHEVROLET

Read the 1966 Road & Track road test of Charlie Hayes' McLaren on the attached DVD

USRRC at Riverside—The Numbers Game

RIVERSIDE — It was called the "Numbers Game" or the United States Roulette Raceway Challenge at Riverside May 2 — and the traffic was fierce, not on the race course, but among the press and workers

The absolute, stark confusion over who goes where at Riverside was due to a quaint computerized numbering system for all passes used by the raceway.

A survey disclosed that all passes were numbered from 30-something to 60-something, and the lower the number the better.

Almost immediately it became apparent that no one had the correct number to reach the necessary area. Drivers were late to the grid as a result of having been issued pass numbers which entitled them to seats in the grandstand at turn seven.

Photographers, who needed to stand in the middle of the course, found themselves with #44 passes, which got them in the first entrance, the parking lot on turn six only, and a ride on the Matterhorn at Disneyland. So-called working press passes were numbered from 0 to 1000 but they all allowed admittance to the paddock only which was full of tow cars and THEY

weren't going that quick; or alternatively, the bridge on the back straight where there was official loitering only.

Then there were a select few of the press who had the magic number admitting them to the press room and/or the press patio. Sadly the significance of this group of numbers was so successfully withheld that their proud bearers had absolutely no idea of what they were entitled to, and so they loitered on the bridge instead.

The workers' numbers game was even more sophisticated. Flag men were given 00 numbers which allowed only Daughters of the American Revolution to get to the refreshment stands. Officials spent most of the time in cars or on bikes on the track, since this was the only way to get from place to place without running into a number-coded guard.

Suppliers spent most of the day outside the gate altogether, they were given numbers which didn't exist at all and were left over from January's late model stock car race.

The new tower was in use for the first time and admittance to that was harder to get than an invitation to the LBJ ranch. The numbers for

entrance to the tower were withheld from ABSOLUTELY everyone including the man who printed the passes. One worker happened to draw the tower number but didn't have the requisite CIA countersignature, and naturally the man empowered to sign was at the top of the tower.

Numbers only count if there are guards on the gates. Since guards are no kind of race-worker dumbells, they work for money. They were not in evidence until about 11 am and until then everyone was civilized and gregarious spending the morning mingling in the pits. Suddenly the loud speaker announced that everyone — regardless of pass number — must leave the pits and go into the paddock area. Then the guards, now on duty, were to check the in people back in. This resulted in an immediately noticeable permanent loss of three thousand people who ended up on the road to March Field.

One official found the answer to the numbers game — very simple really — a light blue jacket with a Riverside Raceway emblem. With this chic bit of attire, one can do anything at the track except get a key to the washroom.

Even loiter on the bridge, which has some of the same advantages.

Drivers Seek to Qualify For Riverside Race Purse

It's the day of decision today around the twisting bends of Ri- | fic Raceway grand Prix at Kent, Wash.; Bob Holbert of

1966 was an eight race series. A crowd of 16,800 saw Buck Fulp winning over two liters at Riverside in a Lola T70 after a tight battle with Skip Hudson in the Lancer sponsored Lola T-70 with Chuck Parsons in a Genie in third. Scooter Patrick won under two liters in a Porsche 906.

The GT category had been eliminated. Supporting races include an SCCA production car race and a new sedan race, the Mission Bell Trophy Race.

Fulp Holds Off Charging Hudson to Cop Riverside

Buck Fulp; Lola T-70

Turn seven at Riverside during the May 1 USRRC, with John Cannon in no. 62 and Jerry Grant in no. 8 side by side followed by Ron Bucknum and Billy Krause in Lolas and Earl Jones' Genie. (D. Ross photo)

Davey Jordan; Porsche 906

Ed Hammill; SR3

By Joe Scalzo
Area Editor

RIVERSIDE, Calif., May 1 - Unsung John "Buck" Fulp and a slinky Lola-Chevy successfully combined to upset the storm warnings here that pointed to a violent victory showdown between superstars Jerry Grant and Charley Hayes.

Fulp, a 28-year-old Dixie-drawling resident of Anderson, S.C., had never won a major race and had never competed at Riverside before.

But he conquered the 95-degree, 182-mi. USRRC tilt with a 99.786 mph average and remained cool in the face of a white-hot challenge in the final eight rounds from second-place Skip Hudson's Lola-Chevy.

Hudson belatedly came hurtling up from mid-field to close furiously on Fulp's leading Lola and was something less than a second behind at the dramatic 70-lap conclusion.

The startling garrison finish of the Lolas came at a time when the crowd of 16,800 had fully anticipated the 2.6-mi. Raceway to be turned into a burnt-out crater from the force of the expected Jerry Grant/Charley Hayes battle which started two weeks ago at the Las Vegas USRRC opener when Hayes charged that Grant had deliberately run off course to pitch rocks at Hayes' own McLaren-Chevy.

But Riverside provided neither Grant nor Hayes the opportunity to re-live their Vegas vendetta.

Grant's Lola-Ford stopped at five laps after Grant embarrassingly missed a gear change and blew up his $8,000 Gurney-Weslake Ford engine. And Hayes' white McLaren fell from the race with a broken ring and pinion on the 27th lap.

At that juncture, dark horse Lothar Motschenbacher seized the lead
(Continued on page 8)

Charlie Hayes; McLaren

Lola T-70's; Buck Fulp leads Ronnie Bucknum

Davey Jordan: *"My first fast ride was in Vasek's Polak's RS-60 (I'd been successful in E production speedsters, a far cry from a Spyder). Vasek was known for a lack of preparation. We went to Del Mar, I thought to test and we did a few laps of practice and he said, "go race". Later on I drove Otto Zipper's Carrera Six; same deal, no preparation, I was the fast qualifier in under two liters, broke the exhaust during the race and DNF'd"*

Bruce Ward: *"My dad, Joe Ward, bought a Bobsy Alfa in 1966, ran the Riverside USRRC in the under two liter category. Qualified behind George Follmer, John Morton and Doug Revson, among others, then DNF'd due to mechanical problems"*

More on:

Buck Fulp Raids Riverside in USRRC Win

(Continued from page 1)

and kept his surprising McLaren-Olds in front clear to the 52nd lap when the overstressed engine shuddered. Fulp took over and passed the remaining 20 on.

Behind Fulp and Hudson were Chuck Parsons in a Genie-Chevy, and Bill Krause in another Lola-Chevy. All were on the same lap, but widely separated. Fifth, down three laps, was a Porsche Carrera Six, a coupe-bodied machine which behaved as nothing so much as an oven to its heat-stricken driver, Scooter Patrick.

The abominable Riverside temperatures robbed the prestige USRRC meeting of at least one potential winner (Ronnie Buckman) and noticeably impeded the progress of another (Krause). Yet heat wasn't a factor in any of the three separate mishaps that interrupted an otherwise trouble-free afternoon.

John Cannon's Las Vegas-winning Genie-Olds blew a tire approaching turn one and went straight on, almost into a chain-link fence, and the Ford GT40 of Al Whatley hit an oil-slick on turn nine and slid for 200 yards, eventually ending off the pavement, but still on its wheels.

Not so fortunate was the black McLaren Chevy of Ralph Salyer, which broke an axle and lurched off the road and into a fantastic

ence of Tracy's Jim Trovers and Frank Coons in his pits.

There were other nervous startees in the field of 31, such as Krause, who had lost his Pacesetter Lola's deck lid at 160mph in morning practice and had to borrow a spare from Fulp, and Chuck Parsons, who had broken two gearboxes in two days with his Genie-Chevy.

Hayes and Grant roared off the starting line as one car, but only got as far as turn seven when Grant made his ill-timed shifting error and irreparably damaged his engine. Hayes' McLaren pulled away from him, as did Fulp's Lola. Grant, however, continued running in third spot until the fifth lap when the Lola locked solid on him and he had to walk back to the pits.

With Hayes leading and pulling away, and Fulp holding second, Parsons' third place Genie made a brief bid to move up, but in doing so the gearbox malfunctioned and Parsons backed off, to eventually finish the long race with a blistered palm from hard-holding the gear lever in place.

Parsons could deal with neither Krause nor Buckman, who passed him on either side on the eighth lap to move into third and fourth positions.

Buckman then took his Lola-Ford

drafting time briefly to spin on turn six without losing much of his 30-plus sec. advantage.

In the meantime, the heat was starting to attack the second place Krause who had Fulp, Hansen, Parsons, and Hudson all go by him. Hansen, however, shortly retired with a broken spindle on his prized Lola.

With the three-quarter mark passed, the frustrated Motschenbacher had his smoking engine break up under him, giving the lead to Fulp for the first and final time.

Hudson passed all those left in front of him with the exception of Fulp. And Dave Jordan, who had replaced Ken Miles in the Otto Zipper Porsche Carrera while Miles tested Fords in Arizona, disappeared into the pits for good with only five laps remaining to leave his color-two-liter lead to teammate Scooter Patrick.

RIVERSIDE USRRC, RIVERSIDE, CALIF., MAY 1.

FINISHERS: 1 — John "Buck" Fulp, Lola-Olds, 70 laps, 185 mi.; 85.76mph; 2 — Skip Hudson, Lamar Lola-Chevy; 3 — Chuck Parsons, Genie-Chevy; 4 — Bill Krause, Lola-Chev; 5 — Scooter Patrick, Carrera 6; 6 — Ed Hamill, Hamill-Olds; 7 — Bud Morley, McLaren-Olds; 8 — George Follmer, Lotus-Porsche; 9 — John Martin, Lotus-Porsche; 10 — Don Skogmo, Genie-Olds; 11 — Budd Clusserath, McLaren-Olds; 12 — Steve Smith, Porsche 904; 13 — Bill Young, Lotus Elan.

Junior Parsons prepares to pass Ed Hamill's Hamill SR2 as they crest the hill entering Riverside's turn seven.   (Richard George photo)

Lothar Motschenbacher tries to go under George Follmer's #16 Lotus-Porsche at Riverside May 1. Follmer finished, Motschenbacher did not.
(Dave Ross photo)

ROYAL WELCOME—Cathiann Vilicich of San Pedro, queen of Sunday's U.S. Road Racing Championship event at Riverside, welcomes fans to the sports car "tripleheader" that includes a full weekend of activity. See adjacent "Motor Sports Inclusive" column for details.

Notable in the 100 mile Mission Bell 100 supporting race, Shelby coupe designer Pete Brock fielded a pair of 900cc Hino Contessa's in an event won by Falcon driver Don Pike. Jim Adams in a fourth overall Cortina won class B, Jim Ryel won Class C and Jim Law in a Saab won class D. Read more in Volume Two, coming in the fall of 2022

Jim Law; *"Pete Brock wrecked his Hino and it was so bent it wouldn't fit in his trailer. I put it on my open trailer, put my Saab in his fancy (and unique at the time) enclosed trailer."*

Brock and Dunham Hino's in the Mission Bell 100

John Morton: *"I stopped at Nickey Chevrolet in Chicago, looking for an Weber carb air horn. They had three racecars in the shop, the Genie run by Dan Blocker for John Cannon and two McLarens for Lothar Motschenbacher and Charley Hayes. I struck up a conversation with Charley and he offered me a job; worked on his car at a couple of races, then on Blocker's."*

Andretti Faces Busy Week, Tests J-Car

BY BOB THOMAS
Times Auto Editor

Mario Andretti, the nation's automobile racing champion, launched a busy work week in the Southland Monday . . . albeit with an interruption due to weather.

His schedule was to begin with testing at Riverside Raceway, move him to Las Vegas later in the week for qualification trials for Sunday's Stardust Grand Prix, bring him back to Ascot Park for a sprint car race at Gardena Saturday night, then send him back to Las Vegas for the 210-mile road race.

At Riverside, the tiny Italian driver is testing Ford's two Le Mans GT machines, the new J-car and its predecessor, the Mark II. The weatherman didn't cooperate Monday . . . neither Mario nor the cars left the garage.

Today, hopefully, he will test as well the Lola-Ford sports car that he drove in The Times Grand Prix Oct. 30. He is preparing the car for Las Vegas where he meets the international set . . . John Surtees, Bruce McLaren, Jackie Stewart, Phil Hill, Jim Hall, Dan Gurney, et al.

This is the first test of a J-car since Ken Miles was killed in one at Riverside in August.

Nothing New

Although the schedule appears to be unusually heavy, especially the Nevada - Gardena - Nevada swing, Andretti says it is "nothing new" for him. Almost matter-of-factly, he said "I've done it before, lots of times."

The three cars he is testing at Riverside for Ford have basically the same

Mario Andretti

And Andretti figured, if anything, to be long on power. The engine reportedly had been tested above 600 horsepower. "It turned out to be 490," said the driver. "Now we're hoping at Vegas it will be up there where it was quoted the last time."

More horsepower is needed, explained Andretti, for the automatic transmission opposed to the more positive manual shift to overcome slippage losses.

"It really worked beautifully at Riverside," said Andretti about the automatic transmission. "Naturally you sacrifice some horsepower that way. I don't know the percentage of slippage. It was a little greater, I think, than it figured to be, but basically the automatic is really something to work with."

He added:

"I know at times I had a definite advantage on certain parts of the track at Riverside."

Transmission Problem

Titus vs. Martin Rematch Looms

By DUSTY BRANDEL

Two prominent California sports car drivers who staged a thrilling battle for national class championships at Riverside International Raceway last fall will have another go at each other next Sunday, May 2, when the U.S. Road Racing championship circuit moves to the 2.6-mile road course at Riverside.

Jerry Titus of Canoga Park and Bart Martin of Hayward will renew the battle in the 182-mile (70-lap) USRRC classic.

Titus will drive the same Webster Special he used to win the national Class D modified title last November. It is powered by a Climax engine.

New Martin Car

Martin will be behind the wheel of a Brabham-Ford recently purchased from the Brabham factory in England. It was campaigned in Europe in 1964 as a factory team car and raced in the Grand Prix at Riverside last October.

The Riverside USRRC is the second in a series of 11 premium events across the nation and offers points for the driver and manufacturer championships. Drivers will be shooting for valuable points as well as $10,000 in prize money.

Worth Points

The first event, a 124-mile (48-lap) race for Grand Touring cars will pay points counting toward the manufacturer's title, was captured by the California Shelby-American, Inc. in 1963-64. It will be followed by a 182-mile classic for sports cars, offering points toward the driving title now held by Sebring winner Jim Hall. Hall and his teammate Hap Sharp will drive Chevy-Powered Chaparrals equipped with automatic transmissions.

Qualifying is on Sat., May 1, and the first race Sunday.

* * *

George Barris, North Hollywood's nationally known custom car king, will have two exciting creations in the fifth annual International Custom Car and Motorcycle show, April 29 through May 2, at the Los Angeles Sports Arena.

The "Cosma Ray," 1965 Grand National custom car champion, is a completely re-styled and re-formed 1964 Corvette, with a V-project design valued at $30,000 and powered by a 500-horsepower Corvette engine.

Another show-stopper will be the "Munster Koach," a star in its own right on the Munster TV series.

More than 400 entries will be on display.

* * *

Everything's a-go-go at Saugus Stadium in preparation for the return of the Pacific Racing Assoc., Super Stock Cars next Saturday night, May 1.

Heading the list of entries set to compete in the 10-event program is 1964 PRA champion "Roarin' Oren" Prosser of Granada Hills, who will be back to defend his title in a brand new Chevrolet.

Former PRA champions Walt Price of San Fernando and Eddie Gray of Gardena have teamed again to campaign for this year's championship. Price will drive a Buick and Gray will tool a Chevrolet. And making his return to Saugus after a two-year absence is Ron Hornaday of San Fernando, two-time NASCAR late model stock car champion. Hornaday will drive a Ford.

They will be shooting for a big slice of $1,650 guaranteed prize money. First event begins at 8 p.m.

* * *

"The Surfers" dragster, driven by Mike Sorokin of Santa Monica, will be out at San Fernando Raceway tomorrow to break the record elapsed time of 206.94 m.p.h. set by Bill Alexander of Glendale.

The powerful Chrysler-powered rail has set records of 7.85 seconds and a speed of 201.78 m.p.h. and is out to beat that record.

Also on hand will be Bill Martin, Burbank, in the Chevy-powered "400 JR."

In addition to the dragster, a full program is set for stockers, gassers and sport cars, beginning at 1 p.m.

* * *

Two newly-built jet dragsters, powered by late-model J-47-33 thrust engines will meet in a special two-out-of-three match race tonight at Fontana Dragway.

The "California Kid" and "Untouchable VI" both have records of 225 m.p.h. through the traps and will go for a 250 m.p.h. record with the new engines.

Eliminations and the first jet race get the green light at 7 p.m.

* * *

Danny Ongais of Carlsbad will wheel his fast stepping slingshot dragster, "the Mangler," in a match race with Larry Faust of Long Beach at Lions' Drag Strip tonight.

Danny's official speed is 206.88 m.p.h. over the ¼ mile and Larry's "Jungle" dragster holds the track record for lowest elapsed time.

Record runs sanctioned by the American Hot Rod Association are programmed tomorrow.

* * *

The National Drag Boat Association will hold its April meet at Ski-Land in Perris tomorrow with an expected entry of 200 boats competing for the cash prizes, trophies and merchandise awards.

YMCA Program Has Huge Field

LOS ANGELES—More than 1100 men and boys represent-

The 1967 USRRC eight race series Riverside stop had a crowd of 10,500 watch Mark Donahue win $4350 in Roger Penske's Lola T-70, followed by Bob Bondurant and Peter Revson. Pole qualifier George Follmer dropped out on the first lap and ended up 21st. Scooter Patrick again won under two liters in Otto Zipper's Porsche 906.

Mark Donohue wins first in Riverside race event

RIVERSIDE, Calif. (UPI)—If anyone hopes to catch hot-handed Mark Donohue of Stony Brook, N. Y., before he makes a run-away of the U.S. Road Racing Championships, they better start plotting.

The New York driver won his second straight USRRC event Sunday at the Riverside International Raceway and now leads in the driver standings with 18 points after the first two races on the circuit.

Donohue let out his Sunoco Chevy and she responded by averaging 105.209 miles per hour for a new course record to erase the old mark of 100.350 m.p.h. set by Texan Jimmie Hall in 1965.

The young driver's time for the 70-laps or 182 miles was one hour, 43 minutes and 47.6 seconds.

Donohue not only captured the plaudits of the 10,500 spectators, but also won top prize money of $4,350 and was presented the stiff challenge from George Follmer of Arcadia, Calif., who had won the pole position with a qualifying record of 111.032 m.p.h.

Follmer took the lead and held it for three laps when Donohue caught up and stayed in front the rest of the way.

But on the 48th lap, Follmer was in 2-1-2 seconds of the lead when he blew his oil line and was forced to retire.

Chevy-powered cars took the first nine places in the race as 16 of the original 31 starters finished. There were no accidents.

Third place on the same lap as Bondurant went to Pete Revson of New York City, who was also driving a McLaren Chevy.

The other top 10 finishers included:

Fourth — Lothar Motschenbacher, Beverly Hills, Calif., McLaren Chevy; fifth—Mike Goth. Corona Del Mar. Calif..

Twiggy Upstages Winner Donohue

BY BOB THOMAS
Times Auto Editor

RIVERSIDE — Mark Donohue found himself first at the finish line Sunday at Riverside International Raceway but a poor second in the winner's circle.

Twiggy was there.

In fact, the "splendid splinter" (apologies to Ted Williams) presented the round-faced race driver from New York with the winner's trophy after he had won the 182-mile U.S. Road Racing Championship event . . . almost as easily as he had won the season's first USRRC race a week ago at Las Vegas. At least at Las Vegas he didn't have to compete with Twiggy.

Guest of Shelby

Twiggy's host at the track Sunday was ex-driver and famed car builder Carroll Shelby, who led his guest to the winner's circle. Wearing a wide grin and with a Texas twang, Shelby said:

"I didn't have a car in

sports car outdistanced runner-up Bob Bondurant's McLaren-Chevy by 55 seconds, roughly two-thirds of the 2.6-mile nine-turn course.

Donohue did not describe his victory as a "country drive" as he did after the Las Vegas win when Follmer—again his only serious competition—dropped out on the first lap.

"Up to the time George went out it was quite a strain out there," Donohue said. "Follmer was never more than six seconds behind me. All it takes in traffic is one slip and things can change in a hurry."

Donohue ran as if he was being chased. His average speed of 105.209 m.p.h. was 5 m.p.h. faster than the former record, set in 1965 by Jim Hall in a Chaparral. The time of the race was 1 hour 43 minutes 47.6 seconds.

After two of the eight races in the USRRC series, it appears that Donohue

the 'breather.' It isn't supposed to do that," he said with an exaggerated shrug of his shoulders.

A ruptured oil radiator had knocked Follmer out at Las Vegas.

Bondurant's teammate, Peter Revson of New York, was third, finishing 81 seconds behind the winner in another McLaren-Chevy. The first three drivers were the only ones among the 32 starters to finish on the same lap.

Fourth place Lothar Motschenbacher lost third spot late in the race when he spun on turn No. 7. He was a lap behind. Fifth was Mike Goth of Corona del Mar in a Lola-Chevy.

Gregory's Timing Off

Winner among the small engine cars was Scooter Patrick of Manhattan Beach. Patrick was 10th overall in his Porsche Carrera 6. Among early contenders who retired with problems were Jerry Grant of San Diego, water pump pulley, broken; 1968

GT 4; 17. Andre Genuer (Seal Beach), Capillo-Chevy; 18. John Morton (Van Nuys); Lotus-Porsche; 19. Chuck Parsons (Carmel), McLaren-Chevy; 20. Jerry Titus (Sherman Oaks), Piper-Buick.

21. George Follmer (Arcadia), Lola-Chevy; 22. Charlie Kolb (Miami), Lola-Chevy; 23. Jerry Grant (San Diego), Lola-Chevy; 24. Frank Matich (Australia), Webster-Olds; 25. Sam Posey (Sharon, Conn.), McLaren-Chevy; 26. Ted Petersen (Newport Beach), McLaren-Chevy; 27. Pierre Phillips (Portland), Lola-Chevy; 28. Ralph Sayler (Hammond, Ind.), McKee-Olds; 29. Skip Scott (Dover, Pa.), McLaren-Ford; 30. Richard Smith (Fresno), Algerio-Porsche; 31. Warren Shamalin (Santa Barbara), Elve-Porsche.

Amateur race results:

PRODUCTION A-D AND MODIFIED C-G (18 laps)—1. Genuer, Capello; 2. Ron Dykes (Marina Del Rey), Mustang; 3. Robert Williams (Santa Monica), Genie-Alfa. Winner's speed: 92.3 m.p.h.
SEDAN RACE (18 laps)—1. Don Pike (Hawthorne), Mustang; 2. Bob West (Hollywood), Mustang; 3. Don Peck (Santa Monica), Mustang. Winner's speed: 89.76 m.p.h.

Peter Revson; McLaren M1C

George Follmer; Lola T70

Fred Baker; Porsche 906

Davey Jordan: *"I drove Haskell Wexler's Lola T-70 a couple of times, filling in when Ronnie Bucknum had schedule conflicts. The car had a 289 Ford, pretty much outclassed by the 366 inch Chevy's everyone else seemed to have. Had a fourth at Laguna once, blew it up the next time I got to drive it."*

Bud Morley went very fast at Riverside, once he straightened things out. (Fritz Taggart photo)

Skip Hudson

Jerry Titus; Piper

Bob Bondurant; McLaren

Jerry Grant

Mike Goth

COMPETITION PRESS &
AUTOWEEK

May 20, 1967   25 Cents

TWIGGY TOASTS MARK AT RIVERSIDE

Simple, Uncluttered Lines Okay For Race Cars, But not Twiggy

By Joyce Uphoff

RIVERSIDE, Calif., April 30 — Twiggy made her racing debut at Riverside at the USRRC. The British model had rather severe lines — simple and uncluttered, but a little small-scale and frail for the race circuit. In fact, next to any Lola or even a McLaren, she drew little attention and even less comment.

Because there was a high breeze, Twiggy was held firmly on one side by boyfriend Justin, and on the other by friend Carroll Shelby (usually seen sponsoring models with more curves and less angles). She showed up in the pits for the last few laps of the race and then rolled over to the winner's circle to greet the victor.

Word got around that Twiggy was there. However, George Follmer, pulling into the pits, out of oil, got more attention from the fans.

Several pit crew members finally noticed the mob of photographers surrounding Twiggy and went over to see whose mechanic was getting all the attention. They realized their error at once, because Twiggy was garbed in clean beige slacks and a brown jacket and had obviously freshly-cut short hair.

As a part of the race scene, Twiggy needs a lot of redesign. In spite of the efforts of the movie Grand Prix to make race fans high fashion conscious, fans are not ready yet for Twiggy.

1968, the last year of the series, had nine races. At Riverside, a crowd of 14,300, the largest in five years, saw Mark Donohue win $4800, this time in a McLaren M6B, followed by Lothar Motschenbacher, Sam Posey and Moises Solana. There was no under two liter category in 1968. Supporting races, SCCA regionals, were won by Scooter Patrick in a Porsche Carrera 6, Fred Plotkin in the Kangaroo Special and Don Pike in a Porsche. More about club racing in Volume Two – available in the fall, 2022

Donohue Wins by Default Over Hall

By BRUCE GRANT
Sun-Telegram Auto Editor

RIVERSIDE — Mark Donohue beat Jim Hall by default yesterday to turn the U.S. Road Racing Championship classic into a test of endurance.

Hall scratched his Chaparral Chevy from the race after a part of the winged car's automatic transmission broke down during a morning practice run.

That left Donohue's McLaren Chevy by far the fastest car in the field of 26 starters. He quickly surged to a 10-second lead over Lothar Motschenbacher, in a McLaren Ford, and gradually stretched that advantage throughout the 60-lap classic.

A broken ignition wire almost created a dramatic conclusion to the race for Donohue. He slowed down suddenly on the next to last lap, obviously with mechanical problems.

ing the starter motor to work the ignition system. I flicked the starter switch on and off as I went around."

Donohue finished 40 seconds ahead of Motschenbacher, of Beverly Hills, who had the third fastest qualifying time. Next came Sam Posey of Sharon, Conn., in a Caldwell Chevy, and Chuck Parsons of Pebble Beach, in a Lola Chevy — one lap behind the winner.

Moises Solana of Mexico City, in a McLaren Chevy; Swede Savage of San Bernardino, in a Lola Gurney Ford; and Jerry Entin of Beverly Hills, in a Lola Chevy, finished two laps in back of Donohue.

Donohue's average speed, as expected, was a race record. He averaged 112.742 miles per hour — almost seven mph faster than he recorded in winning last year's USRRC race here.

grapher. Donohue spun out but quickly got back on the course. "I thought I had run over him," Donohue said, "but when I started out again I didn't feel

(Continued on A—6, Column 1)

Orioles Split With

BALTIMORE (UPI) — The Baltimore Orioles salvaged a split of their doubleheader with the Boston Red Sox yesterday, winning 6-1 behind the six-hit pitching of Jim Hardin after being blanked 3-0 on four hits by Jose Santiago.

It was the third straight win for Hardin, who overcame an early spell of wildness before settling down to throttle the Red Sox. The loser was Jerry Stephenson, now 1-2, who

Andrews, for three fourth.

Curt Bl... out and ... Boog Pow... producing run of th... Dave Ma... center.

Baltimo... in the fift... Belanger,

Donohue leads Motschenbacher

144

ACTION-STOPPING QUEEN —Sharon Kay Terrill, queen of tomorrow's USRRC race at Riverside, stops action by pit crewman as she tours paddock area where cars are being readied for race. Raceway activity begins at 9 a.m. today.

Bud Morley - Lola T-70

Swede Savage - Lola T-70

Chuck Parsons - Lola T-70

Lothar Motschenbacher

Hall Fails to Run; Donohue Takes Race

BY BOB THOMAS
Times Auto Editor

RIVERSIDE — A race that started in mid-afternoon Sunday at Riverside International Raceway ended abruptly about 11 a.m.—the same morning.

Which must threaten some kind of speed record.

To explain: 3½ hours before the race, co-favorite Jim Hall dropped out with a broken car.

And as simply and as early as that, co-favorite Mark Donohue won it.

Unfortunately, that didn't leave too much excitement for the 14,200 sports car fans who turned out in the afternoon for the 156-mile U.S. Road

polis cars when they performed here last fall.

At that, Donohue was "cooling it" during the latter stages of the race and even coasting at times at the end with his ignition trouble.

Second-place Motschenbacher, in a McLaren-Ford, who obviously was giving away some horsepower to his opponent, finished 49 seconds back, or nearly two miles. The rest of the field was strung as far back as one full lap to several laps.

About his spin Donohue

Donohue Has Things His Way For Victory In Road Racing Event

RIVERSIDE (AP) — Mark Donohue of Stony Brook, N.Y., had things pretty much his own way in the U.S. Road Racing Championship despite some anxious moments. The defending U.S. Road Racing titlist won the 156-mile event Sunday at the Riverside International Raceway with an average speed of 112.7 miles an hour. It was seven m.p.h. faster than his winning speed a year ago.

Much of the annual event's drama disappeared 3½ hours before the race when cofavorite Jim Hall of Midland, Tex., had to drop out when his Chevy-powered Chaparral had problems.

Transmission Fails

He said there was a failure in the automatic transmission among other things.

With Hall out, Donohue's Chevy-powered McLaren was at times two miles ahead of second-place Lothar Motschenbach-

Amateurs Will Be Featured On Pro Fight Card

The Auditorium Boxing Club will have an added feature — amateur boxing — on its professional card May 7 in the Memorial Auditorium.

Will Edgington, who is lining up the bouts for Promter Jackie

146

Chapter Five - The Original Can Am

The Can Am began as an SCCA pro series sponsored by Johnson's Wax in 1966. Evolving out of the USRRC, European Group 7 Sports Cars and the loosely affiliated pro races such as Mosport's Players 200 and Riverside's Times Grand Prix, the series effectively had few rules and big prize money, attracting top drivers from all over the world. The Can Am almost immediately became the second richest in racing, surpassed only by the Indy 500. John Surtees and Lola Initially dominated and won the series in 1966 which, Riverside, with L.A. times sponsorship, was named the Times Grand Prix, The last race at Riverside was in 1973 and the Times name left until 1979, when Les Richter and IMSA persuaded them to return. A revival, in 1977, using the Can Am name, based on full bodied converted formula 5000 cars with five liter limit got off to a shaky start but grew as purpose built cars were developed. The series ran through 1986 but the last race at Riverside took place in 1984.

The 1966 season consisted of six races, St. Jovite, Bridgehampton, Mosport, Laguna Seca, Riverside and Las Vegas. At Riverside, the Times Grand Prix, John Surtees won $17,159 in front of a crowd of 81,000 on a hot October day. Jim Hall in a Chaparral was second followed by Graham Hill and Mark Donohue. Surtees was the series champion.

Surtees wins Riverside Grand Prix sports race

RIVERSIDE. Calif. (UPI)— said that he did not believe th
John Surtees, the driving wizard protest would be upheld.
of Surrey. England, was $17,159 So. after fighting off th
richer today after winning the challenges of Jim Hall o
Times Grand Prix for sports Midland, Texas, for the bette

Phil Hill in the Chaparral leads eventual winner Surtees

John Surtees; Lola T-70

Skip Hudson; Lola T-70

Ludwig Heimrath; McLaren

Chris Amon; McLaren

Graham Hill leading Bruce McLaren

Gurney Fined For Speeding

RIVERSIDE, Calif. (AP) — Famed racing driver Dan Gurney was fined $45 today for speeding while on his way to the Riverside Grand Prix last October.

Gurney, of Costa Mesa, Calif., originally had pleaded innocent both to the speeding charge and a charge of reckless driving.

The latter charge was dropped when Gurney pleaded guilty to the lesser charge of speeding.

A California Highway Patrol officer said Gurney was going 70 miles an hour in a 45 m.p.h. zone.

Gurney, who won the Grand Prix in 1964 and 1965, failed to qualify for last October's race.

LATE GURNEY STEPS ON IT, GETS CAUGHT

Race driver Dan Gurney was arrested for reckless driving Sunday morning while on his way to the Riverside International Raceway for a meeting of drivers in The Times Grand Prix for Sports Cars, Riverside police reported.

Traffic officers said they chased Gurney on U.S. 395 for three miles at speeds of 85 m.p.h. until stopping him in the community of Edgemont.

He was taken to Riverside city jail where he was booked and released on $115 bail. Officers said Gurney told them he was late to the meeting at the raceway.

Times GP Crowd Big and Unruly

RIVERSIDE, Calif., Oct. 31 — The largest crowd ever to attend the Grand Prix, 84,000 plus, was treated to better parking facilities, more and permanent concession stands with adequate supplies of drinks to help combat the high temperature, permanent sanitation buildings, and larger and better-placed grandstands to go with one of the highest car attrition rates in the history of the event.

The parking areas were filling up rapidly by 9am and by 10 the grandstands at turn 5, the favorite viewing area, were filled.

The newly leveled-off infield at turn 6 was well set up for spectators, and cars were parked about 50 yards back from the turn with lots of area available for standing room spectators.

The crowd was graced by the usual number of teen age drunks who remained under control as long as police patrolled. After the race when all visible police had left to direct traffic, the parking lot became a raceway for motorcycles and a battling ground for beer bottle throwers.

It was at this point that first aid

Eldon Builds Slot Track at Riverside

RIVERSIDE, CALIF., OCT. 31 — An automobile raceway has opened within a famous raceway.

The formal unveiling of an elaborate and permanent slot car facility, the Eldon Model Car Racing Center, in the heart of Riverside International Raceway took place before the eighth running of the Times GP for

Surprise! Andretti Enters Field for Times Grand Prix

Mario Andretti, the tinymite Italian race driver who recently clinched his second straight U.S. Auto Club national championship, Tuesday became a surprise entry in the ninth annual Times Grand Prix for Sports Cars.

He will drive a special Ford-powered Lola for the John Mecom Jr. team of Texas in the 200-mile, $65,-000 charity event at Riverside International Raceway Sunday.

Andretti joins a team which includes Jackie Stewart of Scotland and Parnelli Jones, the 1963 Indy winner.

Andretti's car will be powered by an aluminum 427-cubic-inch LeMans Ford V-8 engine. Only one other similar engine is entered in the race. It will be used by four-time national champion and two-time 500 winner A. J. Foyt of Houston.

Last May Andretti set an Indianapolis qualifying lap record of 166.328 m.p.h.

Dan and the Johnson Wax Trophy that was awarded race winners. Different from the Series Trophy shown below which floated between two magnets, held in place by guitar strings

Johnson Wax Sponsors
Canada-America Races

The Johnson Wax Co. of Racine and its associate, Canadian Johnson, today announced their sponsorship of the trophy and championship fund for the Canadian-American Challenge Cup Series of International road racing in North America this fall.

A Johnson official, William K. Eastham, said that the company will authorize a permanent Johnson Wax Trophy for the champion driver and will contribute $25,000 to the championship fund.

International racing figure Stirling Moss, who serves as

000. The Johnson Wax Trophy winner will receive $19,250.

Each of the six races will be about 200 miles in length and are expected to attract an international field of the world's top sports car drivers.

"Our support of the Canadian-American reflects the conviction that, as a major international sport, road racing is having a great impact in Canada and the United States," Eastham said.

CanAm Trophy Floats

Bruce Ward: *"My dad, Joe Ward, entered his Bobsy Alfa and was the last place qualifier. A.J. Foyt had lost his qualifying spot after an engine change and the official thought Foyt might make better press than Dad, so ...."*

Dan Gurney

I

Ike Smith: *"Chuck had a used car lot; one day Randy Hilton (of Hilton hotel fame) was there buying a car. He asked Chuck if he was Parsons, the racecar driver. Chuck said yes, so Hilton said, I have my son's Cobra in my garage. He's away in the Navy – wanna race it? Chuck of course said yes; Hilton called Shelby to find out how much and how long it would be to turn it into a racecar. Shelby offered two grand and four weeks; Hilton countered "how much for two weeks"? Shelby said four grand and the deal was done. The car came back on time with a race motor. Then we moved up to a Genie which won Chuck the 1966 USRRC Championship. Later on, Randy got bored with racing; sold Chuck the truck trailer, cars and spares cheaply. Chuck ended up driving for Carl Haas."*

152

Scooter Has Things His Own Way With 910-Powered Porsche 906

By Ron Hickman
Area Editor

RIVERSIDE, Calif., Oct. 29 — The Pennzoil "100" in retrospect should probably have been called the "Scooter Patrick 100" for it was all Patrick's race.

The popular southern Californian had things all his own way, winning by a 16-second margin over Joe Buzzetta's Porsche 906. Patrick's 906 averaged 99.09 mph over 31 laps of the 3.275-mile Riverside long course, as he led from start to finish and completely dominated the 16-car field.

With two wins in his only two starts Patrick winds up with 18 points in the series while Buzzetta's six points for second gives him a total of 19 to edge Patrick by one point in the competition for the Doug Revson Trophy. Mak Kronn and Chuck Dietrich tied for third with 15 points and Fred Baker is fifth with nine.

For Buzzetta the story was strong, but not strong enough as he was simply unable to match the blistering pace set by Patrick, whose fuel-injected 910-engined Porsche 906 is probably the fastest 2-liter car in the U.S.

After an early duel with Monte Shelton, Buzzetta stretched his man broke off. The engine's pistons let go later when Leslie was in fourth spot.

There was one noble experiment involved as well. Dr. Bill Molle, whose Lotus 23 is a perennial top contender in G S/R, opted for more power by adding a second set of plugs and a second distributor. The installation looked neat enough, and ran well in the early going. Halfway through the race, though, some of the many plugs fouled and fouled Molle out of the race after a push start in the pits.

With only 10 cars finishing out of a field of 16 on a 3-mile track, it becomes painfully obvious that the under-2-liter series needs a much larger entry if it is going to catch on the way the other pro series have.

PENNZOIL "100" UNDER-2-LITER CHAMPIONSHIP RACE, RIVERSIDE INTERNATIONAL RACEWAYS, RIVERSIDE, CALIF., OCTOBER 29, 1967

FINISHERS: 1 - Scooter Patrick, Porsche 906 (31 laps, 101.5 miles, 1:01.00.7, 99.9 mph); 2 - Joe Buzzetta, Porsche 906 (31 laps); 3 - Monte Shelton, Porsche 906 (30 laps); 4 - Jacques Duval, Porsche 906 (30 laps); 5 - Henry Candler, Lotus 23 (29 laps); 6 - John Morton, Lotus 23-Porsche (29 laps); 7 - Ed Bowman, Elva-Porsche (29 laps); 8 - Gene Levin, Le Grand-Ford (28 laps); 9 - John Crove, Porsche Spyder (27 laps); 10 - Fred Baker, Porsche 906 (26

82,000 people saw Bruce McLaren win $24,940 in 1967, followed by Jim Hall, Mark Donahue and Parnelli Jones. McLaren was the series champion.

McClaren wins Can-Am at Riverside, Hall 2nd

TIMES GRAND PRIX-BOUND—Dan Gurney, who is winless in sports car racing at Riverside, will be out to rectify the situation Oct. 29 when he competes in the 10th annual Times Grand Prix. The car Gurney will be piloting (above), is an English-built Lola-Ford, similar to last year's model. Photo by Jack Brady

Dan Gurney Has a Point to Prove

BY BOB THOMAS
Times Auto Editor

Dan Gurney, one of the world's great race drivers, still hasn't been able to win a sports car race at his "home" track, Riverside International Raceway,

ORDER YOUR TICKETS TODAY

10th Annual Los Angeles **TIMES GRAND PRIX**

OCT. 28/29 - Riverside International Raceway

TICKETS NOW ON SALE
Southern California Music Co., 637 S. Hill St.

is a 354-cubic-inch Ford, stretched to 377 inches when outfitted with Gurney-Weslake cylinder heads at Gurney's All-American Racer plant in Santa Ana.

"We have the engine in pretty good shape," he said. "We've been closed

Jim Hall's crew works on the Chaparral in one of Riverside Raceway's garages. The car in the foreground is George Bignotti's Lola which Parnelli Jones drove to fourth overall during the GP.

(Jack Brady Associates photo)

154

Sam Posey; McLaren M1B

George Follmer; Lola T-70

Peter Revson; McLaren

Watch the 1967 Can Am Video on the attached DVD

Scooter Patrick; Mirage

Jerry Titus; King Cobra

Gurney leads McLaren, Hall and Jones

COMPETITION PRESS &
AUTOWEEK

November 18 1967   25 Cents

Ford Breaks Mopar Win Streak

McLaren Nips Hall At Riverside

'67 Shelby Models · Meyers Manx ·

Floyd Clymer's
Auto Topics

January 1967 · 50 Cents

· Cars of the Future · Tires '67 ·

- RIVERSIDE TIMES GP
- WATKINS GLEN U.S. GP
- MT. FUJI 200 MILES

AMERICA'S PIONEER MOTORING MAGAZINE · ESTABLISHED 1900

SPORTS CAR GRAPHIC

UK 3'6
Sweden KR. 3.90 inkl. oms

JANUARY 1967 50¢

$400,000 SHOWDOWN

LAGUNA SECA   RIVERSIDE
LAS VEGAS

NEW TRIUMPH GT6/MEXICAN GRAND PRIX / ABARTH'S FUNNY FIATS / YOUR HOT ENGINE: PART ONE / RACING IMP

CHAPARRAL 2E 'FLIPPER'

Dennis Hulme

Peter Revson

Pole qualifier Bruce McLaren won in 1968, picking up the $21,000 first place money, followed by Mark Donohue, Jim Hall and Lothar Motschenbacher. Denny Hulme won the series championship with Bruce in second place.

McLAREN MAKES SHAMBLES OF RIVERSIDE

Donohue Second After Hulme, Hall Pit; Title Up for Grabs at Vegas

By Jack Brady
Associate Editor

RIVERSIDE, Calif., Oct. 27 — The girls were long limbed and scantily clad; the temperature was trying to break 95, the smog was so thick you couldn't see the stark rocky hills that loom over the Riverside course and Bruce McLaren won the 11th Riverside Grand Prix for the second time in as many years, with a comfortable 36-second lead over second-placed Mark Donohue.

So what else is new?

$17,210

As a matter of fact, it wasn't even necessary for Bruce to break his '67 race record in order to qualify for the $17,210 in prize and accessory money and an appropriately colored orange Plymouth GTX. McLaren's race average in 1967 was 114.406mph and he easily won today at a slower 114.353.

An announced 83,000 people watched McLaren take the lead and keep it for the entire 62 laps over the rolling hills of the 3.275-mile, nine-turn, course. Bruce made the comment after the race that, ". . . the Penske crowd was under

the impression they could race with me, but not with Denny, I guess they know better now." It was quite obvious that he was not just there to protect Hulme's bid for the championship.

Hulme and McLaren shared the front row of the 2-2 grid and came away smartly when Dick Keith green-flagged the flying start.

A veritable plague of engine failures, and mysterious maladies that robbed the big 427cid engines of power, left some doubt as to just how long the front runners would last. The intense heat not only played hob with the injector systems, but it made the oily track like glass.

REVSON OUT

Fifth place qualifier Peter Revson brought his Shelby-Ford-McLaren into the pits for good at the completion of the first lap with no fuel pressure. A thoroughly disgruntled crew had juggled two alloy Ford engines for two days and never satisfied themselves as to just where they were losing the battle for power. Finally, what was supposed to be the race engine ventilated its block

(Continued on page 16)

Mark Donohue has a lonely afternoon. Too far ahead of the pack and just far enough behind the leaders, Mark set a steady pace that paid off with a second place-finish, but didn't give him much company. (Jack Brady photo)

McLaren Wins at Riverside

RIVERSIDE, Calif (AP) - New Zealander Bruce McLaren called on all the power and skill at his command Sunday to win the 11th annual Times Grand Prix for sports cars.

McLaren, driving one of the bright orange McLaren-Chevrolet machines he builds in Bucks, England, held the lead in the 200-mile, $101,000 race from start to finish.

Marilyn Fox: *"I became Lothar Motschenbacher's timer and all around gofer One not so funny at the time story - The transporter with race car on board, left Riverside after a practice and test session. The McLaren basically fell off; slid right off the back onto the freeway. Say what?? Yep, right on the freeway. Amazingly, it was not hit, believe it or not. Thank heaven we were in the slow lane and cars were able to go around us - to the side, or just stop. Car was undamaged. Don't think traffic was as crowded as it is these days. Not sure who we blamed but tie downs were double checked after that."*

John Surtees

All the News That's Fit to Print About
NEXT YEAR'S NEW CARS FROM DETROIT!

ROAD & TRACK

OCTOBER, 1968   UK 5/-   SWEDEN KR.450 INKL. OMS   SIXTY CENTS

COMPARING FOUR LOW-PRICE SPORTS CARS
AH Sprite   Datsun 1600   Fiat 850   Triumph Spitfire

Can-Am Challenger

Lothar Motschenbacher's McLaren M6B with Gurney Ford

CANADIAN-AMERICAN CHALLENGE CUP PREVIEW

ROAD TEST OF THE CLASSIC GULL-WING MERCEDES

Donohue Hopes to Cap Biggest Year With Times Grand Prix Win

BY BOB THOMAS
Times Auto Editor

"Why, he doesn't look like a race driver at all," said the cute little blonde in the front row. "He looks too nice."

"Well, he is," responded her escort, who had paid $50 to attend a race driving seminar last week before the running of a Canadian-American Challenge Cup road race at Bridgehampton, Long Island.

OVER COUNTER TICKET SALES START MONDAY

Over-the-counter ticket sales start Monday for the Times Grand Prix at Riverside International Raceway, Oct. 26-27.

Prices are $5 for general admission and an additional $2 or $2.50 for reserved seats.

Tickets may be obtained at the Southern California Music Co., 637 S. Hill St.;

gineering degree from Brown University), has won 9 of 12 races with a Camaro. In the USRRC, which involves the same Group 7 type sports car used in the Can-Am circuit, Donohue drove Penske's Sunoco McLaren-Chevy to victories at Riverside, Laguna Seca, St. Jovite in Canada, Watkins Glen, N.Y., and Mansfield, Ohio.

Aluminum Engine

The car is powered by a 427 cubic inch aluminum Chevrolet engine that was

CAPTAIN NICE — Mild mannered Mark Donohue, one of the top race drivers in U.S. is early entrant in Times Grand Prix.

Lothar Motschenbacher leads Brian O'Neil and Sam Posey

165

ONCEOVER—John Surtees, former world champion and winner of the 1966 Times Grand Prix, checks over the engine in the Lola Chevy he will be driving in Sunday's 11th annual race at Riverside Raceway.

Times photo by Art Rogers

The field rolls out for the start

166

Jim Hall leading Mark Donohue

Sam Posey; Lola T-160

Bret Lunger; Caldwell

Jerry Entin; Lola T-70

Charley Hayes; McKee Mk10

Skip Scott; Lola T-160

John Cannon; McLaren

WORLD'S BEST—Denis Hulme, defending world's champion, powers his McLaren M8-A through a turn in an earlier Can-Am series race. Hulme will be driving the same car this Sunday in the 11th annual Times Grand Prix at Riverside International Raceway. Hulme is the current leader in driver points in the 1968 Can-Am series. His teammate and boss, Bruce McLaren, will also be entered.

Mark Donohue

Skeeter McKitterick: *"I got to drive the Len Terry designed Shelby King Cobra, owned by Mike Koslosky – Shelby built one for Jerry Titus and another for A.J. Foyt but, Foyt couldn't fit in the driver's seat (so I was told) as the foot well was extremely small. The car was more or less designed for Titus. I decided I should try to meet Titus to discuss the car as I had heard less than good reports on the chassis. He was very receptive when I stepped into his*

shop in Tarzana and spent a great deal of time with me explaining the deficiencies and dangers of the chassis and recommended I did not drive it because it wasn't "safe". None of that deterred me after I left his shop as I was pretty awe struck that Trans Am Champ Titus would spend this time with me. One of the experiences in this car at Riverside was that the sliding splined half shafts seized while exiting turn nine and the car responded by spinning the opposite way of the chassis load as the flexible chassis was like spring loaded at that point. I somehow missed everything while revolving in the opposite direction of what would be expected. Well, I went onto drive the car in Nationals winning a few races. One memorable one was racing against a Porsche 908 driven by Steve McQueen. The 908 out handled the King Cobra but I was fortunate to win as McQueen had gear box issues."

John Surtees

In 1969, a crowd of 80,200 watched Dennis Hulme win, followed by Chuck Parsons in a Lola T163 and Mario Andretti in the Holman Moody McLaren. Supporting race was an SCCA regional.

Hulme Wins Times Grand Prix; McLaren Crashes

BY SHAV GLICK
Times Staff Writer

RIVERSIDE—It was a good thing it was Denny's turn to win in Sunday's 10th running of the Bruce & Denny Show.

Driving as precisely as if he were on a slot car track, Denny Hulme went wire-to-wire to win the $102,-234 Times Grand Prix before 80,200 fans at Riverside International Raceway.

Hulme set speed records on every lap as he raced the 201.3 miles around Riverside's nine-turn, 3.3 mile course at an average speed of 121.059 m.p.h. It was Denny's fifth win in the 10 Canadian-American Challenge Cup races. His boss and teammate, Bruce McLaren, has won the other five.

But the familiar 1-2 finish of Hulme and McLaren in their orange-colored McLaren racing machines failed to materialize. The possibility ended with a crash on the 34th lap between turns 1 and 2 when the rear suspension gave way in McLaren's car.

The car plowed off the course, climbed an embankment, hit a race official and then careened crazily along a retaining wall before sliding back down the slope to the middle of the road. McLaren jumped out, unhurt, but most of the orange paint from his car was left on the wall.

The course marshal, Bill Atkinson, of Chula Vista, suffered two broken legs and internal injuries. He was flown by helicopter to Riverside Community Hospital, where his condition was reported as "good."

It was the first time an accident had forced a Team McLaren car out of a race in the Can-Am series and only the second time in 10 races Bruce and Denny had not finished 1-2. It also ended McLaren's bid for his third straight Times Grand Prix victory.

McLaren's car was a total wreck. Bruce will go to his backup car for the final Can-Am race in two weeks at Bryan, Tex. The winner of the Texas race—if it is Hulme or McLaren—will take the $50,000 John-winning Can-Am driver of 1969.

With McLaren sidelined, 44-year-old Chuck Parsons of Deerfield, Ill., moved his Lola-Chevy past Dan Gurney on the 58th lap of the 61-lap race to take second place money. Indianapolis 500 winner Mario Andretti also slipped by Gurney near the end of the race for third place.

Gurney, who had moved into second place when McLaren crashed, drove the final 20 laps with a blown head gasket and his car not only steadily lost power, but Dan nearly passed out from the fumes.

"The fumes about drove me out of my mind," Gurney said. "The head gasket blew and the fumes were blowing right back in the cockpit. I had to kick out the windshield to get some fresh air. But at least we finished a race."

Andretti, driving with an untested Ford aluminum engine flown here Friday night from Charlotte, N.C., has his best-ever Can-Am finish in third place. Mario, who already has clinched the U.S. Auto Club's driving championship this year, was not happy, however.

"The car just wasn't right," moaned the little man who won at Indianapolis last Memorial Day. "Nothing was right. The exhaust was really giving me problems late in the race and I kept losing power. There were no handling problems. I just didn't have any power."

Please Turn to Page 4, Col. 1

Los Angeles Times
Sports
BUSINESS & FINANCE
CC   PART IIi   2†
MONDAY, OCT. 27, 1969

McLaren's Teammate Wins Riverside Race

Hulme Cracks Record at Riverside

Anzac Driver Hits 126 in Trials for Times Grand Prix

BY SHAV GLICK
Times Staff Writer

RIVERSIDE—The fastest lap ever run at Riverside International Raceway and the fastest in the four-year history of the Can-Am series got the Times Grand Prix weekend off to a sizzling start Friday.

Denis Hulme drove his Chevy-powered McLaren through the nine turns of Riverside's 3.3-mile course at a speed of 126.342 m.p.h. This was nearly seven miles faster than the old Riverside track record of 119.683

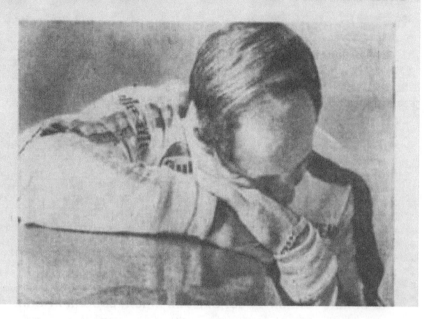

... **TO VICTORY**—Hulme (left) and chief mechanic Cary Taylor are all smiles as they hold winning trophy after the New Zealander's record victory. Hulme won $21,398 in prize money.
Times photo by Don Cormier

Chuck Parsons; Lola T-165

Ike Smith: *"Chuck's best Can Am finish; second in Carl Haas' Simoniz Lola. I was crew chief assisted by Colin Riley. Gary Knutson built the motors; Chaparral aluminum big block, 494 c.i. – about 700 hp.. 195 mph at the end of the straight !! The story behind this, a couple of years before, Masten Gregory missed the race due to not correcting his watch for daylight savings. Carl was unhappy ,offered Chuck the ride"*

Dan Gurney

The track was improving - the dog leg had been added entering turn nine and grandstands, purchased from the Rose Parade were installed. The Goodyear Tower. purchased for $1 and moved from Los Angeles International Airport, provided three levels, operations, media and one for friends of the track and VIP's

Said the L.A. Times Shav Glick of Richter, "He, more than anyone but Bill France Sr., was responsible for the expansion of NASCAR. After they established NASCAR on the West Coast, the series expanded elsewhere. Riverside became a national and international racing institution under Richter's stewardship.

New owners, America raceways kept Richter on as vice president and announced that they would be building a big oval. Of course, that never happened.

(Continued on page 3)

Les Richter Resigns ARI Management Post

LAFAYETTE, Calif. Oct. 20 — Les Richter, president of Riverside International Raceway and vice president of operations for American Raceways Inc., terminated his association with ARI it was learned here today.

Richter's termination with the organization which manages Michigan International Speedway, Texas International Speedway,

Atlanta International Speedway, and a new facility slated for construction in New Jersey, is effective immediately.

The resignation, Richter said, was filed with ARI's vice president Les Share yesterday and confirmed to Larry LoPatin, the corporation's president today.

Richter cited his sudden

(Contined on page 15)

Les Richter Quits ARI Position

(Continued from page 1)

termination as "a difference in thinking in the marketing and promoting of our races.

"While there have been other underlying reasons," Richter said, "the idealistic differences between ARI and myself were the main reason for my action. My interest is to foster bigger and better racing in an attempt to influence more manufacturers to enter the sport," he said.

Richter stated he was of the opinion Larry LoPatin didn't understand the racing business and had little concept of the governing bodies in racing. "The management at ARI doesn't understand the workings of the Automobile Competition Committee of the United States (ACCUS)," he said. "LoPatin had visions of forming a race track owners and promoters association, leaving ACCUS and its member sanctioning groups to issue race dates only.

"I felt because I was the only descenting member of ARI, it was up to me to resign from the organization. I just didn't want to see a continued fragmentation. LoPatin has to realize there is a racing government with which he has to abide," Richter said.

LoPatin, in discussing the resignation, said, "Richter's leaving the corporation came about due to a difference in opinion. He aligned himself with philosophies of various sanctioning bodies which are not totally philosophies of ARI."

It is suggested the problem originally arose out of purse negotiations for the Dec. 7 Texas International Speedway NASCAR 500-mile Grand National stock car race.

The original purse for the race was set at $100,000. To date, the Bryan-College Station, Tex., speedway has posted only $65,000 for the purse plus $18,000 in contingency awards.

Richter said he felt it would be unappropriate for the ARI track to

LES RICHTER
. . . ends association

year. France reported the original purse negotiations would have to be met or the race length of 500 miles would be cut proportionately.

LoPatin accused Richter of siding with Bill France Sr., president of NASCAR, who said the larger purse would be the only one appropriate for the 500-miler.

"This has been one of the most painful experiences of my life," LoPatin said. "But Richter put himself in a position of interfering with our negotiations with NASCAR."

France said it was natural for Richter to attempt to resolve the Texas purse problem. "He's been working closely with NASCAR as our advisor on the West Coast for many years, and with no pay I might add. He generated the Permatex race at Riverside and has been involved in upgrading our

Pacific Coast Late Model stock car division."

It is also reported Richter has been unhappy with ARI procedures for the past few weeks. After the Michigan International Speedway Canadian-American Challenge Cup event on Sept. 28, the corporation terminated several MIS employees. More recently, ARI's comptroller Paul Chover resigned and late last week John Timanus, head of the Michigan International driver's school, offered his resignation.

LoPatin, questioned as to the wholesale lay off, stated, "ARI is concerned with the operation of each individual track. The employees in question were no longer needed, mainly due to the fact they were concerned with the revision construction at MIS prior to the CanAm. In other areas of our operation, we have a roving team which goes from track to track for each individual event," LoPatin said. "Apparently Richter's view of the operation differed from ours."

Richter will retain his position as president of Riverside International Raceway, in which ARI last year invested $2.2 million for track improvements and holds 48.4 percent of the common stock with an option to purchase another two percent.

When asked if the felt he would be able to retain his position at Riverside, Richter said, "I work for Riverside's board of directors. ARI has a minority on the board, so if they vote me to stay, I'll stay.

"All I want to do is find a spot in racing and help advance the sport," Richter concluded.

Coke Pitches 'Real Thing' Slogan

NEW YORK, Oct. 21 — Coca-Cola is undergoing a slogan change—the new title now "It's the Real Thing"—part of a new marketing program designed for Coke for the '70s.

red, will remain the same but will be unified into one system, a vice president reported.

Packaging, vending machines, advertising, trucks, "everything" will have the look of the new design

Mario Andretti; McLaren and Jackie Oliver; TI22

Times Grand Prix This Sunday at RIR

By RYAN REES
Sun-Telegram Auto Racing Editor

RIVERSIDE — This is the big one — the Times Grand Prix — the biggest, richest and most glamorous race of the year in Southern California.

The cars are the fastest road racers in the world. The drivers include some of the best in the world. And the audience, usually near 100,000, includes some of the brightest names from the Hollywood jet-set.

The Times Grand Prix is the next-to-last event on the Can-Am Challenge Cup series of the year. So far, Bruce McLaren and Denis Hulme have captured all nine races and finished second all but once.

In their twin orange McLaren-built, Chevy-powered, cars, the New Zealand duo is a solid favorite in this race. McLaren has won the Times Grand Prix the past two years, the only driver to ever capture the event twice in a row.

He leads teammate Hulme by five points in the driving standings with five wins to Hulme's four.

But it won't be a two-car race although the finish will probably end that way.

Mario Andretti has a 494 cubic inch McLaren-Ford primed and ready, Chris Amon has a new engine for his Ferrari, Dan Gurney had his new Chevy engine sorted out for his McLaren-Eagle, Jo Siffert has the powerful Porsche 917 running and John Surtees will try to make the grid in the Jim Hall-built Chaparral-Chevy.

In addition, Chuck Parsons will be out to hold on to his third place standing in his Lola-Chevy.

Also in the field will be Pete Revson, George Eaton, Lothar Motschenbacher and a host of other local drivers.

McLaren and Hulme have won more than $90,000 in the million-dollar series plus have an additional $85,000 locked up in the Johnson Wax prize fund.

More than $70,000 in prize money is being offered in the Times Grand Prix.

Practice for the Sunday race begins tomorrow at 10 a.m. over the 3.3-mile course at Riverside International Raceway.

There will be practice and qualifying Friday and Saturday, also starting at 10 a.m.

a series of amateur races will begin Saturday at 12:30. Final qualifying will conclude at 11 a.m. Saturday.

Sunday, final practice for the Can-Am will begin at 10 a.m. Amateur races will get underway at 11 a.m. and the Times Grand Prix will start at 1:30 p.m.

Tickets are not available in San Bernardino. The closest ticket outlet is at Riverside Raceway. Other outlets are in Los Angeles.

Jackie Oliver

Mario Andretti

Lothar Motschenbacher

Tony Dean

Ford Will Mount Can-Am Challenge

BY DAN FISHER
Times Staff Writer

RIVERSIDE—Ford Motor Co. will make a 429 aluminum block engine available to outside builders next year in an effort to mount a serious challenge to the Chevrolet-powered cars that have dominated Can-Am racing for three years.

The engine will be the same type that powers Mario Andretti's car in today's Times Grand Prix here.

Though Ford feels sedan racing is more important than Can-Am from the sales point of view, it would like to grab some of the publicity and advertising value attached to the Can-Am series, said Jacque Passino, head of Ford's racing program, in a telephone interview from Detroit.

Aid to Selling

"To a degree, you only have a racing program as an aid to selling cars," Passino said. And other than Indianapolis, Ford will continue to concentrate most heavily on circuits in which the cars bear some resemblance to those you see in dealers' showrooms.

But the "magnificent" publicity Chevrolet has generated, thanks to the domination of Team McLaren in the series, is tough to ignore.

The plan to build the aluminum 429 engine, which is a variation of the 429-cubic-inch engine Ford runs in stock car racing, depends somewhat on how Andretti does in today's race, Passino said. But he felt that Ford is "close to a breakthrough in a relatively light, powerful Can-Am engine.

"We think the engine is capable of being a win-

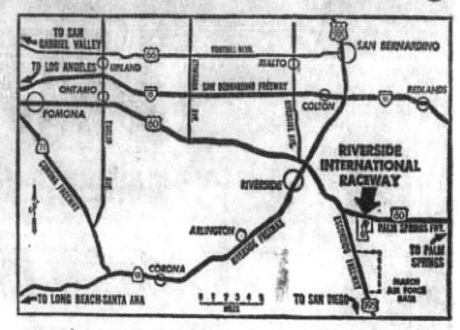

HOW TO GET THERE—Map shows routes to get to Riverside Raceway where the 12th annual Times Grand Prix sports car race is scheduled today at 1:30 p.m.

Times map by Donald Clement

Mario Andretti

Dan Gurney, who switched to Chevrolet power from Ford a month ago, was openly critical of the automaker's approach to the series.

Andretti was obviously upset as he had engine troubles during practice and qualifying.

Gurney, pointing to his 427 aluminum Chevrolet engine, said: "There is no doubt in my mind that's a

tion of the company's 1970 Can-Am plans, it appears to be changing that attitude.

Apparently, the Gurney Ford split was building for some time. He expected to get the aluminum 429 engine that Andretti is driving and lost patience as the series progressed and the company didn't deliver. Passino said that "with Dan, there was always a dispute whether or not the small block, (special) Gurney head route was better than the big block, production head approach."

With Gurney gone, there is no longer an argument and Ford will continue to campaign race engines based on production passenger car power plants.

Low Budget

Gurney says that despite Ford's plans to finally make the aluminum 429 available, he plans to stick with Chevrolet next season and feels he can make his car competitive with Team McLaren in 1970. He said he doesn't know yet what chassis he will

year out of a total $25 million racing budget.

Passino said those numbers are wrong, but the relationship of the Can-Am budget to the total that they indicate (2%) is about right.

Passino indicated that Ford won't try to recruit a builder to field Can-Am cars powered by Ford next year, but it's believed that if the right team could be formed, Ford would change its mind.

In fact, Passino admitted that early in 1968, Ford "tried to make an arrangement" with Bruce McLaren "where he'd use the engine Mario has now," Passino said.

But McLaren made what turned out to be a "fabulous decision," according to Ford's racing chief. McLaren decided to use Chevy power because he felt "Ford wouldn't be ready in time."

Ford wasn't, Passino admitted, and today's race will determine whether or not it is now.

Surtees Enters $70,000 Times Grand Prix

BACK AGAIN — John Surtees of England, winner of 1966 Times Grand Prix, will challenge for title again in sports car classic, Oct. 26 at Riverside Raceway.

Charles Wins With Eagle

John Surtees, former world champion from England, announced Saturday he will drive Jim Hall's new Chaparral 2H-Chevy in the $70,000 Times Grand Prix, Oct. 26 at Riverside International Raceway.

Surtees won the Times Grand Prix in 1966 en route to winning the first Can-Am Series for Group 7 cars.

Hall, the wealthy Texas oilman who helped pioneer Group 7 racing, has spent the past month making improvements on the Chaparral which had its troubles in the early races of this year's Can-Am series.

"Mostly it's been a matter of changing the aerodynamics," says Hall. "For one thing, we've added a wing on the rear, and this seems to help. The car is running considerably better."

Hall, a brilliant designer-driver who holds a degree from Caltech, drove a Chaparral to the U.S.

NEW CHAPARRAL — Jim Hall's revolutionary Chaparral 2H-Chevy, with John Surtees at controls, will contend for honors in the $70,000 Times Grand Prix, Oct. 26 at Riverside Raceway.

Road Racing championship in 1964 and three times has been runnerup in the Times Grand Prix.

In 1965, his partner Hap Sharp won the Times Grand Prix in a Chaparral, beating out Jimmy Clark and Bruce McLaren.

Hall isn't driving this year after suffering multiple injuries in a near-fatal crash in last year's Stardust Grand Prix in Las Vegas.

"I should be ready to go in a couple of months," he says. "I've already done some test driving. My right leg is still crooked but that hasn't bothered my driving. The only problem has been slow nerve returns in my left ankle."

Surtees won the world driver championship in 1964 and also is a former world champion in motorcycle racing. Last week, the 35-year-old Britisher placed third in the United States Grand Prix at Watkins Glen, N.Y.

When Surtees won the Times Grand Prix in 1966, the man he beat out was Hall after a thrilling head-to-head battle before 84,-470 fans. Hall finally surrendered to Surtees' Lola when his Chaparral developed a vapor lock.

McLaren and teammate Denis Hulme are the solid favorites in this year's race, and observers are wondering if anybody will ever catch the New Zealanders who have dominated the Can-Am series since Surtees won in 1966.

Dennis Hulme won $17,500 in November 1970, followed by Jackie Oliver in the TI-22 and Pedro Rodriguez in the BRM. The crowd, despite perfect weather, was only 46,400.

HULME TAKES CAN-AM FINALE

Chaparral 2J Quits Early; Ti22 Second

By Mike Knepper
Managing Editor

RIVERSIDE, Calif., Nov. 1 – It was a non-race, with Denny Hulme's McLaren M8D leading from start to finish to close the final chapter of the 1970 Canadian-American Challenge Cup series at Riverside International Raceway here today.

Jackie Oliver, in the Norris Ti22, did his best to make a contest of it, moving into second place from his position on the outside of the second row of the grid on the first lap and following Hulme the entire distance. But as at Laguna Seca two weeks ago, Oliver just couldn't find the beans under the titanium skin of his immaculate white and blue car and at the checkered was still 8.2 seconds behind Hulme.

PEDRO THIRD

Pedro Rodriguez, BRM; Chris Amon in the STP March; and Lothar Motschenbacher, McLaren M8C, followed Oliver, in that order, to fill the top five spots. Bob Brown, the independent entry from Huntington, N.Y., kept his head in the race and his McLeagle out of trouble to finish sixth, and in seventh was Tony Adamowicz in the Motschenbacher-owned McLaren M12.

Denny Hulme's McLaren leads Bob Brown's McLeagle during action in the CanAm at Riverside. The 1970 CanAm champion went on to add victory number six to his total for the year. (Ed Ingalls photo)

Denis Hulme cools his head with the victor's champagne after winning the Times Grand Prix finale to the 1970 CanAm series at Riverside International Raceway Nov. 1. (Joe Cali photo)

Again missing from the action after grabbing the pole position with a track record of 1:32.49, 128.446mph, was Jim Hall's Chaparral 2J in the capable hands of Vic Elford. After circulating around the 3.3-mile Riverside long-course for two trouble-free days, the crank shaft in the JLO engine that drives the fan system gave up this morning in warm-up. Repairs were made, but at the flag some undiagnosed trouble in the

(Continued on page 20)

GRAND PRIX PARADE—Twenty-nine drivers line up behind the Datsun pace car just before the start of the 61-lap, 201.3-mile race.

CHALLENGER—Jackie Oliver drives Chevy-powered Norris Titanium-22 to second place, finishing 8.2 seconds behind Denis Hulme.

FIERY CRASH—Firemen battle flames pouring from Dick Smith's McLaren-Ford after Fresno driver's car collided with a Ford G7B driven by John Cannon of Canada during The Times Grand Prix at Riverside Raceway Sunday. The cars crashed coming off turn No. 8 of the 17th lap. Neither driver was hurt.

180

Lothar Motschebacher

Pedro Rodriguez; BRM

COMPETITION PRESS &
MAC AUTOWEEK

November 21, 1970   50 Cents

Jackie Stewart Signs for '71 CanAm!

Complete Continental Series Review

Chaparral "Sweeper" Fizzles
Hulme's McLaren Wins Final CanAm

RIVERSIDE

In 1971, a crowd of 57,250 watched Dennis Hulme win $20,337 with teammate Peter Revson second. Jackie Stewart in the Lola threatened until engine problems put him out. Howden Ganley was third in BRM followed by Sam Posey in another McLaren. Revson won the championship.

Hulme, Revson Dominant

By STEVE BEATY   Am title as he became the   lander averaged a record   "I think it's a question of   He was more than 46 sec-
RIVERSIDE — Sunday's   first American to ever win the   breaking 123.727 mph, almost   hard work," said the Can-Am   onds ahead of Revson at the

David Hobbs: *"At the Times GP I drove the Ti22 again, this time under the Delta Tyre banner, again underfunded and no spares. Had no end of issues in practice and started near the rear of the field. In the race I was really going well, and passed car after car and would quite likely been third, fourth at worst, unfortunately I clipped those dreadful tire markers they had at all the high speed turns and damaged the nose, turn two I think, the really fast right hander, and with no spare we were out of the race."*

Titanium Car to Run in Grand Prix

BY SHAV GLICK
Times Staff Writer

Last June 8 several boxes filled with bits and pieces of a Can-Am race car, along with a titanium chassis and a couple of spare engines, were auctioned off by the Internal Revenue Service to satisfy a federal tax lien.

Dean Moon of Santa Fe Springs bid $11,600 for the whole mess, hauled it back to his Moon Equipment Co. warehouse, took an inventory and found many items, such as brakes, suspension components, uprights, etc. missing.

A month later Moon sold the entire package to Terry Godsall, a Canadian industrialist, for $20,000. Godsall is the head of Ti-

TESTING—David Hobbs crests hill in practice run in rebuilt Titanium Can-Am car which he'll drive in Times Grand Prix next Sunday at Riverside.

webs until the Feds moved in.

"Some of the parts walked away," said Hobbs.

It took $6,000 for new parts either through pur-

"We'll also do a bit of tidying up, fixing little things we didn't have time to do before."

Hobbs also hopes his fortunes will change at

Still he feels he has not received the recognition he deserves.

"After 12 years, I'm desperately trying to prove myself. I am trying to get over that plateau that distinguishes the good drivers from the great drivers, at least in the public's, and the sponsors' minds.

"For instance, if Jackie Stewart loses, or the car breaks, everyone says, 'Oh well, it was just tough luck, Jackie, you'll do better next time.'

"When I do exactly the same thing, they say, 'Look at that Hobbs, another lousy ride.'"

Victory in next Sunday's $75,000 Times Grand Prix would put Hobbs over

Start, Finish All the Same at Grand Prix

Revson Conquers 'Worst Pressure'

Enjoyable Day---Hulme

Revson, Hulme With Queen

Peter Revson, left, of Redondo Beach and Denis Hulme of New Zealand pose with queen Shelly Stepanek after winning the 201-mile Grand Prix in Riverside.

AP Wirephoto

185

Ike Smith: *"Jackie Stewart in Carl Haas' Lola was always a threat but we were beset by a number of issues; lost a piston on lap 27 while running second. Jackie was amazing at describing what the car needed though. A download session after practice, before he even got out of the car went something like this – turn two, understeer at the entrance, then ok in the middle, then oversteer on exit; turn six – brakes a little soft, understeer on entrance, then oversteer and so it went for every corner. A pleasure to set the car up with him"* **Compiler's Note** – Ike was crew chief for Carl Haas with both Chuck Parsons and Jackie Stewart. He's now retired and maintaining a Can Am car for the Blain Collection in Visalia, CA.

PENNY LAPS ANOTHER—Denis Hulme (5) pushes his McLaren-Chevy past John Cordts to lap the Canadian driver in the Times Grand Prix Sunday at Riverside. Hulme went wire-to-wire for third straight victory in race. Cordts, in a Lola T-160, blew his engine on 46th lap.

Times photo by Art Rogers

Ike Smith: *"Everyone said it happened at Riverside but it was Watkins Glen – the pits ran downhill. Jackie came in with a flat tire, I stuck the quickjack under the back, picked the car up but Jackie didn't have the brake on, the car rolled forward and the quickjack hit me in the chin. Still have the scar !! Not Jackie's fault, he knew not to touch the hot brakes while not moving."*

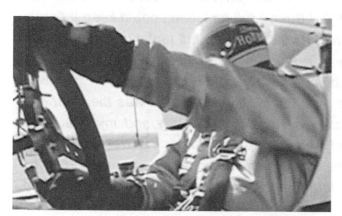

Watch this David Hobbs 1971 Can Am Video on the attached DVD

Tony Adamowicz in Oscar Kovaleski's McLaren

Skeeter McKitterick: *"Driving the King Cobra again for Mike Koslosky, we were the only small block Chevy in the field, deficient in horsepower with only 550bhp to the big blocks 700+bhp. I had a very interesting experience with the chassis; leaving turn seven toward turn eight you may recall there was a rise in elevation and a slight bend to the right going up to turn eight. The car on less the full fuel load would twitch (chassis deflection) to the left as I came of the rise as the car would get a little light! But on full fuel load I could keep it flat up this little rise and bend to the fight. Turns out that it was faster on full tanks then with a light fuel load. During Can Am qualifying I was only running about 165 to 167 mph down the straight but the opportunity arose to drop in behind Denny Hulme in the Mclaren who was exceeding 205 mph. The draft pulled me up to 185; the problem with that was the front end started to lift – the steering went light, the car was shaking violently and my head was buffeting around so bad I couldn't see clearly how deep into turn nine we were going. Fortunately, as Hulme broke for the turn and the speed came down the chassis settled to the ground and I was able to brake into the turn. Nothing left to do at that point except a memo to self " DO NOT, DO NOT try that again!"*

Denny Hulme had things pretty much his own way (top), winning as he wished. The big fright came with the appearance of the 2J Chaparral (above) which sucked its way round faster than the McLaren Team but proved unreliable

Revson, Hulme and Ganley

Howden Ganley: BRM

Roger McCaig

David Hobbs

Fritz Duda's development firm bought the track in 1971 after the owner, Partners American Raceways Inc. got overextended due to bad business moves. Dan Greenwood was appointed as manager. As a race fan and former track announcer, it was thought that Duda might find a way to keep the track functioning. That was not to be the case; the last race was held in July, 1989, with a final driving school in May, 1990, on a shortened portion of the course as construction work began for the new Moreno Valley Mall.

Ron Grable; T160/163 followed by Bob Peckham; McLaren M8C

Davey Jordan; Porsche 908

Riverside group buys Riverside raceways

A change to California ownership of the Riverside International Raceway was announced yesterday by Les Richter, president, as qualifying for Sunday's Motor Trend 500 was under way at the track.

American Raceways held majority interest in the Riverside facility until a group of Riverside and Los Angeles businessmen, known as the Sunnymead Land Investors, purchased the American Raceways stock.

Richter, who will remain as president of both the Riverside and American Raceways, commented that the change in ownership should be beneficial to both organizations. He said that money from the sale of RIR can now help American take care of financial problems at the Michigan International Speedway.

A foreclosure sale on the Michigan layout had been ordered but yesterday's West Coast transaction will not make that necessary, he said.

American Raceways also has partial ownership of the Atlanta International Speedway and majority interest in the Texas International Speedway and had proposed building a track to be known as the Eastern International Speedway near Philadelphia.

Sunnymead Land Investors is composed of Fritz Duda, a Riverside attorney, William Austin, a Riverside Realtor, William Norris, a Riverside real estate land developer, and David Logan, a Los Angeles real estate developer.

Richter reported that the group had purchased 80 per cent of the Riverside stock, but declined to comment on a report out of Detroit that the transaction involved $400,000.

No change in the overall operation of the Riverside track is anticipated, he added.

Pole qualifier George Follmer won $18,2000 in front of 46,300 fans in 1972, leading all but five of the 61 lap race, with Mark Donohue second and Francois Cevert third. Follmer won the championship. The supporting race was an under 2.5 Trans Am, won by John Morton in a Datsun 510. Read more about the Trans Am in Volume Two; coming in the fall, 2022

Caps Can-Am Series Triumph

Follmer Wins L.A. Times Grand Prix

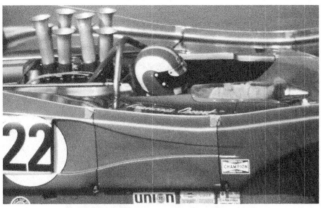

Francois Cevert; McLaren

Milt Minter; Porsche 917

Gary Knutson: *"Hap Sharp fried the seal in the torque converter after the start was delayed. He oiled the track which prompted someone to apply a lot of cement to absorb the oil. Next was someone's idea to have Arciero's helicopter hover over the mess to blow the cement away. It went downhill from there."* Compiler's Note – Gary Knutson was the engine builder (and more) at Traco, McLaren and Chaparral.

Bobby Allison: *"My only drive in the Can Am was with the Shadow team. I loved Riverside, had won there often in NASCAR and Don Nichols offered me a ride after seeing me in the BRE Datsun. The Shadow wasn't difficult to drive for me; blindingly fast; it reminded me of the Supermodifieds I'd driven in the Southeast. Unfortunately Jackie Oliver, who was part team owner wasn't thrilled that I was faster. Then blew his car up and took over my ride. Best part of that is that Roger Penske offered me an Indy 500 ride after seeing how fast I was at Riverside"* **Compiler's Note – Bobby doesn't need much introduction with six wins in NASCAR at Riverside and one in the IROC Series.**

THE WINNER—Happy, relieved and slightly overwhelmed, George Follmer holds hand to head in victory lane. The Arcadia veteran, driving a Penske turbocharged Porsche, won $20,950 in the final race of Cam-Am Challenge Cup series.

Mike Parkes; Ferrari 512

CanAm Closer

It's Icing on the Cake
For the TurboPorsches

Jackie Oliver's Shadow, until a mis-adventure later in the race, had a McLaren in the hands of Francois Cevert to worry about in the early laps. Willi Kauhsen's turboPorsche is just arriving on the scene.

Continued

chicken. A little canny questioning revealed that the turbos (2) were in fact Sweitzers, that the engine was, in fact, a 495cid Chevy (the McLaren's turbo, still on the dyno, is a 430) and that it runs very, very hot. Lee Muir did the engine work, Danny Jones the turbo work and George Bignotti, of all people, was the wizard of the dyno program.

On Saturday morning it turned a couple of :41s (about 10 seconds off the pace) with Oliver driving and then it ate a piston. Oliver is said to have felt it was remarkably easy to drive compared to what he had been led to believe, but as the weekend wore on, he found less and less time to confirm his in-

titial reaction. When practice on Sunday came around, Oliver took it out again and it promptly blew a head gasket. End of TurboShadow threat for this year, and the end of Bobby Allison's ride in the backup car too. But a TurboShadow of some sort will be back in the CanAm in '73 and so, very likely, will Allison.

Peter Gregg had his TurboPorsche back from Germany after its Laguna crash and promptly pranged it in practice. On went a spare nose and *that* one immediately fell apart—spontaneously according to Gregg. His engine had not been overhauled since the beginning of the season and, as a result, was down about 100hp to the rest of the turbos.

The McLarens (Denny's at least) tried going back to the smaller tires on the theory that

the 19-inchers were, responsible for their gearbox trouble, and that necessitated suspension and track changes, but it didn't

Warren Agor couldn't drive his M8F because he fell off a truck while preparing his TransAm car for next year and broke his

TURNING IT ON—George Follmer, in his L&M Porsche, leads pack through the esses just after start of Times Grand Prix Sunday at Riverside International Raceway. Denis Hulme is second and Mark Donohue (on outside) is third just ahead of Peter Revson.

Exuberant Owner Takes His Car on a Victory Lap for $2,000 Fee

Chuck Cantwell: *"In 1969, I went to work for Penske Racing as general manager of our small shop. First I the Trans Am, then with the Porsche 917 in the Can Am, won most of those races. Mark Donohue had a nasty accident early in the season and George Follmer stepped in for him. By the Riverside race Mark had healed and both Penske 917s ran at Riverside. I was a pleasure to race there; Les Richter ran a good operation, at least as I remember anyway. When we weren't racing, I still drove the ninety miles from my house to the track just to watch. I have been happy to write about this; it brings back some memories."* **Compiler's Note – Chuck was Central Division SCCA Champ, moved to California to work for Shelby, the moved back east to work for Penske.**

Sam Posey: A Many-Faceted Race Driver

BY SHAV GLICK
Times Staff Writer

Sam Posey

The Sam Posey most people know is best described in words written by Sam himself:

"I am 29 years old, somewhat overweight and very much over-mouthed. I guess by now I should have learned my lesson and keep quiet, but I never do, I speak out, then regret it later."

That's Posey all right, but there is much more to the man.

He is a painter, writer, furniture designer, cum-laude graduate of the Rhode Island School of Design—and a first-class race driver.

Next Sunday he will drive a Porsche Spyder in the $75,000 Times Grand Prix, final event of the Canadian-American Challenge Cup series, at Riverside International Raceway.

Posey's talents as a race driver—he was fifth in the Indy and Pocono 500s, second overall in the L&M Continental 5000 series and second American in the U.S. Grand Prix this year—are often obscured by the words that pour endlessly and effortlessly from his mouth and pen.

To amuse himself between races he writes about racing and race drivers.

He writes with an insider's touch. He says of Lothar Motschenbacher, who has driven in all but one of the Can-Am races since 1966: "No one has persevered so long and with so much style. Before this important race (Times Grand Prix), which may be his last, perhaps his wife Marilyn will feed him a double ration of the honey he always takes before each race."

Francois Cevert, the blue-eyed Parisian bachelor with the flowing locks, drew this comment: "Ah, Francois. Racing is unpredictable, so it is hard to know how Cevert will do in the race, but win or lose, one thing is certain—forty girls will swoon in the pits at the very sight of him."

Posey can be cutting, too.

"Of the driving of Tom Heyser in the Roman Brio Lola the less said the better. If the track was all straightway, with no bends, Heyser would have a much better chance. But he's a delightful fellow off the track."

Posey calls John Cordts, veteran Canadian driver, "one of the most unkempt drivers in racing. His uniform seems to be left over from World War I."

Peter Revson, last year's Can-Am champion, is "the lame duck of the Can-Am." Revson was winless in eight races this year as George Follmer won the championship. "But Peter's performance in Formula I racing this year has been an inspiration to all American drivers," Posey said.

Please Turn to Page 14, Col. 1

Gary Knutson: *"In 1971, we again used the Chevrolet big block power plant, built in house and with a Reynolds 494 cubic inch aluminum sleeveless block with cast iron liners. On the dyno, they produced 740 horsepower at 6400 RPM with 655 footpounds of torque. These later went up to 509 cubic inches and we adopted this midway through the season. and is very loud. I developed a new intake trumpet design featuring staggered trumpets of two different lengths which smoothed out the power curve."*

One of the largest crowds in Riverside history, 65,166, saw Mark Donohue win $18,700 in 1973, the first season with a fuel economy rule due to the oil embargo. Hurley Haywood was second, and Charlie Kemp third, all in Porsches. Donohue won the championship in the last Can Am to run at Riverside. 1974 saw a shortened five race season with no race at riverside that marked the end of the Can Am. Donohue also won the thirty lap qualifying race and the IROC supporting race, then announced his retirement. Bob Lazier won the Super Vee race. The IROC Series will be covered in depth in Volume Two; coming in the fall, 2022

Donohue Sweeps Riverside, Then Announces Retirement

RIVERSIDE, Calif. (AP) — Mark Donohue won a record sixth straight Can-Am road racing event Sunday and immediately announced he is retiring from competition.

The 36-year-old Brown University graduate said he will participate in the final round of the International 37 years of age, and I feel it is time that I look to something else to occupy my time.

"Except for the last race in the Champions Series at Daytona, I will not compete again in a racing machine.

"I always have said that I was a better engineer than I the field to win the 125-mile second stage in a wire-to-wire performance seldom seen in motor racing.

For his efforts, the stocky blond picked up $17,250 to go with the $96,733 he already had banked from the other seven races in what some ex-

201

Brian Redman: *"In July, 1973, the phone rang. "Brian, this is Vasek" he said. "You know I run Jody Scheckter in Can-Am in Porsche 917/10? Now I have another 917/10 for you to drive at Laguna Seca and Riverside. Come to Willow Springs and test your car, and also you drive Jody's." So one blustery day (is it ever anything else at Willow?) in September, I arrived to see two identical-looking 917/10s sitting in the pit lane. I met crew chief Alwin Springer, and we went over the idiosyncrasies of the fearsome 1100-hp turbocharged monster. After I drove both cars, Vasek asked, "What they like? What they like?" I replied that Jody's car felt different; it had a more solid feel on the road. To which Vasek rejoined, "They same. They same." Following a rather miserable race at Laguna Seca,*

where we had engine problems, we went to Riverside for the final race of the year. Of course, Mark Donohue was in a class of his own in the beautifully developed and prepared Penske owned and Sunoco sponsored 917/30, around three seconds a lap faster than anyone else. "Anyone else" included George Follmer, Jody Scheckter, Peter Gregg, and Hurley Haywood in 917/10s.

Late Friday afternoon, toward the end of practice, I felt something was not right at the back of the car, and an inspection in the pit lane showed a broken rear suspension support tube. On Saturday afternoon, again something was not right. Again, it was a broken chassis tube, but not the same one! By then I was extremely concerned. Remember that in those "good old days" racing was dangerous, and life expectancy not great. Following a sleepless Saturday night, I told Vasek on Sunday morning that I didn't think the car was safe, and I didn't want to drive. "Brian, the guys work all night. The car is perfect, perfect," said Vasek. "Okay Vasek, I'll drive," I replied. In the first of the two heats, the car was very loose but drivable, and I finished second to Donohue. In the second heat, at 200 mph in the fast left-hand kink before Turn 9, something broke. The car went sideways, switched back the other way, and continued in a series of vicious fishtails before eventually coming to halt. I drove back into the pits and Vasek screamed, "What's matter? What's matter?" I shouted that something had broken at the back. The tail was lifted, revealing a broken bottom right rear wishbone Heim joint Only then, on closer inspection, did I realize that the car didn't have the twin parallel links that other 917/10s had, and only then did Vasek admit that the car I was driving wasn't a 917/10 at all, but the original 917 PA driven by Jo Siffert in the Can-Am with a 580-hp motor. The bodywork had been copied from the Scheckter 917/10 and a "spare" 1100-hp turbo engine fitted!

Bob Brown: *"I ran in the Can Am a couple of times at Riverside, first with the McLeagle that Gurney won with, then in the ex Commander Motor Homes M8F. Always reminded of the 200 mph speed down that long back straight. When I think of Riverside, two things come to mind; the great parties at Mission Inn and Dan Gurney".*

AFTERBURNER—Rich fuel mixture in Mario Andretti's car causes flames to belch from exhaust pipes during Can-Am heat race Sunday.

The Grand Prix Scene: 'One Big Party'

BY JEFF PRUGH
Times Staff Writer

RIVERSIDE—To see all the pastel Porsches and twisting turns, it looked as if the California desert had undergone a massive Eu-

who arrived from San Diego the previous night in a camper. "I've been to races at other tracks—at places like Mid-Ohio and Elkhart, Lake and Laguna

fectly out of place for a sports car race. "Fight Smog—Ride a Horse."

Wandering along a hillside overlooking Turn 6, where thousands attended a Molly Bee-Jimmy Wakely-

camper that bore a sign "Coral Tree Racquet Club." They had driven from Marina del Rey to cheer a charter member, a part-time tennis player

an infection. But he can't stay away!"

Not far away, a visitor from Switzerland named Theo Leuenberger, 28, compared Riverside with European road racing.

204

A DAY IN FRONT—Can-Am champion Mark Donohue leads the field on the first lap of the Times Grand Prix sprint race Sunday at Riverside. Donohue, inset, won the sprint, the Times Grand Prix finale and the third heat of International Race of Champions, then announced retirement.

Times photo by Don Cormier

Donohue Heads Porsche Force in Times Grand Prix

German Racers Cars to Beat in Can-Am Finale

BY SHAV GLICK
Times Staff Writer

GRAND PRIX LINEUP

Car. No.	Driver/Hometown	Car	Qual. Speed
FIRST ROW			
6	Mark Donohue (Reading, Pa.)	Porsche	130.089
16	George Follmer (Arcadia)	Porsche	127.708
SECOND ROW			
0	Jody Scheckter (South Africa)	Porsche	127.337
3	Brian Redman (England)	Porsche	123.969
THIRD ROW			
73	David Hobbs (England)	McLaren	123.788
59	Hurley Haywood (Jacksonville, Fla.)	Porsche	123.405
FOURTH ROW			
23	Charlie Kemp (Jackson, Miss.)	Porsche	121.876
96	Mario Andretti (Nazareth, Pa.)	McLaren	121.610
FIFTH ROW			
101	Jackie Oliver (England)	Shadow	121.376
98	John Cannon (Hollywood)	McLaren	121.284
SIXTH ROW			
8	Scooter Patrick (Torrance)	McLaren	119.217
17	Bob Nagel (Bethel Park, Pa.)	Lola	118.600
SEVENTH ROW			
97	Bob Brown (Syosset, N.Y.)	McLaren	118.212
102	Vic Elford (England)	Shadow	117.757
EIGHTH ROW			
13	Sam Posey (San Juan Capistrano)	Ferrari	117.532
9	John Cordts (Canada)	McLaren	117.381
NINTH ROW			
33	Milt Minter (Van Nuys)	Alfa Romeo	117.041
64	Bob Peckham (Tucson)	McLaren	116.963
TENTH ROW			
39	John Gunn (Miami)	Lola	116.947
11	Steve Durst (Medford Lakes, N.J.)	McLaren	116.854
ELEVENTH ROW			
30	Frank Kahlich (St. Clair, Mich.)	McLaren	116.541
34	Tom Dutton (Houston)	McLaren	114.526
TWELFTH ROW			
22	Hans Muller-Perschl (Germany)	Porsche	107.854
2	Gary Wilson (Redondo Beach)	McLaren	96.151

RIVERSIDE — The Times Grand Prix, dominated for years by orange McLarens, moves into the turbocharged Porsche era today.

For the first time since 1967 there is no Team McLaren entry. Instead the front of the 24-car grid for today's $75,000 race, last of the Canadian - American Challenge Cup Series, is filled with 1,200 horsepower German-made Porsches.

Mark Donohue, in the blue and yellow Sunoco Porsche prepared by Roger Penske, is an odds-on favorite. He was won the last five Can-Ams and has clinched the driving championship. He qualified his car at 130,089 m.p.h., nearly three miles faster than George Follmer, who will sit alongside him on the front row in a year-old Porsche prepared by Bobby Rinzler and sponsored by RC Cola.

Donohue and Follmer will be busy today. Each will drive in the final International Race of Champions in addition to the two Can-Am races, a 75-mile qualifying heat at 12:30 p.m. and the 125-mile Times Grand Prix at 3:30 p.m.

worked as a mechanic in every race since 1961.

"I miss the Can-Am in a way," said Hulme, "but in another way I'm happier without it. I didn't enjoy that trans-Atlantic flight every week or so, hopping back and forth between the Can-Am and the Formula I schedules. And I wouldn't have enjoyed chasing those Porsches all year, either."

The second row is also turbo Porsches with the Vasek Polak teammates, Jody Scheckter of South

of the Can-Am is the duel for supremacy among non-turbocharged cars.

David Hobbs, in Roy Woods' Black Label McLaren, worked his way into the crowd of Porsches by qualifying fifth fastest. Hobbs is currently fourth in the Can-Am standings behind Donohue, Follmer and Scheckter. However, Jackie Oliver, driving the UOP Shadow, finished third at Edmonton and second at Laguna Seca in the underpowered black

Jody Scheckter

Riverside track cancels Can-Am

RIVERSIDE, Calif. (UPI) — The sixth and final Can-Am race of the season, scheduled here as part of the Riverside Grand Prix Oct. 26-27, has been canceled, it was announced Tuesday.

"The costs simply aren't justified by the quality of competition being offered," explained Riverside International Raceway president Les Richter.

A Formula 5000 race and two International Race of Champions events will make up the Riverside Grand Prix.

"It is our feeling that events like the Formula 5000 and the Race of Champions more accurately reflect the future of American road racing," added Richter. "We want to concentrate on developing the sport in those areas."

Riverside has been the site of Can-Am races since 1966, the Times Grand Prix, sponsored by the Los Angeles Times. But the Times removed its sponsorship this year.

The 1974 Can-Am series was won by England's Jackie Oliver of the UOP Shadow team. Oliver won four of the five races. The Can-Am finale, as it turned out, was last weekend at Elkhart Lake, Wis.

OFFICIAL
RACE
HEADQUARTERS

Pepper Tree
Appearing Nightly
Dining and Dancing
No Cover   No Minimum

Transportation:
Riverside Municipal Airport: Transportation centers via Golden West Airlines (10 minutes from Holiday Inn)
Ontario International Airport: Transcontinental flights to and from all major cities, and large network of state
commuter services via Pacific Southwest Airlines (20 minutes from Holiday Inn)

The Holiday Inn, Riverside's finest hostelry, just off Highway 60/395 on University Avenue, is proud to have been
selected Official Race Headquarters for all major Riverside International Raceway events. Our service will be
geared to the needs of racing aficionados.

Here the accent is on attentive service, excellent cuisine, live entertainment, and comfortable, modern
accommodations.

Each of the Inn's 128 tastefully appointed guest rooms and suites have been carefully designed to suit the need of
the vacationer as well as the commercial traveler, with individually controlled heat and air-conditioning, color T.V.
background music, and direct dial phones with 24 hour switchboard service. King-sized and water beds are
available.

1200 University Avenue, Riverside, California 92507   714-682-8000

Jody Scheckter; Porsche 917

Brian Redman; Porsche 917

John Cordts; McLaren M8

John Cannon; McLaren M20

Tom Dutton; McLaren M8

Steve Durst; McLaren M8

Sam Posey; Ferrari

Bob Nagel; Lola T-260

Milt Minter; Alfa T33

David Hobbs; McLaren M20

Tony Settember; Lola T-163

Vic Elford; Shadow

Scooter Patrick; McLaren M8

Gary Wilson; McLaren M8

Mark Donohue; Porsche 917

Chapter Six - Single Seat Can Am

  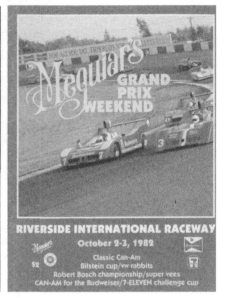

The Can Am name returned in 1977 with a 5 liter center seat formula designed by Carl Haas, the Lola guy, Don Nichols of Shadow fame and Burdie Martin of SCCA to rebody the large supply of Formula 5000 cars. Fuel capacity was reduced requiring pit stops. An under two liter category was added in 1979. Times sponsorship was over; these events were first the California Grand Prix, a name leftover from Formula 5000, then the Budweiser Grand Prix from 1979 to 1981. In 1982 it was the Meguiars Grand Prix. No Riverside event took place in 1983 and the 1984 event, the CRC Chemicals Can Am marked the end of the series. Rebodied Formula 5000's were long gone, interesting purpose built cars had emerged but it was too late.

Patrick Tambay won the 1977 race, the Pepsi Cola California Grand Prix, driving a Lola T333. He won $21,660 and the championship. George Follmer was second and John Morton third. Also on the schedule was an IROC race, won by Cale Yarborough.

Tambay wins his 6th Can-Am race

RIVERSIDE—Patrick Tambay swept to his sixth Canadian-American Challenge Cup victory of the 144 points to win the championship by 36 points over second-place Peter Gethin (108).

Return of the Can-Am

Canadian-American Challenge Cup sports cars return to Riverside International Raceway Sunday after a three-year absence. Above, the Lola Chevrolet of England's Peter Gethin at Watkins Glen early this year.

Patrick Tambay heads field for Can-Am Challenge at Riverside

Series champion Patrick Tambay of France heads an international field of drivers entered in the SCCA Citicorp Cup Can-Am Challenge, the feature race of the Pepsi-Cola California Grand Prix this weekend at Riverside International Raceway.

The season finale of the nine-race circuit is one of three major races celebrating the raceway's 20th anniversary. Sharing the billing are two rounds of the International Race of Champions series, which matches 12 of the world's great drivers in equally prepared Camaros.

Tambay, meanwhile, is expected to con-tinue his domination of the Can-Am circuit, on which he has won five of eight races held in the revival season.

His chief opposition is expected to come from Peter Gethin, England's perennial formula 5000 champion and son of a famed thoroughbred jockey. Gethin won one of the remaining three races and has been the closest challenger to Tambay in two of his victories.

Reentering the series after a tentative early start is the 1973 Indianapolis 500 rookie of the year and one-time dominator of the Tasman series, New Zealand's Gra-

Please Turn to Page 10, Col. 4

Polesitter Alan Jones won $21,050 in 1978, again in a Lola T333, and also won the championship. Warwick Brown was second and Elliot Forbes Robinson third. An SCCA production car race and IROC race were also held.

Aussie Jones wins Can-Am

RIVERSIDE — Australlan Alan Jones led wire to wire yesterday to win the final Can-Am Challenge Cup event of the season and clinch the national championship.

Jones, who started on the pole position with a qualifying speed of 124.165 mph, averaged 115.968 mph around the 2.55-mile Riverside International Raceway road course. The average was just under the course record.

His victory margin was 34 seconds over Warwick Brown, the man he needed to finish ahead of to win the title.

Brown edged Elliott Forbes-Robinson for second by three car lengths. Al Holbert took fourth, 100 feet behind Forbes-Robinson. Geoff Lees of England was fifth. one lap down.

S. Peter Smith; Chevron

John Gunn; GG-4

Rocky Moran: *"This was a great series, still not appreciated by those who compare it with the original Can Am. Maybe it should have had a different name, Great racing; produced drivers who went on to win World Championships and the Indy 500. I drove a Lola T333 for a high school buddy who made a fortune in donut shops; no wins but a couple of podiums. At Riverside, in 1978, had the whole family there watching, a couple of guys crashed in turn six, I ran into the wreckage and that was the end of my race"*

George Follmer had one win in the Prophet

Warwick Brown in the VDS Lola

Shadow - Jean Paul Jarier

Wolf - Michael Brayton

Elliott Forbes-Robinson
Can-Am driver

Can added horsepower help EFR outdistance bad luck?

By JIM MATTHEWS
Sun-Telegram Sports Writer

RIVERSIDE — Elliot Forbes-Robinson, better known as EFR in racing circles, is the guy to watch in the *other* race today at Riverside International Raceway.

The other race is the final event in the Sports Car Club of America's Can-Am series.

Forbes-Robinson, a top competitor during the whole series in these small, exotic cars, will be gaining something he's lacked occasionally through the season — horsepower.

The personable La Crescenta driver is, as they say, due.

EFR, until his disappointing finish at Laguna Seca Raceway in Monterey Monday, had a good shot at winning the SCCA Can-Am Challenge season point title. But, after leading the first 30 laps, a cracked mainfold took him out of both races.

The loss eliminated his chances from catching the Australian duo leading the points battle —

Warwick Brown and Alan Jones, currently whisper close in points. Today's race will decided the series champion, but EFR is a strong contender for victory — moral and otherwise — and he may overtake Al Holbert, who's third in points.

EFR had won two Can-Am races this year in his Spyder, and has been leading or near the front several times when engine problems have forced him out of races. His fourth position in the points race testifies for his consistancy.

"We've just had some bad luck," said EFR. "Several times the engine has just gone away from us when we were doing well."

But today's race will be the first time EFR will be running the larger engine. All season he's had 530 horses and, while he's been quicker around most of the course, some cars were able to pass him through the long straights. The new engine, installed yesterday, churns up 555 horses and will give EFR a little more speed through RIR's

(Continued on E-6, column 1)

Vic Schuppan; Elfin

British Stamp Car's Alain de Cadenet to debut at Riverside

The world's fastest stamp collector will make his Riverside International Raceway debut the weekend of Oct. 14-15 in the California Grand Prix presented by Pres. National City Travelers Checks.

Alain de Cadenet, son of a French nobleman and a racketeer worthy of reminiscence about the "good old days" of sports car racing at Riverside, will drive in the Can-Am feature of the traditional fall weekend of road racing that includes the International Race of Champions series.

De Cadenet, in fact, combines both of his special interests, as he is sponsored by the British Postal Service in the race. His Lola Chevrolet is called the British Stamp Car.

De Cadenet is joined in the Can-Am by the most talented group of foreign drivers gathered for one race since the Can-Am series was revived in 1977. Foremost is Formula 1 star Patrick DePailler, who will drive the Paul Newman-entered Spyder Chevy.

Also making his Riverside debut is Formula 1 driver Jean-Pierre Jarier, a one-time Formula 2 European champion and driver of a world manufacturer's championship Matra-Simca sports car. Series point leader Alan Jones, the Australian who all but has the Citicorp Cup title wrapped up, will duel with No. 2 Aussie, Warwick Brown, and there is yet another Australian entered, Vern Schuppan.

Uncle Sam is represented in the race by veteran George Follmer of Huntington Harbour, Al Holbert of Warrington, Pa., and Elliott Forbes-Robinson of La Crescenta.

TOUGH CORNER—Riverside's hilly Turn 7 was a challenge for Can-Am racers at 1977 California Grand Prix. Can-Am cars return to Riverside Oct. 14-15.

MOTOR RACING

Briton Mixes Stamps and Fast Cars

BY SHAV GLICK
Times Staff Writer

What do stamp collecting and auto racing have in common? Answer: Alain de Cadenet.

De Cadenet, son of a French nobleman and a British actress, is one of England's leading authorities on stamps issued during the reign of King George V—and is one of its better long-distance drivers. His race cars are sponsored by the British Post Office, are British racing green in color and carry the Union Jack depicted as a stamp on the sides.

Although de Cadenet, 31, was born in London and represents his homeland, he spends a great deal of time here with his mother in Hollywood. Valeria de Cadenet took the stage name of Karen Scott when she came here in 1951 to make movies.

"I'm afraid mother never made the bright lights," says her son, "but she had a measure of success as a character actress. And she loves it up in the Hollywood Hills. I can't blame her when I visit and enjoy her view."

Alain has also done some movie work. He taught race driving to Al Pacino and did some of the racing scenes in the movie "Bobby Deerfield."

This year he drove in the Can-Am Challenge series with moderate success but next year he may switch to the IMSA enduro program with its long-distance races, including the Times Grand Prix 6-hour race April 22 at Riverside.

"My main problem this season came from trying to stamps issued in Great Britain during King George V's reign, 1910 to 1936. He later sold his Queen Victoria and Commonwealth collections and in time became one of the most respected George V collectors in the world.

"During my teens when my chums were off fiddling with sports and cars and girls I was busy buying early die proofs and plate proofs, color trials and essays. They cost very little money in those days and now they are the basis of my King George V collections."

His research led to writing articles for the distinguished Philatelic Journal of Great Britain and contributing to Gibbons Stamp Monthly.

His collection has been appraised at between $200,000 and $300,000. More important, he believes, are its intrinsic values.

"Stamps can become a link between parent and child and also be educational. Stamps teach children the use of their hands. You might not think about it but the sorting, pasting, identifying and collecting give an indication of neatness and organization. They also teach geography, history, natural history and even color and symmetry.

"I have tried to follow my grandfather's philosophy in my life. He told me if I ever found myself doing something I didn't think I would remember when I got old, to stop doing it. So now I am doing the two things I enjoy immensely. The stamps are a form of therapy from the racing. The two, one so quiet and so slow moving, the other so loud and fast, form a perfect complement for me."

Alain de Cadenet

Tom Spalding; Schkee

Michael Allen; T332

In 1979, Jackie Ickx won $23,100 in the Carl Haas T333 and announced his retirement. He was followed by Bobby Rahal in the Prophet and Elliot Forbes Robinson in the Newman - Freeman Spyder. Gary Gove won the under two liter category in a Chevron Cosworth. Darrell Waltrip won the accompanying IROC race over Bobby Allison. There was also an SCCA regional and a VW Rabbit Bilstein Cup race.

Keke Rosberg in the Newman - Freeman Spyder

Ickx closes with Can-Am win

RIVERSIDE, Calif. (AP) — International racing star Jacky Ickx has finished his career, with the possible exception of a run at Le Mans next year, and the Belgian driver closed out his career in style.

Locked in a close duel with Elliott Forbes-Robinson for the Can-Am Series championship going into Sunday's concluding event at Riverside International Raceway, Ickx won the race and the point title.

Bobby Rahal of Glen Ellyn, Ill., was second and Forbes-Robinson from La Crescenta, Calif., finished third in the race and second in the 10-race Can-Am Series.

In Sunday's co-feature at Riverside, Darrell Waltrip edged NASCAR rival Bobby Allison to win the International Race of Champions.

Ickx's distinguished career took him literally from a motorcycle to a tank — a stint in the Belgian army — to a sleak and sophisticated Formula 1. On two occasions, he finished second for the world championship.

Why did the 34-year-old Ickx decide to retire?

"Because I've had enough," said Ickx. "I've been doing this sort of thing for 19 years now, and I just think it's time to retire.

"It was a great privilege to do what I've done in racing and I hope I can find something in the future that will give me the same pleasure, be as attractive and interesting to me," he continued. "That's one of the things about quitting something, you can't be sure anything else will ever again be quite so satisfying."

It appeared near the end of the 50-lap race over River-side's 2.547-mile road course that Ickx would finish second, as Keke Rosberg had a comfortable lead. But Rosberg got tangled up with another car and went into the wall on the 45th lap, leaving the door open for Ickx.

The IROC event was a 30-lapper pitting four drivers each from stock cars, formula 1 and Indy-type competition in equally prepared Chevrolet Camaros. Waltrip took the lead on the 10th lap as early pacesetter Neil Bonnett faded, then had only Allison challenge him the rest of the way.

"The way were running, I figured it was going to just be between Bobby and me," Waltrip drawled. "He said he was having some brake problems there at the end, but my car was just fine all the way.

"It was the best driving car I've had in IROC; she didn't understeer or oversteer." Then Waltrip added with a grin, "I would have said she wasn't too loose or too tight, but I've been hanging around to those Formula 1 drivers for a couple of days."

A crowd of 15,000 saw Al Holbert win $25,200 in the his own construction CAC-1 in 1980, followed by Elliot Forbes-Robinson, only six tenths of second back with Patrick Tambay in third. Tambay won the championship with Gary Gove winning the under two liter category in a Chevron. Bob Earl won the supporting Super Vee race and Paul Hacker won the Bilstein Rabbit race.

Holbert Wins Can-Am Race

He Beats Darkness, Forbes-Robinson to the Finish

By SHAV GLICK, *Times Staff Writer*

RIVERSIDE—Al Holbert survived crashes, lost brakes, a chunking tire and gathering darkness to win 1980's final Citicorp Can-Am Challenge race Sunday at Riverside International Raceway in one of the closest finishes in the long history of the sports car series.

Holbert, 35-year-old veteran from Warrington, Pa., was driving a car of his own design and make, a CRC Chemicals Special. He edged Elliott Forbes-Robinson of La Crescenta, in one of Paul Newman's Budweiser Lolas, by less than one second in a race that ended with the winner barely able to see the checkered flag.

The other Budweiser Lola driver, Keke Rosberg, provided the early excitement for an estimated crowd of 15,000.

Rosberg, after trailing pole-sitter Geoff Brabham for five laps, tried to make a pass for the lead between Turns 6 and 7 but as he crept the nose of his Lola alongside Brabham's red VDS Lola the diminishing radius of Turn 7 brought the two cars together. The impact knocked the right front fender off Rosberg's car but he managed to hold his line. Not so fortunate was Brabham, the 28-year-old Australian whose father, Jack, won three world Formula One championships a decade ago. His car was sent spinning into the dirt with fiberglass body panels and dust filling the air.

Holbert Stays Out of Trouble

Holbert, following about 100 yards back, threaded his way through the debris and took the lead. Brabham managed to limp to the pits but there was too much damage for him to continue. Rosberg set out to catch Holbert.

The feisty Finnish driver, fresh from a season on the Formula One circuit, caught Holbert and passed him at the same spot where he had collided with Brabham.

Thirteen laps from the finish of the 50-lap (128.5-miles) race Rosberg had to pit to have flapping body damage taped and the 28-second stop cost him the lead. When Holbert made a fast fuel stop he

managed to come out and retain the lead.

Just as Rosberg appeared ready to make another challenge he was black-flagged by Sports Car Club of America officials to remove left-side bodywork that was rubbing dangerously on his tire. This put him out of contention and he finished fourth behind Holbert, Forbes-Robinson and Patrick Tambay of France, the Can-Am series winner.

Surprised When He Did It

"Kind of poetic justice, wouldn't you say?" a smiling Holbert said. "I had been watching the two (Brabham and Rosberg) and I noticed that Geoff (Brabham) was taking a wide line through Turn 7. I figured Keke would try and take him there but I was a bit surprised when he did it. I think I might have been more conservative. But when he got in so deep and there was no place for either of them to go, it happened."

Holbert, who won his first race at Riverside in a career that first saw him coming here as a pit crew member for the late Mark Donohue in the 1960s, said his major concern was his left rear tire.

"I lost my front brakes when Rosberg passed me and I had to run as safely as I could but then I realized my left rear tire was coming apart. I knew someone (Forbes-Robinson) was closing in on me but I decided in the last five laps to run hard and make my car as wide as I could in Turn 9. And hope my tire wouldn't explode."

Forbes-Robinson Couldn't Pass

Forbes-Robinson moved into a contending position with three laps to go and appeared he could pass Holbert at any time—but he never made it.

"The turbulence that built up when I came close to Holbert prevented me from passing him," Forbes-Robinson said. "I could catch up to him quite easily but I couldn't pass him."

Holbert explained why Forbes-Robinson couldn't pass.

"I can make my car pretty wide when I have to," he said. "I'm so

pleased to win here at Riverside because this is where Mark (Donohue) won his last race and it means a great deal to me to have my name in the record books with his."

It was his second Can-Am win this year. Road America was the other.

John Morton, driving the controversial Frissbee after Riverside favorite George Follmer was replaced Saturday, was never in contention. The white car, with its radical skirt-less ground effects, tangled on the third lap with Colombia's Ricardo Londono and, while the impact appeared to have no effect on the Frissbee, it never moved up to the leaders. On lap 27, Morton pulled into the pits with a broken engine.

Winning Speed: 118.94 M.P.H.

Holbert averaged 118.94 m.p.h. for the 1-hour 4-minute 14.41-second race.

Even though his winning margin over Forbes-Robinson was a miniscule .652 seconds it was not so close as the margin in Sunday's other two races, the Bosch VW Super Vee and the VW Rabbit-Bilstein Cup.

Bob Earl of Novato, Calif., beat pole-sitter David Bruns of Santa Fe Springs in the Super Vee chase by .379 seconds. The closest of all, however, was in the Rabbit race where Paul Hacker slipped by series champion Gary Benson to win by .146 seconds.

For the Follmer family, meanwhile, it wasn't a good weekend. George Follmer, a veteran of 38 major races here since he first drove a Porsche Speedster in a 1960 club race, had his IROC Camaro declared ineligible for Saturday's Trans-Am race. Then car owner Brad Frisselle pulled him out of the Frissbee in favor of test driver Morton.

The only Follmer driving Sunday was Michael, George's nephew. He was in his uncle's Porsche Audi Lola in the Super Vee race. On the second lap Follmer tangled with Michael McHugh in Turn 3 and both cars were knocked out of the race. Follmer had to be pulled from his car by an emergency crew but was not seriously injured.

Patrick Tambay in the Carl Haas Lola T530

Randy Unsbee: *"Patrick Tambay and I became friends during the season. At the final race , we were staying at the same motel. After the race he was throwing team members into the pool ,spotted me, picked me up, made sure someone held my watch and wallet and tossed me in. Later I gave a ride to San Francisco,".*

Friday, October 24, 1980 **PRESS** 1 2

Can-Am at Riverside

RIVERSIDE (UPI) — Bobby Rahal, the rookie sensation of the Can-Am racing circuit last year, has turned superstitious as his winless streak continues through the 1980 season.

"I used to have this pair of red underwear," Rahal said Thursday, "and they were lucky for me until this year. Then I had four straight problems that kept me from winning and I got rid of the red pants."

He's even thinking in terms of odd-even.

"On odd numbered years I do very well," he said, "but even numbered years, forget it. I can hardly wait for 1981."

Rahal is one of the leading drivers in Sunday's Grand Prix Can-Am at Riverside International Raceway with Patrick Tambay of France having already clinched the season championship. But Rahal is shooting for the pole position and a victory to end the season on a strong note.

"We made a decision at the beginning of the season to go with last year's car, updated" the native of Glen Ellyn, Ill., said, "and that looked like the right move after the first couple of races. But since then we haven't looked so good."

Brabham on pole for Can-Am race

Associated Press

Bobby Rahal in the Prophet

Rocky Moran; Lola T332

Vern Schuppan; Tiga CA80

John Morton; Frisbee

222

Gerre Payvis; Lola T332

In 1981, 23,000 fans saw Al Holbert win $23,500 with the Lee Dykstra CAC-2, followed by Jeff Wood in a T530 and Tom Klausler in the Frisbee. Richard Guider won under two liters in a customized March 782. In the supporting races, Again Bob Earl won the Super Vee race and Paul Hacker won the VW Rabbit Bilstein Cup event..

Al Holbert in the CAC-2

Holbert wins Can-Am race

RIVERSIDE, Calif. (AP) — Al Holbert of Warrington, Pa., was a surprise winner Sunday of the Budweiser Grand Prix Can-Am at Riverside International Raceway with a record average speed of 119.391

Patience pays off for Holbert in Can-Am race . . .

(Continued from D-1)

Brabham, the second-fastest qualifier, easily blew away the rest of the 19-car field to lead laps 2 through 41. But he pitted for fuel on lap 40, made one more lap and then came back into the pits with a dead engine.

Bobby Rahal, the No.3 qualifier, lasted only minutes longer than teammate Fabi, going out at the end of lap 22 with suspension problems caused by a flat tire.

That left it to the fortunate Holbert, who had only minor problems except for his unscheduled pit stop. Still, he tried to make it sound good.

"Did I have any problems?" Holbert said, echoing the question. "Everybody had problems. Thank God nobody got hurt. I saw some nasty things out there. The traffic was generally good but some of the new guys apparently are not used to using mirrors. They caused some problems."

However, he was all forgive and forget in light of winning and moving into second in the points standings.

"It's just phenomenal," he said. "Nobody knows what it's like to win here. I've been coming to races at Riverside since I was 11 and to win a race here two years in a row . . ."

Can-Am race notes

With his third Can-Am win this year, Holbert now has 351 points to 407 for Brabham, who got only three points for 13th place. Fabi (15th, 1 point) is now third with 306. There are only two races left in the season. . . . Holbert pointed out his chances of winning looked none too good in the days before the race. "We came to the track with a stiff suspension setup," he said. "I just couldn't drive it. So we lost a day changing that. Then the motor we had in the car just wasn't right; it vibrated terribly. We put another motor in and that one broke. So we lost another day." . . . Ironically, Wood spoke out against other bad drivers. "There was an incredible amount of problems passing backmarkers," he said. "It was just a joke. Most were considerate but the others were just not aware." This was said before he found out about the protests, though. . . . In the companion races, Bob Earl won the VW Super Vee race for the second year in a row, while Paul Hacker won the VW Rabbit sedan race.

Newman fields two-car team for Can-Am Challenge race; Fabi, Rahal are drivers

Actor and racer Paul Newman brings his Newman-Budweiser team to the Can-Am Challenge circuit, a feature of the Budweiser Grand Prix weekend ending Sunday at Riverside International Raceway. The drivers are Italian sensation Teo Fabi and the determined and talented American road racer, Bobby Rahal.

Newman has lent his name to the most exotic of road-racing circuits by fielding a two-car team this season that has excited fans from coast to coast.

Fabi, a former national ski champion whose English has mostly been learned this summer during the racing campaign, is currently battling back from the setbacks he suffered in a duel with young Geoff Brabham for the series driving title. Fabi has won three races, but missed out driving in two of the other four races, allowing Brabham to compile a commanding 99-point lead.

Rahal, the young graduate of formula Atlantic, got his big break and joined the most conspicuous team on the circuit when Indy driver Al Unser reluctantly dropped off the circuit, citing conflicts with his CART Indy car schedule. In Rahal's first start, at Mosport in September, he drove smoothly to a second-place finish behind his teammate.

Newman has steadfastly refused to drive one of his own cars, joking that he is "too long in the tooth" to move up from his current level of competition to the super-fast Can-Am.

Last year's Riverside winner, Al Holbert, is a potent threat to win the race but seems mathematically removed from championship hopes.

Please Turn to Page 12, Col. 1

Al Holbert won $25,800 in 1982 driving a VDS-001. Second was Al Unser Jr. in a Frisbee with Danny Sullivan third in the Newman March 827. Bertil Roos won under two liters in the ex Guider March, now called a Marguey. Unser won the championship. Michael Andretti won the Super Vee race; Wally Dallenbach tentatively won the Rabbit Bilstein Cup race. Vintage races were also on the schedule. Vintage races are covered in Volume Two, available in the fall of 2022.

Holbert Sets Speed Record in Win at Riverside

By SHAV GLICK, *Times Staff Writer*

RIVERSIDE—Veteran sports car driver Al Holbert is a Porsche-Audi dealer in Warrington, Pa., but in a race car he's more at home at Riverside International Raceway than anywhere else.

Holbert, 35, won his third straight Riverside Can-Am with a record-breaking, wire-to-wire performance here Sunday in the Meguiar's Grand Prix. He averaged 120.742 m.p.h. for 60 laps (152.4 miles), breaking the 119.784 record by Jacky Ickx in 1979.

The win thwarted Al Unser Jr.'s hopes of adding the Can-Am championship to the Super Vee title he won last year as a teen-ager. Unser finished second, 45.8 seconds back of Holbert, with Danny Sullivan, last week's Caesars Palace winner, third, more than a lap back of the winner. Unser has 450 points, Holbert 440 and Sullivan 390 going into Sunday's final race at Laguna Seca.

This was Holbert's 10th win in 45 Can-Am starts, moving him into a third place tie with the late Mark Donohue—Holbert's idol when he started racing in New England—in career wins.

"This (win) has a lot of special meaning for me," said Holbert. "I've had a fondness for Riverside since I first came here with my father (Bob Holbert, former national sports car champion) to watch him race in the 60s. And it means a great deal to me to be associated in the record with Mark (Donohue). To share a record with him is to be on a very high plateau."

From the moment the green flag fell to start the race, Holbert was in command. He jumped ahead of Sullivan heading for the first turn. By the 15th lap he had a nine-second lead and by the 20th it was 14 seconds. He maintained enough margin that twice he was able to pit for fuel and not lose the lead.

"The only problems I had were imaginary," said Holbert. "Several times late in the race I second guessed nerup Chris McCarron in the jockey standings. myself but it all worked out. I've always felt that if you

keep working hard, things will keep coming your way.

Holbert won $25,500 from the $138,000 purse.

There was one difference this year from Holbert's last two wins—he was driving for someone else. In 1980-81 he was driving his own car. Last year's winning car, driven by Randy Lewis, finished sixth Sunday. Holbert this year is driving Count Rudy von der Strauten's Team VDS car.

"I had a hard time forgetting it wasn't my car," said Holbert. "When I'm in my own cars, I'm extra careful, especially in traffic. You have to be when you pay your own bills."

Holbert did not join the nine-race Can-Am circuit until after the first race, which Unser won. He took the VDS ride after Patrick Tambay quit to drive for Ferrari in Formula One. Since then, Holbert has won four races.

Next year Holbert hopes to drive an Indy car in the CART series, perhaps for VDS.

"I would definitely like to go champ car racing," he said. "I think I have the patience and the maturity, and the technical background to contribute to a strong effort. I can't speak for VDS, but I believe it's about 50-50 that they'll tackle Indy."

Sunday was a day for second generation drivers.

Michael Andretti, who will be 20 on Tuesday, was never challenged in winning the Robert Bosch VW Super Vee race. The win was the fifth win in nine races for Mario's son. Another 19-year-old, Davey Jones of McGraw, N.Y., finished a close second, with Ed Pimm of Amlin, Ohio, third.

Wally Dallenbach Jr., after finishing second to Gary Benson in the Rabbit Bilstein Cup race, was awarded first place when Benson's car was found to be under weight. Five hours later, the SCCA reversed its decision and awarded the win to Benson. The 20-lap race developed into a four-car battle among Dallenbach, Benson, Paul Schwartzott and Karl Hacker with the lead changing nearly every other lap. Dallenbach's father is a veteran Indy car driver and winner of the 1972 California 500 at Ontario.

There was no Hard Luck Award for the Meguiar's Grand Prix, but if there had it would surely have gone to

Andy Bernstein, 24, a crewman on Rex Ramsey's Can-Am car. Bernstein broke his ankle in a pit accident when he kissed one of the race queens, then tried to jump over a tool box in glee—only to slip in an oil slick.

Lamerok and Laffit Pincay Win

Al Holbert in the VDS

Spend a weekend in fast company.

Meguiar's GRAND PRIX, Oct 1-3, Riverside International Raceway

Toyota Celica Supra Paces the Races

See 72 Hours of Riverside at Meguiar's Grand Prix.

A big weekend of racing roars into Riverside International Raceway October 1-3, 1982, with the prestigious Can-Am Series heading a triple header of motor sports excitement. Along with the high-flying Can-Am cars, hot Super Vees and Rabbits will also wend their way around Riverside's challenging 2.547-mile course.

Leading all the cars around the circuit will be a Toyota Celica Supra, the car with the right stuff. Supra is the Official Pace Car of Riverside and Motor Trend magazine's "1982 Import Car of the Year." An enthusiast's dream, Supra has a fuel-injected Twin Cam powerplant similar to the engines in Formula I race cars. Supra also has variable-assist power rack-and-pinion steering, a close-ratio 5-speed overdrive gear box, ventilated and power-assisted 4-wheel disc brakes, and more. All standard equipment. All the right stuff to pace the races.

Meguiar's Grand Prix Weekend is part of the Budweiser/7-ELEVEN Series for International Can-Am cars and features the Red Roof Inn's 2-liter challenge cars. This action-packed weekend of motor sports excitement promises to be three great days of challenges, speed, skills, and fun. Make your plans now to be there. Spend the weekend in really fast company!

Can-Am. The men. The machines.

Al Unser, Jr., Rex Ramsey, Val Musetti, Al Holbert, John Morton and Danny Sullivan are just a few of the drivers scheduled to race at Riverside for a share of the $100,000 purse. The highly-sophisticated Can-Am cars, powered by 5-liter V8 engines, include Lolas, Prophets, Rals, Frisbees, Chevrons and Phantoms. Can-Am racing means no-holds-barred, wheel-to-wheel action from start to finish.

See the Super Vees to Victory.

Michael Andretti, Jerrill Rice, Mike Rosen, Roger Penske, Jr., and others will be competing for the Robert Bosch Championship and a share of the $30,000 purse. They'll be driving scaled-down versions of Formula I cars powered by highly-modified 1600 cc engines and drivetrains. See many of tomorrow's racing stars today.

Watch the Rabbits Run.

Mark Behm, Gary Benson, Karl and Paul Hachen, Don Knowles, movie star Kent McCord and dozens more will go fender-to-fender in the 1982 Rabbit/Bilstein Cup and its $10,000 purse. The cars are identically-prepared for racing and are basically stock sedans. Watch them run for glory.

The Schedule

Friday, Oct. 1
10:00 a.m.	Can-Am Practice
11:00 a.m.	Super Vee Practice
11:45 a.m.	Rabbit Practice
1:00 p.m.	Can-Am Qualifying (1st session)
2:00 p.m.	Super Vee Qualifying
2:45 p.m.	Rabbit Qualifying

Saturday, Oct. 2
8:30 a.m.	Regional Practice & Qualifying
10:15 a.m.	Can-Am Qualifying (2nd session)
11:15 a.m.	Rabbit Qualifying
12:00 p.m.	Super Vee Qualifying
12:30 p.m.	Classic Can-Am Practice
1:15 p.m.	CSCC Regional Races
3:45 p.m.	Can-Am Practice

Sunday, Oct. 3
9:00 a.m.	Regional Practice & Qualifying
9:30 a.m.	Can-Am Warm up
10:15 a.m.	Super Vee Warm up
11:00 a.m.	Rabbit Warm up
11:45 a.m.	CSCC Regional Races
12:45 p.m.	CLASSIC CAN-AM RACE (10 laps/25 miles)
1:30 p.m.	SUPER VEE RACE (24 laps/60 miles)
2:15 p.m.	RABBIT RACE (20 laps/50 miles)
3:00 p.m.	MEGUIAR'S GRAND PRIX (50 laps/126 miles)

Ticket Information

SPECIAL SUPER TICKET
Good for Friday, Saturday and Sunday
General Admission & Garage ... $20.00 ea.

SPECIAL OFFER EXPIRES BY MAIL OF ALL PERSONS 6:00 P.M. FROM OCTOBER 14
UNLESS MARK W. PURCHASED AFTER OCTOBER 14

SATURDAY ONLY (October 2)
General Admission (children under 12 FREE) ... $9.00 ea.

SUNDAY ONLY (October 3)
General Admission (children under 2 FREE) ... $10.00 ea.

Children under 12 must have valid ticket for grandstands on Sunday.

SEAT PRICES BELOW DO NOT INCLUDE GENERAL ADMISSION TO GROUNDS

Reserved seat Grandstand A (Start/Finish Line)	$4.00 ea.
Reserved Seat Grandstand from Turn 2, 3, 4 and	$6.00 ea.
Reserved Seat Grandstand (B) turn 8	$4.00 ea.
Rows 1 to 26	$6.00 ea.
Rows 27 to 40	$4.00 ea.
Overnight Parking (arrive Fri)	$6.00 ea.

Telephone 714/653-1161
9-5 M-F and for group ticket sales
Make check payable to Riverside International Raceway and mail to 22255 Eucalyptus Avenue, Riverside, California 92508.

OH WHAT A FEELING

TOYOTA

Meguiar's GRAND PRIX WEEKEND

OCTOBER 2-3, 1982

CAN-AM for the Budweiser/7-ELEVEN challenge cup
Robert Bosch Championship/super vees
Bilstein cup - Rabbits — Classic Can-Am

Tickets (714) 653-1161

RIVERSIDE INTERNATIONAL RACEWAY

A pack of Can-Am cars roar out of Riverside Raceway's turn No. 9. The highly-sophisticated sports racing machines will be in action at Riverside's 2.5-mile road course on October 3 for the Meguiar's Grand Prix Weekend.

Showdown for Can-Am title is expected

RIVERSIDE, CA — The 1982 Budweiser/7-Eleven Can-Am series, currently embroiled in a five-race marathon in just 36 days, is heading for what may well be the deciding race of the year when the exotic sports racing cars make their annual visit to Riverside International Raceway October 1-3 for the Meguiar's Grand Prix.

The Riverside event is the 8th race on the season's 9-race schedule, and if the points battle for the coveted Can-Am championship continues as it has from the outset, one of three contending drivers could wrap up the title with a victory at the Raceway's 2.5-mile road course.

Through the season's first five races, which began in May, only two drivers have been victorious—Al Unser, Jr., who captured the first two events, and Al Holbert, winner of the last three races. Holbert took the point lead from Unser with a victory at Trois-Rivieres, Quebec earlier this month, and now leads 270 points to 240.

The third contender is Danny Sullivan who pilots the Paul Newman/Budweiser Team March 827. Despite a disappointing year which has kept him...

A pack of Can-Am cars roar out of Riverside Raceway's turn No. 9. The highly-sophisticated sports racing machines will be in action at Riverside's 2.5-mile road course on October 3 for the Meguiar's Grand Prix Weekend.

MARK C. BLOOME

PLAY SUN BINGO
$500 EACH WEEK

Riverside wasn't on the schedule in 1983 and the series would have been out of business if it hadn't been rescued by Don Walker. He leased it from SCCA and ran it as a private club. His team cars ran with little opposition, Michael Roe winning in 1984 on the VDS-004, followed by Jim Crawford in a March 847 and Horst Kroll in a Frisbee. Kim Campbell won under two liters in a March BMW. Roe won the championship. Other events included Trans Am and Formula Atlantic races, a Russell Formula Mazda race and the Del Taco 10k Run. The series continued on for a couple of years but no more races were held at Riverside.

RIVERSIDE GRAND PRIX
FESTIVAL RIVERSIDE INTERNATIONAL RACEWAY
Saturday and Sunday, October 6-7, 1984.

Michael Roe in the VDS

Juan Manuel Fangio III

Juan Manuel Fangio III

A famous name to compete in Can-Am race

Another second-generation driver bearing the name of a famous predecessor has entered the world of motorsports and will be prominent in the CRC Chemicals Can-Am portion of the Riverside Grand Prix Festival.

Juan Manuel Fangio III, 27-year-old nephew of five-time World Champion Juan Manuel Fangio of Argentina and son of lesser-known driver Borbero Fangio, will make his third Can-Am start of the season at Riverside, where he will drive a 2-liter Ralt RT-2 entered by Mike Ferro's Genoa Racing team

of San Francisco.

A graduate of Formula 2 competition, where he won the 1983 Euro F-2 championship, Fangio made his first Can-Am start at the Dallas Grand Prix earlier this year, qualifying second overall, winning the Two Liter class and finishing third overall in the race.

"Manuel (as he is known) is more than just another second-generation race driver with a famous name," said Don Walker, president of the Can-Am Assn.

"He is truly talented, and has the desire and ability to become

a great driver," Walker said.

Fangio, who was also scheduled to race in the CRC Chemicals Can-Am series event at Sears Point Raceway the week preceding the Riverside event, said that his famous uncle is very much involved in helping promote his career.

The pair visited Europe recently seeking sponsorship for Manuel's 1985 racing activities, which are planned to include either a full-time effort in next year's Can-Am series, a campaign of the Indy car circuit, or both.

Juan Manuel Fangio III

Bill Hill's Marzda - March / Mazda

Can-Am track records falling with regularity to Michael Roe

If he stays true to the record-setting form established earlier this season, Ireland's Michael Roe will probably turn the fastest lap ever at Riverside International Raceway during the Oct. 7 Riverside Grand Prix Festival.

The Irish-born 28-year-old is fast becoming the swiftest driver ever in American road racing. At five of the first seven race tracks hosting the 1984 CRC Chemicals Can-Am series, Roe has set an ultimate track record.

Regardless of who set the rec-ords before him—and there have been some outstanding names like Mark Donohue, Patrick Tambay, Al Unser Jr. and Jacques Villeneuve—Roe has broken them with his Texas Barbecue Sauce/VDS-002 sports racing machine.

This is quite amazing for the young man with a brogue that seems to echo off the green hills.

Only two years ago, he was struggling in the amateur Formula Ford ranks. He won more

Please see ROE, Page 15

Riverside Raceway Will Stay Open Until June of '87 — Maybe Longer

The 26th Winston Western 500, which was to be the last race held at Riverside International Raceway, will be run Sunday but raceway officials now say that it won't be the last race.

"We plan to race at Riverside at least through next June," RIR President Dan Greenwood said. "And there is a possibility that we may run the entire 1987 schedule right where we are."

It was also revealed that the track is negotiating with the Riverside County city of Perris for a racing site 12 miles south of the present track. Plans are to construct a 1¾-mile banked oval to open in mid-1988, with a road course, drag strip and off-road facility to be built later.

Sunday's $404,000 race will conclude the 29-race NASCAR Winston Cup season for the last time. Next year, even if Riverside is still operating, the final race will be at Atlanta International Raceway, a move long sought by followers of the Southern-based stock car racing organization. Riverside has the next-to-last spot on the 1987 schedule.

For the first time since 1978, when Cale Yarborough came to Ontario Motor Speedway with the title already in hand, the championship will not be won in Southern California. Dale Earnhardt, a second-generation driver from Kannapolis, N.C., took care of that a race early when he won the Atlanta Journal 500 two weeks ago in Richard Childress' Chevrolet, clinching his second championship. Earnhardt also won in 1980. His father, Ralph, was the late model sportsman champion in 1956.

The season's final race has been at Riverside since 1981 when it was moved there after the Ontario track was closed.

Even though Earnhardt has assured himself of an additional $550,000 as the 1986 champion, second-place money of $225,000 will be determined Sunday between deposed champion Darrell Waltrip and Tim Richmond, who has won six races this season.

Waltrip has a 21-point margin, 4,015 to 3,994, which means he can collect second money by finishing fourth or better, even if Richmond wins. Last June at Riverside, Waltrip nipped Richmond by four feet to win the Budweiser 400.

Nine other drivers have a shot at a portion of the $2-million bonus payoff by finishing in the top 10. They include Bill Elliott, defending Winston Western 500 champion Ricky Rudd, Rusty Wallace, Bobby Allison, Daytona 500 winner Geoff Bodine, Harry Gant, Kyle Petty, Bobby Hillin and Terry Labonte.

Qualifying will start Friday over the 8-turn, 2.62-mile course at 1:30 p.m. with the $30,000 Busch Pole Award at stake for the driver winning the most poles during the season. Bodine has eight and Richmond seven, but if Richmond wins the pole at Riverside and Bodine qualifies fourth or worse, Richmond will collect the money, thanks to an intricate tie-breaking system.

If anybody besides Richmond wins the pole, the $30,000 will be Bodine's.

"It's make or break for us," Richmond said. "There isn't a whole lot of choice there. We have to get the pole, that's it. But with Harry Hyde and his crew behind me, I think we can do it."

If Richmond wins the pole, the first tie-breaker is no help, since it is the driver who has the most second places. Bodine and Richmond have seven apiece. The next tie-breaker is third places and Richmond has six to Bodine's five.

"I knew we'd been pretty close, but I didn't know it was that close," Bodine said when apprised of the situation. "It means we obviously can't sit around and hope Richmond doesn't get it. We're going to have to do everything we can to win the pole ourselves."

Bodine held an 8-4 advantage over Richmond after he won the pole at Martinsville, Va., on Sept. 18, but Richmond came back to win three in a row at North Wilkesboro, Charlotte and Rockingham, setting track records in the latter two.

Only two drivers, Waltrip and Labonte, have won the pole at Riverside for the last 13 NASCAR races. Waltrip set the track record of 117.066 m.p.h. last June. At that time, however, Bodine and Richmond were second and third, only fractionally behind Waltrip.

For the first time since Riverside began holding NASCAR races, it cannot be said that it is the only road race course on the circuit. Watkins Glen, in upstate New York, joined the schedule last August with a race won by Richmond.

One championship will be determined Sunday even though Earnhardt already has the national title. Either Hershel McGriff, 58, or Chad Little, 23, will win the Winston West crown for West Coast drivers. McGriff, a former Oregon lumberman who is now a copper mine executive in Green Valley, Ariz., has a 10-point lead and needs only to finish to win the first championship of his long career. McGriff has won 14 races at Riverside since 1969.

McGriff won the inaugural Mexican Road Race in 1950, 13 years before his challenger was born. Little, a second-year law student at Gonzaga University, is already assured of being named rookie of the year.

The Winston West champion will receive a $10,000 bonus.

Sunday's race will start at 11 a.m., a hour earlier than originally scheduled.

MORE ON STOCKS—Ron Esau of Lakeside has already clinched the inaugural NASCAR Southwest Tour Grand American championship, but he will face an added challenge Saturday in the season finale at Riverside in the person of Winston Cup veteran **Bill Elliott**, who will drive a Ford Thunderbird for owner-builder **Ivan Baldwin**. Esau, 30, won four of the series' 12 races and assured himself the championship when he won the Suncrest Motorhomes 100 at Willow Springs. Esau will drive **Jim Lee's** Chevrolet, which is usually driven by **Hershel McGriff**. McGriff, who has won the last three Grand American races run at Riverside, will not drive Saturday so that he can concentrate on Sunday's Winston West championship.

Chapter Seven – IMSA

Les Richter had somewhat avoided IMSA due to his loyalty to SCCA, but with his departure and IMSA's arrival at neighboring Ontario, the atmosphere changed as did the financial picture. In 1975, racer / businessman John Greenwood ended up leasing the track for IMSA after some last minute disagreements between IMSA and Riverside management. The event, the Times Grand Prix of Endurance, a six hour, was the first ever run into darkness at Riverside. A crowd of 10,300 saw the factory BMW of Dieter Quester and Hans Stuck win $6500, followed by the other team BMW of Sam Posey and Brian Redman with Peter Gregg and Hurley Haywood's Porsche Carrera in third. First in the under two liter category was the Datsun of Bob Sharp, Walt Maas and Don Devendorf. Indy 500 winner, Roger Ward, finishing 15th, said it was his first night racing experience and was quoted as saying "All the people I have raced with before had the good judgment to race during the day". Race promoter Greenwood blew a motor in qualifying and didn't compete. Supporting events included a B.F. Goodrich Radial Challenge sedan race, won by Dennis Shaw and a Bosch Super Vee race, won by Eddie Miller. Miller went on to win the championship.. IMSA didn't come back again until 1979.

Stuck, Quester capture Six Hours of Riverside

The winning BMW of Dieter Quester and Hans Stuck

Greenwood: Man With Two Hats

BY SHAV GLICK
Times Staff Writer

John Greenwood has a red, white and blue star-spangled Corvette that cost $100,000 and can better 200 m.p.h.

Greenwood loves to race it so much that when he can't find an event to enter, he rents a track and holds a race himself.

That is what the 29-year-old Michigan sports car enthusiast is doing today at Riverside International Raceway, where he will be both driver and promoter in the Six Hours of Riverside, a day-night enduro that is the fifth race in the 14-race Camel GT (Grand Touring) series of the International Motor Sports Assn.

A GT car is essentially a passenger sports car, usually European, such as Porsche Carreras, BMWs, Ferraris and Alfa Romeos. All-American GTs are mass-produced small cars such as the Corvette, Camaro, Monza 2 plus 2 and Capri.

Greenwood and co-driver Milt Minter of Fresno qualified third Friday and will start today's 6-hour race behind two BMW teams. Hans Stuck, winner of last week's Laguna Seca race, and co-driver Dieter Quester of Austria will start on the pole with a qualifying speed of 109.673. The second BMW tandem of England's Brian Redman and Sam Posey of Dana Point will sit alongside with a 108.184. Greenwood and Minter, in the Corvette, were a tick behind at 108.157.

When neither Ontario nor Riverside management showed interest in an IMSA race this year, Greenwood leased the Riverside track. He hired Frank Cipelle, former head of Michigan International Raceway, to run the race, budgeted $150,000 to promote it, and flew home to Troy, Mich., to put a new suspension in his Corvette to accommodate Riverside's high-speed road course.

"I'll be going more than 200 down that long straightaway," said Greenwood the driver. "We're going to run the long (3.25 mile) course so we'll get the full benefit of that long stretch."

"The Camel GT series is the NASCAR of road racing," said Greenwood, now the promoter. "It is the only sportscar racing where spectators can relate to cars they see on the streets. You can't relate much to a Formula 5000."

The IMSA-sanctioned Camel GT and the SCCA-sanctioned Formula 5000 are bidding to become America's premier road-racing series now that the Canadian-American Challenge Cup has been scuttled.

The Six Hours will start at 3 p.m. and run into the darkness.

It will be preceded Saturday by the 100-mile Goodrich Radial Challenge, for compact sedans with street radial tires, and the 50-mile Robert Bosch Gold Cup for Super Vees.

Greenwood is promoting the whole package.

Promoting is not new to the Michigan millionaire. He saved Florida's Sebring, one of the country's most historic courses, when its operators quit two years ago. Greenwood leased the site from the Sebring Airport Authority and is talking about building a permanent racing facility there.

Now he's subsidizing Sebring and renting Riverside for two days. Why?

"I'm not on an ego trip as a race driver. Racing and promoting races tie in with my other interest, my main interest financially, which is selling customized Corvettes and Corvette equipment. Southern California is a major market, so I felt we had to race here. I'm putting on the race to gain exposure."

Greenwood builds individually styled racing Corvettes that sell for $16,000—without an engine. And he builds custom-styled parts for street Corvettes.

"My Corvettes are better customer race cars than the Porsches. Mine are the direct product of my own testing. I do all my own test work. That's why I want my own track at Sebring, so I can test all year. There's too much time in Michigan when we're snowed in.

"When I develop a new idea, I tool it immediately for customer cars. You can buy a Corvette just like the one I race, but there's no way you can buy a factory Porsche that's like the one Peter Gregg will drive today."

Greenwood became a race driver after reading a book by Stirling Moss, Britain's famed Grand Prix pilot. At the time he was a high performance mechanic specializing in Corvettes.

"I took my street Corvette to a parking lot gymkhana and nearly scared myself to death. But I won easily, so I went to a race drivers' school at Waterford Hills and things started happening."

He won the A Production class of the American Road Race of Champions in 1970 and 1971 and co-drove with television's Dickie Smothers to a class win the 1971 12 Hours of Sebring.

Last year it became apparent that Greenwood's car was the fastest GT car in the country. He sat on the pole in six of 10 IMSA races and consistently had the quickest laps during the race. But he won only one, at Daytona, which prompted a competitor to quip: "It's the fastest one-lap Corvette in the world."

Greenwood doesn't care—as long as they're talking about him. The salesman Greenwood, that is. Greenwood the driver can make only about $10,000 if he wins. Greenwood the promoter will consider himself fortunate to break even in his first Riverside venture. But Greenwood the salesman will be more than pleased if fans go home talking about that star-spangled Corvette that went so fast —as long as it lasted.

First Day-Night Race Has All the Thrills of Sundown

BY SHAV GLICK
Times Staff Writer

RIVERSIDE—Things got so slow at the Six Hours of Riverside that Les Richter, president of Riverside International Raceway, was out at the front gate hustling programs. There weren't many customers, either.

Unless you were a BMW (for Bavarian Motor Works) aficionado, Saturday was a long, dull and boring day for the crowd announced 10,300 for Riverside's first professional day-night race. The main suspense was waiting for darkness.

Two European road racing drivers well versed in endurance competition, Hans Stuck, 24, of West Germany, and Dieter Quester, 35, of Austria, led from start to finish, from the heat of midday to the chill of evening. From the moment their BMW teammates, Brian Redman and Sam Posey, took a six-minute pit stop early in the marathon, there was no competition from the 39 other cars which started the Camel GT race.

The domination by the BMW team was so complete that Redman, defending Formula 5000 champion, and Posey, only U.S. driver on the team, came from miles back to finish second, just ahead of the Porsche Carrera tandem of Peter Gregg and Hurley Haywood, both of Jacksonville, Fla.

As early as the first hour, only one car, the Gregg-Hurley Porsche, was on the same lap with the leaders. Redman and Posey did not get back on the same lap with the leaders until the final hour.

Much of the prerace suspense was lost when John Greenwood, the race promoter, withdrew his colorful Corvette after it blew an engine during qualifications Friday. It had qualified third and was expected to be the major challenge to the BMW team.

Greenwood, despite the small turnout, said he hoped to bring the Camel GT to Riverside next year. Hopefully, he'll have the Corvette ready to run, too.

The victory was worth $6,500 to the European pair, who drove 187 laps (617.1 miles) at an average speed of 102.992 m.p.h. on Riverside's twisting 9-turn course. Their margin after 6 hours, 1 minute, 25.3 seconds of racing was nearly a lap, 2 minutes 17 seconds.

Although this was Riverside's first pro Six Hours, it was nothing new to the winners. Stuck, whose father Hans, Sr., was a Grand Prix driver for the famed Auto Union team before World War I, won the Six Hours of Kyalami last year, and Quester, a veteran BMW factory team driver, won the Six Hours of Nurburging.

Darkness slowed some of the American drivers unfamiliar with having only their headlights to find their way around the 3.3-mile "long course," but it didn't slow the Europeans. The fastest lap, in fact, was by Redman in total darkness, 108.7 m.p.h., as he was overtaking Gregg. The fastest daylight lap was 108.06 by Quester.

The Goodrich Radial Challenge for compact sedans was an American Motors parade with Dennis Shaw of Raleigh, N.C., winning in a Gremlin over two Hornet drivers from Atlanta, Gene Felton and Charlie Cook.

Eddie Miller of Vail, Colo., drove a Carl Haas-prepared Lola to victory in the 50-mile Robert Bosch Gold Cup for Super Vees.

Benny Scott, the Black American Racers driver from Hollywood, moved from 34th to seventh in five laps, but spun out on the sixth lap and was towed in from Turn 7. Scott, who finished second last week at Laguna Seca, started at the rear because he was unable to qualify after blowing the engine on his Lola during practice.

CAMEL GT (188 laps)—1. Hans Stuck (West Germany)-Dieter Quester (Austria), BMW, 188 laps, $7,750; 2. Brian Redman (England)-Sam Posey (Dana Point), BMW, 188, $4,075; 3. Peter Gregg-Hurley Haywood (Jacksonville, Fla.), Porsche Carrera, 187, $3,200; 4. Charlie Kemp (Jackson, Miss.)-Carson Baird (Laurel, Md.), Carrera, 185, $2,200; 5. Elliott Forbes-Robinson (La Crescenta)-Milt Minter (Fresno), Carrera, 184, $1,850; 6. Michael Keyser (Towson, Md.)-Billy Sprowis (Mexico), Carrera, 182, $1,500; 7. John Graves (Miami)-John O'Steen (Florrissant, Mo.)-Dave Helmick (Miami), Carrera, 182, $1,250; 8. Jim Busby (Laguna Beach)-Mike Hiss (Tustin), Porsche, 182, $1,000; 9. J. C. Bolanos-Michel Jourdain (Mexico), Carrera, 181, $900; 10. Bob Sharp (Wilton, Conn.)-Walt Maas (Mountain View), Datsun, 172, $1,800 (first under 2.5 liter finisher).

Others included: 15. Rodger Ward (Rosemead)-Bill Freeman (Santa Barbara), Porsche, 165, $700; 16. John Morton (El Segundo)-Jeff Kline (L.A.)-Chris Cord (Beverly Hills)-Salvatore Tomnello (L.A.), Ferrari, 165, $350.

SUPER VEE GOLD CUP (15 laps)—1. Eddie Miller (Vail, Colo.), Lola, 15 laps, $3,250; 2. Howdy Holmes (Alexandria, Va.), Lola, 15, $1,700; 3. Richard Melville (Jamaica), Royale, 15, $1,000; 4. Peter Moodie (Jamaica), Lola, 15, $800; 5. Billy McConnell (Whitmore Lake, Mich.), Essex Tui, 15, $600; 6. Bill Neuhoff (Roanoke, Va.), Royale, 15, $500; 7. Bob Lazier (Vail, Colo.), Tui, 15, $400; 8. Jerry Jolly (Denver), Lola, 15, $350. Others included: 13. Andy Burgraff (El Toro), Royale, 14, $200; 14. Steve Saleen (Tustin), Lola, 14, $150; 16. Ron Dykes (Marina del Rey), Royale, 14, $100; 19. Lee Mueller (Lynwood), Lola, 14, $100; 23. Pete Pittman (Santa Ana), Pittman, 13, $100; 24. Max Schowengerdt (Azusa), Venture, 12, $100; 26. Dennis Blackwell (Santa Ana), Zeltier, 9, $100; 28. Benny Scott (Hollywood), Lola, 5; 30. Dick Ferguson (Los Angeles), Tui, 4. Winners average speed: 104.157 m.p.h.

GOODRICH CHALLENGE (30 laps)—1. Dennis Shaw (Raleigh, N.C.), Gremlin, 30 laps, $2,650; 2. Gene Felton (Atlanta), Hornet, 30, $1,975; 3. Charlie Cook (Atlanta), Hornet, 30, $1,050; 4. Nick Craw (Washington, D.C.), BMW, 30, $575; 5. George Alderman (New Castle, Del.), Datsun, 30, $475; 6. Ray Korman (Gabrills, Md.), BMW, 30, $425; 7. Dan Parkinson (La Canada), Datsun, 30, $375; 8. Byron Weaver (St. Petersburg, Fla.), Gremlin, 20, $325; 9. Gregg Schmidt-Bob McGinty (Ontario), Gremlin, 28, $300. Others included: 17. Arlene Hiss (Tustin), Opel, 27, $125; 17. George Cheyne (North Hollywood), Pinto, 26, $125; 24. Amos Johnson (Raleigh, N.C.), Gremlin, 19 (head gasket), $125. Winners average speed: 86.148 m.p.h.

BMW's outrun field

RIVERSIDE (AP) — Factory prepared BMWs finished one-two in the IMSA GT six hours of Riverside on Saturday at Riverside International Raceway.

Despite a 2½-minute pit stop for brake repairs, 10 laps from the end of the 188-lap, 620.4-mile race, Hans Stuck of Germany and Deiter Quester of Austria won by two laps at an average speed of 102.992 mph.

Taking over second place 12 laps from the end was the second BMW driven by Sam Posey

Brian Redman: "*We finished second in the '75 Six Hour, co-driving with Sam Posey. Had trouble early on with a faulty gauge, a bad sending unit in the oil pressure gauge, but then drove flat - out to finish just behind Hans Stuck and Dieter Quester in the other CSL, on the same lap*"

Riverside Holds a Mini-Sebring

BY SHAV GLICK
Times Staff Writer

The Six Hours of Riverside, a mini-model of the 12 Hours of Sebring and 24 Hours of LeMans, brings international Grand Touring racing to Riverside International Raceway this weekend.

The Camel GT race, sanctioned by the International Motor Sports Assn., will be the first day-night race at Riverside since the 1960s when similar events were staged by the Cal Club. Qualifying is Friday, with the 6-hour race starting at 3 p.m. Saturday.

Two other races, the Goodrich Radial Challenge, a 100-mile event for compact sedans (Gremlins, Hornets, Colts, BMWs, etc.) racing on street radial tires, and the Robert Bosch Gold Cup for Super Vees, a 50-mile race for open-wheeled, VW-powered cars, will precede the Camel GT Saturday. First race is at noon.

MOTOR RACING

With the finish scheduled for 9 p.m., it means that the GT cars (Porsche, Carreras, Ferraris, Corvettes and BMWs) will be driving more than an hour in darkness, with headlights on. The race will be run on the 3.25-mile-long course, giving the more powerful cars a run down

rio and is the point leader after four of the series' 14 races. In most GT races there is only one driver to a car, but in the 6-hour race Gregg will share his Carrera with Hurley Haywood.

Other leading teams include Al Holbert-Bob Hageman, Mike Hiss-Jim Busby, Michael Keyser-Billy Sprowles and Charley Kemp-Carson Baird in Carreras, Hans Stuck (winner last week at Laguna Seca)-Brian Redman and Sam Posey-Dieter Quester in BMWs and John Greenwood-Milt Minter in a Corvette.

The Super Vees raced at Riverside two years ago, but in the interim they have added wings, which figure to make the little buzz bombs about 4 m.p.h. faster. Two years ago they averaged 103 m.p.h.

Benny Scott, a college psychology professor who is working on his Ph.D. thesis at Claremont, will drive a Super Vee. Scott hopes to hone his driving talent so that next year he can become the first black man to drive in the Indianapolis 500. He finished second last Sunday at Laguna Seca.

MOTORCYCLE RACING'—Former national champion **Mert Lawwill**, defending champion **Rick Hocking** and **rookie expert John Allison** of Poway will ride Saturday night in the second annual Cal Rayborn Memorial race at South Bay Park Speedway in

Bert Greenwood: *"IMSA wanted to race at Riverside; management there was not too interested; then made promises they couldn't keep, My brother John hired a long time friend*

and fellow racer, Frank Cipelle, who had helped him promote Sebring and managed Michigan International Speedway, and Frank basically got taken advantage of by the Riverside guys. They agreed to split the cost, then backed out and John had to pick up the tab. The gate of 10,0000 didn't cover the cost and IMSA stayed away until they were wanted in 1979"

Jeff Kline: *"Bruno Borri, who had worked for Otto Zipper, now had Modena Sports Cars in Hollywood and I had raced an Alfa GTA for Otto, so we had this connection.. His customer, Ken Starbird, had just bought a SEFAC aluminum Ferrari Daytona and Bruno suggested that Chis Cord and I drive it at Riverside. He also put John Morton on the entry form in the event we couldn't hack it. It was both Chris' and my first pro race. We qualified 15th. The BMW 3.0 CSL's were the class of the field. We went down the straight with them and then at turn nine they'd disappear not to be seen for twenty minutes and they came by again. We got stuck in fourth gear with two hours to go and limped home, still sixteenth overall. It was the most fun I had ever had to that point of my life (in a car)."* Compiler's Note - Jeff went on to have great success in IMSA, winning the 1987 Camel Light championship.

Porsche RSR's - George Dyer leads Peter Gregg

After a four year gap, the Times Grand Prix came back in 1979. A crowd of more than 43,600 watched Bill and Don Whittington win $14,200 driving a Porsche 935, followed by John Paul / Bob Holbert and George Follmer / Brett Lunger and nine more Porsches. Supporting races included a Champion Sparkplug Series sedan race won by Jim Downing and a Bilstein Rabbit race won by Paul Hacker plus an assortment of vintage races. Read about these in Volume Two; available in the fall of 2022.

WHITTINGTONS WIN TIMES GRAND PRIX

The Whittington brothers, Don and Bill, of Ft. Lauderdale, Fla., won the first Los Angeles Times Grand Prix of Endurance Sunday before 43,600 at Riverside Raceway. The winners, driving a turbocharged Porsche, finished 84 seconds ahead of runnersup Al Holbert and John Paul. The Whittingtons averaged 106.818 m.p.h. for the six-hour run. Details in Sports Section.

The winning Porsche 935 of Bill and Don Whittington

Whittingtons Win Times Race

Brothers Average 106.818 m.p.h. for Six Hours

BY SHAV GLICK
Times Staff Writer

RIVERSIDE—After six hours of racing in which surviving became more important than going fast, the Whittington brothers, Don and Bill, of Ft. Lauderdale, Fla., won the first Los Angeles Times Grand Prix of Endurance in a year-old dual turbo-charged Porsche 935.

Porsches swept the first nine positions as an enthusiastic crowd of 43,600 watched the six-hour enduro on a sunny Sunday at Riverside International Raceway.

Don Whittington, at 33 the elder by four years, drove the final 90 minutes and brought his yellow car to the finish line 84 seconds ahead of the Al Holbert-John Paul Porsche, which was the only other car on the winners' lap.

The Whittingtons, more noted for setting air speed records than race driving, averaged 106.818 m.p.h. for 643½ miles.

"The car ran so smooth we only used one quart of oil the entire race," Bill said. "We ran the new single turbo Porsche at Daytona and had a lot of problems so we decided to go with the old car here. We followed our prerace plan to the smallest detail and it sure paid off."

The only problem they had was a broken seat that "sloshed around everytime we went through a corner."

At day's end the No. 94 car with "Road Atlanta" (the Whittingtons own that race course) on its rear wing was the only car that didn't look as if it had been in a destruction derby.

An oil-slicked surface sent cars skidding, spinning and crashing off course into the dirt—sometimes knocking them out of the race and other times only causing inconvenience, problems for the mechanics, and lost laps.

Two incidents in the second hour at nearly the same place on the track knocked pole-sitter and five-time International Motor Sports Assn. champion Peter Gregg out of contention and put cars driven by Hurley Haywood and Sam Posey out of the race.

Gregg jumped away at the start and built up a 50-second lead in the first half hour. His white Porsche seemed in command of the race when, coming up through Riverside's S-turns, the suspension broke on the right side, sending Gregg sliding sideways through the dirt. The slide also flattened a tire and Gregg limped around the track back to the pits.

Nearly 30 minutes later he returned, in 27th position, 13 laps behind the leader. This didn't deter Gregg and his co-driver, Klaus Ludwig of Germany, however, as they stormed around the track at record speeds, making up three laps to finish

fifth. Gregg's lap of 114.374 m.p.h. on lap 158 was the fastest of the race.

A pack of four or five cars were heading into the high-speed second turn on lap 41 when one car started sliding in the oil. Posey slowed and Haywood, hurrying to make up time lost from starting in the 23rd row, hit him in the rear. The impact knocked Posey's Datsun into a ditch and sent Haywood sliding up an incline, his Porsche afire. Haywood got out and a course worker arrived to put out the fire with an extinguisher—but it didn't work. By the time a fire truck arrived the car was badly burned.

When Posey went out it deprived the hordes of Paul Newman fans from watching old blue eyes perform. He was waiting in the pits to take over when the accident occurred.

Another incident in the esses involving John Paul, in the blue No. 18 Porsche that finished second, cost him the race, according to the driver.

"When Gregg slowed we had just taken the lead," said Paul, defending champion in the World Endurance Driver series. "I was lapping a car when it changed its line, hit my rear wheel and knocked me off the track. By the time I got back to my pits the tire had wrapped around the wheel and knocked my fender off. We changed the tire and had to tape up the things flapping around where the

Please Turn to Page 6, Col. 1

BMW to challenge Porsche domination at Riverside

A potent BMW entry will challenge Porsche domination in the Times Grand Prix of Endurance.

Englishman David Hobbs will co-drive a turbocharged BMW 320i along with Manfred Winkelhoch, ace of the BMW factory driving team and ex-European Formula Two driver.

Hobbs, in his 21st year of racing, is the lead driver for Team McLaren's Winston GT series effort. A popular TV commentator, he's won

seven races two years on the circuit.

Winkelhoch ran a March/BMW in the Formula Two series in 1978, finishing in the top six in four races.

The other factory-backed BMW entry, a four-cylinder BMW 320i, will be driven by Laguna Beach's Jim Busby and Toine Hezemans of Holland.

Busby, winner of five Winston GT races in the last two years, is switching this year from

Porsche to BMW. The Busby/Hezemans BMW has produced 600 horsepower in testing, and Busby reports he's already equalled his best times in the Porsche while testing the BMW at Riverside.

The Times race is the feature of the weekend. Qualifying for the Winston GT cars will be Friday, April 20.

The 44-car starting field will get the green flag at noon, Sunday, April 22.

TRY OUR ROAD SHOW

...Riverside's high-speed road racing course for a weekend of action sponsored by The Times.

This weekend, Riverside International Raceway is the site of Southern California's newest, biggest racing weekend.

Today, beginning at 8:30 a.m., classics and great racing cars from the past roar back to life for the Vintage Sports Car Races. Ferrari, Lancia, Porsche, McLaren, Maserati, Lotus, Jaguar and Cobra ... dueling once again in an exciting wheel-to-wheel spectacle.

David Hobbs   **Peter Gregg**   **Paul Newman**

Tonight, campers can relax and enjoy an evening of disco music and dancing under the stars.

Sunday's day-long action begins at 10 a.m., with the 100-mile Champion Spark Plug Challenge for racing sedans.

And at noon, the highlight of the weekend: The Six-Hour Los Angeles Times Grand Prix of Endurance for Winston GT cars. World-famous drivers like Peter Gregg, David Hobbs and film star Paul Newman will be driving hot Porsche Turbos, Ferraris, BMWs, Corvettes and Datsun Z-cars ... the same cars that race at LeMans, Sebring and Daytona. It will be racing at its best around the demanding 3.25-mile Riverside road course.

And it will be a weekend you won't want to miss.

Tickets are now on sale at Riverside Raceway Ticket Office

SUPER TICKET (General Admission, Paddock & Garage, both days). Each person purchasing a Super Ticket by mail or at Times Special Events will receive a free Champion Spark Plug racing hat $20

SATURDAY
General Admission........................ $6
General Admission plus Paddock $10

SUNDAY
General Admission $8
General Admission plus Paddock & Garage .. $12

Grandstands
Start-Finish $4
Esses $5
Turn 6 .... $6 and $8

Follmer returns to action in Times Grand Prix of Endurance

The last time George Follmer drove competitively in an auto race his Can-Am car ended up on the side of a hill and Follmer ended up in the hospital. That was on Oct. 6, 1979. Two operations and four months in a cast later, Follmer has entered the Times Grand Prix of Endurance April 22 at Riverside International Raceway.

Follmer will be part of the Vasek Polak Porsche entry that could pair him with the likes of Jackie Ickx, Brett Lunger or Peter Gregg.

The 45-year-old Follmer, who owns a Porsche dealership in Pomona, was driving a Prophet Can-Am car at Laguna Seca Raceway when a piece of asphalt lodged in the air box, slipped down the injector system and held the throttle wide open. The car hit a dip and became airborne, flying 70 feet over a fence to land on the hillside between two groups of spectators. Fortunately none of the fans were injured, but Follmer's racing career seemed in serious jeopardy.

"It's darned hard to stop a car going 130 miles an hour when the throttle is jammed," said Follmer. "I still hurt a bit here and there but I'm taking therapy and lifting weights and getting my strength back. I'll be ready for Riverside. It's my favorite track. I've driven just about everything there that moves or has four wheels."

Follmer's brightest moment in racing came at Riverside when he clinched the 1972 Can-Am championship by winning the Times Grand Prix. He drove his first race there in 1960 as a Cal Club rookie in a Porsche Speedster, came out of retirement to win the U.S. Road Racing title in 1965, won the Trans-Am finale in Roy Woods' Javelin in 1971, the Times Grand Prix in a Penske Porsche and the International Race of Champions series in 1973.

Little wonder the popular Southlander is considered to be America's most versatile driver. He campaigned his own Chevrolet-powered Eagle on the USAC champ trail, ran NASCAR for Bud Moore and drove the UOP Shadow on the Formula One Grand Prix circuit, surviving another spectacular crash at Monaco in 1973.

It takes more than a broken tibia, crushed vertebrae and a separated sternum to keep George Follmer from racing.

Danny Ongais / Ted Field; Porsche 935

Dave White / Pat Bedard; BMW 320i

Jim Busby / Toine Hezemans; BMW 320i

Bob Garretson / Skeeter McKitterick; 935

Sam Posey / Paul Newman; 280ZX

Jim Downing / Roger Mandeville; RX-7

239

ENTERED AT RIVERSIDE—Actor Paul Newman, an accomplished race car driver, is shown here with his wife, actress Joanne Woodward

P.L. NEWMAN ENTERED AT RIVERSIDE

Cerwin Vega Goes to the Races!

FEDERATED AND CERWIN VEGA SALUTE THE L.A. TIMES GRAND PRIX!

The thrilling Los Angeles Times Grand Prix comes to Riverside International Raceway Saturday, April 21 and Sunday, April 22, and Federated & Cerwin Vega join in the excitement of this newest, biggest Southern California racing event!

DON'T MISS CERWIN VEGA GRAND PRIX DAYS AT YOUR FEDERATED SUPERSTORES!

Toly Arutunoff: " *Riverside, yeah – 1979; I drove a Lancia Stratos with Jose Marina. - I liked*

the long back straight, gave me a minute to rest as we were constantly passed by the fast guys. Riverside had more challenging corners than most, turn nine, turn one, turn six, made it more fun. Don't remember much else, a long time ago, Read my book !!" Compiler's Note - Toly was also H Prod National champ once upon a time, a Ferrari dealer, racetrack builder (Hallett) and drove in both the Targa Florio and Mille Miglia.

Jeff Kline: *"1979 was my first year in IMSA in a competitive car. This was the second outing of the Racing Beat RX-7, with owner Jim Mederer driving with me. 59 cars in the six hour race, 27 in GTU. Fast guys were Porsche 935's but only on the straights. We were flat out from turn nine to six; no lifting for the esses. A hot day, we only went 113 laps and ended up thirty second overall !! Don Devendorf won in a Datsun"*

240

Rick Knoop: *"Jim Busby connected me with Howard Meister, a Southern California builder who was working the the Aase Brothers to develop the RSR. Alan Johnson,, a pretty fair racer himself and a Porsche dealer was the sponsor. We qualified on the pole in GTO but, unfortunately, the car broke on lap 166. We ended up fifth in GTO and 22nd overall."*

ENTERED AT RIVERSIDE—Actor Paul Newman, an accomplished race car driver, is shown here with his wife, actress Joanne Woodward.

P.L. NEWMAN ENTERED AT RIVERSIDE

Bad breaks kid

If the bad breaks would just leave **P.L. Newman** alone, he might really make a name for himself as a race car jockey. He was all set — under that name — to drive a Datsun 280Z in Sunday's Los Angeles Times Grand Prix of Endurance at Riverside, but teammate **Sam Posey** took the wheel first and put the car out of commission in a minor accident. The brother team of Bill and Don Whittington of Fort Lauderdale, Fla., won it. Posey's mishap kept P.L. — who doubles as Paul Newman in the movies when he isn't driving — off the track all day.

ADDING PADDING—Actor Paul Newman has a piece of padding added to help adjust for size difference between himself and Sam Posey, who will share wheel of a Datsun 280ZX today in the six-hour Times Grand Prix of Endurance.

Times photo by Joe Kennedy

John Paul / Al Holbert 935

The 1980 Times Grand Prix was a sweep for the Dick Barbour team of Porsche 935's. 39,500 watched John Fitzpatrick and Barbour win followed by similar the Bobby Rahal / Bob Garretson car. The top seven were Porsche 935's. First in GTU was the Brad Friselle RX-7. Other events included a celebrity race won by Rick Mears, a vintage race won by Rick Knoop in a McLaren and a Champion Spark Plug Sedan Series event, won by Dennis Shaw. .

SACHS

BARBOUR TEAM/
SACHS 1st & 2nd at RIVERSIDE

Dick Barbour and John Fitzgerald, driving the SACHS Turbo, dominated the Riverside 5 Hour with an impressive win.

Bobby Rahal and Bob Garretson finished 2nd in the SACHS equipped Apple Turbo.

You may not drive a Porsche K3/935 like Dick Barbour and John Fitzpatrick, but SACHS offers you the same quality product and performance in their complete line of shock absorbers and clutches for imported cars. SACHS products are available at better distributors and dealers throughout the United States. Or write or call toll free.

 SACHS
909 Crocker Road, Westlake, Ohio 44145
(800) 321-0784   *Watch for us at LeMans*

Barbour's Intimidation Plan Gets Quick Results and an Easy Win

Fast Pace Knocks Out Top Rivals in Times Enduro

By SHAV GLICK
Times Staff Writer

RIVERSIDE—Dick Barbour's game plan for the Times/Toyota Grand Prix of Endurance was to send John Fitzpatrick out fast and intimidate the opposition.

The plan worked Sunday as Barbour and Fitzpatrick drove their 1980 model turbocharged Kremer Porsche 935 to win the endurance race by three laps over Barbour's other car, driven by Bobby Rahal and Bob Garretson. A crowd of 39,500 watched the five-hour race at Riverside International Raceway.

One lap back of Rahal and Garretson was the Porsche of Hurley Haywood and Bruce Leven, with a pair of 20-year-olds, Dale Whittington and Michael Chandler, fourth, another lap behind. The first seven finishers were in turbocharged Porsches, but none ran like the No. 6 car when Fitzpatrick was driving.

"We wanted to intimidate the other fast drivers so they would turn up the boost trying to keep up with Fitz and drop out," Barbour said. "We really didn't want them out there with us. It looked like our plan worked, didn't it?"

Indeed it did.

Peter Gregg, the IMSA (International Motor Sports Assn.) champion, lasted only 27 laps before he spewed oil all over the track and his Brumos Porsche ground to a stop. Jim Busby and Geoff Brabham, in the BMW that might have given the Porsches a run, stopped after 37 laps with a blown cylinder. Ted Field, fresh from a second-place finish at the Sebring 12 Hours with Danny Ongais, made only 57 laps before his Porsche lost its clutch. Herm Meister and John Mor-

ROADBLOCK—Porsche 911 of Encino's Joel Morenfeld spins out in front of Mauricio DeNarvaez during Sunday's five-hour endurance race at Riverside. DeNarvaez got by without mishap.

Times photo by Jayne Kamin

Defense Wins for Dodgers, and Sutton Leads Applause

By MIKE LITTWIN
Times Staff Writer

Usually, the Dodgers are defensive about their defense. Right now, the defense can take care of itself.

On Sunday, it took care of Don Sutton.

"I wanted to stand out there and applaud," Sutton said after pitching the Dodgers (with relief help from

favorite, position) to rob Gene Tenace of an extra-base hit in the second. Thomas rated it an 8.5. He is not unfamiliar with 10s.

—A Dusty Baker catch in left, robbing Tenace of a homer in the fourth as Hard Bake (Bob Welch's contribution) leaned into the bullpen fence

WINNING WAS EASY—John Fitzpatrick (left) and Dick Barbour struggle to open victory champagne after Sunday's race.

Times photo by Jayne Kamin

Martin Raffauf: "*By the time we got to Riverside, we were not doing too well on our plan to win the IMSA championship. We had won one race and crashed out of the other two. Meanwhile, John Paul had finished all the races and was the leader in the points table. This was Dick Barbour's home track, as it was the closest we would race to his home in San Diego, and his car dealerships in the LA area and he was determined to win this race, While it used to be a six hour race, it had for some reason been reduced to five hours in 1980. The event was sponsored by the Los Angeles Times newspaper, which was owned by Otis Chandler, who was also an IMSA racer from time to time.*

Practice and qualifying went reasonably well for us, and the two cars were once again driven by Dick Barbour / John Fitzpatrick and Bob Garretson / Bobby Rahal. While Dick, Bob and Bobby knew the track very well, Fitz had never seen the place before, but once again, we had an ace in the hole. Our team truck driver was none other than Jack McAfee, a retired, well known Porsche race car driver from the 1950s and 1960s. He knew Riverside like the back of his hand, having won many events there back in his day. Local knowledge, while not critical for Fitz, for sure helped him get up to speed quicker. Pole was taken by the Whittington Brothers but our two cars qualified second (Fitz/Barbour) and fourth (Rahal/Garretson). There were no less than thirteen 935's in the field, either K3 updated ones or the latest factory configuration cars. The competition included, John Paul, the Whittingtons, Moretti, Bruce Leven, Bob Akin / Roy Woods, Randolph Townsend / Bruce Jenner, Peter Gregg / Al Holbert, Mendez / Redman, Ted Field / Danny Ongais, and John Morton / Howard Meister

Sixty cars started the race, and everyone seemed to take off like it was a thirty minute sprint race. Back then, racing was totally different from what we see today in IMSA or the WEC. There were no restrictors, no RPM limits, no boost limit, no fuel limits, you just went as hard as you dared. The 935, if assembled correctly would run easily for 24 hours at about 650 horsepower. How long it would run at 1.4-1.5 bar of turbo boost and 750+ horsepower was anyone's guess, but it was almost guaranteed that something would eventually break at that level. The things that usually failed were the turbos and/or the head gaskets on the engine due to overheating. In any case, Don Whittington took off like he was in a 30- minute sprint race. Fitz stayed right with him, and passed for the lead after two laps. Fitz was the maestro of boost control, frequently changing the boost several times during one lap and he would routinely get more speed out of the car with less wear and tear than most of the others. By the first hour, our cars were running 1-2 and they would stay that way to the end. Several, such as Peter Gregg, Moretti, Danny Ongais, John Paul and the Whittingtons had engine and mechanical failures and dropped out. In the end, our two cars, separated by a few laps, crossed the line together. Bruce Leven and Hurley Haywood were third, a lap behind the second-place car. At this point in time in IMSA history, that was a pretty impressive accomplishment as competition was very tough. Anyone could buy the latest 935 equipment and run at the front. For a team to finish 1-2 in a 5-hour IMSA race in 1980 took good preparation, organisation, pit work, strategy, and above all good driving. We had all of that at Riverside.

That night at the airport on my way to a meeting in Atlanta, I ran into Al Holbert. We were on the same plane to Atlanta, and chatted while waiting to board. When he saw that I had Dick Barbour racing team kit on, he remarked that this was a very good result for us. His view was that to finish 1-2 in an IMSA race was a pretty impressive achievement, and complimented us on it. We thought we were doing things right, but to have a two-time former IMSA champion (eventually to become five-time champion) who was one of your main competitors tell you that, well that made it even more special."

Jeff Kline: *"In 1980, Racing Beat ran a two car team; Jim Downing and I in one car, Walt Bohren and Takashi Yorino, Japanese Mazda champ, in the other. Sponsored by Akai, we had this huge VCR and cameras in the car, state of the art for 1980 – they didn't work !! I qualified fifth in GTU, broke an apex seal and was out by lap three. Finished 22nd in GTU. My teammate, Walt, only went 130 laps"*

FRONT RUNNER—Don Whittington and brother Bill will start their Sun System turbo Porsche from the pole position in today's Los Angeles Times/Toyota Grand Prix of Endurance at Riverside. The Whittingtons have been racing cars for only about two years.

WHITTINGTON PORSCHE WINS POLE

Sets Trials Mark of 119.642 m.p.h. for Times Grand Prix

By SHAV GLICK
Times Staff Writer

RIVERSIDE—Defending champions Don and Bill Whittington will start on the pole in Sunday's annual Los Angeles Times/Toyota Grand Prix of Endurance, a five-hour race around Riverside International Raceway's 3.3-mile road course.

Don drove their Sun System twin turbocharged Porsche 935 to a record 119.642 m.p.h. Friday, bettering Peter Gregg's 1979 speed of 117.862. He and Bill, who won last year's six-hour race for their first IMSA (International Motor Sports Assn.) win, will share the ride again Sunday.

John Fitzpatrick, in a Dick Barbour Sachs-sponsored turbo Porsche, will be alongside Whittington after posting a lap at 119.537.

"We won the pole at Road Atlanta and Bill Whittington won the race," Fitzpatrick said. "Now they've won the pole so it's our turn to win the race."

Gregg, all-time IMSA winner with six championships, including last year, is third at 118.229. This is faster than his record of last year and he did it in the same car. Gregg's is the only year-old model among the leaders.

Can-Am driver Bobby Rahal, driving a second Barbour car, was a surprise fourth at 116.631.

A turbocharger hose disintegrated on the second lap of Whittington's 20-minute qualifying period and it was touch and go if the crew could repair it in time for Don to run a fast lap.

John Fitzpatrick

"I was so mad when I got back in the car that I didn't drive well," said Don. "You never drive well when you're upset and I was plenty upset. It was panic time. Fortunately, I settled down and the tires got warmed up and we made our quick time on the very last lap."

Bill Whittington, in another Sun System turbo Porsche, had even worse luck qualifying. He spun on the oily track coming out of high-speed Turn 9 and damaged the car.

"We would have liked to run both cars Sunday but now we won't," said Don. "Actually, we were going to run three cars. Now it'll be two."

Dale Whittington, youngest of the brothers, qualified last year's winning car in 13th place with a speed of 112.663.

Dale will drive with Michael Chandler of Dana Point. The two raced against one another last year in Super Vees. Chandler was the U.S. Auto Club's Mini-Indy runner-up last year but this will be his first time in a turbocharged Porsche.

"Dale did a great job with that car," said Don. "It's not tricked up like the new Kremer models. It's virtually the same car we drove last year. He's about in the same position as we were (the Whittingtons were seventh at the start last year) and he went nearly as quick as I did last year."

Don qualified last year at 112.813 m.p.h., just a tick faster than Dale.

Fitzpatrick, a veteran Porsche driver from England who now lives in La Jolla to be near Barbour's racing headquarters, was not at all disappointed with his position.

"Poles are mostly for sponsors," said Fitzpatrick, who had never seen the Riverside track before Thursday. "It doesn't mean much in an endurance race but it's nice for the sponsor. Riverside is a nice track, the kind I like with high-speed corners. And the car was set up just right so I didn't have to make many changes. I'd say our chances for Sunday are very bright."

Qualifying records were also set for the Champion Spark Plug Challenge race for compact cars and in the GTU

Please Turn to Page 10, Col. 1

Possibly the first GTP car; Jim Busby's BMW March Chevrolet

Danny Ongais / Ted Field; Porsche 935

John Paul / Preston Henn; Porsche 935

Bob Akin / Roy Woods; Porsche 035

Werner Frank / Roger Schramm; Porsche

Nobuhide Tachi / Tim Sharp; Dome Celica

Anatoly Arutunoff; Lancia Stratos

Chris Cord / Jim Adams; Dekon Monza

John Casey / Rick Knoop; Mazda RX-7

Vic Manuelli: " An IMSA story - We were in the registration line at my first IMSA event, the six hour. In walks Mears, Ongais and Ted Fied - We moved aside and Peggy Bishop said," hey, you stay right there You were here before them"! WOW. Felt accepted, lol. No wonder IMSA was so popular. - I first raced at Riverside on a Honda 450, later on joined the Pantera Club, did some club events there. Then, a racing opportunity came along - I got a sponsorship deal with Lone Star Beer. They sent a truck to our pit area and off loaded around ten cases which we provided to all the SCCA worker's for their after race socials, The best experience - Flat out in my Pantera; around 180 mph and seeing the blue passing flag waving - and a couple of 935's and Lola's go screaming past into turn nine - A pucker factor for me."

Don Devendorf: Fast Driver in IMSA Slow Lane

By SHAV GLICK
Times Staff Writer

Nine cars had finished when Don Devendorf completed the Times 6-Hour race last year, but from the commotion in his pit area you'd have thought he—not the Whittington brothers—had won.

In his own way, Devendorf had won. You see, he drives in the International Motor Sports Assn.'s GTU (for cars with less than 2.5 liters in displacement) class and his underpowered Datsun ZX had just beaten all the other Datsuns, Mazdas, Porsche 914s and 911s and Lancia Stratos in its very competitive division.

In most of the IMSA season the GTU cars have their own events, usually 100 miles or less, but in endurance races such as Daytona, Sebring and Sunday's Times Toyota 5-Hour at Riverside International Raceway, they intermingle in the same race with the turbocharged Porsche 935s and other race cars.

Don Devendorf

"It presents some unusual circumstances in that our more talented drivers, in slower cars, end up running against less-talented drivers in faster cars," said Devendorf, the GTU champion, who won 9 of 14 races last year. No other driver won more than one.

"You spend a good deal of time looking in your mirrors for faster cars, especially on their own car and make it run better."

Devendorf is not a professional race driver, however, in the sense he makes his living in a car. Quite the opposite.

A graduate engineer in electronics from Cal State Long Beach, class of '66, Devendorf heads the radar research and development program at Hughes Aircraft Co. He oversees a section of 32 engineers in esoteric thinking, including a "black program" of top-secret priority.

"My engineering background provides us with a more scientific approach to racing," said Devendorf, who joined John Knepp, a physics major from the University of Utah, to form Electramotive in 1973.

"We take a stock Datsun engine and retool it to our specifications," Devendorf said. "We use standard pieces but with our modifications. Porsche, for instance, builds special parts for its race cars. We use parts from the factory catalog. We have found that the Japanese use high-quality material in their stock equipment."

One of Electramotive's extras is the use of its own instrumentation, designed by Devendorf, to measure down force, air drag, road friction and aerodynamics. And the engines are tested on a computerized dynomometer.

"You've got to use every facility available to keep up these days. The Mazdas are coming at us with all we can handle at Riverside. They'll have three factory RX-7s, one each for Brad Frisselle, Walt Bohren and Jeff Kline, with Japanese co-drivers. They didn't like it when we won all those races last year and they got shut out except for the 24 Hours at Daytona. They even sent their No. 1 driver over from Japan, Yoshimi Katayama, to beat us but he didn't do it. Now they're back in force."

Katayama was the lead driver when a Mazda RX-7 won at Daytona, but in two later races he was beaten by Devendorf.

"The Riverside race will be interesting," Devendorf said.

25 cents a lap. For some reason I always seemed to do well so the next thing was running slaloms in parking lots. Every time I'd do well someone would egg me on to the next level and now I'm racing Datsun ZXs."

Devendorf, a California Interscholastics Federation champion in the side horse and parallel bars at Westchester High, credits his gymnastics ability for some of his driving success.

"Dexterity, agility and balance are all helpful in driving," he said. "A driver has to have excellent coordination and so does a gymnast. I think you will find that most successful drivers had some background, or native ability, at skill sports such as gymnastics, diving or some other hand-eye-and-foot sport."

Devendorf paid his dues as an amateur driver before gaining factory support from Nissan.

"I've heard people say I got to the top because I had factory support. Well, I think they have it backwards. The truth is, the factory sponsors drivers with the talent. Contrary to popular belief, they are a great boon to competent drivers who do not have the money to buy a ride. I could not race at this level as an independent. It's too expensive."

Devendorf won three Sports Car Club of America national championships, two in Triumphs and one in a Datsun 1200, before catching Nissan's eye. In 1973, driving for Sun and Moon Datsun, he won 20 straight SCCA C Sedan races and decided to step up to a B-210. This led him to Knepp and the two started Electramotive.

Their garage was in a basement underneath a bar in El Segundo and when the ice melted in the bar the water dripped in the shop. This year Electramotive moved to spacious new quarters in the same area.

Sun and Moon, two distributorships in Whittier and Lakewood, are still with Devendorf and will be the major sponsors of his car in Sunday's race.

Rocky Moran: *"Dan Gurney asked me to drive the Toyota GTO car at a number of races. Co drivers included Willie T Ribbs, Juan Fangio, Dennis Aase, At Riverside, we all got cooked by the side exhaust, redesigned for the next race. Guess Dan was happy with my performance as he signed me up for the GTP team!!"*

A crowd of 46,352 saw John Fitzpatrick and Jim Busby win in 1981, collecting $18,500. Fitzpatrick and Busby, in their own Porsche Kremer 935, survived a protest by the Chuck Gaa built Porsche 935 of John Paul Jr. and Sr. who finished second. This race was also part of the World Sportscar Championship. Supporting races included a father / son celebrity race, won by Bobby Unser with his son Bobby Jr. in second and a Champion Spark Plug sedan series race, won by Joe Varde in a Mazda..

RANDY McBRIDE / Los Angeles Times

Jim Busby, left, and John Fitzpatrick waive from winner's circle after winning the Times/Toyota six-hour race Sunday.

Fitzpatrick's Team Wins It
The Pauls Lose 6-Hour Race on Track and on Appeal

By SHAV GLICK, *Times Staff Writer*

RIVERSIDE—John Fitzpatrick, whom long distance driving veteran Brian Redman called "the finest Porsche driver of all time," had to call on all the cunning of a decade racing the West German cars to win Sunday's Times/Toyota Grand Prix of Endurance.

Fitzpatrick and Jim Busby drove 656.7 miles in 6

J.L.P. Racing, the Paul entry, but it was rejected by the stewards. Ironically, an almost identical protest was filed Friday by Stropus claiming that Paul, not Fitzpatrick, had the fastest qualifying lap. That time Stropus won the protest when IMSA officials admitted they missed Paul's fast lap.

UPI photo

Popular guy at the track

John Fitzpatrick's crew leaps on his car for a victory lap after Fitzpatrick won the Los Angeles Times Grand Prix of Endurance at Riverside International Raceway Sunday.

Martin Raffauf: *"Garretson Enterprises was running all the cars for Cooke - Woods racing in 1981 including Roy Woods' and Bob Garretson's 935's as well as two new Lola T600's*

that had been ordered. We had run the 935s at Daytona and Sebring, and Atlanta, and would again at Riverside. The T600 would debut at Laguna Seca, the week after Riverside. We had won Daytona, 2nd at Sebring and 3rd at Atlanta, so were looking for a good result at Riverside. Brian Redman and Bobby Rahal would drive one car, Bob Garretson, Roy Woods and Ralph Cooke the other.

John Bright, from Lola Cars UK had come over and joined our team in California and would be the crew chief on the T600 effort. He accompanied us to Riverside, just to watch, as he said he knew nothing about Porsche 935 "street cars". Friday night Bobby Rahal and Jerry Woods took John out to "see the town". Most of us went back to the hotel early, as we had a big weekend ahead. There was some commotion and noise in the early am just past midnight at the hotel, as I was in the next room to Jerry and John. I paid it no mind as I was half asleep anyway. The next morning we had trouble getting John up and going. Where are my boots he asked? Jerry said, well we had to leave them outside the door. He goes out and there are his shoes with vomit all over them. He exclaims loudly, "Hey someone has thrown up all over my boots"! Jerry Woods says, well that would be you last night !

John needed most of Saturday to recover, good thing we didn't need him for anything during the race. Rahal was laughing most of the day as he figured he had given John a good indoctrination to Riverside and IMSA. We finished 3rd and 4th with the two cars in the race. The T600 would have a successful debut the following week, with Brian Redman winning the race, and eventually the 1981 IMSA championship. Bob Garretson would go on to win the FIA World Endurance Championship with his 935. It was a mighty fine year. Good times and the IMSA of old was a little different than it is today"

Actor Paul Newman will team with Masahiro Hasemi in a Datsun ZX Turbo in the GT class in Times/Toyota Grand Prix at Riverside April 25-26.

This Year, Newman Hopes He'll Star in Times Grand Prix

Actor Paul Newman, who missed last year's Los Angeles Times Grand Prix because of a movie commitment, will drive a Datsun ZX Turbo in the GT class in this year's Times/Toyota Grand Prix of Endurance April 25-26 at Riverside International Raceway.

Newman, 55, has won a national championship in D Production (1976) and C Production (1979), and also drove a Porsche Turbo to a second-place finish in the 1979 Le Mans 24-hour race.

Newman will be paired with Datsun Japanese factory driver Masahiro Hasemi at Riverside. With Hasemi behind the wheel in a recent test session at Daytona Beach, Fla., the Datsun ZX Turbo, a 4.2 liter, V-8 powered car, was timed in excess of 200 m.p.h. Newman will debut the ZX at Road Atlanta next Sunday.

Newman now owns his own racing team, which will feature three-time Indy 500 winner Al Unser

and Italian Formula Two star Teo Fabi in the 1981 Can-Am series.

Newman's '79 C Production victory, his most recent triumph, came on Riverside's twisting course.

Tickets for the Times/Toyota Grand Prix can be obtained at the Times Special Events, 212 W. First St., Theatre Jewelry Center, 655 S. Hill St., Los Angeles, Riverside International Raceway box office, and all Mutual and Ticketron agencies.

Skeeter McKitterick: *"In 1980, I drove the Roy Woods DeKon Monza with George Follmer. The car had a Fischer Engineering twin turbocharged small block Chevrolet that put out 1,100 HP!! Roy rented the track on a private testing date; George had me do the bulk of the driving while we attempted to get the horsepower to the ground, we finally backed down the turbo to stop spinning the wheels in fourth gear on the back straight. We also went through three gearboxes in one day – they weren't up to the challenge of the power the Chevrolet was developing. Even with the boost down where Dennis Fischer figured we were still making 800 horsepower. We got up to sixth or seventh against all the 935's before mechanical issues put us out."*

Only four women are entered in the Times/Toyota Grand Prix of Endurance this weekend at the Riverside International Raceway and two are co-drivers: Kathy Rude (left) and Divina Galica.

This Team Will Have a Woman's Touch

By TED GREEN, *Times Staff Writer*

People with only a passing interest in auto racing generally don't pay much attention to endurance drivers in the slower, smaller-car classifications. After all, there is no Andretti, Foyt or Fittipaldi in the pack.

However, one driving team figures to attract more than a passing glance during this weekend's Times/Toyota Grand Prix of Endurance at Riverside Raceway.

The teammates' names are Kathy Rude and Divina Galica.

Car owner Dave Kent of Hawthorne has teamed the two women in his Mazda RX-7 and, so far, no one can really accuse him of pulling a publicity stunt. Running in the GTU class (which means the engines must displace less than 2.5 liters), Rude and Galica finished ninth in 12 Hours of Sebring. More than 70 cars started in their division.

Rude, 23, is a native of Washington state who now calls Anaheim home. She likes life in the fast lane so much, she says, she hopes to drive in the Indy 500 before too long.

Galica is a London veteran of hundreds of European races, including Formula One and Formula Two.

Rude has driven professionally for three years, Galica for seven,

as a 19-year-old freshman. Now she's getting ready to take the California state exam in her new sidelight, cosmetology (skin care).

Galica is perhaps better known as captain of the British women's Olympic ski team in 1968 and 1972. She also skied in the 1964 Winter Olympics. Between 1968 and 1972, she was rated in the world's top 10 in both downhill and slalom.

Runs Two Other Cars

It is driving skills, car owner Kent says, that attracted him to both women. Kent, who has factory support from Mazda, runs two other cars on the GTU circuit. Two men, Lee Mueller of Westminster and Walter Bohren of Monterey, will share one of them at Riverside.

Says Kent: "Kathy co-drove at Daytona and impressed me very much. Based on her age and performance, I'd says she has a helluva future. I felt if she could do as well as the guys in equal equipment—and equal is the key word—her career could skyrocket.

"Then the thought occurred to me that it would be neat to have a woman co-drive with her, so we can pit two women against two men in equal cars. There aren't that many women drivers to choose from, but Divina is quite good.

Girls draw attention. If they do well, it adds to the cake."

Kent also says: "Women, as a rule, haven't had a real good opportunity in competitive equipment. Even Janet Guthrie (the first woman to drive at Indy) . . . the crew she had was far from George Bignotti or Roger Penske. We consider ourselves that caliber in this type of racing. And I think Kathy is better than Janet Guthrie."

"Publicity stunt? Not at all," Rude said. "Dave was really happy with Daytona and he felt it would be really nice to help someone starting out in their careers. Women usually don't get top-notch cars no matter where they race."

Rude said she tested an Indy car at Ontario in 1979 and got it up to 174 m.p.h.

"There aren't a lot of girls in racing," she said. "I think people have the false impression that it's a macho, masculine, brute sport. Actually, it's concentration, finesse, knowing how to handle a car—it's really more analytical than anything else."

Rude aims high. "I'd like to drive Indy cars, GT's at Daytona, and race in Europe at Le Mans," she said.

The team of Rude and Galica, incidentally, represents half the women scheduled to run at Riverside. Karen Erstad of Anaheim Hills

David Hobbs / Marc Surer - BMW March

Sixth Overall for Hobbs and Surer

TOYOTA FATHER/SON RACE DRIVERS

UNSER SR. AL UNSER SR. SIR JACK BRABHAM WALLY DALLENBACH SR.

UNSER JR. AL UNSER JR. GEOFF BRABHAM WALLY DALLENBACH JR.

AND GENE HACKMAN OTIS AND MICHAEL CHANDLER

Stommelen / Meister; Porsche 935

Jim Mullen / Rick Knoop; Mazda RX-7

Al Gebhardt / Bruno Beilke; BMW M-1

Chris Cord / Jim Adams; Dekon Monza

Kenper Miller / Dave Cowart; BMW M-1

Frank Carney / Dick Davenport; 280ZX

Paul Newman / Masahiro Hashemi; 280ZX

Jim Downing / Irv Hoerr; Mazda RX-7

Kathy Rude / Divina Galicia; Mazda RX-7

Sam Posey / Fred Stiff; 280ZX

The Lola T600 of Ted Field and Bill Whittington won in 1982 in front of a crowd of 46,000, followed by the Al Holbert / Harald Grohs Andial Porsche 935. Jim Cook and Jim Mullen won GTU in the Trinity Racing RX-7 and the Almida / Soto Porsche RSR won GTO. In addition to the six hour, there was a Champion Spark Plug Series sedan race, won by Irv Pearce in a Spirit and a ten lap veteran / rookie race featuring drivers like Jack Brabham, Parnelli Jones and Roger Ward in identical Toyota Celicas. John Paul Jr won with Michael Chandler second and Parnelli Jones in third. Read about the supporting races in Volume Two; available in the fall of 2022..

Field and Whittington win Toyota Grand Prix

By BILL FROLOFF
Desert Sun Sports Writer

RIVERSIDE — Six hours of all-out speed.

That's what it took Sunday for Ted Field and co-driver Bill Whittington as they drove their Interscope Racing Team's Chevrolet-powered Lola to a resounding two-lap victory over Al Holbert and Harald Grohs in the fourth annual Los Angeles Times-Toyota Six-Hour Grand Prix of Endurance at Riverside International Raceway.

A crowd estimated at 46,000 watched as Field and Whit...

of the race with a 114.549 33rd lap, earned $9,700. The third-place finishers, Jim Busby of Laguna Beach and Vern Schuppan of Australia, earned $5,550.

Later on, Paul Jr. and John Paul Sr., his father and co-driver, were knocked out of the race when the engine in their Porsche Turbo blew out. The Pauls, who were going for an unprecedented six straight victories, managed to complete just 79 laps. Their car had also been leaking fuel for about five laps before leaving the race.

The Winning Lola T-600 of Ted Field and Bill Whittington

Akins team has something up its sleeve for Riverside — tubular frame

Bob Akin will co-drive with England's Derek Bell in the Riverside grand prix April 25.

Bob Akin's Coca-Cola/Paradyne Racing Team will debut its new tubular-framed Porsche 935-K3 at the April 25 Times/Toyota Grand Prix of Endurance.

Akin will co-drive with England's Derek Bell on Riverside International Raceway's 3.25-mile, nine-turn road course. Bell teamed with Belgium's Jacky Ickx to win last year's 24 Hours of LeMans, Bell's second victory at the famed French circuit.

Akin hopes to improve on his last three performances at Riverside. In 1979, he, Rob McFarlin and Roy Woods combined for a fourth-place finish. Akin followed that with a fifth place in 1980 with Woods/Ralph Kent Cooke.

Last year at Riverside, a variety of minor mechanical problems relegated the Akin/Mauricio De Narvaez/Skeeter McKittrick team to a 23nd-place finish.

Akin is a veteran road racer who began campaigning in SCCA events in 1959. In 1979, he won both the 12 Hours of Sebring and the 6-Hour Watkins Glen Trans-Am event. Last year, he finished second to Brian Redman in the 24 Hours of Daytona. Akin has twice finished fifth in the World Challenge for Endurance Drivers championship standings.

A die-hard vintage car buff, Akin is a familiar sight in the U.S. and Canada driving one of his classic, which include a 1959 Cooper Monaco and the ex-Peter Revson L & M Lola T-222.

When he's not racing, Akin is president of Hudson Wire Company in Ossining, N.Y., a leading producer of specialty wires for aerospace and electronics industries.

Rich keep getting richer

The richest road racing series just got richer. The R.J. Reynolds Tobacco Co. sponsors of the Camel GT Endurance Championship. The Times/Toyota Grand Prix is one of those races. The $150,000 Camel GT point

262

AP Laserphoto

WINNING TEAM — Bill Whittington (left) and his partner Ted Field show their prize trophy after winning in the Times/Toyota Six-Hour Grand Prix of Endurance Sunday in Riverside. The team drove a black Interscope Lola T-600, the first Lola ever to win in the Times race.

David Hobbs: *"I loved Riverside, it was such a fast track to drive on, could get very sandy sometimes and I never liked those damn tyres, but the corners were awesome, Turn 9 was bit of a ball breaker, but hey, in those days most corners were as unsafe as hell but it flowed really well, was a very satisfying track to do well on. Passing was not that difficult either so all in all a terrific spot. Plus you could see the underside of a B52 flying by about every five minutes, also pretty cool!!"*

Jim Adams - Lola T600

Bob Akin - Kremer Porsche 935

263

John Greenwood - Protofab Corvette **Roger Mandeville - RX7**

Danny McKeever: *"When I saw the houses going up off in the distance, I knew the end was coming. A great place to race; loved the 3.3 mile circuit. I taught a lot of guys who were there for the first time., many IMSA guys, NASCAR drivers, Off roaders. Drag racer John Force told everyone "Danny taught me to turn right and left"* **Compiler's Note** - Danny was chief instructor for Cal Club Region, SCCA, has run the Fast Lane Driving School for decades, trained the Toyota Celebrity Race drivers and won more than a few races. Buy his book "Professor Speed" on Amazon or at Autobooks in Burbank

Bruce Mallery: *"I was co-driving Vic Manuelli's GTO Pantera. Things were going OK, running mid pack in GTO and trying to stay our of the way of the Porsche 935's and new GTP cars. Coming through the esses, the rear end got loose and I spun the car in turn 5.*

The car came to rest sideways in the middle of the track with the engine stalled. As I looked back down the track towards turn 2, I could see a line of cars headed my way at over 100 mph. Fortunately, the corner workers got them slowed down and there was room to pass on both ends of the car. Ted Field, Lola T-600, was leading with John Paul Jr. right on his tail in his Porsche 935. As Ted moved left at the last second to miss me, John Paul Jr. saw me too late to avoid locking up and sliding into me. I saw the crash later on ESPN and realized that the Pantera hopped into the air and rotated about 45 degrees. After this, I got the car restarted and drove to the inside of turn 6, out of the way. I had been hit directly on the left front wheel and there was no body damage. The crew brought a new wheel and tire with a jack and lug wrench so I could fix the damage. Unfortunately, the brake rotor and suspension were also damaged so we retired the car on the spot. I wasn't injured, so I just went home that evening. When I got to my office on Monday morning, several of my co-workers asked if I had seen the local paper; which I hadn't. On my desk, were several copies of the morning's Orange County Register with a picture of the crash on the top half of the front page in color. Color was fairly new for newspapers then so it really stood out. I immediately went to the Register's offices and "borrowed their negative" to make my own negative and lots of various sized copies. Almost 40 years later, I still remember the events that day like yesterday."

Skeeter McKitterick: *"In 1982, I drove the Golden Eagle Racing Rondeau, powered by a Chevrolet small block. Had a decent effort in prerace weekend testing, managed a first for me in this category of chassis of getting through turn two flat (with very stiff springs) but, the exit was a bit busy and the car was too nervous to drive for a long period of time. While tire testing for Firestone we also found we were running very high tire temps; in excess of 270 degrees; the tires were bubbling! Got up to third towards the end of the first hour, then we lost a valve cover gasket."*

The team of John Fitzpatrick, Derek Bell and David Hobbs in a J. David Porsche Kremer 935 collected $25,000 for their win in 1983, followed by the Al Holbert / Jim Trueman March 83G and the Bob Wollek / Mauricio de Narvaez Porsche 935. The fifth overall Wayne Baker / Jim

Mullen / Kies Nierop Porsche 934 won GTU and the AAR Toyota, driven by Wally Dallenbach Jr, Whitney Ganz and Dennis Aase won GTU. The race was marred by the fatal crash of Rolf Stommelen in the second J. David team car. Supporting races included a Champion Spark Plug Series sedan race, won by Joe Varde in a Dodge Charger and a Renault Cup event. Read about the supporting races in Volume Two; available in the fall of 2022..

John Fitzpatrick - *"The J David Dominelli team was a dream team; Max Crawford, Glen Blakely and Mark Popov"* Compiler's Note – Read more about J.David in Chapter Thirteen.

David Hobbs: *A tragic race; Derek Bell and Rolf Stommelen were driving the other Fitzpatrick car, the famed Whale tail that John and I finished fourth overall and class winner at Le Mans the year before. Rolf clipped the wall at turn seven but didn't think he had done any damage and kept his foot in it with terrible consequences, at the end of the main straight the tail came off sending him into the end of the wall around turn nine, killing him instantly. Fitz was devastated, we all were, we had all had a very jovial breakfast that morning at the HoJos on University Ave and were one and two in the race. Fitz thought we should keep going with the other car, as the organizers did not want to advertise the fact that Rolf had died, which pulling the other car out would have signaled, so Derek joined me and we went onto win the event, but not a great celebration.*

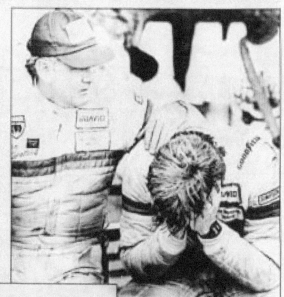

Stommelen Dies After Crash

Three-Time Daytona Winner Hits Barriers at Riverside Raceway

By SHAV GLICK, Times Staff Writer

RIVERSIDE—Veteran German endurance driver Rolf Stommelen, 39, died of injuries Sunday after a fiery crash midway through the Times/Datsun 6 Hour race at Riverside International Raceway.

Stommelen died at Riverside Community Hospital of cardiac arrest caused by unspecified injuries after his Porsche 935 knocked over two two-ton concrete barriers and then cartwheeled more than a hundred yards down the track. No other car was involved.

Stommelen, a three-time winner of the Daytona 24 Hour race (1978-80-82), was driving a turbocharged Porsche owned by John Fitzpatrick of San Diego. Fitzpatrick's other car, driven by himself, David Hobbs and Derek Bell, won the six-hour race.

The winning car led 82 of the last 88 laps (out of 196) after a mixup in pit stops and a flat tire halted the early pacesetter, a Chevrolet-March driven by Al Holbert and Jim Trueman. Hobbs took the checkered flag in the Porsche, a lap and 34 seconds ahead of Holbert. The third-place car, another Porsche 935 driven by Bob Wollek of France and Mauricio DeNarvaez of Columbia, was four laps back.

Stommelen was running in second place 15 minutes from the halfway point when the rear wing apparently lifted coming down the long Riverside backstretch.

Please see STOMMELEN, Page 10

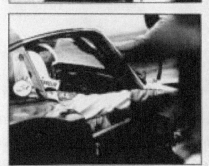

The Cost of the Race: One Car . . . and One Life

Far left, top to bottom, Rolf Stommelen, a three-time winner of the Daytona 24-hour endurance race, straps on his helmet for the last time, helps his partner out of the car and takes over the wheel for his fatal ride at Riverside International Raceway Sunday in the Times/Datsun 6 Hour race. Above, teammate Derek Bell, with car owner John Fitzpatrick (left), breaks down after he hears the news that his friend is dead. Left, the wreckage is hauled away.

Wayne Baker / Kies Nierop; Porsche 934

Rolf Stommelen / Derek Bell; Porsche 935

Al Holbert / Jim Trueman; March 83G

Boy Hayje / Roberto Moreno; BMW320i

S

keeter McKitterick: *"I drove Ian Dawson's GRID SP1, powered by a Cosworth DFV with Randy Lanier at Riverside in 1983. The car was an absolute dream to drive; loved this car as long as Ian was present to dial the car in. The chassis was very sensitive to set up. Ian was Mario Andretti's engineer at Lotus when he won the F1 World Championship and the car was basically the Lotus F1 chassis with a full body work developed by Ian. We tarted thirteenth but broke and ended up 55th*

Foyt and Andretti are teammates in a Porsche today

By Tom Cheche

A special brand of excitement is being generated in advance of The Los Angeles Times Grand Prix today at Riverside (Calif.) International Raceway, over the pairing of what may be the two greatest American race drivers of all time as co-drivers.

A.J. Foyt and Mario Andretti will co-drive a Porsche 935 turbo in the 6-Hour IMSA GT race, marking several significant firsts. It will be the first time the two drivers have been teamed together, and it will be the first time Andretti has driven a Porsche race car of any kind.

There is no other race car over the past decade that has so epitomized motor racing invincibility as the Porsche 935 turbo, and there is no driver who is as well known around the world as Andretti. It is almost incredible that Andretti has never driven a 935, and Andretti himself admits he is amazed to realize he has never driven one.

THE CAR THEY WILL drive is the Preston Henn-owned 935 turbo formerly known as the Andial 935. It is one of the most radically designed 935's in competition, and it is almost new. The car made its racing debut last year at Riverside with Al Holbert turning some astounding times before the machine parked with some mechanical problems.

After Riverside the car sat idle until this year, when Foyt was made a last-minute teammate of Bob Wollek and Claude Ballot-Lena, two Porsche veterans. Foyt and company drove the car to victory in this year's 24 Hours of Daytona. Wollek is one of the most experienced Porsche drivers in the world, and he described the Andial car as the best 935 he has ever driven.

And so what we have this weekend is two of the finest drivers in the world teaming up in what may be the best 935 turbo in the world.

As Andretti tells the story, he was in Detroit last week for a press conference. One morning he was having breakfast with his son, Michael, who

Auto racing

is a professional driver. Along with the two Andrettis were several other people, including Glenn Davis, late of Army football fame and now director of special events for the L.A. Times.

Now, it turns out that car owner Henn has two Porsche 935s, and during breakfast, Michael Andretti was asked about the possibility of driving one of those cars in the upcoming L.A. Times Grand Prix. Mario, overhearing all this, and knowing that Foyt was planning to drive the ex-Andial car at Riverside, piped up with, "Well, if Foyt is so hard up for a ride, tell 'em I'll co-drive with him."

"I thought they had the rides all locked up, and I never really expected them to take me up on it. But one phone call and five minute later it was all set," Andretti said.

You mean Foyt didn't have a thing to do with it?

"Oh, no. He didn't even know about it until it was set."

Well, what were you doing, just agitating?

"Yeah," chuckled Andretti. "I guess you could say that."

AND SO IT WAS set. Andretti arrived on Wednesday to get the car set up for the race, with Foyt arriving today. The driving schedule has yet to be worked out. As for the differences in the handling preferences of the two drivers, Andretti says he doesn't anticipate any problems.

"I'll just set the car up the way it's comfortable for me, and most of the time it's okay for the other driver. If not, we can make some changes. But a car either feels good or it doesn't, and that's a fact."

Sunday's L.A. Times GP should be a fun day for Foyt and Andretti. And for Mario, a fun weekend would be appreciated. He was in Atlanta last weekend for an Indy car 200-miler and wrecked his No. 1 car. Andretti was left with a bruised jaw from the crash.

Next day, things went from bad to worse.

"We thought we needed about 1 more m.p.h. out of our backup car to make it competitive under racing conditions on Sunday. We had been running between 192 and 195 m.p.h. laps in the full race setup, and I thought we needed about 197.

"Well, late Saturday we made some wild guesses, and it backfired in spades. We lost 10 m.p.h."

And adding insult to injury, on Sunday Andretti found out he didn't need the extra speed anyway.

"As it turned out, we didn't need more than 190 on race day. After we made our guesses we wound up at 184 with a bad bottoming problem and a car so loose I was constantly afraid it was going to spin."

GLC 1983 Road
Atlanta RS 1st
Performance Sedan

RX-7 1982
Daytona GTO
Champion

Watch for Mazda
B2000 in upcoming
off-road events

RX-7 1983
SCCA PRO
Rally Champion

If you're at a race right now, chances are we are, too.

Whether the race is on a twist-ing road course or across an unforgiving desert, chances are good that Mazda is there.

We're currently campaigning cars in IMSA racing, the SCCA PRO Rally series, and in SCORE and other off-road events.

We're more than a little involved in racing. Because at Mazda, racing isn't a token commitment. It's a total commitment.

mazda

The more you look, the more you like.

John Fitzpatrick Favored to Repeat Riverside Win

By SHAV GLICK, *Times Staff Writer*

John Fitzpatrick

Bob Garretson

RIVERSIDE—San Diego car dealer Dick Barbour arrived here a year ago with some rather pretentious goals for his racing team: Finish 1-2 in the Times/Toyota five-hour race and win the IMSA championship, the 24 Hours of LeMans and the Porsche Cup.

With the help of driver John Fitzpatrick and car preparer Bob Garretson, Barbour accomplished them all, a remarkable feat in the fiercely competitive world of big-bucks racing. Then, late last year, Barbour abruptly quit the sport, both as a driver and as a car owner.

What was once the Barbour Racing Team has split, Fitzpatrick going one way and Garretson the other. And now the two are battling one another for supremacy in 1981.

Fitzpatrick, with Jim Busby as co-driver in a twin turbo Kremer-Porsche 935, is favored to repeat as winner in Sunday's Times/Toyota six-hour race at Riverside International Raceway.

Among Fitzpatrick's chief rivals are expected to be two Garretson-prepared Porsche 935 turbos, one driven by Daytona 24 Hour winners Brian Redman and Bobby Rahal, the other by Garretson (the third Daytona 24 Hour winning driver), Ralph Kent Cooke and Roy Woods. Last year Fitzpatrick and Barbour finished first here, followed by Rahal and Garretson.

Although Fitzpatrick is a three-time winner of the Porsche Cup—given annually to the best of the company's drivers the world over—and one of Europe's formost GT

Please see RIVERSIDE, Page 17

John Fitzpatrick: *"Riverside was my favorite track in the U.S., probably because I won there three times. However, It holds both good and bad memories for me as Rolf Stommolen was killed there in 1983 in my Porsche 935. I had started with him in that car and after the accident I moved over to the second car with Hobbo and Bell and we won. Rolf was taken to the hospital and died on the way there. I wasn't told until after the finish of the race that he had died. We were living in San Diego at the time and my wife had just had our first child. Rolf and Marlene were good friends of ours and it hit Sandra very hard and was the main reason for me stopping driving at the end of that year. The car was repairable but we decided to scrap it out of respect for Rolf."*

Pictured above is the class #7, Mazda RX-7, one of the cars competing in the Times/Datsun Grand Prix of Endurance April 23–24.

Mazda drivers show themselves as strong competitors in four IMSA races run this year

Though just four races have been run in the International Motor Sports Assoc's Camel GT series, (three in IMSA's Champion Spark Plug Challenge series), at the Times/Datsun Grand Prix race weekend slated for the Riverside International Raceway April 23–24, Mazda drivers have already established themselves as strong competitors in a number of divisions.

In the GTO (Grand Touring Cars with engine displacements more than 2.8 liters), class #7, the Mazda RX-7 will be driven by the Racing Beat team of Anaheim. With drivers Pete Halsmer, Rick Knoop and Bob Reed at the wheel, Racing Beat's 13B rotary engine-powered Mazda finished first in GTO and third overall at the Daytona 24-Hour in February. The third overall placing was the best ever recorded by a Japanese manufacturer at Daytona.

Halsmer and Knoop hope to take the #7 RX-7 into Riverside's Camel GTO victory circle as well.

In the Camel GTU division, (GT cars with engine displacements of less than 2.8 liters), where the RX-7 runs with the smaller 12A rotary engine, Mazda drivers have won three of the four races held in 1983.

At the Daytona 24-Hour, Kent Racing's #92 RX-7 finished tops in GTU. Lee Mueller, Hugh McDonough and Terry Visger co-drove the car. For Riverside, the Hawthorne-based Kent team will field a two-car effort. Mueller and Visger will driver #96, while George Follmer and Rocky Moran will be behind the wheel of the #92 RX-7.

Mazda's Roger Mandeville won the first professional race run through the streets of Miami when his #38 RX-7 captured the victory in the Miami Grand Prix GTU competition on Feb. 26. Mandeville finished second in the 1982 season's GTU drivers' standings. He'll share the driving at Riverside with Amos Johnson.

Mandeville's friend and rival, 1982 GTU drivers' champion Jim Downing, will also be on hand at Riverside. Downing, who will co-drive the #63 RX-7 with John Maffucci, is currently tied with Mandeville for third place in the 1983 GTU drivers' standings.

The men who stand first and second thus far in the 1983 GTU drivers' points are Mazda drivers Jack Dunham and Jeff Kline. Dunham and Kline teamed with Jon Compton to win GTU at the 12 Hours of Sebring on March 19, but will go at it together only in the shorter Riverside endurance race. The Dunham/Kline pairing will be in a #66 RX-7 at Riverside.

Another strong Mazda contender scheduled to run at Riverside is the #82 Trinity Racing RX-7. Joe Varde is the lead driver for #82. He finished third among GTU drivers during the 1982 season.

On the strength of its drivers' performances, Mazda already holds a lead in the GTU manufacturers' championship standings over Porsche, Datsun and Toyta. Mazda won the GTU manufacturers' crown in 1980, 1981 and 1982.

In the Champion Spark Plug Challenge series, which features competition between race-prepared street sedans, Mazda has the early-season lead in the drivers' and manufacturers' title races.

Both the older rear-drive cars, such as the Mazda RX-3 and AMC Spirit, and the newer front-wheel drive cars, such as the Mazda GLC, Renault Le Car, Honda Civic, Nissan Sentra, Dodge Challenger and Ford Escort, are expected to play in the action at Riverside.

Only the front-drivers, which compete in the ProFormance class, are eligible for points counting toward the manufacturers' title. To allow time for the race teams to make the transition to front-drive cars, however, the older rear-drive entries are still allowed to run, and their drivers can chalk up points that go toward the drivers' title.

Consequently, Mazda finds itself up top in both categories. Sacramento racer Dave Jolly has grabbed the lead in the drivers' standings after taking his #31 RX-3 to victory at Daytona, and finishes of eighth at Sebring and third at Road Atlanta. Next to Jolly for the season lead is Amos Johnson and his front wheel drive Mazda GLC.

So far in 1983 Johnson was first in the ProFormance class at Daytona and first overall, (as well as in class), at the Champion Spark Plug Challenge race at Sebring.

Johnson's efforts have given Mazda a 10-point edge over Dodge and Volkswagen in the series' manufacturers' points. Nissan, Renault and Honda also are on the board already.

Roger Mandevile leading Jeff Kline; both in GTU RX-7's

Racing's the pits for women drivers without owner's bucks

By SHAV GLICK
Los Angeles Times

RIVERSIDE — Why aren't there more women race drivers?

Shirley Muldowney has proven they can beat the men by winning the world drag racing championship. And Janet Guthrie attracted a lot of attention when she became "The First Woman to Drive at Indianapolis" in 1977.

Since Guthrie drove her last Indy 500 in 1979 and also drove in a few NASCAR Grand National races, no woman driver has been in either Indy cars or Grand National stockers.

"It sounds dumb, but it's more difficult for a woman to get sponsorship," said Desire Wilson, "and without sponsorship you can't get rides at Indianapolis or in Formula One."

Wilson and five other women drivers are among the 86 teams entered in today's 6-hour main event of the Times-Datsun Grand Prix of Endurance at Riverside International Raceway.

"I don't think I proved my point, that I was capable of driving there," she said. "In fact, I've proved my point everywhere I've raced. Each time a woman moves up, though, she leaves the same thing. 'What's a girl like you doing here?'"

Wilson was lapping Indianapolis Motor Speedway at around 192 mph before a string of six blown engines kept her from qualifying. Teddy Yip's Eagle Cosworth.

Wilson has been racing against males since she was 9, driving successfully built by her father in South Africa. She "retired" from racing at 13 but, at her father's insistence, returned to the sport when she was 19.

That was 10 years ago, and the slender 5-foot-6, 128-pound racer has a long list of accomplishments. In 1976, she won the South African National Formula Ford championship, and the following year won a "Driver-to-Europe" award, similar to one Indy Schecklter won a few years earlier.

"I was newly married, so Alan and I chucked we would take it and go to Europe for three months," she said. "We've been gone six years now."

Alan Wilson became director at the Brands Hatch track in England, a position he left earlier that year to design and direct construction of the New York Grand Prix circuit in Flushing Meadow.

"I don't think I could have done all the things I did without Alan's support," Desire said. "I have been very fortunate to be doing something I can do with my husband."

Her most significant achievement was winning the aurora British Formula One championship driving a Theodore reef in 1980. It was the only time a woman has won a Formula One race.

Wilson is driving a Porsche-March 80G with the car's owner.

San Bernardino, Page 09

Al Holbert and Jim Trueman drove the March to a third place finish

In the 1984 Times Grand Prix, a crowd of 42,750 saw Randy Lanier and Bill Whittington win in a March Chevrolet after a long pit stop dropped the Derek Bell / Al Holbert Porsche 962 to second. Five laps back was the Kenper Miller / Mauricio de Narvaez March. The Mazda team of Roger Mandeville and Amos Johnson won GTO and Elliott Forbes Robinson won in GTU. Supporting races included the Champion Spark Plug Series sedan race, won by Bobby Archer, a Jim Russell School Pro Series single seater race and the Renault Cup spec series. Read about the supporting races in Volume Two; available in the fall of 2022.

RICK CORRALES / Los Angeles Times

Winners Bill Whittington (left) and Randy Lanier celebrate win in Times 6-Hour race at Riverside.

6-Hour Race Is Decided in Final Stop

By SHAV GLICK,
Times Staff Writer

RIVERSIDE—After six hours of racing Sunday at speeds up to 190 m.p.h., the Times/Nissan Grand Prix of Endurance at Riverside International Raceway came down to a 15-second differ-

Read More About Bill Whittington and Randy Lanier in chapter Thirteen

The Kreepy Krauly March 83G of Sarel van der Merwe and Tony Martin finished sixth

Holbert's admits error costs him a victory

Examiner news services

Al Holbert committed a big error yesterday, and he didn't hesitate to admit it.

"It was my fault. I really made a mistake," said Holbert, after delaying taking the wheel during a pit stop in the Los Angeles Times Grand Prix of Endurance at the Riverside International Speedway, where he and teammate Derek

Motor sports roundup

Bell finished second.

"We had never gotten a good fuel flow count. The crew wasn't sure how much fuel would go in and how fast. I had an idea and I was concentrating on that.

"Derek yelled, 'Let me out. I can't stay in any more.' And I just wasn't ready to get into the car. It was my mistake."

The error resulted in a one minute and two seconds-long pit stop, and dropped the Porsche 962 behind Bill Whittington and Randy Lanier of Florida. The winners drove a new Chevrolet March to post a 4.9-second victory, averaging a race-record 110.451 mph in completing 204 laps or 663 miles around the 3.25-mile, nine-turn road course.

The pit stop came with just 24 minutes remaining in the race. Bell, who was part of the winning team in last year's race, had just spent more than a half-hour erasing Whittington's 14-second lead and passing him for the top spot, but was forced into the pits for fuel and a driver change.

Last year, Holbert came to Riverside with a brand new car and was leading by 18 seconds with less than half an hour remaining in the race when a rear tire blew out and cost him the victory.

A Ford Mustang prototype which had won the pole position Saturday at a record 124.387 mph ran strongly in the early stages yesterday but encountered problems with its turbocharger and made several lengthy pit stops before the car was taken out of the race with transmission problems.

Finishing third was a team of Kenper Miller of Pittsford, N.Y., and Mauricio DeNarvaez of Colombia. Fourth was John Morton of El Segundo, Calif., and Tony Adamowicz of Los Angeles, followed by a team of Chuck Kendall of Flintridge, Calif., and Jim Cook of Los Alamitos, Calif.

In the 100-mile Champion Spark Plug Challenge road race, also an IMSA event, Bobby Archer drove a Renault Encore to victory in 1 hour, 6 minutes and 2.4 seconds.

Archer, of Duluth, Minn., finished 12 seconds ahead of Dave Jolly, of Sacramento, driving a Mazda GLC.

In Martinsville, Va.: Geoff Bodine's first Grand National victory was worth far more than the winner's share of the $250,300 purse in the Sovran Bank 500 at Martinsville Speedway.

Bodine raced into the lead 46 laps from the end on the way to the victory that earned his team $29,800.

However, the triumph for the 35-year-old New York state native, now living in Pleasant Garden, N.C., also earned the team, owned by Rick Hendrick of Charlotte, N.C., the ninth and last available spot on NASCAR's Winner's Circle program.

That program, for race winners who run the entire 30-race circuit, provides appearance money for each race. In the case of Bodine's All-Star Racing team, it will be worth $99,400 over the rest of the 1984 season.

"That's just great," said the elated Bodine. "It's going to mean a lot for our team."

The beaming driver said of the victory that had eluded him in his first 68 Grand National starts, "It's just one of the most exciting and gratifying things in my life.

"Everybody on this team has worked very hard for it. We've struggled a lot, but this will give all of us a real big boost."

Bodine wrested the lead from defending Winston Cup champion Bobby Allison on the 452nd of 500 laps around the Virginia track's .526-mile oval.

At Zolder, Belgium: Italy's Michele Alboreto drove his Ferrari to an unchallenged victory in the Belgian Formula 1 Grand Prix, dominating the race from the moment he took off in the pole position.

He completed the 70 laps (185.4 miles) in an average speed of 115.245 mph, despite stopping for a quick tire change in the second half of the race.

Derek Warwick of Britain, in a Renault, finished second, 42.386 seconds behind the winner.

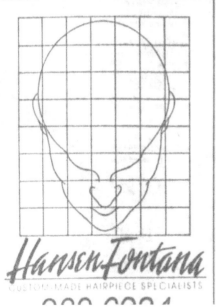

Ike Smith: *"Billy Scyphers decided he wanted to race a Ferrari; didn't go well with 3.3 liters in GTO !! So we moved his operation from San Diego to Salina, built a tube frame Corvette that was pretty fast. Testing one day, we were faster than Dennis Aase in the GTO Toyota. Dan Gurney saw Colin Riley working on the Corvette, knew we were a threat. The performance of that car got us a Chevy factory deal."*

Polesitter Bobby Rahal / Klaus Ludwig; Zakspeed Mustang GTP DNF'd

GTO Winner Roger Mandeville and Amos Johnson

Bob Akin / John O'Steen - Eighth Place Finisher

1984 marked the first serious discussion about moving the track. Looking back on it, none of this seemed realistic

Parade of Wheels
by Floyd Freel

Riverside Raceway Relocation Plans

Riverside International Raceway officials have endorsed plans for a proposed multi-use regional park near the City of Corona, as part of their relocation process announced last February.

Board Chairman Fritz Duda said the Raceway has committed to begin working immediately with City of Corona and Riverside County officials in planning the new park which will include an automotive oriented industrial park as part of its overall design.

"The park concept is well suited to our relocation plans" Duda said. "We have been assured by both the City of Corona and the County that all of the requirements we established for relocating our facility, including a time schedule, can be met," he added.

A study completed earlier this year shows that the Raceway and its testing operation is one of the major contributors to the economy of its primary region, with a total impact ranging from $92,000,000 and $137,000,000. The new site should have that impact because of its convenience to all of Southern California, according to Raceway officials.

Plans for the regional park and motorsports complex were announced by Riverside County Supervisors Nor-

ton Younglove and Melba Dunlap along with Corona City officials.

Younglove, who has been working closely with Raceway officials in their site search ever since relocation plans were announced eight months ago, said the proposed regional park and its excellent site would benefit a four-county area, including Riverside, San Bernadino, Los Angeles and Orange counties.

The regional park site is adjacent to the Prado Flood Control Basin, just north of the Riverside Freeway (Highway 71 and I-15). It is convenient to all of Southern California's major population centers and is appproximately 25 miles southwest of the existing Riverside Raceway site.

The City of Corona, which is adjacent to the freeway regional park and motorsports complex site was once known as the "Indianapolis of the West," having hosted the annual Corona Road Races in 1913-14 and 1916, when such auto racing legends as Barney Oldfield, Earl Cooper, Ralph DePalma, Bob Burman and Eddie Rickenbacker raced around the perfect circle course now known as Grand Boulevard.

Raceway officials said that while it is too soon to talk opening dates, County and City officials believe the new park site will be completed by the end of 1986.

In keeping with relocation plans announced last February, the existing Raceway will remain in operation through the 1986 racing season, which concludes with the Winston Western 500. This year's Winston event is set for November 18 and advance ticket sales are the highest in the race's 22 year history.

A New Riverside International Raceway Slated to Be Built in Corona Area in 1987

By SHAV GLICK, *Times Staff Writer*

RIVERSIDE—The long-awaited word on the relocation of Riverside International Raceway came Friday when Riverside County officials announced that a new track will be built in the Corona area, near the Prado Dam.

The complex, to include an oval track, road course and drag strip, is expected to be ready early in 1987.

Racing will continue at the old site through the 1986 season, according to Fritz Duda, raceway board chairman.

The facility will be part of a multi-use regional park to be developed jointly by the county of Riverside and city of Corona on land under lease from the Army Corps of Engineers. The site is north of the Riverside Freeway (Highway 71 and I-15) between the Prado Dam and the Corona airport. It is about a mile from the Green River golf course, where Riverside, San Bernardino and Orange counties meet. The access off-ramp from the Riverside Freeway is Serfas Avenue.

Duda had announced last February that the closing of Riverside International Raceway was inevitable because housing developments are encroaching on it.

"There will be no concrete stadium, like Ontario, and there will be no night racing," Duda said. "We want to develop a place where families can come and enjoy afternoon racing in a park-like atmosphere. Unlike Riverside, where most of the facility is dirt and dusty, we plan to have a grassy setting."

All of the major sanctioning bodies now using the track—NASCAR (stock cars), IMSA and SCCA (sports cars) and NHRA (drag racers)—have expressed enthusiasm over the new project.

"I would certainly expect CART (Indy cars) to become part of our schedule again when the oval track is complete," Duda said. CART canceled the California 500 last year, saying the Riverside road course did not meet its standards.

"If this doesn't go, it could leave major league auto racing without a market in Southern California," Duda said. "Ontario is gone and so

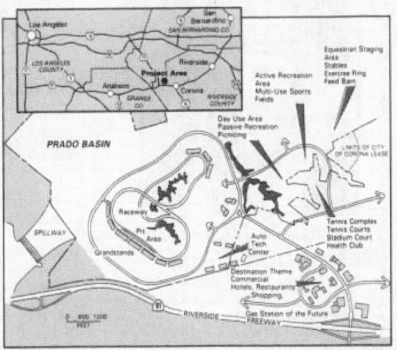

The new Riverside Raceway will be part of a regional park near Prado Dam in Corona. The track is expected to be ready in 1987.

Times Map by Don Clement

is Orange County Raceway, and Riverside is next. We don't want any mistakes this time, so we plan to have representatives from each sanctioning body assist in designing and planning the new tracks."

The proposal calls for an oval speedway between 1½ and two miles in length, a road course a minimum of two miles long and a quarter-mile drag strip. The name will remain the same: Riverside International Raceway.

"We don't plan on having weekly drag racing, but we would like to put on one or two major races, such as the World Finals, each year," Duda said.

Most of the spectator seating will be on grassy picnic knolls, like those at such tracks as Laguna Seca in Northern California, Watkins Glen, N.Y., and Elkhart Lake, Wis. There will be areas for RV parking with spectator viewing. The Butterfield Stage Park for RVs is already part of the park.

About 25,000 grandstand seats will be scattered about the course.

In addition to major races, the California Motor Sports Center will be available for uses similar to

those that keep the current track busy about 250 days a year. These include track rental to clubs such as the California Sports Car Club, American Road Racing Assn., Pantera Owners Club, Vintage Auto Racing Assn., and Porsche Owners Club; companies for TV commercials, equipment testing by manufacturers and racing teams, smog emission testing and the Jim Russell British School of Motor Racing.

Supervisor Melba Dunlap, in whose district the proposed park lies, noted that the facility will also have non-racing attractions.

Other proposed recreational uses include a tennis complex, health club, interpretive center and meeting rooms, jogging trails and an equestrian area with stables, exercise rings and feeding barn.

County and city officials expect within 30 days to prepare a request for proposals and preparation of a master plan and environmental impact study for the proposed regional park/motor sports complex. Results of the study will determine the cost of the multimillion-dollar layout.

Al Leon / Art Leon; March

Allen Glick / Billy Scyphers; Ferrari 308

Bill Van / Bruce Leven; Porsche 924 GTR

Wayne Baker / Jack Newsum; Porsche 935

Chuck Kendall / Jim Cook; Lola T-600

Albert Naon / Diego Montoya; Sauber BMW

Jim Downing / John Maffucci; Argo Mazda

Clay Young / Doug Grunnet; Fiero

Logan Blackburn / Don Devendorf;

Bruce Jenner / John Bauer; Thunderbird

45,960 spectators saw the B.F. Goodrich Porsche 962's dominate in 1985, The race, shortened to 600 kilometers from the previous years six hours, was won by John Morton and Pete Halsmer with teammates Jim Busby and Rick Knoop in second. Five laps back was the third place Tullius / Robinson Jaguar. Jim Downing and John Maffucci won the Camel Light category in an Argo - Mazda; John Jones and Wally Dallenbach won GTO in a Mustang. Jeff Kline and Jack Baldwin won GTU in the Malibu Grand Prix RX-7. Fiero driver Bob Earl said "track conditions were terrible, with pieces of cars and tires everywhere."Another odd incident – after a multi car crash in turn three which brought out the pace car, second place Brian Redman's Jag was hit by a BMW. In the supporting races, Kal Showket won the Champion Sparkplug Challenge race and the Renault Cup event was won by Parker Johnstone. Saturday had two SCCA events. Read about the supporting events in Volume Two; available in the fall of 2022.

Morton, Halsmer drive Porsche to enduro win

By KATIE CASTATOR
Sun Sports Writer

RIVERSIDE — Nissan named it, and claimed it would be a showcase for its new Nissan GTP ZX-T.

But the experimental car, co-driven by Don Devendorf and Tony Adamowicz, ran into driveline problems and out of development time. Thus Nissan's car never left the garage Sunday at Riverside International Raceway in the Los Angeles Times-Nissan Grand Prix of Endurance.

So what the crowd of 45,960 got instead was Tire Wars, and a poster-picture, one-two finish by two blimpless B.F. Goodrich/Porsche 962s. John Morton of El Segundo and Pete Halsmer drove the winning car — the first-ever Camel GT victory for a car equipped with Goodrich tires.

Morton led the twin sister of his black-and-white Porsche, co-piloted by Jim Busby and Rick Knoop of Laguna Beach, over the finish line by a winning margin of 0.138 seconds. Time of the 600-kilometer race (373.75 miles) was 3 hours, 27 minutes, 25.673 seconds. The winner's average speed was 108.110 mph.

It gave the Goodrich people, which sponsor both cars, a perfect opportunity to shoot a new promotional picture, and it left that other tire company without a first or second place for the first time in the history of the Camel GT series.

In past Camel GT races, 83 of the 86 winners have rolled across the finish line on Goodyear tires. The Goodyear people also lost at Daytona in 1980 and Sebring in 1983.

And until the third-place-running team of Bruce Leven-David Hobbs in the Bayside Disposal/Bridgestone Porsche 962 went out with mechanical problems on the 85th lap, it appeared Goodyear would be locked out of the top three spots. Bob Tullius and Chip Robinson drove the factory-backed Group 44 Jaguar XJR-5 to a third-place finish. Bob Akin and Jim Mullen finished fourth in a Porsche 962.

On the 111th lap, the Busby-Knoop Porsche (No.67) caught up with its stablemate (No.68) and followed it around the 3.25-mile course without attempting to pass. Both cars ended the 115-lap race with their lights on. It appeared to be a set-up ending sure to please the cars' backers, and a film-script writer if Hollywood ever decides to make it into a movie.

"Set up! Set up! Shame on you," Busby scolded. "Actually, I got on the radio and said we were going to turn the lights on. I said: 'Is that a Hollywood finish?'

"What we wanted to do was get the cars together. We knew that the 68 car had led for a good portion of the race. We had a slight braking problem in the 67 car. So we decided, heck, we've got four or five laps to run, the 68 car is going to win the race so that's what we did. It makes a nice picture and everybody is happy."

John Paul Jr., who started the race in a Buick March, had the first-lap lead coming out of the esses but took himself out of the race when spun out at Turn 8 and had to wait for the full field to pass before pulling back on the track. He moved from 52nd place to 13th place by Lap 4, but his car developed electrical problems.

"All the wiring melted and filled the cockpit with smoke," he said. "It got so bad, I couldn't see any more, so I pulled off."

Polesitter Al Holbert, who shared a ride with Al Unser in another Porsche 962, gained the lead after Paul spun out. He increased it to a full-minute over the rest of the field until his turbocharger went bad and required 21 minutes to replace. Holbert was later involved in a three-car scrap and finished in 11th place.

Holbert, who has four seconds at Riverside, has never won a race there.

"It always seems to be one thing that keeps me from winning," said Holbert. "This time it was the turbocharger, and we haven't had a turbocharger problem in a long time."

John Jones and Wally Dallenbach Jr. finished fifth overall and won the GTO class in a Motorcraft-Roush Ford-Mustang. Jim Downing and John Maffucci (RGP 500 Disk Brake Mazda Argo) finished first in the Camel Lights class. Paul Lewis and Scott Pruett finished first in the GTU class in a Mazda RX-7.

Two local drivers failed to finish. Don Kravig of Redlands, one of three drivers of a Porsche 934, left the race after 20 laps; Doug Barnhold of Fontana in a Nissan 280ZX was knocked out after 46 laps.

280

Four divisions of racing guarantee weekend of excitement on demanding 3.25-mile track

It's not any big news story that Al Holbert and Derek Bell are among the early favorites in this weekend's Times/Nissan Grand Prix of Endurance.

The pair drove their Lowenbrau Porsche 962 to victory at Miami, and added second places at Daytona and Sebring.

Holbert currently leads the Camel GT point standings with 58. Bell is second with 50.

Yet, nothing is certain in racing, and nobody knows that better than Holbert. He's finished second at Riverside International Raceway four times. The past two years have been particularly galling to the three-time GT champion.

In 1983, a late-race tire problem ruined his chances. Last year, an unexpected, time-consuming driver change cost him

John Jones, a 19-year-old Canadian who races with a Mustang, leads the GTO point standings with 55.

speedy, nine-turn road course.

Among that machinery is the Conte Racing Buick-March of John Paul Jr. and Bill Adam.

Adam will be a factor this weekend.

Randy Lanier, the defending race and Camel GT champion

IMSA history to win the GT title and be named "Most Improved Driver" in one season.

A new Porsche 962 will be in the hands of Jim Busby and Rick Knoop. Knoop stands third in the GT standings on the strength of two third-place finishes and one sixth place.

The addition of David Hobbs makes co-driver Bruce Leven's Bayside Disposal Porsche 962 a force to be reckoned with. Hobbs scored a fine second-place finish at Miami before signing on with Leven. Hobbs co-drove to victory here at Riverside in 1983 with John Fitzpatrick and Derek Bell.

Pete Halsmer and John Morton, both versatile drivers, will field another Porsche 962 at Riverside.

The Rick Knoop / Jim Busby Porsche leads the Brian Redman / Hurley Haywood Jaguar

The Tim Coconis / Argetsinger Lola T-616 Polimotor leads the Adams / Hotchkis March

Rick Knoop in the BFG 962, entering turn seven

Rick Knoop: *"As I was catching my teammate Morton, the leader, he was slowing a bit due to engine problems. Team Manager and Owner Jim Busby made the decision that we should continue to run one and two with Morton taking the win. Made for a photo finish, great ad for B.F. Goodrich. Morton and Halsmer had done a great job and it was only fitting that they hung on to win."*

The Baldwin / Kline RX-7 leads a pack of GTP cars

John Morton: *"A long way from when I came here in 1962 to attend Carroll Shelby's driving school and drive the first Shelby Cobra ever built. This was a great win for Goodrich, a great win for Busby and a great win for Porsche, and the greatest thing that's ever happened to me. We actually had five laps on the third place car. a lot of attrition which benefitted us"*

Jim Busby: *"It sure didn't hurt that all these guys (Morton, Halsmer, Knoop and himself) are local guys who know their way around Riverside," "It'll be a sad day for me if Riverside ever closes because this track has meant so much to me and to racing, but if this is the last IMSA race here, I'm sure glad we won it. I ran my first year on this track." "We had a lot of luck today but we also some great preparation," Busby said. "This was a remarkable win for such a new team using street-construction radial tires on our race car. I always thought we'd do it, but I didn't know it would come so soon. It was a tribute to our crews."*

Pete Halsmer: *"I came to Southern California from Indiana in 1970 and raced here as an amateur for about eight years and won a couple of Formula Vee races," he said. "I lived in Huntington Beach and I'd work awhile and race awhile until I finally caught on as a professional driver."*

Jeff Kline: *"In 1985. I drove a GTU RX-7 with Jack Baldwin for the Malibu Grand Prix sponsored and factory supported team, owned by Ira Young, a Canadian real estate developer. An "All Star Team" - Clayton Cunningham was the team manager who would go on to run the Nissan 300ZX factory team and Infinitis at Indy. Dan Binks, who went on to even more success with Corvette, was the crew chief. Baldwin was the 1984 GTU champ.*

Jack and I made a great team, except he was at least seven inches taller than me and eighty pounds heavier. My seat insert looked like a "Barcalounger". This 600k race was a challenge as the GTU class had some of the best drivers in IMSA including Tommy Kendall, Lee Mueller, Bob Earl, Jim Downing, Chris Cord, Steve Millen, Bill Auberlen, Scott Pruett, Bob Bergstrom and Dominic Dobson, probably a few more. Lee Mueller was on the pole in a Mercury Merkur. He was quick, but we didn't think a turbo four banger had much of a chance to finish and he dropped out at 39 laps. The GTU class had 20 entries, making it the largest and most competitive class in the race.

The best attribute of the Mazda rotary was as long as you didn't seriously over rev or get a

piece of foreign material in the intake, you would finish. It is really fun to drive a race car that revs to 14,000 rpm. The race went smoothly, we completed 103 laps and finished two2 laps ahead of another RX7 driven by Tom Kendall and his brother. I truly enjoyed the focus required to drive the car as fast as you could and not crash or break the car. GTU had an extra challenge in that you spend a lot of time looking in your mirror. GTU cars would go down the back straight at Riverside and hit 165 / 170mph but the fastest cars in GTP would hit close to 200mph. Driving a GTU car fast meant you had to judge the closing speed of faster cars and make room for them and not sacrifice lap time. Riverside was very difficult because you had the fast esses and if a few GTP cars were racing for position, there was a chance of getting punted out of the way in their haste to get by. There were 29 DNF's in this race out of 59 starters. We thought this might be the last Riverside. - Turned out there were a few years left.

John Morton and Bob Akin

John Fitzpatrick: *"So about Riverside - The track layout was superb, good for both the drivers and the spectators. The esses were amazingly fast and quite a challenge to take flat. There was a good selection of varying corners that really tested the set up of the car. Les Richter was a great guy and always made us feel welcome and the fans were very enthusiastic.*

When we took delivery of the 956 in early 1983 we flew it out to the workshop in San Diego and did our testing at Riverside. I don't remember the lap times but it was considerably faster than the 935's and stuck like glue to the track. The downforce was so much higher than anything I had previously experienced and after a few laps I was struggling to keep my head up straight. I did get a Can Am win with it, at Road America. I was sad to hear that Riverside had been sold for housing development etc. but I suppose that is the way of the world these days. To sum up, Riverside holds good and bad memories for me, but that's racing."

Ed Swart / David Christian ; BMW M-1

Roy Newsome / Bill McVey; Mazda RX-7

John Kalagian / John Lloyd; March

Frank Honsowetz / Doug Barnhold; 280ZX

Forbes-Robinson / McKitterick; Fabcar

John Klug / Lou Sell; Porsche 935

John Jones / Wally Dallenbach; Mustang

Bob Earl / Dominic Dobson; Fiero

Army great Glenn Davis got caught from behind this time.

Really 'Mr. Outside'

Glenn Davis admittedly has lost a step or two since he and **Doc Blanchard** were terrorizing Army's football opponents in the mid-1940s.

But he was left in an embarrassing position before The Los Angeles Times-Nissan Grand Prix of Endurance auto race in Riverside, Calif., Sunday.

Davis, director of special events for The Times, had finished a meal in his hotel room when, dressed only in his shorts, he opened the door and pushed the tray into the hall. Alas, the door was spring-hinged, and before Davis could react, it closed behind him.

Davis took the tablecloth from the tray and did his best to cover himself. Then he knocked on the door of the adjacent room. A woman answered, and Davis explained his plight. She was wary at first, but she called the desk, and Davis was rescued.

Davis denies it, but as he left, the woman reportedly said, "Now, I know why they call you Mr. Outside."

First and Second - Morton, Halsmer, Knoop (with champagne) and Busby

Motor Racing / Shav Glick

Greenwood Denies That Riverside Will Close

Stories and rumors that Riverside International Raceway will close after this season have been categorically denied by Daniel Greenwood, president of the 28-year-old road-racing facility.

"I would like to put an end, once and for all, to all the stories I have heard, and been asked about, that Riverside International Raceway is not going to operate in 1986," Greenwood said. "We are committed to sales through the entire year, and our contracts with sanctioning bodies, such as NASCAR and SCORE, are firm."

One national motor sports publication intimated that the Times/Nissan Grand Prix of Endurance last April would be the last International Motor Sports Assn. competition at Riverside, and an East Coast newspaper reported that NASCAR had a provisional schedule for 1986 without races at Riverside in June and November.

"As far as NASCAR is concerned, our 1986 season will end at Riverside, just as it will this year," said Jim Foster, vice president of the stock car racing organization, by telephone from Daytona Beach, Fla. "They tell us they're operating through 1986, so we plan to be there."

Greenwood, former vice president of corporate relations for the Los Angeles Olympic Organizing Committee, also heads an RIR team that is searching for a relocation site for 1987 and beyond. Last October, it was announced that the new site would probably be in the Prado basin, near Corona, but recent developments have expanded the search.

"We are studying five sites, three in Riverside County, one in San Bernardino County and one in Los Angeles County," Greenwood said. "The Prado basin site, where we had planned to move, does not look as certain as it did a few months ago.

"At one point, I would have said it was 70-30 that we would build our new facility there, but now I would say it is no better than 50-50. Feasibility studies of Prado are continuing by the county of Riverside, the city of Corona, the (Army) Corps of Engineers and our group, but because of some unexpected problems, we felt we needed to explore other potential new locations."

The San Bernardino site is in Glen Helen, a regional county park about 10 miles northwest of the city of San Bernardino. The Los Angeles County site is reportedly near Magic Mountain in the Newhall-Saugus area.

"We would like to remain in Riverside County, to keep the continuity of the name, but our main commitment is to have a major motor sports complex in Southern California," Greenwood said. "We would like to have an oval, perhaps a mile-and-a-half or two-mile track, as well as a road-race course and a drag strip, plus garage and office space."

Greenwood said he hoped to have a relocation site determined by Sept. 30, either Prado or one of the others. Plans call for the first race at the new location to be the Times-sponsored IMSA endurance race on a road course in April 1987.

SPEEDWAY BIKES—The Nissan American Speedway Final Saturday night at Long Beach Veterans Stadium, is the first qualifying round for U.S. riders that will ultimately lead to the 1985 World Final Aug. 31 in Bradford, England. Five riders will advance to the Overseas Final July 14, also at Bradford. Favorites among the 16 riders Saturday night are six from the 1984 British League season—**Bobby Schwartz, Lance King, Shawn Moran, John Cook, Rick Miller** and **Sam Ermolenke.** King, 21, of Fountain Valley, tied for second place in last year's world final with Denmark's **Hans Nielsen** behind winner **Erik Gundersen** of Denmark. Other qualifiers include **Mike Faria, Brad Oxley, Alan Christian, Keith Chrisco, Mike Curoso, Keith Larsen, Mark Dwyer, Jim Lawson, Gene Woods** and two-time national champion **Kelly Moran,** who has finished fourth in each of the last three world finals. . . . **Shawn Moran** and **Bobby Schwartz** qualified for the World Pairs final by winning a semifinal round last Saturday in England. The finals are set for June 15 in Poland. . . . The Speedway Magazine Cup all-scratch championship is

scheduled Wednesday night at San Bernardino's Inland Speedway. . . **John Cook** will delay his return to England so that he can ride Tuesday night at Ventura.

STOCK CARS—**Jim Robinson,** defending Winston West champion and well on his way to winning more money this season than has ever been won in a single year in the 31-year-old series, will be at Mesa Marin Raceway in Bakersfield for Saturday night's Suncrest Motorhomes 200. The bearded garage owner from North Hollywood has won $12,430 in four races this season and leads **Hershel McGriff** by nine points and rookie **Glen Steurer** of Simi Valley by 14. Robinson won the 1982 Winston West race at Mesa Marin and was second to **Sumner McKnight** last October. . . . Ascot Park has scheduled a quadruple card Sunday night that includes Cuch Motorsports pro stocks, Figure 8s, bomber oval cars and a women's main event. . . . Modifieds will return Saturday night to Saugus Speedway for a 17-event program. Claimer stocks will race Friday night at Saugus. . . . **Dick Shepherd** and **Barry Bradshaw** will continue their pro-mod battle Saturday night at Bakersfield Speedway in Oildale.

SPRINT CARS—There have been 11 different winners in 19 races in the Kraco-California Racing Assn. season. **Brad Noffsinger** has a 19-point lead over **Eddie Wirth,** with **Mike Sweeney** only one behind Wirth, going into Saturday night's feature at Ascot Park. . . . **Bubby Jones,** defending CRA champion, will skip the

Ascot race to drive in a $25,000 winged sprint event at Baylands Raceway in Fremont, Calif.

OFF ROAD—**Roger Mears** will use his new Nissan King Cab desert race truck for the first time Saturday in the annual Baja International in Ensenada. It will be Mears' first desert ride in more than a year. **Neil Woolridge,** three-time South Africa desert motorcycle champion and winner of the Springbok race, will ride a Kawasaki 500 with **Roland Geiger** in the 447-mile race that will start, then end in Ensenada after looping across the peninsula to San Felipe. . . . Only three cars left the starting line last Saturday in Anaheim for the North American leg of the 35,000-mile American. The only American starter was **Jim Arnold** of Garden Grove. The cars are scheduled to return June 20 and leave for the South American leg.

DRAGS—The SoCal Timing Assn. will hold its June speed trials Sunday at El Mirage Dry Lake. This is the SCTA's 40th consecutive season. . . . Riverside International Raceway's monthly program is also scheduled Sunday.

HONORS—**Parnelli Jones, Henry Banks, Joe Boyer** and **Floyd Roberts** were added to Auto Racing's Hall of Fame at the Indianapolis 500 old-timers' dinner. . . . **George Moore** of the Indianapolis Star received the Ray Marquette Memorial Award for his "contributions to auto racing . . . as a journalist and humanitarian."

RIR may not relocate at Glen Helen, or anywhere else

Gary Patton
... County parks director

By KATIE CASTATOR
Sun Sports Writer

Gary Patton would like a firm agreement by November with an acceptable racing concern to build a motor racing complex at Glen Helen Regional Park in Devore.

He doesn't believe, however, that Riverside International Raceway, Inc., will be that party.

"We have four unopened proposals (from candidates) and Riverside is not among them," said Patton, San Bernardino County Regional Parks Department director.

"It's my opinion the Riverside people do not intend to build a race track anywhere."

In February, 1984, Riverside Raceway revealed it would leave its home in Edgemont at the end of the 1986 race season because of the building boom of family dwelling units, which have steadily moved closer to the raceway grounds.

Prado Basin near Corona was originally chosen as a relocate site. But Dan Greenwood, president of RIR, announced in late June that his company had dropped that plan because the area was the home of an endangered bird and the site of an Indian burial grounds.

"They knew there was no way they could build a track in the Prado Basin," Patton said. "Then why did they go to the trouble to attempt to put one there?"

It has been speculated by some racing insiders that RIR never did plan to rebuild. Announcements that they would rebuild were supposedly a smoke screen so race sponsors and sanctioning organizations would not become uneasy about their future in Southern California.

But Greenwood still contends his people are working to find an acceptable location to build, saying that Glen Helen and Albers Hill near Lake Elsinore are among four sites still being considered. He said he was asked not to disclose the other two sites. Indian Dunes north of Los Angeles was dropped from the list because there were too many problems.

"We've been waiting to meet with a couple of San Bernardino County Supervisors on the Glen Helen site," Greenwood said. "I'd say it will be another 30 to 60 days before we make a deal anywhere or know for a certainty what we will do."

Greenwood did admit there is a possibility RIR will be unable to find a suitable location.

"If we cannot find an acceptable site at an appropriate cost we'd then announce publicly we had stopped looking and will stop operations the end of 1986," Greenwood said. "While we intend to build a new facility, we have the race dates, the sanctioning bodies and everything else to consider.

"We could wait until December or January of next year to pick a site and still be open in time (for the 1987 season). But we'd like to make a decision sooner so (in case RIR does disband) somebody else could step in (and pick up the race dates)."

Asked why RIR had not officially submitted a proposal to the County Parks and Recreation Department for the Glen Helen location, Greenwood said that most of the information asked for on the proposal was historical information about racing business and projections for the future.

"For us, a private company, to bare our soul doesn't seem to make sense," he said.

Patton said the proposals from the four candidates will be screened by a committee of seven San Bernardino County people who will be appointed in the next week to 10 days by the County Board of Supervisors.

Riverside Raceway Considers Move to Valencia

Negotiations between Newhall Land and Farming Co. and Riverside International Raceway officials may bring a combined oval-road track and drag strip to the Valencia area by the end of the year.

The now-defunct Indian Dunes off-road facility is one of two sites near Valencia that Riverside officials are considering leasing. Both sites are owned by Newhall Land and Farming.

"We've talked in generalities," said Daniel Greenwood, president of Riverside International Raceway. "The negotiations have been very preliminary. By next week we'll have a clearer idea as to whether it will go forward."

Greenwood said that engineers have seen both sites and deemed them feasible for a racing facility. There are problems, however, with rising property values in the area and poor access roads.

"Property values are obviously an issue," Greenwood said. "The roads are definitely a problem. But we think it can be compensated for."

Robert Wilke, executive vice president of Newhall Land and Farming, confirmed the talks but declined to discuss details.

"'Negotiations' is too strong a word," Wilke said. "Our main discussions have been with county people [about reopening the off-road track]."

The Los Angeles County sites are among several being considered by Riverside officials in the Southland, according to a spokesman. Three others are in Riverside County, and one is in San Bernardino County.

Michelle Pappalardo from Burroughs.

The City lineup: Karen Walker and Teri Rupe, El Camino; Vincent, Chatsworth; Stephanie Remington and Diane Kennedy; Michelle Van Kirk and Kim Green, Cleveland Borrego, Monroe; Diane Lopez and Katrina Garcia, Syl Hernandez and Rosi Castro, Bell; Lisa Bautista and Sus Banning, and Lisa Cantor from North Hollywood.

Information: (818) 341-7314 or (818) 843-2150 ext. 170.

■ Robinson Leads Going Into Mesa Marin

Jim Robinson of Reseda is the leader in the NASCAR Win point standings going into tonight's Suncrest Motorhomes half-mile Mesa Marin track in Bakersfield.

Going into last Sunday's Budweiser 400 at Riverside In Raceway, Robinson was tied with Hershel McGriff of Brida But McGriff had engine problems and was forced to drop out race. Robinson finished 13th overall and second among Win drivers.

The top Winston West finisher was Glen Steurer of Si Steurer finished 11th overall at Riverside and currently Winston West standings. Steurer also will be competing for first-place check at Mesa Marin.

■ Las Vegas Night in Canoga Park

Racing at RIR certain through '86

By KATIE CASTATOR

Prado Dam area dead as site for Riverside raceway

By LARRY HICKS
Sun Staff Writer

Once an apparent certainty, the Prado Dam area near Corona has been killed as the site for a new Riverside International Raceway complex, the company's president said Wednesday.

fered with plans to expand the Riverside raceway, which is east of Riverside near Edgemont.

Greenwood said he guessed about two months ago that the Prado site was going sour.

"We saw it coming," he said. "That's why I've been looking acti

Price Cobb and Rob Dyson won $26,500 driving a Porsche 962 in 1986, followed by Darin Brassfield anf Jochen Mass in another 962. Third was Bruce Leven, Paolo Barilla and Bob Wollek, also in a 962. The Downing / Maffucci Argo Mazda won Camel Light; Jack Baldwin and Jim Miller won GTO in a Camaro and Roger Mandeville won GTU in an RX-7. A horrendous crash involving Lyn St. James, Chip Robinson and Doc Bundy made the news, with fortunately no injuries. Other races include an SCCA regional, a Champion Spark Plug Series race, won by Amos Johnson, and a Sports 2000 event. Read about the supporting races in Volume Two, available in the fall of 2022.

Dyson, Cobb have their day, win Enduro at RIR

LORI SHEPLER / Los Angeles Times

The Porsche 962 of Rob Dyson and Price Cobb negotiates the Riverside track en route to checkered flag at a slow average speed of 95.948 m.p.h.

Rob Dyson: *"Our first time at Riverside; exciting, fast, hot, dusty ... we had a brand new, fresh from the factory ten day old 962, chassis #120, one of the last ones built. Drake Olson had destroyed ours at Atlanta; took a while for a new one to arrive. I was driving, along with Price Cobb. So every practice our crew chief, Pat Smith, was making changes, ride height, shock settings; just setting the car up as we practiced, something usually done in testing. We were running the long course, the last time IMSA would use that (the following year and last year we raced at Riverside, we used the shorter 2.5 mile course) Price qualified well and found we could run at that pace for the entire race. We were second when Price turned the car over to me and, well, it helped that some of our competitors crashed and broke."*

The start

The Busby / Morton 962 DNF'd

Team captain Jim Busby (left inset) and John Morton will drive this Porsche 962 in Sunday's Grand Prix of Endurance at Riverside.

John Hotchkis / Jim Adams; Porsche 962

Gordon Spice / Relly Bellm; Spice Pontiac

Watch this Jim Busby video on the attached DVD

Dyson-Cobb Porsche Endures Amid the Crashes

By SHAV GLICK
Times Staff Writer

RIVERSIDE—A 10-day-old Porsche 962, fresh out of the box from Weissach, West Germany, outlasted the finest long-distance racing machinery in the world Sunday to win the Los Angeles Times/Ford Grand Prix of Endurance.

Car owner Rob Dyson, 39, of Pleasant Valley, N.Y., who was substituting for his regular team driver, and Price Cobb, 31, of Dallas finished the six-hour race at River-

■ *A horrible accident luckily has a not-so-horrible ending. Mike Downey's column, Page 6.*

side International Raceway ahead of three other Porsches. But the German parade was aided by a spectacular crash early in the second hour that destroyed Chevy Corvette and Ford Mustang Probe prototypes and a Jaguar.

In the accident, the Probe of female driver Lyn St. James rolled

■ *For Rick Murray and his crew, Sunday turns out to be the pits. Pat Ray's story, Page 6.*

up and over a fence before crashing upside down in flames, and the Jaguar driven by Chip Robinson took off like an airplane before coming back to earth dancing on its tail like a wave-walking marlin. Miraculously, the drivers, including Doc Bundy, who started it all in the Corvette, walked away from

the scene with nothing more than bruised bodies.

In a later accident, a Chevy Camaro driven by Les Delano of New York, slid through the dirt, pierced a wire fence and rammed into a spectator's camper parked near the second turn. A 12-year-old boy suffered a broken arm and was taken to Riverside Community Hospital.

The accidents caused the pace car to parade around the 3.25-mile course for 90 minutes while crews picked up debris and replaced dam-

Please see RACE, Page 6

Watch the entire race on the attached DVD

Dicing With Death in the Tight Turns at Riverside Raceway

RIVERSIDE—The Corvette was on the left. The Mustang was in the middle. The Jaguar was on the right. All three cars were doing at least 160 m.p.h. as they polished off the 35th lap. All three drivers had just thrown it into fifth gear as they crossed the START/FINISH line of the Times/Ford Grand Prix of Endurance and hummed toward turn No. 1.

There was room for one of them on the curve, maybe two.

Not three.

Doc Bundy, in the 'Vette, thought he had enough room, and thought he had enough varoom. He came up behind Chip Robinson's Jag on the straightaway. "I thought about taking him on the outside. Then I said, 'Well, that's a little risky move.'"

He looked for an opening behind Lyn St. James instead. Bundy knew her Mustang Probe very well. He used to drive that car, last year, before changing sponsors. And the year before that, he drove Robinson's Jag XJR-7. Even won the 1984 Miami Grand Prix with it.

Now they were virtually side by side. Three Sunday drivers. Three road hogs on pavement where honking the horn cannot help.

Bundy wanted by. "The Ford was coming slow off the corners," in his opinion. It also had bumped against his car three times in one turn alone, just before St. James relieved Pete Halsmer at the wheel, Bundy said.

His own car's momentum was considerable and Bundy was braking lightly with his left foot, reluctant to hold back. When the Jag kept to the right, Bundy believed he would rear-end it if he stayed in that lane. So, he veered the 'Vette to the inside.

He was below and left of the Mustang, in its blind spot. The turn was at hand. Bundy felt he had the speed and the space. "I'm through. Clear," he convinced himself.

As the cars banged together, the horror began.

The Mustang swerved wildly to the right, smashing into the restraining wall and bursting into flames. The Jaguar was airborne. It flipped completely, then thrashed on the track like a beached shark. The Corvette spun out of control and crashed into the guard rail. It, too, caught fire.

St. James saw a spray of dirt and fuel against the windshield, sensed the fire behind her as the car overturned, clutched

MIKE DOWNEY

the wheel, "closed my eyes and waited for it to end," she related to a Ford spokesperson later.

When the Mustang came to a rest, upside down, St. James unbuckled her belt and scrambled out, her wrists and ankles throbbing, her helmet and uniform charred. Bundy also got free quickly and ran to her car.

"Are you OK?" he yelled.

"Why did it happen?" St. James asked back. "Why did it happen?"

"I don't know," Bundy said. "I don't know."

It was over, and, in proper auto-racing fashion, it was over in a hurry. A track worker, Charlie Kuhlman, was rushed to a hospital with first- and second-degree burns from fighting the fires. St. James, said the Ford spokesman, Kevin Kennedy, had a bruised foot and: "She's sore and shook up."

But all three drivers walked away.

More than once Sunday, the murmur of

"worst crash I've ever seen" could be heard in the pits and bleachers of Riverside International Raceway. This had been an accident for the ages, or for the 11 o'clock news shows, at least, or for the more gruesome opening moments of "Wide World of Sports."

To see it in person was to feel not only the thrill of danger, but the chill of violent death. You saw those explosions and you told yourself you had just seen somebody die.

You rushed to the scene of the accident, inspected the hole in the wall, examined the twisted wreckage of the three machines and cringed. You saw the metal intestines of the Jaguar dangling over the sides, and the front left tire dislocated to the steering wheel's right. In the garage, six mechanics covered the Jag gently with a sheet, like assistant coroners covering a corpse.

Having seen all that, you could hardly believe it, 70 minutes later, once this arduous six-hour race had resumed, that the driver with whom you were sitting did not have an ache or a pain.

Bundy, 38, a Vietnam veteran from Gainesville, Fla., said almost nonchalantly: "When I hit the wall, I was already on fire.

It seemed like it took me 10 minutes to get out of the car, but it was only a couple of seconds. In racing, we're so used to speed that a fraction of a second seems like a long period of time."

Bundy said he still was not sure who hit who first. He sensed that St. James saw him in her blind spot at the last instant, tapped his car, then caromed into Robinson's.

"If you've got to lay fault, well, I'll accept the fault because I took the riskiest move," Bundy said. "But I thought I had a clear lane, especially with the speed she was traveling . . .

"It's easy to say in retrospect that I should have waited. And those two could have dealt with whatever they had going. But in racing, when there's a hole, you're paid to make the move to the hole. I don't want to point a finger at anybody, because to me, it's just a racing accident."

You wondered if Bundy happened to recall an old, popular song in which a Corvette and a Jaguar sped together into a turn.

"Hey, that's right," he said. "Dead Man's Curve."

That one was just a racing accident, too.

Bob Wollek / Paolo Barilla Porsche 962

Lyn St. James' Ford Probe disintegrates while Chip Robinson's Jaguar tumbles during an IMSA race in Riverside, Calif.

Vic Manuelli: *"I was right behind the horrific wreck where Bundy collided with Lyn St. James and the Jag , four hundred yards back when all hell broke loose. I radioed my pit, drove thru the intense smoke and several more laps under caution. That they all survived was amazing."*

Paul's Buick on pole for six-hour Enduro

Sun News Services

RIVERSIDE — The Buick Hawk driven by John Paul Jr. will start from the pole position in today's six-hour Los Angeles Times-Ford Grand Prix of Endurance Camel GT sports car race.

Paul Jr., 26, of Lawrenceville, Ga., roared around the nine-turn Riverside International Raceway course Friday in a record time of 1 minute, 30.103 seconds. He averaged 129.851 miles per hour, eclipsing his own record, set in 1985 of 1 minute, 32.254 seconds and 126.824 mph.

The second starting position

last International Motor Sports Association Camel GT race at Road Atlanta, pulled a muscle in his back during practice on Friday. Co-driver Doc Bundy qualified the car in the seventh starting position.

The team recruited Camel GTO driver Wally Dallenbach Jr. to replace Van der Merwe, who is consulting a sports medicine specialist in Riverside and will be unable to drive due to a back injury.

Veteran sports car driver Greg Pickett will take Dallenbach's place in the GTO-class Camaro.

In other Saturday activity

ADVERTISING **SPECIAL** SUPPLEMENT

TIMES GRAND PRIX OF ENDURANCE

The Nissan GTP, Number 83, heads into a turn in last year's Los Angeles Times Grand Prix. Top racers this year are, at left, Geoff Brabham, top, and Chip Robinson, and at right, Al Holbert, top, and Price Cobb.

Jeff Kline: *"I was co-driving with Don Bell in his #01 GTP Light Royal-Buick. The car broke after 12 laps and I was out of a ride. Joe Varde was in the #06 Alba Buick and was entered with a co-driver who was also a sponsor. He practiced in the car, but after the race started, he decided he was out of his depth and did not want to drive. Joe was already out driving and his crew chief found me and asked me to take over. When Joe came in after about 75*

minutes, he was surprised to see me get in. Later in the race when I got in for my second stint, I was pulling out of the pits at the same instant that Lyn St. James, Chip Robioson and Doc Bundy got together in a major crash right in front of me. Stuff was flying everywhere and I was happily surprised that all survived.

Later, in the last hour of the race, I was passing the #90 Delano / Petery Camaro in the esses. I was on the inside but the Camaro driver moved over on me and we touched. The Camaro went flying off to the left, hit a bank about 75 yards from the track, jumped the fence and hit a camper car with spectators in it, injuring a twelve year old boy. I was unaware of it until I came around the on next lap and saw the accident and a full course yellow. The spectators sued the driver, not sure how that came out, but we finished 22nd and 5th in GTP Light."

Team That Finishes Together Stays Together

By SHAV GLICK,
Times Staff Writer

Jim Busby has been racing or managing cars on the International Motor Sports Assn. Camel GT circuit since 1975, but the most memorable of his 96 races was last year's Times Grand Prix of Endurance at Riverside. And he didn't even win.

Busby was driving with Rick Knoop in a Porsche 962, but he was also manager of the team that included a companion car driven by John Morton and Pete Halsmer.

Late in the 800-kilometer race, Morton, in car No. 68, was leading. But closing rapidly was the No. 67 car, with Knoop driving. No one else was close. Busby was in the pits waiting for the Morton-Halsmer car to take the checkered flag when he noticed that Knoop was gaining with every lap. Busby, the team manager, had to make a decision.

Should he let the car he had driven win by signaling Morton to slow? Or should he signal Knoop to let up and allow Morton to win? Or should he put up the "race for it" sign and let them fight it out?

"It was the hardest thing I've ever had to do around a race track," Busby said. "A lot of people watching figured we were slowing down the 68 car so we could have a nice picture of our two cars for a poster, but that was far from the case.

"I had just turned over the 67 car to Knoop when the engine in the 68 car blew with four laps left. Knoop was picking up 17 seconds a lap, but the race really belonged to Morton and Halsmer. They had done a better job and deserved the win.

"What we didn't want was to have them start racing one another and maybe knock each other out of the race so we decided to radio Knoop and tell him not to pass the 68 car. We showed '68-67' on the pit board for them both to see. We didn't want them tangling and letting some other car win. We felt a 1-2 finish would be a whole lot better than 0-0."

The margin of victory, 0.138 seconds, was the closest finish in IMSA history.

Now Busby is planning strategy again as manager of the two-car team

Busby Had to Make a Tough Choice Last Year; Defending Result (Victory) May Be Tougher

for Sunday's Times/Ford six-hour race, but he has made one significant change. This year, he will share a car with Morton.

"No, it wasn't a case of if you can't beat 'em, join 'em," Busby said, laughing. "It just worked out that way. We will have Jochen Mass and Darin Brassfield in the other car, so we feel good about defending our championship at Riverside with two solid cars."

The Busby team's fortunes will have to change, however, if there is to be another 1-2 finish. Crashes have plagued the team in the young 1986 season, especially the No. 68 car.

Jan Lammers crashed 68 in the 19th hour of the 24 Hours of Daytona, destroying the chassis.

There was no No. 68 at Miami while a replacement from Germany was awaited, and it no sooner arrived than Busby rolled it during a prerace test at Sebring. It could not be repaired in time for the race and was withdrawn.

Two weeks ago, at Atlanta, Mass and Brassfield drove it to a sixth-place finish, but it wasn't handling properly, apparently still suffering from its Sebring crash.

No. 67, which Busby and Morton will drive at Riverside, has been only slightly more fortunate. It finished third at Daytona after leading for more than 11 hours.

Miami, though, was double trouble. Busby crashed it during practice. Three days of around-the-clock repair work had it ready for the race but then Brassfield crashed while running third.

In the Sebring 12-hour race, it finished second, eight laps behind the Porsche 962 of Bob Akin, Jo Gartner and Hans Stuck.

"I was very uncomfortable in the 67 car that day," Busby said after driving less than an hour of the once-around-the-clock race. "I was still somewhat rattled from flipping the 68 car, so I withdrew myself from the race. I'm glad to get credit for finishing second, but Morton and Brassfield did all the work."

At Atlanta, where a Corvette driven by Sarel van der Merwe and Doc Bundy snapped Porsche's 16-race IMSA win streak, Busby and Morton finished fifth.

"We have two fully sound cars again," Busby said. "Both ran well at Atlanta, so we're back up to full strength. We expect to be double tough on our home track."

Busby, of Laguna Beach, and Morton, of El Segundo, were weaned on Riverside's high-speed 3.25-mile road course.

"Riverside is very special to me," Busby said. "My dad took me to my first race there in 1957, when I was 14. We sat up in Turn 6 and I thought, 'Gee, I've got to do this some day.'

"I have tested there as long as I can remember and I won there in '81 with John Fitzpatrick, so I have a lot of personal attachment to the track."

Morton's roots at Riverside go back to 1962 when he attended Carroll Shelby's driving school and drove the first Shelby Cobra.

"The Riverside track is the first thing I remember seeing when I came to California," Morton recalled. "I had a special feeling, learning to drive a race car there, and it's never gone away. Every time I go there, I have that special feeling.

"It has been the focal point of my career. I have won several races there and last year's was certainly the most important one I ever won. When I heard the track was going to close, I wanted to win the final IMSA race there and that's what I thought I'd done last year. But now there's another race and I still want to win the last one. So that means we'll have to win again Sunday."

The Porsches should benefit from the return of the Times race to six hours from the much shorter 600 kilometers of last year, which lasted only 3 hours 27 minutes.

"Riverside is good for the Porsches because the course is so long," Morton said. "That 1.1-mile backstretch lets the Porsches really wind up. It is a very difficult course because it is so

fast. Ground effects make it almost like racing on a speedway.

"Up through the esses [a series of switchback turns] there is very little letting off the throttle, so the element of high speed never goes away. It presents us a danger not found elsewhere on a road circuit. Because of that, you can never relax."

Busby sees his main competition coming from another Porsche 962, driven by Al Holbert and Derek Bell, last year's IMSA champions.

"Al is always tough to beat," Busby said. "He's a great driver and has a great team. He's never won an IMSA race at Riverside, so he'll be bearing down extra hard, but we feel confident that we are capable of beating him.

"This year you can't discount the other makes, either. For years IMSA races were a Porsche show, but this year the Chevy, the Jaguars, the Buick and the Ford are all tough.

"The pace will be much faster than last year, even though the race is longer. I think it will make for the wildest and most competitive road race seen at Riverside since the old Can-Am series in the early '70s."

Busby, 43, has won six Camel GT races, the first at Ontario Motor Speedway in 1976 while driving a Porsche Carrera. That same year he was named IMSA Driver of the Year. He also has two class victories in the 24 Hours of LeMans, in a Group 5 car in 1978 and with Doc Bundy in the IMSA GT class in 1982.

When BF Goodrich decided to field a two-car IMSA team last year, the tire company sought out Busby to manage it. One of his first decisions was to name himself as one of the drivers.

"I'm like Holbert in that I manage the team and drive, too," he said. "I love to drive and I don't want to step down. Not too far down the street I'll probably have to quit, but not right now.

"Some of the decisions I have to make, like the one last year at Riverside, are tough, but I always want to do what's best for the team first.

"I want all of us to win. And if one car can't win, I'd like to see them finish second. We did it last year—and even if we weren't trying for it, made a hell of a poster, didn't it?"

1987 was the last year for IMSA at Riverside. Using the shorter 2.5 mile course for the first time, John Morton and Hurley Haywood won in a Jaguar XJR7, followed by the Chip Robinson / Al Holbert Porsche 962. First place payoff was $36,500. In third was another 962, driven by Darin Brassfield and Wally Dallenbach Jr, First in Camel Light was the Jeff Kline / Don Bell Spice. In a separate 300 kilometer race GTO / GTU race, Chris Cord won GTO in a Toyota; Amos Johnson was the GTU winner in an RX-7. Additional events included a Sports 2000 race, won by Randy McDaniel and a three hour Firehawk race on Saturday won by Parnelli Jones in a Nissan 300ZX and an International Sedan series race on Sunday, won by Parker Johnstone in an Acura. Read about the supporting races in Volume Two; available in the fall of 2022.

John Morton: *"This was a very special win for me, having started my career at Riverside at Shelby's Driving School. This was to be the last IMSA race at Riverside and the last Jaguar race for Bob Tullius. The Chip Robinson / Al Holbert Porsche had led most of the race and we were fortunate to be able to pass them with two laps to go and hang on for the win."*

Grand Prix decided in closing seconds

RIVERSIDE (AP) — The winner of the Los Angeles Times Grand Prix of Endurance wasn't determined until the final seconds of the race at Riverside International Raceway.

John Morton and Hurley Haywood, in a Jaguar XJR7, were victorious Sunday.

Robinson. It was the first win for the Jaguar team this year.

Haywood, 38, of Ponte Vedra, Fla., had driven the first part of the event.

It was the fourth second-place finish at Riverside for Holbert in the past eight years. Holbert, the defending Camel GT

and Wally Dallenbach, Jr., with Rob Dyson and Price Cobb fourth in another Porsche.

Don Bell and Jeff Kline won the Camel Lights class race in their Pontiac Fiero GTP.

Earlier in the day, actor Paul Newman

spin in turn seven of the 2.54-mile Riverside road course, but at the finish, his Dan Gurney-built Toyota held off Tommy Riggins' Chevrolet Camaro for the win. It was Cord's sixth career victory in 78 starts.

Al Holbert Is Denied Again at Riverside— on Next-to-Last Lap

By SHAV GLICK
Times Staff Writer

RIVERSIDE—Al Holbert has been coming to Riverside International Raceway almost since it was built in the late '50s.

He watched his father, Bob, win here. And he has been here every year since the International Motor Sports Assn. came to Riverside in 1975.

He has won 47 Camel GT races, more than any IMSA driver in history. He has won at every IMSA track except Riverside.

He finished second here in 1979, 1982, 1983 and 1984.

He has often said that the one

■ *Newman crashes: Paul Newman is uninjured in a crash in the GTO-GTU race won by Chris Cord. Shav Glick's story, Page 12.*
■ *They're organized: Bob Tullius' Jaguar racing team is fine tuned for victory. Tracy Dodds' story, Page 12.*

wood beat the Porsche 962 of Holbert and Robinson by 2.7 seconds.

It was a particularly sweet win for Jaguar owner Bob Tullius, as the other $200,000 team car had crashed during practice here last Tuesday

AL SEIB / Los Angeles Times

Jaguar being driven by John Morton holds on to a slim lead as it goes on to win The Times Grand Prix of Endurance by just 2.7 seconds.

Vic Manuelli: *"We lost a multi disc clutch, the crew pulled the gear box out as I jumped into my tow vehicle and drove to closest auto parts store for a Ford truck clutch assembly to install. Lost a hell of a lot of laps, but finished."*

301

Winning Team: Here's an Organization That's Organized

By TRACY DODDS
Times Staff Writer

The pit crew works quickly to send the Tullius Jaguar back into the endurance race in winning time.

LADIES...
Start Your Engines!

Gregg Dallenbach St. James

Times Grand Prix of Endurance
April 24-26, Riverside Int'l Raceway

Top female race drivers Lyn St. James, Deborah Gregg and Robin Dallenbach will be battling wheel-to-wheel against the best male endurance drivers in the world at the Times Grand Prix of Endurance.

They'll be part of a new format at Riverside Raceway featuring, on Sunday, an International Sedans race (9:45 a.m.), 300K battle for GTO/GTU cars (10:45) and, at 1 p.m., the 500K Times Grand Prix of Endurance for the 200mph GTP and Camel Lights cars.

This Weekend!

Times Grand Prix of Endurance
April 24-26, 1987
Riverside International Raceway

David Hobbs / Bruce Leven; Porsche 962 Ninth Overall - Sixth in GTP

UCLA Junior Will Compete in Two Events of Times Grand Prix at Riverside

By SHAV GLICK,
Times Staff Writer

Jack Baldwin won consecutive International Motor Sports Assn. GTU driving championships in 1984 and 1985, and Tom Kendall won in 1986.

So, in racing's version of the rich get richer, they will become teammates Saturday in a Chevrolet Camaro for three hours in the Parnelli Jones Firestone Firehawk race during the Los Angeles Times Grand Prix of Endurance at Riverside International Raceway.

Kendall is only 20, and Baldwin will be 39 next month, but Baldwin is the big kid of the team.

"When I cut myself, I bleed Chevy motor oil," Baldwin likes to say. "When Chevy asked me if I'd like to drive in the Firehawk series, they told me I could pick my teammate. Well, when I heard that Tom Kendall was switching to a Chevy, who else would I have chosen? I like the idea of having No. 1 on the side of my car."

Kendall, who, at 19, won last year's Firehawk championship as well as the GTU title, drove a turbocharged Nissan 300ZX last year with Max Jones. The winning car will also be at Riverside but will be driven by Kendall's brother Bart and his father Chuck, other members of the family racing team from La Canada-Flintridge.

Both Baldwin and Kendall will be doing double duty this weekend. On Sunday, both will be driving in the combined GTO-GTU race of 300 kilometers. Baldwin will be in a Chevy Camaro, naturally, in the GTO class, while Kendall will be in the winningest car in IMSA history, the red, white and blue No. 75 CCR-prepared Mazda RX-7 that has won four GTU championships (Jim Downing in 1982, Baldwin in 1984 and 1985, and Kendall last year).

An identically prepared Mazda will be driven by older brother Bart, a 21-year-old senior at Stan-

Tom Kendall

ford majoring in economics and communications.

Tom Kendall, who became the answer to a racing trivia question last year when he (1) became the first driver to win two IMSA championships in a single season, and (2) became the youngest driver to win any IMSA championship, is a junior at UCLA majoring in economics and business.

This year he is pursuing both championships, but is also branching out.

During the Long Beach Grand Prix three weeks ago, he drove in his first Trans-Am race and finished second behind Scott Pruett in a three-year-old Mercury Capri that his father used to drive.

"It was quite a boost in horsepower for me, but I got a kick out of it," Kendall said. "My GTU car puts out about 300 horsepower and the Trans-Am car was almost 600 so it was quite a difference. I was pleased with my finish considering it was a last-minute deal we threw together."

Kendall qualified third—the first nonturbo car—and ran in the top five for 48 of 60 laps. He moved into second place on lap 50 when Elliott

Forbes-Robinson dropped out, but he had to fight Bruce Jenner for second place.

"I was falling apart," Kendall said. "At the end, my hood was lifting up on the straightaways, and my transmission temp was off the gauge. I just kept going, and finally got to the end. I'd like to try some more when they don't conflict with my other racing."

Kendall also wants to run in the Sports Car Club of America's Escort Endurance series, a showroom stock class similar to the Firehawk series. However, the opening race is Saturday at Sears Point Raceway, north of San Francisco.

"I tried to figure out some way I could drive half the race at Riverside, turn the car over to Baldwin and fly to Sears Point, but it just didn't work out," Kendall said with a smile. The Riverside 3-hour race starts at 3 p.m. and the Sears Point 6-hour enduro at 4:15 p.m.

If Baldwin had a Chevy waiting at Sears Point, he's also the kind of a guy who would have tried to figure out a way to drive in both races.

"I'm just the classic hot-rod kid chasing a dream," Baldwin said. "On the other hand, I'm only in racing for one thing, and that's the money. But that doesn't mean what it sounds like. What that means is that the more races I run, the more money I make.

"I'll run anything—as long as it's a Chevy. When I was a kid growing up in Florida, I wouldn't even let a Ford in my driveway."

Kendall, on the other hand, isn't as particular. He'll drive anything, as long as it has four wheels.

"I've made a point of getting as much experience as I can in different kinds of cars," he said. "Not only does it accelerate learning, but in this business one can never tell which door opportunity will knock on. And experience gives you something intelligent to say when you open the door."

When the door opens, Kendall

will be ready. He maintains a B average at UCLA between races.

Kendall grew up around race cars driven by his father. In 1981, when he was 14, Tom was on the crew when his dad and Dennis Aase won the GTO division of the Sebring 12 hour race in a Carrera and Road America in a BMW.

Both Tom and Bart will be driving in their third Times enduro. Together, they finished second in 1985 in the GTO class and last year Tom was fifth in the GTU Mazda and Bart was fourth, driving with his father, in a Camel Lights Mazda Lola. Tom has also won the last two Firehawk races at Riverside.

"We consider Riverside as our home track," Tom said. "Both Bart and I are familiar with the track and that helps when you're in traffic, and there are so many cars in the Firehawk race that we'll see some pretty heavy traffic. What I want to do is to translate my success in Saturday's race into the GTU race."

Kendall is second, six points behind John Finger and a Mazda, after three races in defense of his GTU championship. He finished fourth at Daytona, second at Miami and fourth at Sebring.

"In Miami I was leading on the last lap when Luis Mendez ran over the back of me and let Finger get by, and at Sebring I had a big lead when I got in a pit accident with Danny Sullivan when he was driving A. J. Foyt's Porsche. That's two races we should have won."

If you're wondering, there's another Kendall coming along. John, 12, races motocross and plans to race karts in the near future.

Claire, the Kendalls' wife and mother, says she isn't planning on racing, but just in case, she graduated from the Bob Bondurant School of High Performance Driving at Sears Point.

"When I went to Bondurant's school, my mom went with me," Tom said. "She passed me once, but I had to put her down. It was because I ran out of gas."

Jeff Kline: "In 1987 I came to Riverside certain this was to be the last race there. We thought the bulldozers were due very soon after this event so this was the race everyone wanted to win. It was 500 kilometers (312 miles), using the short 2.54 mile ourse. I was driving the Pontiac Spice GTPL. formerly Camel Light; slightly smaller cars limited to three liters, sponsored by AT&T Computers and Collins & Aikman, a GM supplier. Everything was first class; my co-driver was Don Bell, a very good teammate. The team was very professional and most of the crew came from the UK and the Spice team in Group C. I didn't realize it at the time, but 1987 would be the pinnacle of my career. We had an exceptional year by any standard. winning six races. I was on the pole 15 times set 15 lap records and set 13 fastest race laps and 13 racing lap records

The Riverside short course was great fun and as this race was only for GTP and GTPL, I didn't have to dodge those pesky GTU cvars (I was once one !!). There were 21 entries, 12 were GTPL. There were many great drivers in GTPL including Jim Downing, Skeeter McKitterick, Charles Morgan, Steve Durst and Mike Brockman. I was able to put the car on the pole and set a GTPL record. Don started the race and had a great race with Steve Durst in the Jiffy Lube Spice Pontiac. Fuel was good for about an hour and the plan was that I would get in at the first stop and finish the race, about 2 hours more.

When Don came in, the Jiffy Lube Spice had about a 40 second lead. I got in and Mike Brockman got in the Jiffy Lube car. I drove qualifying time laps for the next ninety minutes and caught Mike at turn six and passed him easily. We finished sixth overall, first in class and about thirty seconds in front of Mike and Steve. I set fastest race lap. It was one of the best times I ever had in a race car."

Chip Robinson / Al Holbert Porsche 962 - Second overall

Chip Robinson, quoted in the L.A. Times - *"I've has not been back to Riverside since last years crash, not even to test. He and Holbert will start work Friday when the track opens for practice. Several changes have been made since last year's six hour race, which was run on the full 3.25-mile course. This year the race will be approximately three hours long and will be run on the 2.54-mile short course that eliminates Turn eight and cuts almost in half the long back straightaway. Robinson applauds both changes.*

"Riverside is a dangerous race track," he said. "And what I'm saying has nothing at all to do with my accident last year. Any time you're at a dangerous race track, the least amount of time you spend on it the better. Three hours is twice as good as six hours. "I don't know of any track in the country, probably the world, where conditions are as dangerous as they are up through the esses (a series of quick right- and left-hand turns between Turns two and six) where people go off into the dirt and send up a cloud of dust that totally obscures a driver's vision. "You can be going 170 to 180 m.p.h. up there when almost without warning, you can't see a thing. You don't know what's up ahead but you can't stop, or even slow down much, for fear you'll get rammed from behind. "To me, it's inexcusable that nothing has been done about it in all the years Riverside has been there. I don't know of any other track with that problem. You would think they would plant grass, or pave it, or put in some sand pits, or something. It's so potentially hazardous that it seems obvious to me that something should be done." Robinson went into the esses "blindfolded," as he put it, in the 1985 race. He didn't like it then and he doesn't like facing the possibility again this year.

"Dangerous or not, I have to approach Riverside the same way I approach any race track," Robinson said. *"I have to go as fast as I can to win the race. That's what Al Holbert hired me to do, to win. So far, this season has been a little disappointing."*

Paul Newman

Doc Bundy

John Hotchkis

Brian Redman / Chris Kneifel - Qualified Sixth / Finished 17th Overall / 8th in GTP

Steve Durst / Mike Brockman; Spice

Pete Halsmer / Scott Pruett; Mustang GTP

Brian Redman / Chris Kneifel; Porsche 962

John Hotchkis / Jim Adams; Porsche 962

Howard Cherry / Chip Mead; Fabcar

Doc Bundy; Corvette GTP

Jim Downing / John Maffucci; Argo

Elliot Forbes Robinson; Nissan GTP

Lyn St. James; Mustang

Les Lindley; Camaro

Fred Staffilino: Fiero

Tom Gloy; Mustang

Mike Downs; Firebird

Paul Newman; Nissan 300ZX

Tom Kendall; Mazda

Vic Manuelli; Capri

The racetrack we couldn't kill

Riverside to continue for 10 months, maybe longer

Riverside isn't dead. Reports of its death, too, were greatly exaggerated.

After our "Riverside Requiem" cover story by Pete Lyons (AW, July 25), we received dozens of letters from readers reminiscing about the loss of their track. One letter, from Ed Ewegen of Costa Mesa, Calif., began, "I've endured at least five 'official' last races at Riverside ..."

Well, Ed, it's not over yet.

Rumors of Riverside's miraculous recovery arrived in the mail in the form of a press release from the Skip Barber Racing School. There it was. For immediate release: "The 15th location (of the school) with a base operation at Riverside International Raceway beginning Nov. 11, 1988."

A call to Sue Little, operations manager at Riverside, clarified the situation: "Yes, we've seen the end of 'major' motorsports, but we'll continue limited operations for at least 10 months. That will include the driving school, test sessions, club racing and possibly Cal Club SCCA events.

"We're talking to Cal Club right now," Little noted. "But we'll definitely continue

Riverside survives despite the bull(dozers)

club racing—the Porsche Owners Club, the Alfa Romeo Club—hosting non-spectator events. This is something we're able to do to support them."

Only phase one of the project that impinges on Riverside is underway. It affects a small section of the old track from Turn Eight to the Bosch bridge. Downhill from Turn Six to Seven, the track has been extended back to the right-hander at Nine, shortening the course, but lengthening its life.

But there's no word on how long Riverside will be able to continue operations. "Ten months, that's all we're predicting now," said Little. Are you listening, Ed? ∎

AUTOWEEK OCTOBER 31, 1988

Fact - A few SCCA regionals were held in 1989 as well as Skip Barber schools. The last driving school was held in May, 1990, using a shortened section of the remaining track. Rocky Moran recalls testing the AAR GTP Toyota in the fall of 1989 on a small portion of track still remaining. Unfortunately the GTP Toyotas never got to race at Riverside.

Chapter Eight - Formula One

Formula One came to Riverside on a warm, almost hot, November in 1960, after an unsuccessful appearance at Sebring the year before. Sebring organizer Alec Ullman had hoped that the move might increase interest; in fact, with the championship already decided, some teams chose to ignore it, notably Ferrari, and the L.A. Times opted to not participate. The crowd, said Ullman, was a disappointing 25,000. Sterling Moss qualified on the pole in a Lotus Climax and won, followed by Innes Ireland and Bruce McLaren. The supporting races included formula juniors, won by Walt Hansgen in a Cooper BMC, with Bill Krause in a Lotus Ford second and two classes of sedans, with Hansgen winning with a Jaguar and Jim Parkinson in an Austin.

MOSS WINS U.S. GRAND PRIX

Pit Stops Slow Brabham As Ireland Takes 2nd

By DENNIS SHATTUCK

RIVERSIDE, Calif.—If Stirling Moss really did have a mechanical jinx, he obviously left it in England when he departed for the second Grand Prix of the USA. Moss, the fastest man in racing today, ran flawlessly for 75 laps to win the U.S. GP in relatively easy fashion Nov. 20 at the Riverside International Raceway.

Moss may have wished off a tiny portion of his noted ill fortune onto World Champion Jack Brabham, however. Brabham, slowed by two quick pit stops, just couldn't regain enough ground to challenge Moss and finished in fourth place. A

Moss Wins U.S. Grand Prix; Ireland 2nd, McLaren 3rd

STIRLING MOSS
. . . front runner

By JERRY DIAMOND

RIVERSIDE, Nov. 20. —Stirling Moss of London closed the 1960 world championship racing season here today with a brilliant win in the Grand Prix of the United States.

The cocky 31 year old British champion ran a front running race in a Rob Walker team Lotus for 70 of the 75 laps to finish 38 seconds ahead of Innes Ireland of England, also piloting a Lotus.

Third went to Bruce Mc-Laren of New Zealand, driv-

pit stops. He finally finished fourth.

For the crowd of 25,000, the 275 mile feature lacked much of the excitement usually associated with America's only championship Formula I contest.

Brabham led the 23 car field off the grid, followed by Moss, Dan Gurney, Ireland and John Surtees. On the third lap, Joakim Bonnier of Sweden moved his BRN into fourth spot behind Gurney.

On the fifth lap, Brabham's Cooper spurted flames on the back street and the cautious Aussie pulled into the pit, yielding the lead to Moss.

Brabham returned seconds

breakdown would foil his attempt to win the feature.

Holding a six second lead after 15 laps, the sure-handed, 11 year veteran increased his advantage to 14 seconds after 25 laps, then 22 seconds after 40 laps.

NEVER PUSHED

Moss admitted that he never pushed once Brabham made his first stop.

"I don't like to say I stroked the car for the entire run but I never really opened it up," the Britisher said.

Lap statistics upheld Moss's brief summary of strategy. Not once in the 2 hour, 28 minute marathon did his Lo-

Santa Monica driver placed sixth.

In the preliminary event for compacts, Wally Hansgen headed a one-two sweep of the 100 mile race for Jaguar. Augie Pabst, driving the other Briggs Cunningham owned Jaguar entry, finished second.

1—Stirling Moss, Great Britain, Lotus; 2—Innis Ireland, Great Britain, Lotus; 3—Bruce McLaren, New Zealand, Cooper; 4—Jack Brabham, Australia, Cooper; 5—Joakim Bonnier, Sweden, BRN; 6—Phil Hill, United States, Cooper; 7—Jim Hall, United States, Lotus; 8—Roy Salvadori, Great Britain, Cooper; 9—Wolfgang von Trips, Germany, Cooper-Maserati; 10—Chuck Daigh, United States, Scarab; 11—Pete Lovely, United States, Cooper-Ferrari; 12—Oliver Gendebien, Belgium, Cooper; 13—Howart Crane, United States, Maserati; 14—Henry Taylor, Great Britain, Cooper; 15—Maurice Trintignant, France,

Riverside Brings Formula I Racing to Southland

By PAUL WALLACE

The U.S. Grand Prix at Riverside Nov. 20 will bring to the West for the first time an International Formula 1 race.

This is quite a big thing for Southland racing fans. But I have been surprised at how few — including many sports car nuts — really know just what Formula I racing is.

Formula I is the highest refinement of automobile road racing. A Formula I race is to the best modified sports car meet what thoroughbred

0-10 FOR FREE—

racing is to quarter horses in the turf world.

A sports car—even a full-house modified machine — must be equipped so it could be licensed to drive on the streets.

Such competitive sporting autos as the Birdcage Maserati, would offer ineffective, if not impossible, around-town transportation. But it still must be equipped with at least two seats, a spare tire, a battery, lighting and generating accessories and fenders.

A Formula I or grand prix car is hampered by no such weight-adding, power-sapping paraphernalia. It is 100 per

CLASSIC MASERATI FORMULA I CAR ... Riverside Entry

Beach's Danny Jones the 1960 California Racing Association sprint car championship last weekend at Ascot.

Jones took over the lead in CRA's season capper when his arch rival, Don Davis, pitted for fuel on the 80th lap. Then he came around to find a tow truck, on the track to push a stalled car, right in his path. Jones had to hit the wall to miss it.

Out of the race, he was given Louis Vasel's mount to finish the chase. But with the machine running way back in the field, it was a futile gesture.

MOSS LEADS QUALIFIERS FOR GRAND PRIX AT RIVERSIDE

BY DICK HYLAND
Times Staff Representative

RIVERSIDE — A modern bit of the old world will be transplanted here today when the 75-lap Grand Prix of the United States is run over the 3.275 mile Riverside Raceway.

Twenty-five of the same great drivers and the same fast Formula One cars that have raised road racing enthusiasm to the point of madness in Europe will line up on the starting grid for the green flag at 2 p.m.

A half hour of ceremonies will precede the big race. Prior to these, at 12 noon, a 30-lap compact-sedan race will be held.

Moss Timed in 1:54.4

On the front row today will be England's Stirling Moss, Australia's Jack Brabham and Riverside's own Dan Gurney, on the basis of Saturday's qualifying times.

Moss was the fastest in a

Lurani trophy, Hansgen won $1,000.

Fourteen of the top road racing drivers in the world for 1960 are scheduled to be among the starters in the Grand Prix. They include world champion Brabham, who has compiled a record never equalled in the sport's history. The 1959 champion, he has won five of the eight national Grand Prix races this year.

Brabham, a practical Australian automotive engineer, will drive a car he helped design, a Cooper-Climax. So will Bruce McLaren, New

Cyclones Top COP, 14-6

STOCKTON — The Iowa State Cyclones Saturday night defeated the College of the Pacific Tigers, 14-6, on two second half touchdowns.

Zealand runner-up for the world title. It is estimated that all of the cars in the Grand Prix cost in the $30,000-$40,000 range to build.

Formula One cars are ultra streamlined single seaters without starters, headlights or fenders, have four and five speed gear boxes that assist the drivers to drop from 180 m.p.h. to 40 m.p.h. and back up again in a matter of yards. Their fuel is limited to 100/100 octane commercial aviation gasoline. Their engine sizes are limited to 152½ cubic inches.

Entries by car number:
1—Jack Brabham (Australia), Cooper.
2—Bruce McLaren (New Zealand), Cooper.
3—Ron Flockhart (England), Cooper.
4—Stirling Moss (England), Lotus.
5—Tony Brooks (England), Cooper.
7—Olivier Gendebien (Belgium), Cooper.
8—Henry Taylor (England), Cooper.
9—Phil Hill (U.S.A.), Cooper.
10—Innes Ireland (England), Lotus.
11—John Surtees (England), Lotus.
12—Jim Clark (England), Lotus.
14—Roy Salvadori (England), BRM.
15—Joakim Bonnier (Sweden), BRM.
16—Dan Gurney (U.S.A.), BRM.
17—Graham Hill (England), BRM.
18—Maurice Trintignant (France), Cooper-Maserati.
19—Ian Burgess (England), Cooper-Maserati.
20—Bob Drake (U.S.A.), Maserati.
21—Brian Naylor (England), Maserati.

Brabham leads Gurney and Moss

GENUINE TREAT is in store for Southern Californians when they are introduced to Grand Prix Formula 1 type of racing at Riverside Raceway, Sunday, Nov. 20. It's the 2nd US Grand Prix, a world championship 250-miler, the 1st of which was staged last year at Sebring, Fla. Above is start of that race. Starting grid in top photo shows, from left, the 3 Coopers of the late Harry Schell, world champion Jack Brabham, and Stirling Moss. No. 2 in 2nd row is Tony Brooks, Ferrari. At start (lower photo), Brabham (8) and Moss (7) jump into the lead, with Bruce McLaren (9, Cooper), the eventual winner, coming up fast on the inside (far left). Best F1 drivers and cars in the world are entered at Riverside, where compact and Formula Junior races are set for Saturday, Nov. 19. (MOTORACING photos by Gus V. Vignolle and Jack Brady)

Frank Shefffield: "My favorite Stirling Moss at The 1960 US Grand Prix incident. I was Jack-of-all-specialties at Turn Seven on Wednesday or Thursday. As the only one there: I was Observer, Flagman, Turn Marshal, and Emergency Crew, all in one. I had a headset, a fire extinguisher, and a set of flags.. By Sunday I had promoted myself through flagman at several different turns to Turn Marshal at Eight. Near the end of the race, Moss was a minute or so ahead of the second place car, Innes Ireland, and with about four laps to go I reckoned he (and I, and everyone else) was bored and marking time to the finish. I had been using the blue flag ("look out for overtaking traffic") conscientiously for the entire run. I just casually strolled a step or two closer to the course and flipped the flag out so Moss could see it. He did, and I saw him give a quick look in his mirrors and nod his head. I thought, "Ho, good joke!"*

Next time he came by he was travelling perceptibly faster than in the immediately previous laps, and at just a critical point, he was out of shape and his car was sliding right at me! I jumped and scrambled, and he gathered it up and motored around, head back and laughing. Ho, better joke."

HAPPY TEAM—Mary and Alec Ulmann, who make up an unusual man-and-wife combo for sports car racing promotions, stage the 250-mile World Championship for Formula 1 cars at Riverside Nov. 20.

It's Stirling Moss in a Breeze!

STIRLING MOSS of Great Britain whips the Rob Walker Lotus-Climax around turn 6 at Riverside Intl. Raceway on his way to victory in U.S. Grand Prix, Nov. 20. He took the lead on lap 5 when Jack Brabham, Cooper-Climax, made a pit stop, and was neverheaded from there on. Other photos on Page 1 and 5. (Photo by Bill Norcross)

READY TO GO—Top drivers in this weekend's U.S. Grand Prix at Riverside are welcomed by Carroll Shelby, right. From left, are: Henry Taylor, John Surtees, Roy Salvadori, Innes Ireland, Tony Brooks.

Dan Gurney; BRM leads Jack Brabham; Cooper Climax

Grand Prix Called Brilliant, Fascinating

By PAUL WALLACE

The past weekend's U.S. Grand Prix at Riverside Raceway was even more impressive than I had expected.

The Formula 1 cars—the synthesis of 60 years of automobile development — are magnificent racing machines.

An amusing sidelight was to see these drivers in to the track on the public roads from their temporary garages in Riverside as a Morris Minor, entered in the sedan race, was trundled in on a fancy trailer.

The European Grade 1 drivers in GP cars are as much artists as craftsmen and watching the combination made it clear why grand prix racing breeds such a devoted afficionado clan.

* * * *

ADD TO THESE ingredients the color, excitement and drama of a world championship event, the most refined form of road racing, and you have a show of brilliance and fascination.

The cars do everything noticeably better than sports racers and the drivers are able to realize their potential for blindingly fast motoring to a higher degree in them.

The devotees the race brought to Riverside from far parts of the world were a marked contrast to local sports car types who often seem to be more conscious of their own impression on each other than of the race itself.

The people who follow the Formula I circuit around the globe—the real connoisseurs—were as happy and excited as kids at a birthday party, enjoying themselves hugely and not at all shy of showing it.

After my exposure to the grand prix' glamor and warmth, its Coopers and Lotuses, its Brabhams and Masses and Irelands and the Count Giovanni Lurunis and Gregor Grants, I may be spoiled for a time for local sports car events.

* * * *

WITH A BIG weekend of football games and too little space for them all in the sports section, the race got abbreviated treatment here Monday.

So, late or not, I'd better recap some of the details lost to the blue pencil in my Monday stories.

Stirling Moss in Rob Walker's dark blue Lotus won

MOSS FLYING LOW AT RIVERSIDE
Eventual U. S. Grand Prix winner Stirling Moss of England in the No. 5 Lotus overtakes three cars in Turn 7, including the Cooper of Brian Naylor (No. 21), the Scarab (No. 23) of Long Beach's Chuck Daigh and the Cooper-Maserati of Wolfgang von Trips.—(Staff photos by Bryan Hodgson.)

BRM CARS IN FORMATION
The BRMs of Jo Bonnier (foreground) and Riverside's Dan Gurney were very fast but proved predictably unreliable. The machinery in the tail is a disc brake attached to the transmission instead of the rear wheels.

ACTION IN TURN SEVEN
Young Bruce McLaren (No. 3) swings his factory team Cooper wide to miss the spinning Tony Brooks in one of the Yeoman Credit team's last year's model Coopers. Brooks stalled and was out of the race.

fancy-car exhibition of the year.

It is open and free to the public.

Chuck Daigh in the Scarab

The teams garaged in the University Avenue area of Riverside and some drove to the track

Surtees

Maurice Trintignant

Jack Brabham; Cooper Climax

Phil Hill; Cooper Climax

Stirling Moss; Lotus Climax

Bruce McLaren; Cooper Climax

Early U.S. Grand Prix action: Stirling Moss leads Dan Gurney through Riverside's Turn 8.

GRAND PRIX OF THE U.S.

BY DENNIS SHATTUCK

FORMULA ONE for 2.5-liter racing cars rattled its final gasp in the Grand Prix of the USA, yet, like a phoenix, from its ashes may arise a newer, brighter creation—at least for American fans of road racing.

The final FIA meeting in the 6-year-old Formula brought to California, under the aegis of Alec Ulmann and his Automobile Racing Clubs of California/Florida, the fall Grand Prix circus and a quality of machinery and driving never before seen in those parts. If the 2.5-liter

6-7 aficionados by huge smiles and friendly waves of the hand during the entire last half of the race. Despite bad luck in both previous appearances at Riverside (sports car events), Moss carries tremendous popular appeal. Mounted in the fastest car developed under the Formula, Moss was the odds-on choice for victory long before the race was started. His Lotus was never really pressed after twice World Champion Jack Brabham made the first of two brief pit stops. Brabham seemed to have inherited some of the ill fortune that had dogged Moss during the past two seasons.

Unlike the first modern Grand Prix of the U.S. held at Sebring, Fla. in 1959, the second GP was almost a financial, as well as an artistic, success for its organizers.

The February 1961 Road and Track covered the race - read the article on the attached DVD

Oliver Gendebien; Cooper Climax

Augie Pabst, who replaced Moss, and Walt Hansgen drove Jaguars in the sedan race

STRATEGY — Shown planning their strategy for the Compact Sedan Race this coming weekend is Henry Henkel, right, Western sales manager, Rootes Motors. This is the first time the competition team representing Rootes Motors has ever raced in the United States. Other members are, left to right, Norman Garrad, competition manager; J. T. Panks, managing director, Rootes Motors Inc., and Paddy Hopkirk, Ireland's top racing driver.

Chapter Nine - Midgets and Sprint Cars

 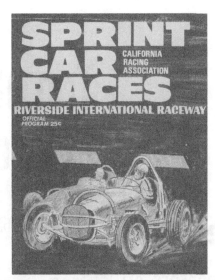 

Midgets first raced in 1958, running the course in reverse. On January, 1958, J.C. Agajanian brought out the crowd that raced at Ascot, with the idea of running on a shortened version of the road course, in a counter clockwise direction. A crowd of 6000, on a cold, windy day, saw Johnny Tolan win in the Bill Krech Offy.

Then on Memorial Day weekend, sprint cars ran a CRA sanctioned 500 mile race on Saturday, midgets a five hundred miler on Sunday and a stock car race was scheduled for Monday (Read about that in Volume 2). The midgets and sprint cars again ran the road course counter clockwise. The midget race was won by one armed racer, Allen Heath after battling Jim Hurtubise. Hurtubise spun and was overtaken by Parnelli Jones for second. The

VAN NUYS PILOT in Sunday's 500-mile late model stock car race at Riverside International Race way is Bob Osborne. Race will be passenger car counterpart of famed Indianapolis 500-mile Memorial Day classic.

PRACTICE SPIN—Howard Gardner, son of late Chet Gardner, is one of top-notch leadfoots entered in tomorrow's 500-mile big-car race at Riverside Raceway. Memorial Day event will be first of three 500-milers planned at Riverside tomorrow, Saturday and Sunday.

VALLEY RACE CAR TO COMPETE—This sprint race car will compete in the 500-mile Big Car Race at Riverside tomorrow. Owner and builder shown here, is Lee Knox, Modern Muffler Co., 11726 Ventura Blvd., Studio City. Sponsor is Mitchell Muffler Co., Alhambra. Driver Roy Prosser of Pacoima will be at the wheel.

sprint car show had 48 starters (only 18 finished) and was won by Bud Rose in the Joe Gemsa owned Kurtis Offy that had starred in the 1950 Clark Gable film; "To Please A Lady". Both races lasted more than five hours.

The race weekend was poorly attended, 12,000 fans, despite its billing as a replacement for the Indy 500, with promoters announcing they had lost as much as $50,000 on the event.

Raceway In Special Offer

RIVERSIDE (UPI)—Sponsors of three 500-mile races at Riverside International Raceway Friday, Saturday and Sunday today offered qualifying shots to cars that failed to make the grade at Indianapolis.

An offer to pay air freight for cars unable to qualify for the Indianapolis Memorial Day classic was made Monday by Galard Slonaker, president of the group sponsoring the local races.

The 500-miler for Indianapolis-type cars will be run Memorial Day. A 500-mile race for midget cars will be held Saturday, followed by a late-model American and European stock car 500 on Sunday.

Trio of 500-Milers In Riverside Begin

One of the biggest spectacles in automobile racing, the big three 500-milers at Riverside International Raceway, tops the Southern California sports scene this long Memorial Day week end.

Up for decision are three important speed classics, the 500 for major race cars Memorial Day, the 500 for mighty midgets Saturday, and the 500 for late model European and American stock cars Sunday.

All three events will be flagged off promptly at 11 a.m. at the starting line of the tricky, two and one-half mile course which is located approximately at the junction of Highways 365 and 60.

The coveted pole position for the big car event tomorrow will be occupied by Tiger Nick Valenta, the San Fernando leadfoot who won it by turning in the quickest time of the day on the first day of qualifying.

On the pole in the first row for the midget 500 on Saturday will be Lloyd Corbin, the Garden Grove tooler who was the fastest in his division on the first day of qualifying.

And the No. 1 spot in the stock car chase on Sunday will be anchored by Danny Graves of Gardena.

He wheeled his 1957 Chevy around the fastest on the first day, the traditional time when pole positions are won no matter what times are turned in during the remaining days of time trials.

The race cars and mighty midgets will circle the paved raceway counter-clock-wise while the European and American stocks will whirl around clockwise.

And the racers, both midg-ets and Indianapolis-type cars, will be given the starting flag from a flying start while the stocks will be flagged away from a standing position.

Aerial salutes will mark the important stages of each race, one being fired at the 100-mile mark, two at the 200 and so on until the checkered flag falls on the hoods of the winners.

Crowds in the excess of 75,000 are expected to watch the top-notch drivers from three racing associations gun for upwards of $50,000 in purses and prizes.

The events are sanctioned in order by the California racing Association, the United Racing Association, and the National Association for Stock Car Racing (NASCAR).

They are sponsored by Crown-America, a racing organization headed by Galard (Al) Slonaker with Charley Curryer, an old hand in the speed fraternity the director of racing.

This marks the first time in the colorful history of automobile racing that three 500-mile races have been staged on consecutive days and the first time that European and American cars have competed in the same races.

Rose Surprises at Riverside

Another Rose Wins A 500

JUNE 4, 1958

Bud Never Lost His Touch

TEN YEARS to the day after Mauri Rose won the Indy 500, Bud Rose (no relation) coped the Riverside, Calif., 500-miler. He's shown here with starlet Diane Gannon and promoter Charlie Curryper (face observed at left) receiving his trophy. (Walt Mahony photo)

..BUD ROSE (whose real name is Harry Eisele) shown in action on a conventional (left hand) turn at the Riverside (Calif.) International Raceway on his way to victory in the May 30 500-mile race sanctioned by CRA. Bud drove a car which has been in the MGM studios prop room since the 1950 filming of "To Please a Lady." Bud came out of retirement for the race. (Walt Mahony photo)

Rosie Rouselle leads Colby Scroggin

Johnny Woods

Veteran Butch Rose Wins Riverside 500-Mile Race

BY JACK CURNOW
Time Staff Representative

RIVERSIDE, May 30 — Bud (Butch) Rose, more familiar to the older racing fans than the youngsters, came out of retirement to show the kids the short way around the tricky 2.6 mile Riverside raceway road course today.

The South Pasadena star of yesteryear, who's been in retirement since winning the 500-miler at Oakland Speedway in 1952 (except to make a movie at Indianapolis) covered the 500-miler in 5 hours, 54 minutes and 57 seconds.

He was tooling a 270-cubic-inch Offenhauser, the same car which the late Mac Hellings drove to second place behind Bill Holland at Indianapolis.

Henry Second

Hank Henry of Tucson finished second, seven laps back of Rose in a Chevy-powered sprint car. Rip Erickson of North Hollywood, driving a GMC, wound up third.

Promoters estimated the crowd at between 10,000 and 25,000 but this observer would say not more than 7500 fans were on hand.

Rose drove a heady race (it figured he wasn't going to blow up early against the kids). He started in 19th position in a 46-car field, took the lead briefly early, made a pit stop at the 68th lap and lost it. He was running second to Scotty Cain in a Buick Special and exchanged the lead with him a couple times. Cain hit the fence on Turn 6 on the 140th lap and Rose took over again, never to be headed.

The three-day race carnival continues here tomorrow with a 500-mile midget race featuring many of the same drivers who raced sprint cars today. Sunday it winds up with a NASCAR stock race.

Persuaded by Gemsa

Rose, who weighs 240 pounds and admits to 52 years, was talked into racing today by Joe Gemsa of El Monte, who bought the Offie three weeks ago from MGM studio. It was the bus in which Rose doubled for Clark Gable in the movie "To Please a Lady." Gemsa and Rose both are old-timers and raced together for many years before each gave up competition.

Gemsa now operates race cars for a living while Rose has his Rose Engineering Machine screw shop in Los Angeles. The combine picked up about $2000 of the guaranteed $10,000 purse.

Rose made two pit stops and his crew gets a lot of credit for today's victory. He stopped at the 68th lap and took on 60 gallons of fuel in a minute and 30 seconds. His next stop was on the 138th lap and took 2 minutes, 10 seconds. His crew changed a left front wheel, then Rose decided he'd rather use the original, and it was replaced.

21 on Track

There were 21 cars still running after the grueling marathon.

When Diane Cannon, queen of the racing week end, gave Rose a smackeroo in victory lane, the veteran quipped, "I wish this had happened 20 years ago."

Here are the first 10 finishers announced by Walt James, prexy of the sanctioning California Roadster Association:

1. Bud Rose (Offie); 2. Hank Henry (Chevie); 3. Rip Erickson (GMC); 4. Don Davis, Phoenix (Pontiac); 5. Bud Sterrett, Long Beach (Maserati); 6. Leon Conner, Newhall (Chevie); 7. Rosie Rouselle, Long Beach (Offie); 8. Peloins Holmes (Merc); 9. Dick Hakins (Merc); 10. Cecil Burnaugh, Chevie.

Start Cool

Midgets

Allen Heath won the 500 mile midget race

Promoters of Riverside Raceway Drop $50,000

RIVERSIDE (UPI) — Promoters of three 500-mile races at Riverside International Raceway over the Memorial Day week end Monday counted financial losses which may go as high as $50,000.

Attendance for the three-day event totaled a meager 12,000 fans, despite its billing as a possible rival to the Indianapolis 500-mile classic.

started the race but only 19 finished.

The 500-mile race for midget cars on Saturday was captured by one-armed Allen Heath, Northridge. Jones was second and Joe Benter, San Diego was third.

The 500 miler for big cars was won Friday by Bud Rose.

Bud Rose giving directions to the trophy girl, future actress Dyan Cannon

Roger Ward and Don Edmunds

Parnelli Jones: *"This weekend stands out as I raced in all three 500 mile races. Not the greatest success; I broke in the sprint car race, finished second in the midget race; followed Hurtubise in third until he spun and moved to second. I led the stock car race for 400 miles, driving Vel Miletich's 56 Ford, until, with a four lap lead, the motor blew and a I hit a guardrail"*

Billy Cantrell

Speed Age Covered It Well !!

RIVERSIDE

CALIFORNIA got more racing Memorial Day weekend than it usually gets all year. Championship cars, midgets and late-model stocks took over the Riverside International Motor Raceway in turn for 500-mile races on successive days.

Bud Rose, West Coast racing veteran, won the big-car event in an elapsed time of five hours, 54 minutes, seven seconds. His car, a former Indianapolis machine, was the same one he drove as Clark Gable's double in the film "To Please A Lady."

On Saturday the midgets took over. Allen Heath, the indomitable West Coast driver who lost his left arm in a racing accident three years ago, took the checker in a Ford V8-60 midget after a seesaw battle with Jim Hurtubise and Parnelli Jones.

Sunday dawned bright and clear for the NASCAR Grand International for American and European stock cars, a new wrinkle in American racing. But at the 11 a.m. starting time there was no sign of action. Up in the Pagoda, NASCAR president Bill France refused to let the race begin until he had cash in hand for the purse. Crown-America officials, the race promoters, immediately sent a Brinks armored truck on a tour of the box offices. An hour later the truck had picked up over $11,000, and France accepted a $4,700 check for the balance. France asked the drivers if they were willing to race, since NASCAR couldn't guarantee the check. With a rousing "Let's go!" they charged for their cars.

A few minutes later the green flag flashed and a solid mass of 46 cars — Fords, Chevrolets, Pontiacs, Plymouths, two Citroens, a Goliath and a 4CV Renault — roared away through the Esses. This time it was a fight among Jones ('56 Ford), teammate Eddie Gray ('57 Ford) and Jim Reed ('57 Ford), the New Yorker who had flown out after driving the Trenton 500 on Memorial Day. Gray took the checkered flag after Jones retired with a blown engine and Reed spun into the guard rail. ●

The big cars take off on the first lap of the Riverside 500. Bud Rose took home the hardware.

Heath, the only one-armed pro race driver now active, poses with his trophy after midget win. Parnelli Jones pulled down second money.

Bud Rose (43) leads Allen Heath through Riverside's Turn No. 7. Rose used same car to double for Clark Gable in Hollywood movie.

The real Scotty Cain story – *"The car was a Kurtis 500B that belonged to Ed Walsh, got wadded up in practice at the Speedway and was shipped back to Glendale where Ronny*

Ward (Roger's brother) worked as a master fabricator. After he repaired the chassis it was turned over to some hatchet mechanic who made it into a poor man's sports car to run with Cal Club SCCA. It was then sold to Jim Williams who hired Hal Grist (CRA driver and yellow flagman) who took the ride contingent on me being the crew chief. The car was pretty shabby so I went to meet Frank and he took a liking to me. (I think he was terrified that this 21 year old

kid was going to disgrace the Kurtis brand) He came to my house and determined what basic stuff I needed and gave (gratis) parts and instructions. Great guy! Cut to the chase - I lived about a mile from Walt James and had partnered with him on a late model stock car, so when the three day Riverside deal was announced (500 miles for NASCAR stocks, CRA Sprints and URA Midgets (!) I entered the car. Walt stopped by and gave me a list of what I had to do to pass safety tech. By then Williams was AWOL and had no money. Walt suggested Cain as a driver since he had some connections and could arrange for the car to be made legal. Grist could not match the deal. Scotty was a hired gun, period. The first time he saw the car was the weekend before Memorial Day when he showed up to qualify - (mid-pack). Race day we get there late and Cain is furious. I just get him calmed down as I'm strapping him in when Williams shows up unexpectedly, pushes me aside and tells him "Sweeney tells me we're gonna win this thing so I want you to bring it in two laps before the end so I can take the checker." No driver I ever knew would take kindly to that, under any circumstances. Our strategy was to run gasoline with an 80 gallon tank. The CRA guys all

ran alky and had smaller tanks. Cain was running four seconds under his qualifying time, leading by nearly two laps around the 420 mile point when he came into the uphill section leading to the esses. We ran the track counter-clockwise for safety but that meant that the metal fences ends were facing the wrong way. Coming up that short stretch the front wheels came off the ground and when he corrected the fence post caught the crotch between the torsion bar arm and the right hub and broke

the axle. The only thing that saved his life was the headers. The nailhead Buick had 4 individual pipes and the steel wheel/hub/brake drum assembly (probably weighed 50 pounds min) tore off the first 3 but the 4th one held and deflected it. There was a perfect Firestone SS170 tire tread mark on the top of his hat. He was dazed but unhurt. He got out of the car and walked across the track directly in the path of Rip Erikson who just barely missed him. Scotty blamed the car for the axle breaking and left the track."

Bettenhausen, Templeman Head Riverside Race Field

Tony Bettenhausen, 1951 national driving champion from Tinley Park, Ill., and "Shorty" Templeman, 1956 and '57 national midget champion from Seattle, head a star-studded entry list, including a dozen other Indianapolis drivers, for this afternoon's 100-mile USAC midget auto race at the Riverside International Raceway.

Besides Bettenhausen and Templeman, the other Indianapolis drivers who'll see action in the five event program over the paved 2½-mile road racing course include George Amick, Don Edmunds, 1957 Indianapolis "rookie of the year" from Anaheim; Bud Clemons; Johnnie Tolan, 1952 national midget champion from Norwalk; Dempsey Wilson; Billy Garrett; Danny Oakes; Bill Homeier; Earl Motter; Bill Cheesbourg and Ray Crawford, 1954 Mexican Road Race winner.

* * * *

OTHER TOP entries, seeking to take home the $5,000 purse J. C. Agajanian is offering

TONY BETTENHAUSEN
Won Title in 1951

against 40% of the gate, include "Bullet" Joe Garson, former Pacific Coast midget champion: Lakewood's Jerry Unser,

1957 national stock car champion; Indianapolis rookie Art Bisch, who finished fifth in last year's coast midget standings; Bob Cortner, 1957 BCRA midget king; Harry Stockman, Don Horvath, Jimmy Moorehouse of Santa Ana, Larry Dunham of Norwalk and Jimmy Hayes of Long Beach.

Qualifying will start at 11 a.m. and the first race, the 3-mile trophy dash for the fastest six cars, will start at 2 o'clock. There is also a pair of 12 car, 10-mile heat races before the 40 car, 100-mile feature.

* * * *

TOLAN SET the pace in qualifications Saturday with an average speed of 92 miles an hour on the 2½ mile course. Amick had the second best time of 90 mph and Templeman was clocked at 87 mph.

Roger Ward of Los Angeles suffered facial and nose injuries when his car spun into a bank on the sixth turn. The front end of the car was demolished.

James Matson: *The big oval at Riverside basically used turn nine of the road course and at turn three a connector road was added to the back straight to make an oval. uphill some one way and downhill the other.*

24 cars attended the first CRA race, June 25, 1960, was a 30 lap feature won by Bob Mathouser who started from the eighth position in the Morales Brothers Offy.

Tim Kennedy: *"I got out of the Coast Guard in 1962, ended up in L.A. at among other things, sprint car races. I became the CRA publicity director, edited the first CRA yearbook and complied all the records. CRA ran seven races at Riverside, the last in August, 1965. Drivers didn't want to travel as far as Riverside after Whiteman Stadium's third mile and Speedway 605's half mile opened in 1966. A number of drivers preferred the clay dirt tracks as it reduced tire costs; they went to Ascot and El Cajon."*

The California Racing Association held sprint car races on the half mile paved ovel oval from 1960 through 1966.

Ned Speth Speeds to Victory In Riverside Sprint Car Race

RIVERSIDE — Ned Speth led all the way Friday night to win the California Racing Association sprint car main event at Riverside International Raceway, but Jim Roessler of San Bernardino stole the show.

Roessler moved from 12th to third before 1,582 fans, the

ord of 11:36.24 in his Bismuke Chevy. He was challenged most of the way by second-place finisher Jimmy Miller of Lakewood. Fifth was Hal Minyard of Crestline.

Roessler was the fast qualifier and took second place in the three-lap trophy dash.

Fast qualifier — Jim Roessler, San

Minyard, East Lead Parade Of Sprint Cars to Riverside

RIVERSIDE — Sprint cars compete at Riverside Raceway's half-mile oval tonight for the first time in four years.

Hal Minyard of Crestline and Jay East of Colton have joined the elite 50-driver field.

9-8 Thriller

Action starts with qualifying at 7 o'clock. A three-lap trophy dash leads off racing at 8, followed by four 8-lap heat races, a 15-lap semi-main and a 30-lap feature.

Minyard, defending California Racing Association champion, will pilot the Leonard Surdum sprinter, a Chevy-powered

Chapter Ten - Go Karts

Go Karts ran at RIverside almost from the beginning to the end. the long course used turn eight; the short course turned onto the back straight at seven, much like the short sports car course.

Steve Sharp: *"Totalled my kart at my first enduro here, won the next day in a borrowed Caretta. Lot of drugs in those days, one of my buddies said he'd dropped acid before his race - crazy times indeed !! I was friends with famous rockstar Lee Michaels at that time, he had a Mercedes bus and he and his bass player both raced"*

Karter Magazine - 1981

Kevin Sterner: *"I raced both the long and short courses in the 200cc stock class. Great track"*

Go Karts race at Riverside

B

Nine national champions will participate in the final road race

Riverside Raceway Set To Hold Go-Kart Race

Riverside International Raceway will be the scene today of

Dan Meray: *"Loved that track. Ran it with SCK. Drove 200 cc twin and 250 cc Zip superkarts"*.

GO-KART RECORD

RIVERSIDE, Calif. (AP) — Ken Fox of Glen Ellyn, Ill., set the fastest time Friday at the trials for the U.S. National Karting Enduros when he took his twin-engine Class C-Open go-kart around the 2.6-mile Riverside Raceway course at an average speed of 85.42 m.p.h.

The races are Sunday and Monday. In Friday's trials, Martin Wilcox, 31, of Roswell, N.M., broke both feet and ankles and his left elbow when his kart went out of control and hit a wall at an estimated 70 m.p.h.

US Go Kart Title

David Gard of Sacramento this week won the national sprint point championship for go kart racing in Riverside. In taking honors he was first in the class A super lightweight class.

Previously he had won the governor's cup, the territorial cup and the Oregon State championship.

Moon Over Riverside

Without doubt, Kathey Hartman and Lynn Haddock are the most successful IKF Kart racers EVER. Between them, they have more Duffies than anybody probably ever will again. However, that's not what this story *is* about.

Let's go back to Riverside International Raceway in 1978 or 1979. For some reason that I never understood, four Karters decided to get "cheeky" and pull a prank on Kathey. Maybe it was because she won all the time, or that she was a WOMAN or maybe they just were being ornery. Whatever the reason, they decided to surprise her as she went under the bridge on the back straight and showed their collective rears. By the way, I mean that literally not figuratively.

Riverside had this HUGE long back straightaway that stretched for almost a mile. You came onto the back chute right out of the pretty tight scoring turns and looked down at what seemed like an endless straightaway. You then ran slightly downhill until you went under a bridge that allowed traffic in and out of the track while races were going on. From there the track went slightly uphill, into a kink to the left. Then you bent around to the right into the famous (infamous?) turn nine. The second generation turn nine was a lightly banked 180 degree that had this intimidating steel wall on your left. In one of the faster singles, this was a flat out turn but if you wanted to keep your momentum up (momentum was everything at Riverside) you let the Kart drift up toward that steel wall.

If you were doing it right, you came off the corner about a foot off the wall. From there, you went down the pit straight and got your signals from your buds. A kink to the left just past the pits, and a right into the famous Riverside "esses." All the time going uphill, left, right, left, up to turn six. Around six to the right, downhill, then uphill and over the crest. A little to the left into scoring, around to the right onto the back chute. A lap at Riverside. Got it?

About midway through the hour, as Kathey (leading of course) approached the aforementioned bridge she was greeted by the sight of four guys just off the track to the right with their pants down giving her a quad-moon. I understand she almost drove off the track. After the race when Kathey told her husband John Hartman about it, he threw a fit. Kathey supposedly wasn't that upset about it.

Now you gotta understand that I know who the four "culprits" were but I'm not going to rat them out even after all these years. Guess all four and you will win the not-yet-famous "Moon over Riverside" award. Incidentally, I was in that same race and they didn't (thank goodness) moon me.

Amazingly, I am in possession of several photos of the incident. Email me at wcpeacock@bak.rr.com and I'll pass them on. Submit your guesses to me, and I'll let you know how you did!

—Joe Karter (aka Bill Peacock)

Cover of the July 1984 Kartech magazine featured a nice big story about Kathy written by Rhonda Hens-Brown.

The karts are Kathy, Ted Fasano (I'm "almost" positive), and Kel McIntee. Note Kel waving his fist in approval. This photo (of the karts) was actually taking on the next lap after Bones came off the bank and back across the track.

Here's a pic of Old "Joe Karter" aboard his Dick Peck Hornet taken at Riverside WAY back in the day (probably around 1963).

Timothy Dwyer: *"In 1966, I had a Bultaco powered FKE, broke the frame, drove around found a friendly farmer who welded it up - A great time - Best was the gas station; free gas for your kart (and tow car too) - huge fields back in the day. I miss Riverside."*

Bobby and Scott Pruett

Lake Speed before his ride off the track in turn seven.

Ed Mitchell locked real good in Open Heavy until he lost a plug.

Doug Milliken on his way to another Reed Heavy win.

RIVERSIDE INTERNATIONAL RACEWAY

Domes a country mile ahead in Open Lite.

The burning of Domes hat after his win.

Chuck Hammond continuing to do a fine job for Karters everywhere.

The winners - Doug Henline and Mike Burris.

The reopening of Riverside International Raceway to karts was an event long awaited by karters and when the day arrived people seemed to come out of the woodwork to try out the track once again. Guys showed up for this race who hadn't raced their enduro all season. Three years of legal hassels and bad feelings between the track and karting organizations had only whetted the appetite of the drivers to get on the flat out course.

The course opened on Saturday to an avalanche of karts and a dirty track. The result was three ambulance runs in the first session of practice. It turned out not to be an omen for the weekend for the races all ran smoothly after that. The Pre-Grid entry, however, ended up with a badly broken ankle and will be out for the remainder of the season.

Because the race weekend corresponded with the IKF April Rules Meeting, several Board members came out to catch some of the Sunday action. Gene Rice, Lake Speed and Hohn Markham of New York all could be seen milling around the pits greeting old friends. Lake Speed decided to give the Riverside course a try and went out for the C-Open race in a Hartman car. Witnesses say that his engine stuck about ten feet in the air as he was going off of the blind turn seven. Chalk another one up for the track.

The juniors started off the race day on Saturday with the Las Vegas contingent again taking a stronghold on the trophies. However, in this weekends Reed race, Lincoln Addis and Allen Holt had some strong opposition in Mike Siebler. After a wire-to-wire race between the three, Siebler came up with the wind, his first in enduros. The stock class saw another first time winner in John Hillbish. The formidable sprint driver, Ron Tull, showed he is also a threat in enduros by capturing second.

The Reed Light win went to Kathey Hartman who really had to fight for it this time. For the first part of the race it was a real battle between Hartman, Rod Whorton and Ed Hundley driving Roger Folland's "don't-stick-the-engine-cuz-it's-the-only-one-I-have" special. Twenty minutes into the hour Hundley drove into Whorton which put Ed out and slowed Rod down enough to give Kathey the win.

Another super close contest in the heavyweight reed class. Picture a race to the finish between Doug Milliken and Steve O'Hara. O'Hara studies Milliken's moves and beats him through scoring every lap; he has the end of the race planned. Milliken outsmarts O'Hara in the last 20 yards of the race by changing tactics and diving under Steve at the line winning the race by half a kart length. The race was won by twelve years driving experience and as someone said of Doug Milliken, "he was not" born in a closet.

The Stock Light race belonged to Bobby Shiffert. The past Junior Grandnational Champion continues to come on strong in the senior classes backed up by his uncle-mechanic, Ed Shiffert. Ed Hundley settled for a second after some early dicing with Shiffert. Gary Rosenbaum and Jim Heck both drove fine races for third and fourth.

What can you say about Stock Heavy except that Swanhuyser did it again. Six out of seven races this senson ain't bad. This time he had lasting power to his credit for there was a strong showing from David Conner, who eventually blew a motor, Dave Knapp, who broke a crank and Don MacDonald who just wasn't as fast. Bruce Swanhuyser is a good bet for winning the nationals in this class.

Darryl Domes, driving the Mike Colver, ESP sponsored entry in Open Light, literally blitzed the

---

Ed Hundley second in Stock Lite.

Bob Shiffert Stock Lite winner

Sam Winkler and Bob Meli in C-Open action.

Mike Burris on his way to Open Heavy victory.

Terry Hannum seems to be getting everything together.

RIVERSIDE INTERNATIONAL RACE RESULTS

100cc McJunior
1. Mike Siebler
2. Lincoln Addis
3. Allen Holt
4. David Conrady
5. Kenny Queen
6. James Gray

Stock Junior
1. John Hillbish
2. Ron Tull
3. Allen Holt
4. Mike Weber
5. Kenny Queen
6. Fred Dodge

100cc Mc Heavy
1. Doug Milliken
2. Steve O'Hara
3. Steve Derksen
4. Fred Hashimoto
5. Dan Eggleton
6. Henry Shaw

Stock Light
1. Bob Shiffert
2. Ed Hundley

3. Gary Rosenbaum
4. Jim Heck
5. Ed Swopes
6. Tony LaRocca

Stock Heavy
1. Bruce Swanhuyser
2. Don McDonald
3. Tom Osterkamp
4. Terry Bilton
5. Ed Swopes
6. Mike Thermos

Open Light
1. Darryl Domes
2. John Bottcher
3. Kirk Feyerabend
4. Geroge Ito
5. Ernie Sisley

Open Heavy
1. Mike Burris
2. Don McDonald
3. Frank Snyder
4. Tim Holt
5. Bruce Swanhuyser

B Limited
1. Don McDavitt
2. Tim Harris
3. Walt Burns
4. Bill Rozhon
5. Wayne Dunlap
6. Ron Miller

200cc Mc
1. Bob Allman
2. Mike Blakely
3. Steve Hawks
4. Jack Nelson
5. Bill Butek
6. Robert Wenz

100cc Mc Light
1. Kathey Hartman
2. Rod Whorton
3. Doug Milliken
4. Howard Combee
5. Steve O'Hara
6. Ruben Serrano

B Open
1. Terry Hannum
2. Eldon Callen

3. Dave Martin
4. Chuck Holden
6. Howard Combee

C Open
1. Terry Hannum
2. Bob Meli
3. Ron Black
4. Dale Estes
5. Sam Winkler
6. Jack Feyerabend

FKE
1. Don McDonald
2. Jim Haney
3. Richard Burman
4. Eugene Bemis
5. Barry Blume
6. Jeffrey Frost

Reed Open
1. Kathey Hartman
2. Mike Thiele
3. Cleve Potter
4. Ron Wahlman
5. David Newman
6. Mike Savin

125cc Mc
1. Hollis Brown
2. Doug Milliken
3. Wally Bayes
4. Les Ewert
5. David Hashimoto
6. David Fuller

Reed Novice
1. Russell Kataoka
2. Allen Conrady
3. Chuck Avery
4. Dennis Wood
5. James Parry
6. Harold Rank III

100cc Expert
1. Doug Henline
2. Darryl Domes
3. Terry Gunn
4. Bobby Shiffert
5. Tom Holt
6. Kevin Cogan

field. Even with a pit stop he led wire to wire and lapped just about everyone. The winning of this race brought on the hat-burning ceremonies at the end of the day whereby Darryl set fire to race-weathered canvas hat to commemorate his first win in a long time. John "the Flying Hornet" Bottcher took a commendable second.

Open Heavy went to SCK president, Mike Burris. Like most of the races this weekend this win was hotly contested. Eddie Mitchell, driving his best race in a long time, and Bruce Swanhuyser gave Burris a race for his money. Mitchell "was determined" but blew a clutch and Swanhuyser was forced to make a pit stop so the victory went to Mr. Burco for his staying power.

The enduro veterans showed their stuffy in B Limited which was won by long-time driver Don McDavitt. Tim Harris another B Limited veteran took second; Walt Burns, who is always right in there, placed third. This race was a comeback for Bill Rohzon taking fourth in his Cardas sponsored kart.

Bob Allman showed what racing is all about in his B Reed win. After getting off the line late he moved consistently forward and when he hot in front he was gone. Nice showing by Allman.

Terry Hannum has had his best season this year and his worst luck, what with running out of fuel and spinning out. He finally succeeded in breaking Tom Holt's B Open win streak at Riverside and did so handily. Hannum went wire to wire in the lead and as someone said, "If Hannum goes an hour he's hard to beat." He repeated his success in C-Open. Even with a bad start he passed Bob Meli, CRA candidate for Rookie of the Year, on the fourth lap and was adios. Lake Speed's trip off the track at turn seven also make the race interesting.

The 125cc race was the scene of the Hartman

rent-a-motor act. Hollis Brown borrowed a motor and a new pipe from Gary Hartman. Since Hartman was busy with his own stuff he told Hollis to just follow the instructions that came with the pipe when putting it on. Hollis did just that and even though he had no practice time, he ran the race cold turkey and won. Doug Milliken ran with him all the way but settled for second. Wally Baynes and Ken Crites also ran good until Crites was bumped off the track.

In other races, Mike Thiele's win streak in Reed Open got busted by Kathey Hartman in a good contest. The race also marked the comeback of IKS entry Ronnie Wahlman. Reed Novice was the scene of Russell Kataoka's last novice win as he has accumulated enough points to graduate to the regular Reed classes. Don McDonald took the FKE victory over Jim Honey who fell back after a couple of pit stops. Third went to Richard Burman who drove his best race in a long time.

The 100cc Expert Race was again the outstanding event of the weekend. This race has developed into an all-out, serious car race among the sports' best Open drivers. This race was won after a super tight eight laps by Doug Henline followed closely by Darryl Domes. Terry Gunn and Bobby Shiffert also ran a race to the finish with Gunn narrowly taking it.

There were other interesting sidelines to the Riverside weekend. Jack Sabin was seen walking around the pits with his fourth cast in two years. Also, George Giannini set a record by putting more pistons in a motor than has ever been done before. With the end of the day beers and the famous Darryl Domes hat-burning ceremony, Riverside International Raceway again belonged to the karters and again was the scene of some of the finest in racing competition.

Rocky Moran: *"I had a laydown 125cc two stroke kart, ran a lot of one hour enduros. We used the short course; wow was it fast !! I think we had to lift at six and again maybe at nine. Pretty exciting at 120 mph. My biggest competitor was Duffy Livingstone, who basically invented the go kart and one fast guy. I hung out at his shop in Monrovia and learned a lot"*

Dave Clark: *"This is my twin enduro kart at the very last race ever held at Riverside, April, 1989. The back straight had been ripped up to start construction for the mall (where the Lowe's is now was the original back straightaway - the Champion bridge also used to be there). So, they made a new road from turn seven over to the dogleg through the infield, so we could race."*

Go Karts in 1963

Bob Suchy - *"I heard a radio commercial advertising road racing go karts, went to check it out with my brother. After that went to Orange County Kart Supply and bought a lay down with a 125 Mac. Great times at Riverside; Raced there in 1977 and 1978, then again from 1985 to 1987 with my 2 younger brothers."*

Bill Pyles: *"The last race at Riverside, April 15, 1989 - We used a modified course that did not involve turn 8. We took a short cut at left hand turn 7 and then turned right onto the back straight. The esses were bumpy as hell. A friend of mine had a homebuilt laydown; Yamaha Heavy; lost control in the esses and backed into the armco barrier and broke his back. Fortunately he recovered after three weeks in the hospital. Pretty inconvenient as he lived in Arizona. Other than that - Really miss Riverside, always fun"*

Steve Leistokow: *"We almost got hit by a enduro kart that launched off the inside of turn six. He hit right below where they are standing"*

12,200 spectators watched John Cannon, in an Eagle, win the first event of the SCCA Continental Championship (then called Formula A) at Riverside in April 1969. Second was Lothar Motschenbacher in a McLaren M10 followed by Tony Adamowicz in another Eagle. John Milledge won the accompanying Formula B race in a Brabham Ford.

CANNON CAPTURES CONTINENTAL OPENER

By Ron Hickman
Area Editor

RIVERSIDE, Calif., April 20 — The new SCCA Continental Championship series for Formula A machinery got off to a rousing start as John Cannon put the Malcolm Starr Eagle-Chevy into the winner's circle after a wire-to-wire win from pole position in today's Riverside Continental Grand Prix.

Cannon, rich in track experience and preparation with the new Eagle

Milledge Takes F/B-C Event In Brabham

By Ron Hickman
Area Editor

RIVERSIDE, Calif., April 20 — It was almost no contest in the Formula B-C companion feature race to the F/A Continental Grand Prix on Riverside International Raceway's 2.6-mile road circuit here today.

Jon Milledge of Mountain View, Calif., put his Brabham-Ford on the pole with a new qualifying lap
(Continued on page 26)

after several hundred miles of tire testing, made a shambles of the previous Sports Car Club of America F/A records. He took pole position with a 1:20.43 lap, nearly seven seconds quicker than the standard established by Jerry Hansen's Lola at the American Road Race of Champions last November.

BREAKS DAN'S RECORD

To top this, Cannon's average speed for the 45-lap race on the 2.6-mile Riverside International Raceway course eclipsed the 45-lap record set by Dan Gurney in a USAC Championship car at the Rex Mays 300 last year. Cannon's race winning average speed was 112.998mph, compared with Gurney's mark of 112.189mph.

LOTHAR SECOND

Lothar Motschenbacher was second in a spanking new McLaren M10A-Chevrolet, 50 seconds behind Cannon. Tony Adamowicz, Eagle, was third, six seconds behind Motschenbacher. These two drivers were the only ones on the same lap with the winner at the finish.

Jerry Hansen's McLaren-Chevy was fourth, half a minute behind Adamowicz, with George Wintersteen's Lola T142-Chevy fifth, another 30 seconds back of Hansen.

Qualifying took place in three
(Continued on page 24)

Lothar Motschenbacher (11), in his very fresh McLaren-Chevrolet, gets past the Lola-Chevrolet driven by Bud Morley in the Continental Championship premiere race for Formula A cars at Riverside International, April 20. Motschenbacher finished second behind John Cannon after starting in 13th position. (Jack Brady photo)

Cannon Pilots Chevy to Victory at Riverside

Continental Grand Prix queen Ava Zamora motions to start the race as the flag goes down. Moments later, the field makes its first turn, and hours later, winner John Cannon accepts the trophy from queen Ava. Cannon won in a Chevy.

Cannon Captures Riverside Title

By TOM REINKEN
P-B Correspondent

RIVERSIDE — Formula A racing may be the way to fly. At least that was the opinion of John Cannon just after he sped to victory in the first annual Riverside Continental Grand Prix before 12,200 here at Riverside International Raceway Sunday.

Cannon, originally of England and now residing in Pasadena, led from flag to flag, covering the 45-lap, 117-mile distance in one hour, two minutes, 7:48 seconds. He averaged 112.998 m.p.h. over the nine-turn road course, breaking the record formerly held by Dan Gurney.

"This could be the series," said Cannon, relaxing in the raceway's press headquarters.

He stressed money as one of the factors in building the series. "You could make it luxuriously on $75,000 in this series.

That will only get you started in Can-Am," Cannon reasoned.

Top Name Driver

He also believes the series needs a top name driver to make it more popular. He mentioned one specifically.

"I'm dissappointed that Donohue (Mark Donohue, current Trans-Am and USRRC Champion) isn't driving this series."

The series should be more competitive than Can-Am, according to Cannon, because of the restrictions on engine size and weight. "There aren't going to be any super-exotic cars," he predicted.

Can-Am cars are heavier and harder to handle than are the Formula A machines Cannon stated. He called the formula cars mentally more demanding.

Riverside is the first of a 12 race trail in an attempt by the SCCA to bring an American equivalent of the European Grand Prix to the United States.

This is actually the third year of existence for the Formula A

Seagren Defends

343

Tony Adamowicz

Bobby Brown: *"My first race at Riverside - The opening race of the 1969 Continental Series. The first thing I noticed was the skies were brown and my eyes were burning from the smog. We didn't have that yet in New York. I liked the track, the tires in the esses got your attention, then at turn six, you had to focus to avoid being distracted by the huge crowds in*

the stands, so close to the track. I drove an Eagle, had a good race, finished ninth.

The next day, doing tire testing for Firestone, I had a horrendous crash. Early in the morning, cold tires, cold brakes, entering turn nine way too fast. End over end a few times, destroyed the car; I

fortunately only had a mild concussion and was back racing in two weeks. Firestone bought me a new car the next day; they were great about paying for motors and other broken parts, even the car when we were testing." **Compiler's Note** - Long Island Chevy dealer Bob Brown started out in a Corvette, then moved to a Cobra from famed Ford dealer Jack Griffith. In the 1969 Continental season he had a number of top five finishes. Later he raced in Europe, in the Can Am and currently is winning in vintage racing.

Sam Posey / Ron Courtney Crash

From the New York Times; July 11, 1976: I brought the Eagle out of Turn Six, a 180-degree right hand turn, and accelerated down the undulating straight toward Turn Seven, which was a fairly slow lefthander. The approach to Turn Seven was sharply uphill, and from the car the turn itself was invisible behind the hill. As I entered the braking zone I pushed the brake pedal - and it went right to the floor. I tried to pump the pedal. but it stayed on the floor. No brakes! I was going 140 miles an hour.

The spectators were on my right; Turn Seven would be coming up to my left. I twisted the wheel to the left, purposely provoking a high-speed spin just as the car swept up the hill toward the turn. At that instant I had a flash of what was about to happen: I would spin through the turn, off the far side of the track and into the bank. Spinning the car would reduce the speed of impact, but it would still be a serious crash. "The car is going to take a beating in this one," I thought as I hurtled over the crest of the hill.

And then grim anticipation gave way to horror as I saw what had not been visible from the straightaway: another car sitting sideways in the middle of the road, directly in my path. Dark blue, with chrome sparkling in the sun. I felt my car going backward in its spin. Then I was into the other car with a terrific collision, my engine and gearbox tearing into the soft fuel tanks like a battering ram. A mighty wrenching free - flight - my front wheels silhouetted against the sky - my car starting to roll over in midair - an explosion of flame far below me. Now I was upside down and falling; the road came up to meet me.

My car landed upside down, slid off into the dirt and stopped. It was bright in the cockpit. The rollbar had held up and I could see out between the ground and the edge of the cockpit. People's feet appeared in my little window. They lifted the car enough for me to wriggle out.

345

There was smoke everywhere and people running - my God! The other car - the driver's still in it - I've got to get him out! I started toward the car, which was bent in the middle like a splintered branch. Someone grabbed my arm and spun me around. I was looking into the anguished face of one of the corner workers.

"He's trapped! Can't you see that?" he shouted. 'We're going to have to cut him out of the car." They led me over to the side of the road. Suddenly, very dizzy, I sat down. A little later, someone handed me a cup of water. "How is he? I asked. "I don't know. They think he's still alive."

The other driver's name was Ron Courtney. There was nothing I could do to help him. And as I went back over the sequence of the crash - the pedal going to the floor, my attempt to pump the brakes, my decision to pitch the car into a spin with a trajectory away from the spectators -I knew that I had acted under extreme pressure exactly as I would have if there had been time to deliberate every maneuver.

Presently, the wreckers came to remove the shattered cars. As I watched the remains of the Eagle being hoisted off the ground, it occurred to me to be thankful for the way it had held up in the crash, It was inherently a strong car, but during the winter it had been made even safer by installation of a heavier rollbar and an automatic fire-fighting system: that extra insurance had probably saved my life. I couldn't sleep that night. My mind was used to shutting out disappointments - this was something new. I watched all the late movies and then sat outside on the steps in the cool night leaning hack against the door.

I knew that, in Riverside. Ron Courtney was still on the critical list and was fighting for his life. I tried to make sense out of the extremes of horror and ecstasy that had been encompassed in the last two weeks, but they were as incomprehensible to me as sounds that are beyond the range of human hearing.

To my unspeakable relief, Ron Courtney lived through his ordeal. Then he sued me - Me, and almost every other individual and company that had been even remotely involved in the accident. I had never heard of one driver suing another for something that happened on the track, for as long as racing has existed, the participants have recognized that it is a dangerous activity and that those who race do so at their own peril Indeed, every driver must sign a waiver of liability to that effect before he is allowed on the track. But did precedent mean anything? I didn't know anything about law. All I knew was that Courtney had retained as his lawyer the famous Melvin Belli. In the first weeks after I was sued, I struggled with a bewildering morass of lawyers and depositions. The initial assumption was that I would be covered by the Sports Car Club of America master insurance plan, but on closer inspection it was discovered that the policy did not apply to driver-versus-driver lawsuits. I was on my own.

Fans and racing people from all over the country wrote to me to express their indignation at what Courtney had done. At first I was indignant, too and hitter. As a driver I had done all the right things in the car, and yet I was being victimized by this lawsuit.

But slowly I began to understand the situation from Courtney's perspective. Frightfully injured, hospitalized for months, medical hills exhausting his financial resources, at some point he must have wanted to lash out in any direction that might produce some money for him and his family.

Four years and eleven months after the complaint was served on me, the lawsuit was settled out of court. Throughout all that time it took only a word, or a phrase, or some idle thought in the middle of the night to bring the dull dread of the suit to the front of my mind, and to recall the horror of the day it represented.

John Cannon and the trophy girl

Davey Jordan; Eagle

347

**Davey Jordan, Scooter Patrick, Miss Formula Racing Association,
John Timanus, Lothar Motschenbacher and Alan Johnson**

Scooter Patrick puts the new Garner TS5 through its paces during a recent test session at Riverside Raceway. Three of the cars, powered by American Motors 305cid V8s, will be fielded by Jim Garner's American International Racing team in the Continental Championship. Other team drivers are Dave Jordan and David Hobbs.

In front of a crowd of 14,500, John Cannon won again in 1970, collecting $5950. Cannon, this time in a McLaren, led every lap; followed by Davey Jordan in an Eagle and Chuck Parsons in a Lola. Cannon would later be the season champion. In the companion Formula B race, Mike Eyerly won in a Chevron Ford.

Cannon Runs Away With Riverside Continental Opener

(Continued from page 1)
Special Lola T190-Chevy, recovered from a first-lap spin which dropped him to 24th place to finish third, right on Jordan's tail.

Fred Baker's McLaren M10-Chevy was fourth, another 10 seconds back.

Two laps behind Cannon, Spence Stoddard's Competition Development Lola-Chevy captured fifth place, with an eight second margin over John Gunn's Surtees-Chevy. Eric Haga, in an identical car to Stoddard's, hounded Gunn for the last 25 laps, but fell four seconds short of catching him at the finish.

RON'S REFLECTION

Although Cannon was not pressed at the finish, he drove much of the first 33 laps with his mirrors full of Ron Grable's Lola T190-Chevy. Grable, who had qualified second, was the only one able to challenge or run with the winner, closing to within a few lengths on several occasions. On Grable's 34th lap his throttle stuck open going into turn 6—and even simultaneous application of the brakes, downshifting and the ignition kill button couldn't keep him from a solid smack into the boiler plate wall just beyond the end of the water-filled crash barrier.

The resulting impact separated

Repeating his 1969 performance, John Cannon scored the victory in the Continental Grand Prix at Riverside April 19, leading from start to finish in his Hogan McLaren M10B. The race was the first of 14 in the pro Formula A series.

(Robin Robin photos)

Cannon's Racer New, but Well Tested

BY SHAV GLICK
Times Staff Writer

RIVERSIDE—It is almost an axiom of motor racing that new model cars are never quite ready when the green flag drops on the opening race of the season.

Engines arrive late from the factory, the suspension doesn't act right, there isn't time to tinker with the carburetion, the brakes are sticky.

The lament along the pit wall is the same. "If we only had another couple of days, or another week. If we'd just got a little earlier start."

...in under any circumstances, but if it does . . ." he said with a knowing wink.

Cannon has had the reputation of being a master driver on the wet stuff. He stunned the Can-Am Series with his win in the rainy 1968 Monterey Grand Prix while driving an all-but-obsolete car. As a youngster in a home made car he first attracted notice in 1963 by bolting to a temporary lead in the rain at the Canadian Grand Prix.

Cannon is defending champion, having won last year's race wire to wire in an Eagle.

Cannon has not only ... ... seen the track, Cannon has a ride for the Memorial Day race at Indianapolis in a four-year-old turbocharged Ford owned by Rolla Vollstedt. It was driven in the 500 last year by Larry Dickson.

"Indianapolis is very important to me," he said. "In long-range terms I want to learn as much as possible this year and come back in '71 really ready to race. Having an older car could be an advantage for a rookie because I won't have to be worrying about sorting it out."

day during qualifying runs for the Continental Grand Prix at Riverside International Raceway.

Smothers, driving a Lola-Chevy, was burned when a fire extinguisher in the car exploded. He was sprayed with a chemical which is used to inhibit gasoline-type fires. Although his left shoulder and arm were burned, he is expected to attempt to qualify his car today.

Busby, of Newport Beach, lost control of his Eagle Chevy on a curve and the car climbed an embankment and hit a guard rail. Busby was ...

Davey Jordan: *"Long story, I was driving for Johnnie Crean (of Fleetwood Motorhome fame). He had bought Surtees TS5's but they all had rear suspension failures in testing so he bought some Eagles from Gurney. Crean and James Garner had partnered in this deal (American International Racing) to use AMC motors; the AMC motor deal fell through so I go to drive a car with the motor out of Garner's Daytona Lola. Cannon was the fast guy in qualifying and all through the race, with me chasing Ron Grable and Chuck Parsons, Grable blew up, Parsons got a wheel off and I passed him for second. Freddy Baker was fourth. I won $4050, probably most of of which went to Crean. Did well in some other races, led the championship for a while"* Compiler's Note - Davey won numerous SCCA Championships in a Porsche Speedster, then drove a variety of Porsche 904's, Carrera Sixes and campaigned the Shelby Toyota 2000's in C Production"

RACE QUEEN

The business of auto racing may be a serious one when the race is on, but there are plenty of moments before and after when a little light banter is in order. Above, television comedian Dick Smothers talks things over with Miss Continental Grand Prix, Candy Martin, of Villa Park, in front of Smothers' Manhattan Beach discotheque. Dave Jordan, who will compete against Dick and the rest of the Continental field today, loaned the car for this scene taken in front of Cisco's during a recent press party. Smothers has been driving as both a professional and amateur for the past three years but will be attempting his first full professional season with today's Continental. Miss Martin, whose 36-23-35 chassis you'll see presenting the winning trophy in the L & M Winner's Circle after today's race, is a Miss World contestant and was first runnerup in the recent California Citrus Queen contest.

Dick Smother's with Davey Jordan's Eagle and Miss Continental Grand Prix

Cannon Continues His Winning Ways With Riverside Continental Victory

His Motor Oil? ...VALVOLINE!

John Cannon, whose end-of-the-season charge barely fell short of winning the Continental Series last year, is back again and must be regarded as a top contender for the 1970 title. In winning the 100-mile race April 18-19, at Riverside, Cannon averaged 113.577 m.p.h. and finished two and a half minutes ahead of second place winner Dave Jordan. Both Jordan and Chuck Parsons, who finished third, relied on Valvoline Racing Oil.

The Formula B title went to Mike Eyerly, another Valvoline user. Eyerly was the Formula B-C champ in the 1969 competition.

Take a tip from these champion drivers . . . get Valvoline for *your* car. It's the Champions' Choice!

VALVOLINE OIL COMPANY

 Division of Ashland Oil & Refining Company
Ashland, Kentucky

Gus Hutchison and Rich Galloway

Dick Smothers

Speed Age Covered the 1970 Race

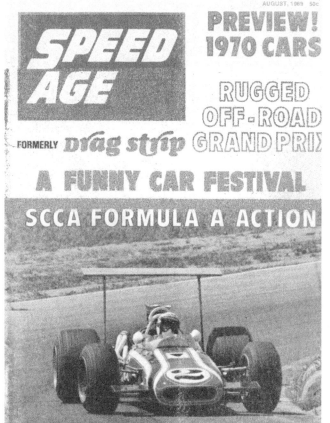

AUGUST, 1969 50c

SPEED AGE

FORMERLY drag strip

PREVIEW! 1970 CARS
RUGGED OFF-ROAD GRAND PRIX
A FUNNY CAR FESTIVAL
SCCA FORMULA A ACTION

by Hans Von Graubert

Formula Racing Comes of Age on the American Scene as the SCCA Begins an Exciting Season with the

Riverside Continental Grand Prix

Read the entire article on the attached DVD

In 1971, 13,075 fans saw Australian Frank Matich win in a McLaren M10B, powered by a Repco - Holden V8, by finishing second in each heat. Ron Grable won one heat as did Sam Posey but neither did well enough in each to equal Matich's two seconds. Second by virtue of a third and fourth was Jim Dittemore in the Kastner Brophy Lola T192, followed by Sam Posey in a Surtees TS8. Total payout to Match was $7700. Weather was peculiar, the day starting in rain and hail and finishing in sunshine.

Matich finishes second twice, captures L&M prize at Riverside

Race winner Matich in the McLaren Holden passing Rex Ramsey in the ASD Mk.1

CONSISTENCY WINS TOP L & M PRIZE FOR MATICH

Frank Matich (R) finished second in a pair of races to win the over all point title in the L & M Continental Grand Prix at Riverside Raceway. Ron Grable (4) held the lead until a crash forced him out of the race only four laps from the end. Jim Dittemore (rear car) finished second in over-all points.

Matich Takes Grand Prix

Frank Matich, in the car at the right, was the over-all point winner at Riverside Raceway's Continental Grand Prix. Trailing him in order are Ron Grable and Jim Dittemore.

UPI Telephoto

Ron Grable; Lola T190 Chevrolet

RIVERSIDE'S MISS SEARS PRESENTS TROPHY
Debbie Wilson, Miss Sears, Riverside, presents the L & M Continental Grand Prix over-all point trophy to Frank Matich following Sunday's competition at Riverside Raceway.

Jim Gustafson: *"I remember this race like it was yesterday, my first time at Riverside. I was excited be here; when I was in high school back in the Midwest, I would read all the car magazines, and enjoyed vicariously the extensive coverage of races at Riverside. My first day at the track, was on Friday, practice day for the opening round of the U.S. Formula 5000 championship. Over 35 cars were entered for what promised to be a great season for the series. My not so favorite memory: I had just pulled into the circuit and noticed a big cloud of dust in the esses. I ran over to see what was happening; the track was red flagged and it got real quiet. A driver from Utah, Mel Andrus, had crashed his Lola T-142 and was killed. This was my first introduction the RIR, I couldn't have been on the property more than 5 minutes. Despite this, I couldn't wait to start racing here, and did so many times later, but I've never forgotten my first day at RIR, and poor Mel's last."* Compiler's Note - Jim started out in Formula Ford, moved up to a T-190 in Formula 5000, then to a March 73A.

Formula A's rev up today

By ALLEN WOLFE

RIVERSIDE — Formula A cars, the renowned failures of the Questor Grand Prix, hope to accomplish today — rebuilding their tarnished image.

Less than a month ago, American drivers were humiliated by an overwhelming performance from European Formula 1 drivers in the $251,675 race at Ontario Motor Speedway.

★ ★ ★

Top qualifiers

1. David Hobbs, Russ, England, McLaren-Chevy, 118.339 mph.
2. Sam Posey, San Juan Capistrano, Surtees-Chevy, 117,170.
3. Frank Matich, Sydney, Australia, McLaren-Repco, 116,760.
4. Dr. Lou Sell, Fullerton, Lola-Chevy, 116,140.
5. Brett Lunger, Wilmington, Del., Lola-Chevy, 115,542.
6. Skip Barber, Carlisle, Mass., STP, ...

billed as the great "international conflict."

The confrontation ended with a verdict of "no contest."

... View, Calif. — was able to finish in the top ten, limping home a disappointing seventh.

Today, Riverside International Raceway will be the scene of the third Continental Grand Prix for formula A-5000 machines. One important element is missing — the Europeans.

"We're back in our own element — racing against each other," says Sam Posey, who tangled with John Cannon and was one of the early casualties in the Questor race. "The Questor was nothing more than a great circus — it just wasn't a proper match."

Driving Championship in Europe." Posey says "I should think that they would have tremendous spectator appeal.

... but unfortunately the majority of fans are ignorant of that fact.

"Race fans don't identify with these names, they want to see guys like Mario Andretti, Peter Revson and Mark Donohue."

Although the Continental series is about to embark on its third season — with an increase from $20,000 to $35,000 is guaranteed

awards per race — Posey feels the series has reached its "make or break" point.

... to draw some respectable crowds or the people who put up the money won't do it again next season."

The threat of rain hung over today's race with 30 cars scheduled to get the green flag in the first of two 100-mile heats at 1 p.m. after a 45 minutes recess for fuel and minor repairs. The second heat will get under way at 2.

★ ★ ★

ANDRUS DIES IN RIVERSIDE CRASH

David Hobbs: *In 1971, I qualified on the pole in a McLaren; got caught out on dry tires at the start, spun and the %#$&@% car wouldn't restart. I did go on to win the championship that year.*

357

Sam Posey

Nick Dioguardi; Surtees TS5

Lou Sell; Lola T-192

Eppie Weitzes leads Ron Grable and Jim Dittemore

The 1972 L & M Grand Prix, was the last race on the 1972 calendar. A crowd of 12,000 watched Brian Redman win both heats, using the 2.5 mile "short" course and pocketing $17,800 in the Bobcor Sid Taylor Chevron Chevrolet, followed by Sam Posey in a Surtees TS11 who ran second in both heats and Graham McRae who had a third and a fifth in his own McRae GM1.

Redman Finds Formula for Victory

By TED GREEN
Sun-Telegram Sports Writer

BRIAN REDMAN
... Continental winner

RIVERSIDE — The Continental Formula 5000 road racing series ended in controversy at Riverside Raceway yesterday, as Britain's Brian Redman won both heats in the eighth and final event of the season, the L & M Grand Prix.

Redman, a veteran international driver from Colne, England, ran away with the first 38-lap heat when countryman David Hobbs blew an engine on the 29th lap aftr riding Rdman's tailpipe throughout the race. Sam Posey of San Juan Capistrano was second, trailing by 37 seconds.

In the second 97-mile chase before a crowd of 12,000, it was stictly Redman and Posey. The likeable Briton passed Posey on the second lap of the 2.5 mile course and maintained a four-car length advantage to the finish line, but Posey's crew filed a protest with Sports Car Club of America officials immediately after the second heat.

Posey maintains he was passed by Redman under a waving yellow caution flag. There is no passing permitted under the yellow, as Posey had slowed down to avoid a slower car's spinout.

"I have never been penalized in any racing since I began in 1959," the 25-year-old Redman said. "It would not have been to my advantage because I only needed to finish second by 37 seconds or less to be the overall winner.

"It's not easy to see flags at this course in the first place," Redman continued emphatically. "If it was a caution situation, the black flag should have been thrown."

Apparently agreeing with Redman, SCCA officials upheld Posey's protest but fined Redman $100, a mere slap on the hand compared to the other option—disqualification.

Controversy aside, the series championship was decided on the first lap of the first heat when Brett Lunger, the only man with a chance to catch series leader Graham McRae, was involved in a four-car crash.

McRae, a native of Wellington, New Zealand, led Pomona's Lunger by 18 points as the day began and needed only an overall finish of sixth or better for the title.

When Lunger crashed, though, the excitement was gone.

McRae won four of the eight Continental races, as he demonstrated superior driving ability by navigating on tracks he had never seen before. This was his first road racing year in America, but victories at Laguna Seca (May 7), Watkins Glen (June 18) and Road America (July 16) put the 32-year old McRae in a superior position to snatch the series from Hobbs, last year's champion. McRae was third.

"Thank goodness it's finished," McRae said. "I've been racing every week in Europe and America and have gotten pretty tired in the second half of the season. I didn't really want to get in the car today — the beach seemed more inviting."

McRae, who designs the chassis on all his Formula cars, was asked if he took it easy, knowing he needed only to finish to win the series.

"I was flat out on the car but it just wouldn't go," he said. "I would have liked to challenge for the lead, but we've had engine troubles lately. I was 20 miles an hour slower in the straightaways, so there was no way for me to win. I'm just happy it's over."

Lunger, the 25-year-old surprise of the L & M circuit, appeared to have avoided the first-lap crash between George Follmer and Eppie Wietzes. He made it through some flying debris, but was bumped by Bob West, who was trying to pass on the inside.

"West went up on the dirt and hit me broadside," said Lunger, who finished third in the series. "He actually vaulted over my car. You can see a black tire mark on my helmet."

Lunger came back in the second heat to finish third behind Redman and Posey, when his crew pirated needed parts off the car of Haggar teammate Hobbs, who was finished for the day after he blew in the first heat.

Driving the same Chevron Chevrolet he piloted to consecutive seconds at Road Atlanta and Lime Rock, Redman drove two flawless races, averaging 116.737 m.p.h. Hobbs, the top qualifier at a track record of 121, persistently rode Redman's bumper in the first heat, but Redman would not give in. The two Britons roared by the start-finish line time and again only a few feet apart, but Hobbs could not overtake him.

(Continued on B–8, Column 3)

Brian Redman: *"In 1972 I came to Riverside for the first time, driving the factory Chevron B24 F5000. Towards the end of the race, I was slip-streaming Sam Posey in his Surtees TS11 coming towards Turn 9, flat out at 170 mph. Suddenly, Sam apparently lifted and I swerved to avoid nim. I was now in the lead and won. A protest was lodged that I'd overtaken Sam under the yellow flag. The Chief Steward came to me and in a strong Lancashire accent said: "Now then Brian lad, I'm Sam Smith from Accrington" - a town 7 miles from where I lived in Burnley - "as one Lancashire lad to another, dids't tha' see t'yellow flag or not?" I truthfully replied that I had not. "Right lad, your't winner" said Sam. Later, a gentleman came up to me and introduced himself as Carl Haas, American importer for Lola race cars and Hewland gearboxes. Carl said he was forming a partnership with Chaparral legend Jim Hall to run F5000 in 1973, and would I like to drive for him?"*

Under the Hood

L&M Field Is Diverse

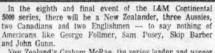

By TED GREEN
Sun-Telegram Racing Writer

Scanning the roster for Sunday's L & M Grand Prix at Riverside Raceway, you might get the impression the United States is holding a special session on the West Coast.

Although there may not be any politicians, a good number of racing ambassadors from around the world will form the most diverse international field ever assembled at the Riverside road course.

In the eighth and final event of the L&M Continental 5000 series, there will be a New Zealander, three Aussies, two Canadians and two Englishmen — to say nothing of Americans like George Follmer, Sam Posey, Skip Barber and John Gunn.

New Zealand's Graham McRae, the series leader and winner of three of the first four races, needs a sixth place or better finish to take home all the marbles.

Brett Lunger of Pomona, the leading American driver, is 18 points behind McRae and is the only driver with a chance to catch the New Zealander.

Horst Kwech, who was born in Australia, has been racing in this country for 10 years. His countrymen, Kevin Bartlett and Bob Muir of Sydney are a strong double-entry.

L&M champion David Hobbs (Upper Boddington) and Brian Redman (Colne) form Britain's contingent. Hobbs has only one win this year — as opposed to five in 1971, having been plagued all season with engine problems. Redman, a veteran Formula driver in Europe, has two straight second place finishes.

Eppie Wietzes of Ontario leads the Canadian delegation.

He won the Watkins Glen L&M race and is fourth in the driver standings. Horst Kroll of Toronto is the second Canadian.

The first heat of the L&M 5000 begins at 1 p.m., but if the national anthems of all the countries represented are played, the start may be slightly delayed.

Stock Car Notes

A broken engine Sunday in the Delaware 500 at Dover Downs International Speedway could cost Bobby Allison the 1972 NASCAR Winston Cup Grand National driving championship.

Going into the race, the Alabama driver trailed Richard Petty by 32.9 points. Following Allison's departure on the 331st mile of the 500-mile event, he fell 113.9 points behind Petty, the defending titlist from North Carolina, who finished second to David Pearson.

Petty's point total is 7,226.90, while Allison has 7,113. There are five races remaining on the National Association for Stock Car Racing schedule in which Allison can start a comeback. The first is Sunday in the Old Dominion 500

Formula 5,000: 'Most Competitive'

BY SHAV GLICK
Times Staff Writer

Over Labor Day weekend there were three major auto races, the California 500 for Indy-type championship cars at Ontario, the Southern 500 for late model sedans at Darlington and the L&M Continental 5,000 for formula cars at Lime Rock.

At Ontario Roger McCluskey won by more than a lap (2½ miles). At Darlington Bobby Allison and David Pearson were seven laps (10 miles) ahead of

MOTOR RACING

the third place car. But at Lime Rock Brett Lunger's margin was measured in seconds (11) and yards (450).

THE FORMULA 5,000—Sam Posey takes turn in Chevy-powered Winston Delta Surtees which he will drive Sunday in LGM Grand Prix at Riverside Raceway.

got the kinks out Graham has had his troubles."

Lunger is the busiest rider on the circuit, racing the L&M series in the U.S. and the Formula II and 5,000 series in Europe. He raced in a F/2 race last Sunday in Belgium and will fly to London Monday for another next week.

MOTORCYCLE RACING—

Three days of racing are in store for Ascot Park fans, climaxed by Sunday afternoon's 8-mile national on the half-mile dirt oval. The shift from night to day for the national poses problems for Ascot favorites. Gene Romero, 1970 AMA No. 1, describes it: "Racing at Ascot at night is like racing on fly paper. In the daytime it's like wax paper." Two veterans, Dick Mann and Jim Rice, who do not like night races, will join newly crowned national champion Mark Brelsford and Gary Scott as favorites. Friday night Romero, Mert Lawwill and Kenny Roberts will join the Ascot regulars for a flat track show. Saturday night will be a T.T. steeple-

Hobbs, Posey Top Riverside Record

Sam Posey, Loretta Swit and Brian Redman

COMPETITION PRESS &
AUTOWEEK®

OCTOBER 14, 1972   50 CENTS

Redman Wins
RIVERSIDE
But McRae New Champ

STEWART
IN CANADA

Sandy Shepherd ran ninth and twelfth in his Lola T300

Pomona's Lunger Chasing McRae for L&M Crown

RIVERSIDE — At the 1971 L&M Grand Prix at Riverside International Raceway, people heard a lot about a new driver named Brett Lunger of Pomona.

A year and a half later, Brett Lunger is near the top and is the only driver remaining with a chance of catching series leader Graham McRae for the 1972 L&M Continental 5000 championship.

Lunger is seeking his first major championship title Sunday in the L&M Grand Prix at Riverside, the last race in the eight race series.

He trails New Zealander McRae by 18 points going into Riverside's race. If Lunger

ever be able to do," he says. "One of the keys to the success is being able to race nearly every week."

There's nothing like winning to spawn success but Lunger has managed to maintain his original goals.

"I have one major objective in auto racing," he says, "and that is to make a good living by racing cars. There's nothing in today's world I would rather do, and I consider myself lucky to be doing something I enjoy."

Lunger doesn't tell you he works hard to maintain his success. Although he won only once race in 1971, he received as much publicity as

he went.

The hard work paid off 1 year with third place in [] championship standings and much better sponsorship 1972.

Carl Hogan, head of Haggar-Hogan team, hi him ostensibly as the No man behind defending se champ Cavid Hobbs.

However, a quick look the standings going into last race—Hobbs is eig Lunger second—should you who's No. 1 on that te

BRIAN REDMAN WINS CONTINENTAL AT RIVERSIDE

Valvoline drivers finish 1-2-3 at Riverside.

Brian Redman won the L&M Continental 5000 race at Riverside Speedway. Redman, driving the new Valvoline/Chevron, averaged 116.737mph. Sam Posey finished second.

Graham McRae placed third overall and was declared the Series champion in the final point standings.

As you can see more professional race drivers at Indy, on dragstrips and on road race courses rely on Valvoline than any other brand. You can rely on Valvoline for your car, too.

Rex Ramsey: *"We ran this race with a car that we hand built, even poured the wheels out of mag. and spun them to finish in Red Legrand's shop in the San Fernando Valley. We built the chassis, headers, wing. suspension, body and even did the porting on the 302 Chev. that we built out of used parts from James Garner's blown up Daytona Coupe Lola that we bought for $600. Airheart gave us the brakes. We took the car to the last race, in Canada, the first with this car, and it rained so hard that everything was floating down the pit lane. None of ours, since didn't have any spares. Finished ninth, came back to Riverside and DNF'd."*
Compiler's Note – Read more about Rex in Chapter Thirteen.

John Cannon

The 1973 race consisted of two 60 mile heat races, with the top ten moving to the feature race. Brian Redman, driving a Lola, won, by winning one heat and the main event, picking up $18,250 for his efforts, followed by Jody Scheckter in a Trojan and Tony Adamowicz in a Lola. SCCA regional races accompanied the event with familiar names as class winners; Dick Starita, Dennis Aase, John Ryals and Jeff Kline. Read about the supporting races in Volume Two; available in the fall of 2022.

Redman Wins at Riverside

Examiner News Services

England's Brian Redman headed for Monterey and next Sunday's second leg of the L&M Formula 5000 race at Laguna Seca considerably more solvent than he was at this time last week.

Along with his Lola-Chevy, Redman was packing along $18,250, his reward for winning yesterday's $60,000 L&M Championship Series opener at Riverside International Speedway.

For the first 19 laps, Redman trailed Brett Lunger's Lola-Chevrolet. Then, when Culver City's Lunger was forced to take a pit stop with suspension troubles, Redman took over the lead on the 20th lap.

Pulls Away

He steadily drew away from South Africa's Jody Scheckter, who wound up the 40-laps over the 2.54 Riverside road course in second place, 12½ seconds back.

Redman's average speed of 118.413 mph was a course record for the distance.

Lunger spent only seconds in the pits, but by the time he returned to the race he was running seventh and managed to finish in sixth place.

Scheckter, who also finished second to Redman by less than a second in a heat race, won $10,550 for second place.

Lunger won his 60-mile heat race easily to share the front row with Redman for the start of the championship race.

With Lunger at the front and Redman and Scheckter in pursuit, the trio maintained a three-car duel for the opening half of the race, well ahead of the remainder of the pack.

Tire Wobbles

Redman confessed an out-of-balance tire made him believe he had a flat tire at one point, but he con-

BRIAN REDMAN
On to Monterey

tinued on. Scheckter, who posted the fastest qualifying speed of 121.677, had handling troubles, which he said prevented him from closing

ground on Redman.

Last year's series champion, Graham McRae of New Zealand, was forced out of his heat race with overheating problems in his McRae Chevrolet after moving from eighth at the start to third.

In the main race, McRae started 21st but diced his way into 10th before the overheating forced him out after only 11 laps. He wound up 23rd.

Two Spins

In the second heat race, Eddie Miller of Vail, Colo., spun out into a guard rail and Bobby Muir spun in the same spot, landing on top of Miller's car. Neither was hurt. Muir was even able to start the 101-miler, finishing 16th.

Bob Booth of Oakland, crashed his Formula V racer during a preliminary event yesterday and was hospitalized with a broken leg, the weekend's only injury.

The results:

[results list, illegible]

Redman prefers Riverside

By KEVIN CLOE
P-B Staff Writer

RIVERSIDE — It's a new season, but Brian Redman is picking up where he left off at the Riverside International Raceway.

The English driver made it two consecutive victories at the Riverside Raceway Sunday afternoon when he piloted his Steed Lola T-330 to a convincing victory in the opening of the 1973 L&M Continental Formula 500 Championship Series.

Driving under a new racing format, Redman fought off South African Jody Scheckter in the first heat of the two-heat qualifying session and then took advantage of Pomona's Brett Lunger's pit stop to pick up the victory in the main event.

Last year in the L&M finale of the eight-race series here, Redman captured both heats on his way to the win and finished fourth overall in the series standings.

"We were having trouble right from the start with the oil pressure," noted the defending Riverside champion. "We were losing from eight to 40 pounds of pressure for most of the day and still lost from 10 to 15 pounds during the last third of the race."

Redman shot into the lead on lap 20 of the 101-mile championship race when Lunger pulled into the pits for a 16-second checkup after sliding into turn 7.

Previous to that, Lunger claimed the lead right from the green flag at the start of the race after taking the second qualifying heat by more than 26 seconds over Australian Max Stewart.

The Pomona resident did set a track qualifying record on the 18th lap of the second heat when he piloted his Haggar Lola T-330 through the 2.54-mile Riverside course in 1:15.33 minutes for a speed of 121.388 miles per hour.

Scheckter, who was making his first appearance at Riverside, finished behind Redman in the first qualifying heat by only .48 of a second. The South African star held the lead over Redman in the heat for the first 19 laps after sit-

ting on the pole, but relinquished it midway through turn 9.

After passing Scheckter on the outside, Redman opened the advantage to a second and a half with only four laps left and then just held on for the victory.

Lunger's only serious challenge in his qualifying heat came from Tony (A to Z) Adamowicz for the first ten laps. But after making contact in turn 6 with Len Guneau, 'A to Z' dropped to fourth place and never really regained any momentum.

Before a crowd of 14,100 Redman pocketed $18,250 for his victory as part of the $60,000 total purse.

Scheckter finished second,

while Adamowicz was third, David Hobbs fourth, Peter Gethin fifth, Lunger sixth, Stewart seventh, Eppie Weitzes eighth and Gus Hutchison ninth — all finishing on the same lap as Redman.

Redman was clocked at 118.413 miles per hour in the 40-lap main event.

Lunger's record-setting lap during qualifying will go into the books as a separate standard.

In recapping the race, Redman reflected, "This has been a diabolical weekend. I can't remember when we've had such a bad weekend with the cars."

If this was a bad weekend for the Lancashire resident, then his competitors better

Scheckter debuts at Riverside

RIVERSIDE — David Hobbs calls him a "bloody nuisance." Brian Redman says he's a half-second quicker than Mark Donohue and Skip Barber says although he makes a lot of mistakes he is still one of the best drivers in the world.

The man they are talking about is 23-year-old Jody Scheckter, a South African who has set formula road racing in Europe on its ear.

"He is nothing short of phenomenal," says America's young road racing hopeful, Brett Lunger. "I've seen him do things on a race course I couldn't believe."

Even George Follmer, a man who is conservative when it comes to passing out compliments, is raving about Scheckter's ability.

"If his car is competitive in the L&M series," Follmer says, "he will blow everyone else's doors off."

Scheckter, who drives with what most people call "high-speed abandon," will be making his first driving appearance in the western United States this Sunday in the L&M Championship season opener at Riverside International Raceway.

The youngster from East London, So. Africa, will be driving a brand new Winston Delta Trojan designed and prepared by the successful Syd Taylor racing team. He enters the event as one of the favorites despite the best field ever assembled for an American formula 5000 race.

Among the international stars Scheckter must compete with are Englishmen Brian Redman, David Hobbs, Derek Bell and Peter Gethin; Australians Frank Matich, Graham McRae, Max Stewart and Bobby Muir; and Americans Lunger, Barber, Tony Adamowicz and Jerry Grant.

the first time he had ever driven a Formula 1 car — in fifth position and was running near the front when an accident sidelined him.

In the So. African Grand Prix earlier this year, he stunned both the field and his countrymen by qualifying on the front row with World Champion Emerson Fittipaldi and was running in first place before mechanical problems set in.

"He makes a lot of mistakes because he runs so hard," says Barber, who ra...

Bret Lunger

Redman waits for chance, wins again in L&M race

By TED GREEN
Sun-Telegram Sports Writer

RIVERSIDE — Brian Redman is a lot like golf's Bruce Crampton — unspectacular but unnervingly steady.

He would rather outfox an opponent than outrun him. He waits for the slightest mistake with unnerving patience and when it finally comes, he pounces like a hungry cat.

Repeating a script he authored at Riverside International Raceway only seven months ago, Redman took advantage of an error by front-running Brett Lunger yesterday to capture the opening race of the 1973 L&M Championship.

A crowd of 14,100 under overcast skies watched Redman, a 36-year-old road racing veteran from Colne, England, grab the lead from Lunger midway through the 100-mile sprint after the Pomona driver had temporarily skidded off the 2.54 mile course.

Redman Riverside King

RIVERSIDE, Calif. (AP) — Brian Redman of England has won the first race of the 1973 L&M Formula 5000 championship series but he says he won't be able to race in the series next event this weekend at Laguna Seca.

Redman captured Sunday's $60,000 101-miler at Riverside International Raceway, taking the lead on the 20th lap when Brett Lunger, who had set the pace from the start, was forced to stop with suspension trouble.

FROM THEN on Redman drew his Lola-Chevrolet away from South African Formula One champion Jody Scheckter and wound up winning the $18,250 first place money with a margin of 12½

seconds and an average speed of 118.413 over the 2.54-mile road course.

Redman, a Ferrari team driver, said he is committed to running in this weekend's World's Manufacturers championship race at Spa, Belgium.

Scheckter, who had set the best qualifying speed of 121.077 was second in a Trojan-Chevrolet to win $10,550 and also finished second behind Redman in their preliminary 60-mile qualifying heat.

Lunger, of Pomona, Calif., won his heat race to join Redman in the first row and jumped to the early lead in the main event.

He led until the suspension

trouble forced him to duck into the pits for a 16-second stop and by the time he got back out was back in seventh. Lunger battled his way as far as sixth before the race ended.

THIRD PLACE went to Tony Adamowicz of Torrance, Calif., in another Lola-Chevrolet and he won $6,000.

David Hobbs finished fourth in a Lola-Chevrolet and fellow Englishman Peter Gethin was fifth in a Chevron-Chevrolet.

Graham McRae of New Zealand, who won the series last year, had overheating troubles and completed only 11 laps.

L&M CONTINENTAL CONTENDER — Jerry Grant, making his return to road racing at Riverside Raceway, relaxes between sorting-out laps in his new Formula 5000 racer. Grant, who is most famous for his "almost win" last Memorial Day at Indianapolis, apparently has decided to abandon the United States Auto Club Championship Trail for the lucrative L&M Continental series. Two sixty mile qualifying heats and a 100 mile Grand Prix race will open the 1973 Formula 5000 season at Riverside this Sunday. Jerry will compete against some of the biggest stars in world racing. Twelve of them are top international formula race car drivers. No less than ten are given an even chance to win the series opener and a lions share of the $60,000 purse.

L&M road race series in 1973 debut Sunday

The L&M Championship, fast becoming the number one road racing series in America, makes its 1973 debut at Riverside International Raceway Sunday with an all-star international cast of drivers.

Forty-six entries have been filed for the $60,000 season opener, with 12 top foreign drivers meeting the best American racers in open-wheel, formula car racing.

Graham McRae of New Zealand, the defending series winner, and Brian Redman of England, last year's Riverside victor, head the list.

McRae and Redman by no means have a lock on things as the series opens. In the seven-year history of the series, 1973 figures to be the most competitive ever with over a dozen drivers given an outright chance to win.

Among them:

—Jody Scheckter, a brash, young newcomer from South Africa; very fast; has a violent driving style.

—David Hobbs, the old-pro from England; top equipment, top driver.

—Brett Lunger, the young American who plans on being the first Yank to win the L&M driving title since 1968.

—Peter Gethin, the diminutive Englishmen who was fastest in the early season races in Europe.

—Derek Bell, another front-running Britisher who has teamed with the experienced American team of Lothar Motschenbacher.

—Jerry Grant, almost won Indy a year ago; plans to run the L&M series this year.

—Tony Adamowicz, the last American to win the L&M Championship (1968); racing for the powerful Roy Woods Racing Team.

—Eppie Wietzes, Canada's best road racer and a winner on last year's tour; like Scheckter, drives with abandon.

And the list goes on.

Practice for the L&M Championship opens tomorrow and continues Saturday along with a schedule of sports car racing.

Sunday, April 29 will feature a total of six races, three of them highlighting the colorful Formula 5000 cars of the L&M Championship. Three sports car races will round out the program.

The large field of competitors for the L&M race will be split in two for two qualifying heats of 60 miles each. The top 10 finishers in each heat plus foar selected starters will make up the 24-car starting field for the L&M Championship. The first heat race begins at noon with the $60,000 L&M Championship taking the green flag at 3 p.m.

Graham McRae

Jerry Entin: *"I had a lot of experience at Riverside, first drag racing my Corvette, the driving "Ol Yeller and a Cheetah in the USRRC and, later a couple of McLarens and a Lola in both the USRRC and Can Am. After a few seasons in F-5000, I retired and ran a team, partnered with Sid Taylor to run Jody Scheckter in a Trojan T-101. We managed to win the championship".*

Sid Taylor, Jerry Entin, Ron Bennett, Jody Scheckter and Kerry Agapiou

Brian Redman: *"In early 1973 I started testing a new Lola T330 in England with Lola owner Eric Broadley and crew chief Jim Chapman, at the same time a T330 was sent to Chaparral in Midland , Texas where Jim Hall and his crew, Franz Weis and Troy Rogers were doing the same thing. In late April we all arrived at Riverside for the first race of the new season. During each practice and qualifying session, I drove the Broadley car and Jim Hall's. In spite of all the work we'd done in the U.K. I chose the Hall car; it had better balance and was more stable in the fast corners. I passed Jody Scheckter on the outside of Turn 9 to win the race, then missed the next two races due to driving the Ferrari 312 PB in Europe. In spite of winning 5 races to Jody's 4, he had more points due to running more races and won the 1973 championship"*

Brian Redman in the Carl Haas Lola T330

John Gunn – March

Gus Hutchinson

Skeeter McKitterick: *"Mike Koslosky bought an Eagle for me to drive in F5000. Preparation was always impeccable and very professional. I ran the car in some Nationals Continental series races pretty much drama free other than the one time I touched another car at the start of the event and folded back the front canard over the air inlet to the radiator, by halfway through the race my feet were being fried; the brake pedal was so hot that when I*

crossed the finish line I had to immediately pull over. The corner workers at start finish had to help me out or the car as I couldn't stand up on my third degree burned feet. – off to the doc in the paddock for some care; I declined the ambulance ride to the hospital, as after all I had my new girlfriend with me and wanted to show her I was tough! She later became my wife; lucky for me she was a physical therapist as there was more than once I needed her skills after stopping too quickly against some barrier somewhere along the line. Later on we moved up to a Chevron and a T-332 Lola"

VALVOLINE 1-2 AT RIVERSIDE

At the 1st L&M Championship Formula 5000 event at Riverside International Raceway on April 29, Brian Redman finished on top with a record speed of 118.413mph. He was driving a Jim Hall/Carl Haas Lola T-330. In a Sid Taylor Trojan T-101, Jody Scheckter trailed him to finish 2nd.

Both drivers were running on Valvoline® racing oil. In fact 16 out of the 24 starting cars had Valvoline in their crankcases.

Valvoline stands up to the toughest conditions. That's why pros like Brian Redman run on Valvoline. And why more professional race drivers at Indy, on major drag strips and on road race courses run on Valvoline racing oil than any other brand.

Now, doesn't that tell you something about the kind of motor oil you should run on?

Valvoline. We have the right kind of motor oil for every kind of car, every kind of driving.

Valvoline

For the man who really cares about his car.

A crowd of 30,000 saw Mario Andretti win $16,750 in 1974, beating Brian Redman and Warwick Brown, all in Lolas. Originally a Can Am was part of the program, but was cancelled so the supporting event was the IROC race, won by Bobby Allison. Read about the IROC Race in Volume Two; available in the fall of 2022.

Mario wins at Riverside

By OWEN KEARNS JR.

RIVERSIDE — Bobby Unser's high-priced turbocharged Indianapolis car only lasted 10 laps Sunday but its performance in the 100-mile Riverside Grand Prix sobered

Redman and another competitior.

Third heat of the International Race of Champions, which will be televised by ABC in February, went to Alabama's Bobby Allison, who

Jim Gustafson: *"In the spring of 1974, I purchased a Lola T-190 Formula 5000 car. I had been raced in Formula Ford when a friend put this car up for sale, at a very reasonable price. Despite not having a lot of racing experience, I decided I needed a car I could do a little pro racing with so I took the car to Riverside and it tried to kill me. This model Lola had an extremely short wheelbase, only 88". The previous owner attempted to upgrade the car by putting Lola T-192 bodywork on it. These two models were very similar. After realizing his mistake, Eric Broadly of Lola, made the new model's wheelbase 10" longer. With the new body on the old model, the front nose and wings extended much farther forward of the front wheels, and put a lot of downforce on the front of the car so it was really out of balance. Not knowing any better I went out for practice - Turn one was very fast and the car would get a little light as you went over the tunnel that went under the track. My first time at speed thru there resulted in me doing a high speed 360. There were concrete walls on both sides of the track at this point. Luckily for me, I didn't hit a thing. Over the course of the summer I made a lot of changes to the car, and in the fall entered the big pro Formula 5000 race. Key points about the race - Bobby Unser showed up in Dan Gurney's Olsonite sponsored Eagle Offy and both Mario Andretti and Brian Redman had their helmets stolen just before the race on Sunday. Mario had to borrow a helmet from Johnny Rutherford, and Brian grabbed the closest one he could find, and it barely fit. I spun on oil in my heat race along with James Hunt and others, and didn't qualify for the main event. I got rid of this car soon after this, but kept the memory."*

Bobby Unser

Sam Posey, blowing a engine in the Talon

James Hunt; Eagle

Brian Redman

Skeeter McKitterick: *"We purchased the Vel's Parnelli Jones Viceroy sponsored Mario Andretti Formula 5000 car. Vel's delivered the car to our team at Riverside and had Mario present to set the car up and introduce me to the Lola. I was able to wedge myself into Mario's seat and set a decent time first time in the car 1.8 seconds. slower than Mario on the day. My best race in the car was at Riverside for the season ending race and as it turned out the last F5000 race in history. In my qualifying heat I had a really good dice (side by side in turn nine a few times) with John Cannon in the March 761, basically the F1 chassis with a small block Chevy, for fourth in the heat. We started the main race according to finishing position in the qualifying heat races and had a good run in the final race running with Vern Schuppan, Brett Lunger, Teddy Pillete, Warwick Brown and John Cannon. Unfortunately we had mechanical issues and did not finish."*

Andretti (inside) and Unser

John Morton: *"Francisco Mir, identified as a "wealthy Argentine expatriate" although he had a Ferrari garage in Santa Monica started a F-5000 team from scratch. He was apparently well thought of by the Ferrari community, had taken a Daytona to LeMans once. No one lasted too long with him; Lella Lombardi, James Hunt, EFR and a few more. Ryan Falconer, who was building his motors, recommended me. At Riverside in 1974, I was seventh and Lella was ninth. He was a hard guy to deal with - used to lock us in the shop (me and crew chief Joe Cavaglieri). bring us lunch, then lock us in for the rest of the day, afraid we we're going to steal something"*

Riverside track cancels Can-Am

RIVERSIDE, Calif. (UPI) — The sixth and final Can-Am race of the season, scheduled here as part of the Riverside Grand Prix Oct. 26-27, has been canceled, it was announced Tuesday.

"The costs simply aren't justified by the quality of competition being offered," explained Riverside International Raceway president Les Richter.

A Formula 5000 race and two International Race of Champions events will make up the Riverside Grand Prix.

"It is our feeling that events like the Formula 5000 and the Race of Champions more accurately reflect the future of American road racing," added Richter. "We want to concentrate on developing the sport in those areas."

Riverside has been the site of Can-Am races since 1966, the Times Grand Prix, sponsored by the Los Angeles Times. But the Times removed its sponsorship this year.

The 1974 Can-Am series was won by England's Jackie Oliver of the UOP Shadow team. Oliver won four of the five races. The Can-Am finale, as it turned out, was last weekend at Elkhart Lake, Wis.

Michael Brayton's Eagle getting fuel

A crowd of 56,700, the largest since 1968, saw Mario Andretti in a Lola T332, lead all forty laps to win in 1975. First place paid $19,450. Mario was followed by teammate Al Unser with Brian Redman in third..

Mario wins Grand Prix

RIVERSDE, Calif. (UPI) — Mario Andretti breezed to the winner's circle in the California Grand Prix for Formula 5000 cars and Bobby Allison captured the International Race of Champions in similar easy fashion Sunday to climax a hectic weekend of racing at Riverside International Raceway.

competed in during the weekend.

"I couldn't believe it," said the smiling Nazareth, Pa., veteran, "I finished all four races."

Andretti was challenged only briefly in the first lap of the 40-lap, 100-mile Formula 5000 as he finished 15.676 seconds over Al Unser, his Viceroy-Lola

IROC finale at Daytona Beach, Fla., on Feb. 13.

Only nine drivers from the original 12-man field remain in competiton for the $212,000 purse. Eliminated Sunday were five-time NASCAR Grand National champion Richard Petty and Formula 1 stars Jody Scheckter of South Africa and Hunt.

Andretti leads RIR qualifying

Sun-Telegram News Service

RIVERSIDE — While his chief rival was having his problems, Mario Andretti was busy showing why he has been dominating the last races of the SCCA-USAC Formula 5000 season.

Andretti, driving a Parnelli Jones Viceroy Lola, toured the 2.54-mile Riverside International Raceway course at an average speed of 126.4 miles-per-hour in the first day of

Motor racing

practice for Sunday's $60,000 California Grand Prix Formula 5000 race.

Today's events start at 9 a.m. with more Formula 5000 practice runs. Another qualifying session for the 5000 events is scheduled for noon.

The second in a series of four International Race of Champions will begin at 2 p.m. It will be followed by more 5000 practicing and qualifying.

Andretti's top rival and USAC series champion,

Brian Redman, found the going a bit rough. He crashed his Lola into the wall earlier in the day and, even though he wasn't injured badly, his car was too badly damaged to be repaired for Sunday's race. It was Redman's second smashup into a crash wall in two weeks.

Redman's crew, headed by Jim Hall, set about

preparing a back-up car for the race but it won't be as fast as the original.

In other practice runs, Andretti's teammate, Al Unser, was clocked at 126.134 and Grand Prix racing star Jody Sheckter followed him at 125.389.

In practice runs for today's race Bobby Allison was the fastest finisher in one of the equally prepared Camaros to be driven by the 12 invited world class drivers. Allison's average speed was 100.371 m.p.h.

ι-powered offenses meet

Jim Gustafson: *"I was entered in this big season ending race, probably the zenith of this series, in my 1973 March 73A. I arrived on Thursday, the day before the track opened for practice and was staying at the track in a rented motorhome, and arranged for my chief mechanic to stay with me. Billy had a day job and made the drive out from Long Beach, only to find he was late, and registration was closed. With no other place to stay, Bill decided to sneak into the track thru a back gate, but was caught by security. After Bill explained he was part of my crew and would be signing in next morning, they released him. Well, next morning I was paid a visit by the director of SCCA Pro Racing, and was read the riot act. I was told I must go to see track president Les Richter and apologize. I had heard he was a no nonsense fella, former LA Rams and NFL Hall of Fame guy. So, I never did go to meet him. I'm not ashamed to say, I was too scared. I now look back and wish I did, how often do you get a one on one with a legend like that"* Compiler's Note: Jim didn't qualify for the race, along with twelve others !!

Brian Redman: *"We were back for the final F5000 race of the year plus the IROC race. In one of the worst racing weekends of my career, it all started to go wrong on Friday morning when the left front tire on my Lola T332 burst on the apex of fast Turn 9, I went straight across the road into the wall, hard. My helmet broke the plexiglass screen at each side of the cockpit. Next in Saturday's IROC race, I was leading Richard Petty when he gave me a gentle tap in the esses spinning me through the dirt, I rejoined but coming fast into Turn 9, a stone jammed the throttle open, and I went head on into the Turn 9 wall. Sunday we had the second IROC race to be followed immediately by the F5000 race. I was having great difficulty holding my head up due to neck muscle damage during the F5000 accident on Friday and when I got out of the Camaro, my dark blue racing suit was black with sweat. The F5000 backup car was the unloved T400, which I'd never raced. I finished third, behind Mario and Al Unser, Sr. but won my second championship."* Compiler's Note – Brian Redman was the winningest driver in the Formula 5000 series with three championships

Redman hits wall, needs backup car

RIVERSIDE — Mario Andretti and Al Unser, who have dominated the last races of the SCCA-USAC Formula 5000 season although they lost the championship to Brian Redman, continue to lead the speed parade into Sunday's finale at Riverside International Raceway.

Bad luck continues to dog Redman, who crashed hard into the Turn 9 wall Friday and put his car out of the race. Redman will have to drive his less competitive backup car Sunday.

Andretti's fastest prac-

tice lap Friday in the Vel's Parnelli Jones Viceroy Lola was 126.408 mph on the 2.54-mile road course, and Unser was clocked at 126.134 in a nearly identical car.

Redman, sixth fastest in his backup Boraxo Lola T-400, was topped by grand prix driver Jody Scheckter, former drag racing champ Danny Ongais and a star of the Long Beach Grand Prix, Tony Brice.

In practice runs for today's International Race of Champions heat, Bobby Allison turned in the fastest time with a 100.371 clocking.

Practice times:

The 1976 race, the last race in the last season of Formula 5000 was won by fast qualifier Al Unser in the Vel's Parnelli Jones Lola T332 followed by Jackie Oliver in the Dodge powered Shadow and Brian Redman in the Carl Haas Lola T332. Unser's win paid $19.950.

Al Unser Easy Winner Over Oliver and Redman

Rocky Moran: *"I got to drive Jack McCormack's Talon, along with Sam Posey and John Woodner. Broke something and didn't start. But the next year I had had a ride in a Lola T332, broke that after 23 laps"* Compiler's Note – Rocky moved into the Can Am ranks in 1978 and then into Indy cars and the Gurney GTP Toyotas

Unser coasts to F-5000 win

By PAUL OBERJUERGE
Sun-Telegram Sports Writer

RIVERSIDE — Cale Yarborough and Al Unser won the two featured events at Riverside International Raceway Sunday, but Bobby Unser was more impressive and Brian Redman got a more important victory.

NASCAR's Yarborough grabbed a first-lap lead in the early race — the third leg of the International Race of Champions — and cruised to

tively have not made it. The engine went dead on the last turn and I just coasted across the finish line after taking it out of gear."

Unser had qualified for the pole position, and led the rest of the 33-car field by as many as 17 seconds before easing off the last few laps. He averaged 121.555 miles per hour in his blue and white American Racing Team Lola T-332.

Unser finished second in the

"There are a lot of conflicting dates with USAC races," the dark-haired 37-year-old said. "It would be nice if something could be worked out, but it doesn't seem too likely."

Unser earned $19.950 for his win, Oliver got $12,300 and Redman picked up $9,500.

Al by no means was the only Unser to have a good day at RIR.

Yarborough upheld the reputation of the "good 'ol boys" in the IROC

Formula 5000 in trouble

RIVERSIDE, Calif. (AP) — Brian Redman of England is on the verge of his third straight Formula 5000 road racing championship as the 1976 season ended here Sunday with a 101.6-mile sprint.

The result could be historic. Redman might be the last champion the ailing series will have.

The entry list for the Riverside finale is the most formidable of the year. And the crowd possibly will be the best. But this has not been a good season for North America's premier road racing series.

Competition has continued to fade since the glory days of 1974 and 1975 when Mario Andretti, Bobby and Al Unser, Johnny Rutherford and others gave the series immense popular appeal. The series is now — with a few exceptions — a haven for Formula 1 hopefuls or has-beens, who have done little to spur interest or dwindling gate receipts.

Only seven races were on the schedule this season; one track was visited twice. There really hasn't been a good crowd all season, and promoters are wary about next year. The series no longer is visiting places like Atlanta, Seattle, Long Beach, Laguna Seca, Ontario and others that it used to.

Promoters at most of the healthy road racing circuits already have made discreet inquiries with the U.S. Auto Club to see if larger, more powerful Indianapolis cars could be booked next year instead of F-5000.

USAC announced last week its intention to give up its co-sanction of the series with the Sports Car Club of America. The two sanctioning groups had once envisaged a common formula for F-5000 and Indy cars, but no one was willing to make the first move.

Dan Gurney, who builds cars for both series, was one of F-5000's strongest boosters, but now he has switched his emphasis to building a new Indy car. An F-5000 prototype with much promise now is only collecting dust in his shop.

The Shadow cars have been running this season and may not be back next year. Al Unser's team also is doubtful for 1977.

The SCCA is talking about a six- to nine-race schedule next year, but veteran George Follmer said: "I don't really know of any tracks that want them back."

Follmer was champion this season of the SCCA's revived

Brian Redman

Oliver, Redman, Jones and Ongais

Chapter Twelve – Indy Cars

Riverside native Rex Mays won the big car race at Ascot in 1936, then was killed in a similar race at Del Mar in 1949. It was only appropriate that the first Indy car race since 1949, held at Riverside in 1967, be called the Rex Mays 300. First, Dan Gurney tested there to convince Les Richter that it would be a good show.

MARCH 1966

RACEWAY

THE OFFICAL PUBLICATION OF RIVERSIDE INTERNATIONAL RACEWAY

EXCLUSIVE REPORT
Gurney tests Indy car at Riverside

USRRC Preview   **Daytona 500**
Championship Trail   **Drags-Sports Cars**

Read this Raceway Magazine article on the attached DVD

The claimed attendance in 1967 was a disputed 38,000, with terrible weather, cold and overcast for the November 26th race as polesitter Dan Gurney in his own manufacture Eagle won $31,525. Second was Bobby Unser in the Wilke Eagle, followed by Mario Andretti in the Clint Brawner Hawk. A.J. Foyt's fifth place secured him the USAC championship.

GURNEY GETS USAC WIN ON 'HIS' COURSE

Lloyd Ruby spun his Ford-powered rear engine Mongoose on the initial lap of the 300-mile Rex Mays Memorial USAC championship car race at Riverside Raceway Nov. 26. At left Gordon Johncock (left) and Jerry Grant are about to go around the spinning Ruby.

At right George Follmer (#17), Jerry Titus (#11), Lothar Motschenbacher (#96) and Charlie Parsons begin to thread their way through the first lap incident. Ruby worked his way up to finish fourth. (Dave Lundeen photos)

Gurney Wins Rex Mays 300; Foyt Clinches Driving Title

RIVERSIDE, Calif. (AP) — Despite a rash of protests, Dan Gurney broke his jinx yesterday, driving his powerful All-American racer to a victory in the first running of the Rex Mays 300-mile race for Indianapolis-type cars.

A. J. Foyt, Houston, Tex., finishesd fifth but still won the United States Auto Club national championship for a record fifth time. He beat Mario Andretti who had been aiming for his third consecutive championship.

Gurney, of Corona Del Mar, Calif., long a favorite at the Riverside International Raceway, drove spectacularly, coming from behind to take the lead in the last of the 116 laps.

After the race, Clint Brawner,

ie Ginther, meanwhile, lodged a protest against the capacity of Andretti's fuel tank. It, too, was found to be legal.

Unser Second

Finishing behind Gurney, who took home $31,525, was Bobby Unser of Albuquerque, N.M. Unser, who pocketed $10,150 in second place money, had taken the lead late in the race when Andretti, of Nazareth, Pa., had to stop for fuel. Andretti won $7,600.

Two favorite drivers — Jim Clark of Duns, Scotland, and John Surtees of Limpseld, England — dropped out with mechanical problems early in the race.

At the start, Gurney jumped into a short lead with Clark pushing all the way.

Clark took the lead on the 23rd

gine trouble.

Gurney resumed the lead.

A. J. Foyt, of Houston, Tex., was knocked out of the race briefly as his car swept through a series of turns near the start-finish line.

He and Al Miller of Roseville, Mich., tangled in the turns and drove off the course, disabling both cars.

Foyt jumped into the car driven by Roger McCluskey, of Tucson, Ariz., who had taken second place behind Gurney when Clark dropped out.

Foyt made one lap in McCluskey's Ford-powered machine, stopped in the pit to check a tire then sped back onto the track to stay in contention.

Gurney lost the lead several

SCREAMING EAGLE—Dan Gurney pilots Eagle to top speed of 117.735 m.p.h. in Rex Mays 300 qualifying.
Times photo by Joe Kennedy

Gurney on Pole in Rex Mays 300

DUEL FOR LEAD — Dan Gurney (48) of Corona del Mar, Calif. and Bobby Unser (6), Albuquerque, N.M., race almost side by side around turn during closing laps of the Rex Mays 300 at Riverside (Calif.) International Raceway. Gurney took the lead on the next-to-last lap and won, with Unser second. Left background is Johnny Rutherford. (AP Wirephoto)

COMPETITION PRESS &
AUTOWEEK

December 16, 1967   25 Cents

GURNEY'S RIVERSIDE VICTORY !

Daytona R
amps

Starting Grid - Gurney and Clark

DAN GURNEY GETS A KISS FROM HIS WIFE AT RIVERSIDE RACEWAY
He drove his Indianapolis type car to victory in the Rex Mays 300 race.—(AP)

Dan Gurney

Coming up in the *Good Season*
at Riverside International Raceway

THE REX MAYS "300"

NOVEMBER 26, 1967

Indy cars and drivers in the Los Angeles area
for the first time in more than 30 years

The final event on the
United States Auto Club's
"Championship trail."

Non Championship F/1 Race Set for Riverside

RIVERSIDE, Calif., Aug. 9 — ACCUS, meeting in Los Angeles last week, has granted a full FIA International listing for a F/1 race at Riverside Raceway in Nov. 1967.

The announcement came at the conclusion of the meeting when the committee, consisting of representatives from USAC, NASCAR, SCCA and NHRA, took action on a sanction request submitted through SCCA last week by Raceway President Les Richter.

"We are extremely delighted to have the race date granted," Richter said when informed of the August ACCUS action. "The addition of such an event to our calendar helps fulfill our plans to conduct a well-rounded schedule of premium races at the Raceway.

"A race of this type and caliber, which is open to leading drivers from Europe, as well as the United States, is something that has been in great demand by our fans."

Exact date of the race according to Richter is Thanksgiving weekend of next year, Nov. 25 and 26. A full international listing on the world calendar of racing events means that several types of cars are eligible to compete although Richter says the event would probably be restricted to F/1 cars.

"Now that we have the calendar listing," Richter went on, "we intend to proceed immediately with final plans as to distance, prize money, and entries.

"We are hopeful of having European drivers participate since many of them will be in this country at that time of year. Pitting them against top-notch American drivers will provide an exciting event."

The November race, which will be sanctioned by SCCA and conducted by the Cal Club Region, will not be a world points race counting towards the driving championship. FIA rules permit only one such race per country and Watkins Glen currently has that listing.

There is no restriction on drivers, however, and Richter said he plans to extend invitations to such top-ranking European stars as Indianapolis winners Jimmy Clark and Graham Hill, plus Bruce McLaren, Jackie Stewart, John Surtees, and Jack Brabham.

In this country, Richter said he plans to invite drivers from all the major sanctioning organizations, men such as Dan Gurney, A.J. Foyt, Parnelli Jones and Mario Andretti from USAC, Jim Hall, Hap Sharp, Ken Miles, Bob Bondurant and Ritchie Ginther from SCCA, plus several of the NASCAR drivers who are experienced open cockpit competitors such as Bobby Johns and Cale Yarborough.

A previous F/1 race, this one the official Grand Prix of the U.S. was held at Riverside in 1960 and was won by Stirling Moss in a Lotus before a disappointing crowd.

Observers noted at the time of the announcement that a preliminary race was required to be run on a venue the year before in order to qualify it for a grand epreuve.

Outcast Mitter Climbs to Crown

By D. O. Cozzi

FRIEBURG, Germany, July 31 — Gerhardt Mitter virtually clinched the prestigious European Hillclimb Championship for Porsche with his mountain win here today.

Driving a 2-liter eight-cyl. prototype, Mitter won the Frieburg-Schauinsland climb over his closest rival and last year's champion, Ludovico Scarfiotti.

Scarfiotti totalled just two secs. more than Mitter's time in the required two runs up the 6.9-mi. hill.

The December 1st Rex Mays 300 of 1968 drew a crowd of 36,000 and was won by polesitter Dan Gurney once again, leading from start to finish and collecting $18,050 for the win. Bobby Unser was second and won the USAC championship followed by Mario Andretti. This was the last race for turbine cars. Accompanying events included a celebrity vintage race and an air show..

GURNEY WINS REX MAYS 300

Bobby Unser Nips Andretti For USAC Title

By Del Owens
Autoweek Managing Editor

RIVERSIDE, Calif., Dec. 1 – Dan Gurney and Bobby Unser, finishing second a lap off the pace, were the big winners here today at the 116-lap, 301.6-mile Rex Mays 300 United States Auto Club Championship car road race.

Gurney, driving the Olsonite Eagle-Gurney Ford, successfully defended his 1967 Rex Mays win, roaring to victory at an average speed of 111.689mph to break his own record of 108.391, set during last year's 300-mile event. The Santa Ana, Calif., driver/builder pocketed $18,050 for his win.

Unser, in the Rislone Eagle-Ford, by finishing second, captured the USAC National Driving title, 6.8 points ahead of Mario Andretti.

Andretti and Unser, the only challengers for the 1968 crown, brought their title bid to the Rex Mays, the final race on the 1968 USAC calendar, separated by only 308 points. Andretti, by completing the distance no less

(Continued on page 12)

The final appearance of the Indy turbines ended as both cars were demolished in a crash against a boiler plate retaining wall during the Rex Mays 300 USAC Championship car road race at Riverside, Calif., Dec. 1. Mario Andretti, replacing

Joe Leonard in the Parnelli Jones Firestone Lotus-Turbine when his own car went out with engine failure, had only completed one lap in the car when he tangled with Art Pollard in the Granatelli STP machine. Neither driver was injured.
(Bob Perry photo)

Gurney Wins Rex Mays 300; Unser USAC Driving Title

397

Gurney Garners Pole at Riverside

By MILES OTTENHEIMER
Staff Writer

RIVERSIDE — Determined Dan Gurney blazed to a new Riverside Raceway record here yesterday to garner the coveted pole position for today's Rex Mays 300 mile battle for Indy type cars.

Gurney drove his Ford powered Eagle Racer around this tricky, 2.6-mile course at a speed of 118.556 to shatter his own record of 117.735 set in the Rex Mays race last year.

Second fastest qualifier after two days of trials was Mario Andretti, while San Jose's Joe Leonard in one of the two turbine powered cars in the

DAN GURNEY

the 41 qualifiers will start today's race, which is the second longest competition scheduled by USAC, next to the Indy 500.

LEONARD PROBLEMS

Earlier yesterday, Leonard had some break problems with his bright red turbine machine, but he came back toward the end of the session to turn his fastest time.

The other turbine, piloted by Art Pollard, experienced problems yesterday too. All four wheels locked on the car and it went into a spin, but wasn't damaged. Nonetheless Art is a doubtful starter for today.

Andretti, who is after his third national driving title

Gurney and Andretti

398

PARNELLI JONES GIVES MARIO ANDRETTI MOTORBIKE RIDE

Al Unser; Lola Ford

Joe Leonard; Lotus Turbine

Daring Dan Wins It Again With Castrol Motor Oil!

California's Dan Gurney surprised no one on December 1, 1968, when he wheeled his screaming Eagle around Riverside's 2.6 mile course to capture the Rex Mays 300 for the second straight year!

Also to no one's surprise, Dan had Castrol Motor Oil working with him inside his 305cid pushrod Ford engine, (with his specially designed Gurney heads), as he easily lapped the entire USAC field.

Gurney's Eagle screamed to a new track record of 111.689mph, cracking his own record of 108.39lmph, set during last year's 300 mile event.

"Of all the oils I might have picked—and I've tried alot of them—," says Gurney, "I settled on the new Castrol XLR racing oil because this multigrade oil is fortified with Liquid Tungsten to give superior performance under the most severe service. I recommend Castrol XLR for any car, racing or not, if the owner really cares about his power plant."

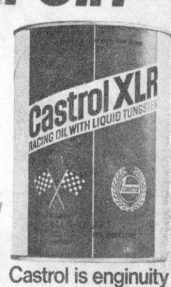

MOTOR OIL

Castrol is enginuity

Skip Scott; Lola Ford

Mark Donohue; Eagle Chevy

A.J. Foyt; Coyote Ford

Jack Brabham; Brabham Repco

Watch the 1968 Rex Mays 300 on the attached DVD

In the last race of the 1969 season, an unusually late date in December, Dan Gurney won the pole and finished third. First place Mario Andretti won $19,850 in the Brawner Ford with Al Unser second. Considered the most exciting race of the year, the disappointing crowd of 18,500 was blamed on the pre Christmas date and increase in ticket prices. "That size crowd didn't even cover the $75.000 purse, the richest USAC event outside the Indy 500, and was compared to 36,000 the year before, 50,000 at stock races and 77,000 for sportscar races", said track publicity director Jack Matthews. Some new innovations, this would be the last race for four wheel drive and the first with automatic transmissions in some cars. The automatics were developed by the Spar brothers of B&M fame. Indy cars wouldn't come back again until 1981 under CART.

MARIO ENDS '69 WITH REX MAYS VICTORY

Gurney Dominates, Finishes Third Behind Al Unser's Lola

By Del Owens
Managing Editor

RIVERSIDE, Calif., Dec. 7 — Mario Andretti capped his most successful season in U.S. Auto Club Championship car racing by posting a come-from-behind, 37-second margin of victory in today's USAC finale, the Rex Mays 300.

The 120-lap race over Riverside International Raceway's revamped 2.54-mile road circuit wasn't decided until the 117th lap when Dan Gurney's race-dominating Eagle-Ford slowed with differential failure. Gurney, who had held as much as a 1:50-second lead over the field, decreased his speed with 10 laps to go, and just three circuits before the checkered, was passed by Andretti in the sweeping right-hand turn nine. Two laps later Gurney was also passed by Al

Unser's Vel's Parnelli Jones Lola-Ford to bring his Olsonite-sponsored machine home in frustrating third; 1:2 behind the winner.

Andretti completed the 300-mile affair in 2.47 for an average speed of 109.451mph. The Nazareth, Pa., driver collected $19,650 out of a total $75,000 purse for his victory in the STP-sponsored Brawner-Hawk 255cid Ford.

MARIO'S RECORD

With today's victory, the 29-year-old Andretti became the first driver to top 5000 points in USAC's Championship car division. In six years of racing in the division, Andretti has posted 30 wins and a total of 19,414 Championship points.

Finishing behind the top three was Bobby Unser in the Bardahl Eagle-turbo Ford. Last year's USAC National Champion entered the race second in the standings behind Andretti but lost the position to brother Al when a last-lap pit stop

(Continued on page 18)

Review Next, Then Vacation

LAFAYETTE, Calif., Dec. 9 — Autoweek's annual 1969 Review will be published next week.

The issue will present a complete wrapup of activities in all major competition series, as well as automotive milestones during the past year.

The issue will also mark a two-week interruption in publication as the Autoweek staff enjoys their annual vacation.

Rex Mays 300 winner Mario Andretti pushes his Hawk-Ford ahead of George Follmer's Lotus-Plymouth. Bill Simpson's Gilbert-Chevy follows. Follmer was running fourth when he spun and finished 14th, Simpson ran out of fuel in the final turn but finished eighth.
(Autoweek photo)

COMPETITION PRESS & AUTOWEEK

Vol. 19, No. 50

December 27, 1969

AUTOWEEK THIS WEEK

Rindt Auto Show
● Jochen Rindt staged his annual auto show in Vienna and included Art Arfons' "Green Monster" as one of the cars on exhibit. Jackie Stewart also guests with Arfons on

Mario Breaks USAC Records With First Riverside Win

(Continued from page 1)

for consultation denied him the possibility of overtaking the faltering Gurney for a third-place finish. If Bobby Unser had been able to garner the third-place Championship counters, he would have remained second in the National standings, 15 points ahead of Al Unser.

TRACK TAKES TOLL

The 300-miler didn't see a single competitor in the 30-car field void of mechanical problems. Only 16 cars were running at the finish, with many at a greatly reduced speed.

Gurney took the immediate lead at the green after three pace laps—two scheduled and an additional circuit when Gurney came down to take Shim Malone's flag far ahead of the field.

As Gurney went into the lead from his record-breaking pole position, Andretti slipped past Mark Donohue's Sunoco Eagle-Chevy, dropping the second-fastest qualifier to third. Andretti, who said earlier this year that he wouldn't let Gurney have an easy race at Riverside, proved his statement by putting his bright red machine at the head of the pack on the seventh circuit.

MARK STAYS CLOSE

Two laps later, Gurney repassed Andretti while Donohue stayed in close striking distance in third.

Johnny Parsons Jr., driving the

Victorious trio in the Riverside International Raceway winner's circle—USAC's 1969 National Champion Mario Andretti, car owner Andy Granatelli and Firestone's Bill McCrary. (Jean Beeching photo)

Joe Hunt Magneto Drake Offy-powered dirt car, completed only one lap when his mount became locked in gear on the pace lap. John Cannon dropped out of the race after two laps when the borrowed turbo Ford powerplant in his Vollstedt dropped a valve. The Vollstedt crew spent last night

Donohue playing three-car bumper tag at the head of the pack, Roger McCluskey settled his Coyote-Ford into fourth, three seconds behind the leaders, with Gordon Johncock's Gilmore Broadcasting Eagle-Ford in fifth, Bobby Unser sixth, Gurney's Eagle teammate Swede Savage in seventh, and

made an attempt to take the lead, out-pulling both Gurney and Andretti on the long back chute, but fell back to third when the cars entered the sweeping right hander heading toward start-finish.

MUTHER TANGLES

Rick Muther became a spectator

of road racing, spun in front Muther, leaving little room to pa Muther's Two Jacks Lola-Of clipped the rear of Session's handing the Lola

MOD MARIO ANDRETTI, sporting side-burns and the sign of the times, accepts the winning trophy and $19,650 for his triumph in the Rex Mays 300 at Riverside International Raceway. Andretti averaged 109.44 miles an hour in a Ford.

Student and Teacher

Former San Bernardino driver Swede Savage listens as Dan Gurney explains a point about driving during practice for the recent Rex Mays 300 at Riverside Raceway. Gurney says when his driving days are over he would like to have a stable of young drivers racing cars he's built.

Wally Dallenbach finished seventh; here leading Bill Simpson

Mark Donohue

Al and Bobby Unser

AUTOMATIC SHIFTS GET TEST SUNDAY IN REX MAYS 300

BY SHAV GLICK
Times Staff Writer

The era of the four-wheel drive in U.S. Auto Club racing ends Sunday in the Rex Mays 300 at Riverside, but a new era may be ushered in during the same race—and in the same two cars.

Andy Granatelli's flaming red Nos. 20 and 40, driven by Sam Posey and George Follmer, will be steered around Riverside Raceway's 2.5-mile Indianapolis-type car course for the last time by four-wheel drive, but they also will have an automatic transmission.

Last year the Rex Mays 300 marked the final ride of Granatelli's turbine, legislated out of existence by USAC as the four-wheel drive was this year.

Plymouth Engines

Both Posey and Follmer will have Plymouth stockblock engines and torqueflite automatic transmissions in their racing cars.

The transmissions were developed by two young Van Nuys engineers, Bob and Don Spahr of B & M Automotive Products in cooperation with Chrysler engineer George Wallace. Bob, 35, and Don, 31, have been developing drag racing transmissions for 16 years and were given the task, by Chrysler, of creating a workable automatic for road racing cars.

Posey, a rapidly-rising, 24-year old driver from Sharon, Conn., drove with the automatic transmission in a road race at Kent, Wash., and came away enthused with the innovation.

"The automatic was worth more than a second a lap, at least," said Posey Friday as he prepared to qualify for Sunday's 300-mile race.

"It reduced manual shifting from 16 shifts to two a lap," he said. "And it freed my left foot, letting me ride the brake going through turns, so I could keep the engine running at full power. Even though shifting becomes an intuitive, almost mechanical, movement by a race driver, its elimination gives you more time to think about what you're doing."

Posey thinks enough of the automatic transmission that he is having one installed in the Dodge Challenger he will drive in next year's Trans-Am sedan series.

The success of the automatic transmission in its first race is due to a remarkable testing device developed by the Spahrs called the Environmental Drive Train Development Lab. It tests transmissions under a variety of stresses like a dyno does for engines.

"I wish it were possible to test other aspects of a car as accurately as this does for transmissions," praised Posey, who plans to move his Trans-Am project headquarters to Los Angeles to be near B & M Automotive and the

Willow Springs testing track.

"There's nothing like Willow Springs in the East," said the young driver. "In fact, there is hardly any place to test cars back home."

Posey will be making his first ride at Riverside since a spectacular crash during practice for the Continental Grand Prix wrecked his Formula A car last April.

Dan Gurney Fastest in Riverside Trials

RIVERSIDE—Dan Gurney drove his Ford-powered Olsonite Eagle around Riverside International Raceway's 2.5-mile course at 118.513 m.p.h., nearly two m.p.h. faster than any other driver during Friday's three-hour qualifying session for Sunday's $85,000 Rex Mays 300.

The Corona del Mar driving veteran has sat on the pole and won both previous 300-mile Rex Mays races.

Another three-hour qualifying session, from 2 to 5 p.m., will be held today, with the fastest 30 cars starting Sunday at 1 p.m.

in the Mays race, long USAC road race of the year.

Trans-Am driving champion Mark Donohue is second behind Gurney at 116.731 m.p.h., a fraction ahead of Al Unser, 116.720. Indianapolis winner Mario Andretti is next at 115.830.

1. Dan Gurney (Corona del Mar), Eagle-Ford, 118.513 m.p.h.; 2. Mark Donohue (Media, Pa.), Lola-Chevrolet, 116.731; 3. Al Unser (Albuquerque), Ford, 116.720; 4. Mario Andretti (Nazareth, Pa.), Hawk-Ford, 115.830; 5. Bobby Unser (Albuquerque), Eagle-Ford, 113.924; 6. Swede Savage (Santa Ana), Eagle-Ford, 113.36; 7. A. J. Foyt (Houston), Coyote-Ford, 112.781; 8. Johnny Rutherford (Ft. Worth), Eagle-Ford, 112.697; 9. Gordon Johncock (Hastings, Mich.), Eagle-Ford, 112.689; 10. Roger McCluskey (Tucson), Coyote-Ford, 112.079; 11. George Follmer (Arcadia), Lotus-Plymouth, 111.721.

Women Scribes Invading 'Never-Never Land'

By ALLEN WOLFE

The liberalization of the American woman is almost complete and absolute. The stepping stones to this freedom were laid on Aug. 26, 1920, when women's suffrage (the right to vote) was ratified through the 19th Amendment.

In 49 years since that momentous day, the "delicate sex" has invaded the heretofore solely male domain of sports. With the banner of equality as their bible, women have become an integral part of the American sports scene.

Lee Breedlove donned a crash helmet in 1965 and streaked 310 mph over the Bonneville Salt Flats in Utah. Babe Zaharias compiled an auspicious record in track and field and golf spanning 25 years, and led by Diane Crump, a brave band of girls stirred up controversy in the field of thoroughbred racing through their efforts to turn it into a "co-educational" sport.

Despite this overwhelming tide of female influence, the United States Auto Club (USAC) has remained staunch and steadfast in the face of it all. That is, until now.

Since 1909, USAC and its former counterpart, the American Automobile Assn., succeeded in banning women from the pits and garage area of all the races that came under its jurisdiction. To this date, no woman has trod the hallowed ground known affectionately as Gasoline Alley at the Indianapolis Motor Speedway. However, that may be altered on May 30, 1970.

In an unprecedented move, USAC competition director Henry Banks lifted the ban prohibiting women journalists from the pits and working garages last weekend at Riverside International Raceway. It occurred during qualifying for the Rex Mays 300, final step in the 18-race series for Indianapolis Championship cars.

But the clemency was only temporary.

"It must be emphasized that USAC changed its policy for the Rex Mays race only and does not apply to other USAC sanctioned events," said Banks. "The entire matter of working press credentials for women will be reviewed at a later date.

"There is a tremendous interest in covering auto racing today by female reporters and photographers," continued Banks. "As the sport continues to grow and involve more and more legitimate news women, we will have to recognize their needs and re-evaluate our policies regarding them."

A vanguard of 10 women registered to cover the Rex Mays race, with the majority of them taking at least one trip to the pits for qualifying.

P.S. to Henry Banks: But Henry, what about women mechanics?

DATSUN DEALER

Dusty Brandel: "Before this, Bob Russo and Deke Houlgate, the p.r. guys, would bring drivers up to the administration building for interviews. Banks came to an AARWBA (American Auto Racing Writers and Broadcasters) meeting and we yelled and screamed about not being allowed in the pits. Someone said, "if we don't write about you, you won't make any money" and that struck home so he made an exception for the USAC race at Riverside only. Took a couple of years for them to come around at Indianapolis" Compiler's Note - Dusty was the first woman allowed in a NASCAR garage (1972) and the first women allowed in the Indianapolis Motor Speedway Press room (1971). She is a member of the West Coast Stock Car Hall of Fame and a recipient of the Squier Hall Award for NASCAR Media Excellence.

USAC First: Female Scribes In Racing Area

RIVERSIDE, Calif., Dec. 7 — A "first" in U.S. Auto Club history was recorded here today when authorized female writers and photographers were allowed in the garage and pit areas for today's Rex Mays 300.

Henry Banks, USAC's director of competition, said the long-time ban on women in these areas was being lifed on a trial basis only.

The decision, he emphasized, was made concerning road courses only at this time, in particular this race. Further policy decisions, which may affect all types of USAC events, will be announced following a review of today's trial run.

The matter of women in the working pit and garage areas at USAC races was presented at a meeting yesterday morning of the American Auto Racing Writers and Broadcasters Assn., attended by Banks.

He was asked to consider a change in USAC policy in view of the fact there are an increasing number of women who are legitimate qualified writers and photographers covering the auto racing circuit.

Banks issued a statement shortly after the meeting, lifting the ban for the Riverside race.

Riverside International Raceway's Dusty Brandel and automotive journalist Jean Beeching flank USAC's Henry Banks in the track's garage area. The two distaff members of the fourth estate were prime movers in opening the gates to qualified automotive journalists and photographers at the Rex Mays 300.

Swede Savage; Eagle

Back for the first time since 1969, the 1981 L.A. Times California 500 looked much different from the previous events. CART was the sanctioning body. Only one Offenhauser made the field, John Mahler in the Trench Shoring Penske Offy. 51,246 fans braved the hundred degree August temperature to see Rick Mears in the Penske Cosworth win $30.915. Second was Gordon Johncock in a Wildcat Cosworth followed by Bill Alsup in another Penske. Only nine of the twenty eight starters made it to the finish line. Polesitter Geoff Brabham led seventeen laps before mechanical problems forced him out. The supporting event was a NASCAR Winston West race. The supporting Stock Race .is covered in detail in Volume Two, available in the fall of 2022.

Mears survives Cal 500 battle of attrition

For Jerry Karl (left), who crashed into Turn 8 wall after collision with Johnny Rutherford, it was rough day at Cal 500. For winner Rick Mears, however, it was another story.

Heat, mishaps trim field to 9 finishers

By JIM SCHULTE
Sun Sports Writer

RIVERSIDE — The predictions for Sunday's California 500 called for a high attrition rate. Expect 40 to 50 percent of the 28-car field to not be around for the checkered, the doomsayers intoned, because of the effects of the heat on machine and man, coupled with several of the drivers' unfamiliarity with a road course.

Boy, were they ever wrong. Try 66 percent.

When Rick Mears crossed the finish line first after 500 grueling kilometers (314 miles) over Riverside International Raceway's twisting layout, his was just one of 10 machines his still running. Only nine of those were competing Indy-cars.

The 10th was the track's tow truck, which would have probably finished seventh based on total miles driven. It was that overworked.

Mears, on the other hand, hardly worked at all while ending the five-year Unser Brothers domination of this race.

His Penske PC-9B Cosworth ran flawlessly and he missed a pair of spectacular crashes and successfully dodged numerous other shunts, spins and lesser mishaps to post a huge margin of victory over Gordon Johncock, who was almost a full lap down.

The rest of the survivors in order were: Bill Alsup and Michael Chandler (both a lap down), rookie Bob Lazier (three laps back), Dick Simon (five), Herm Johnson (seven), Scott Brayton (eight) and Bobby Unser (11). The name of the tow truck driver was not available.

"I knew it was going to be a long, hard race, which it was," said Mears, who earned his first RIR road win. "It took its toll. A guy was really going to have to pace himself to finish. I thought that coming into it and that's the way it turned out.

"I felt that 300 miles in this kind of temperature (95-plus) on this track, it was definitely going to take a pace to make everything live. That's what I tried to do."

He succeeded with ridiculous ease, taking the lead on the 45th of the 95-lap grind and then just waiting for a challenge. It never came.

"The last 30-40 laps or so I was just watching

(Continued on C-4, column 1)

You'd never know it from looking at the wreckage of his car here, but Jerry Karl was uninjured after a collision with Johnny Rutherford, who also was unhurt, in the Times/California 500 at Riverside.

Herman Johnson spins out in Turn 7 Saturday during qualifying for Times 500 at Riverside.

Steve Chassey: *"An awesome track - A hot and dusty day in August, not the best time of year for Riverside and unfortunately I wasn't the fastest road racer at that time. Driving Max Dowker's Eagle, I blew the motor after 42 laps, just as I was figuring the track out. Lot of attrition, only nine cars running at the end."*
Compiler's Note - Steve started at Ascot and Saugus in California with stock cars. After a stint in Vietnam, he went on to sprint cars and was CRA Rookie of the Year, He had 44 starts in Indy Cars, ten at the 500 and had two wins in the USAC Silver Crown Series.

Michael Chandler

Gordon Johncock

Johnny Rutherford

411

Rick Mears, in a Penske Ford survived 130 degree track temperatures and won $33,591 in 1982. Only four cars were running at the finish; Tom Sneva in second in a March Cosworth Johnny Rutherford in third in a March Cosworth and Roger Mears in fourth in a Penske Cosworth. In the supporting events, the 200 kilometer Winston West race was won by Rick McCray and the Toyota father / son celebrity race was won by Bobby Unser.

Mears leads 4 survivors to AirCal 500 finish line

By BILL JOHNSON
Sun Sports Writer

RIVERSIDE — Rick Mears, surviving a driver attrition rate more commonly associated with demolition derbies, kept his car running long enough to reach the winner's circle and capture his second consecutive AirCal 500 Sunday at Riverside International Raceway.

Taking advantage of the demise of Kevin Cogan's vehicle (blown piston) on lap 50, Mears took over the lead from the pole sitter and never relinquished it, running the required 95 laps (500 kilometers) in 2 hours, 42 minutes.

All the 30-year-old from Bakersfield really had to do was keep his Gould Charge Penske PC-10 Ford from blowing its engine or frying its transmission to secure the victory and capture the $33,391 first prize.

Mears' car was one of only four running at the end of the race, tying an Indy-car record set in 1974 in a 200-mile race at Trenton, N.J. It also was the smallest field of finishers in an Indy-car race since 1978 when five cars were running at the end of a 500-mile race at the Ontario Motor Speedway.

It was a combination of the heat (an estimated 130 degrees on the track surface) and the taxing, serpentine RIR road course that prompted vehicles to break down at an alarming rate. Engines, transmissions and gear boxes were especially susceptible to failure Sunday.

"In a race like that you just have to concentrate on being smooth, not taking any chances, shift it nice and easy and try not to over-rev the motor," said Mears, who cruised the track at an average speed of 115.944.

"Some of those guys were driving awful hard and using up their cars. I just wasn't going to do that."

Some of those guys would be the race's big names, Mario Andretti and Indy-winner Gordon Johncock, both of whom were out of the race by the 10th lap.

Andretti, in fact, blasted away from the field at the start of the race and held the lead for those first 10 laps before he left the race when his STP Wildcat developed electrical problems.

Johncock, Andretti's teammate, departed even earlier — on the seventh lap — when the gear box on his STP Wildcat failed.

Mears was the only finisher who ap-

(Please see Mears, C-4)

AirCal 500 road race to be held at Riverside

RIVERSIDE — For years the oval race tracks of America were the breeding grounds for future Indy Car racers. What it took was a heavy foot and the ability to turn left.

Not so anymore. Four of the 12 races on the PPG/CART schedule are now run on twisting road courses, with more in the offing in 1983.

Next road race on the slate is the Los Angeles times-sponsored AirCal 500 Sunday at Riverside International Raceway.

The season's first road race, the Cleveland 500K on the runways of

ico 150 in Mexico City.

Premier road runner on the circuit is Mario Andretti. He traversed the world for seven years in Formula One series, won 12 races and became just the second American to win the World Driving Championship, doing so in 1978.

The Penske pair of Kevin Cogan and Rick Mears started their careers in road racing, Cogan in F-Atlantic and Mears in off-road vehicles. Al Unser Jr., currently leading the Can-Am series, will make his debut on the Forsythe team running with Mexico's Hector Rebaque, a veteran sports car

Johncock comes to Riverside as leader of pack

Gordon Johncock is having the kind of year race drivers dream about.

As the CART Indy Car World Series heads to Riverside Aug. 29 for the $230,000 AirCal 500 — the only appearance of the Indy Cars in California this year — this is what Johncock has done:

• win three of six races, including his second Indianapolis 500,

• finish in the top five of all six races to date, and

• win almost $300,000, more than he's ever won in an entire season.

But if it sounds like he's running away with things, he's not. In fact, his 1982 success has been anything but easy. Witness the Indy 500: with 10 laps to go, he had a 14-second cushion on Rick Mears. Fighting an ill-handling STP Wildcat, he barely held on in a thrilling last-lap

duel, beating Mears to the checkered flag in the closest Indy 500 finish in history.

At the season's next race in Milwaukee, it was again Johncock and Mears, one-two. And, at the Michigan 500, Johncock was again leading with Mears, clicking off a half-second each lap, closing to within two seconds of Johncock when Mears' right tire blew, sending him into the wall.

If that wasn't pressure

enough, Johncock then had to battle teammate Mario Andretti

Johncock, currently leading the '82 CART/PPG point standings with 137, has added incentive to win the AirCal 500 — revenge. In 1981, Mears beat Johncock in the Times California 500 in a race Johncock thought he had won. He intends to even the score Aug. 29.

Mears, the defending PPG Indy Car World Series Champion, added five more 1981 wins to his California 500 laurels. He earned more than $300,000 and became the "fastest" member of racing's "Millionaire's Club," reaching the million-dollar mark in career earnings in only his 58th career start.

This season, Mears, winner of the 1979 Indy 500, has won two races and finished in the top

Please see JOHNCOCK, page 2

Father/son teams to race in Toyota challenge

The AirCal 500 at Riverside International Raceway has 14 entries in the Toyota Father/Son Race, to be held at 12:15 p.m. Sunday, Aug. 29.

Seven father-and-son racing teams will be competing against each other at speeds of up to 150 mph over a 10-lap course. Prize

money will be $20,000. The race will be held prior to the 1982 AirCal 500 for CART Indy Cars.

Three division winners will be named in the 25-mile event: the first-place father and first-place son, plus the winning father-and-son team, based on a points system.

Three-time Indy 500 cham-

pion Bobby Unser and Bobby Jr. return to defend their title at Riverside. At the 1981 Times/Toyota Grand Prix of Endurance, the Unsers not only won the team title, but also finished father and son team, based on a sweep the event.

They'll be challenged by for-

Please see FATHER, page 2

413

1983 was the last year Indy cars raced at Riverside. Moving on to Long Beach, which had become a happening of its own, no one missed the hot August Riverside weekends. Now called the Budweiser 500, Bobby Rahal in a March Cosworth won $39,380 at this last event in front of 51,500 spectators on a hundred degree day. Second was Teo Fabi followed by John Paul Jr. Supporting races included the Warner Hodgdon 200 kilometer Winston West event, was won by Herschel McGriff and the Dominos Pizza Celebrity Challenge, a 10 lap Formula Ford race won by Parker Stevenson, all of which will be covered in Volume Two, available in the fall of 2022.

The Sacramento Bee • Monday, August 29, 1983 D5

Rahal's Luck Finally Improves As Fabi Stalls In Pits

Bee News Services

RIVERSIDE — Bobby Rahal's luck changed Sunday on the way to victory in the Los Angeles Times-Budweiser 500 Indy-car race.

Rahal, who had run well in nearly every race this season without coming out on top, this time took advantage of pole-sitter Teo Fabi's ill fortune in the pits.

"We've been on the verge (of winning) in every race," said Rahal, the 30-year-old driver

Motor Sports

from Dublin, Ohio, who was the CART rookie of the year in 1982 when he won two races. "Little things kept happening to us to keep us from winning.

pit stops were fantastic. We had to be patient to not run out of fuel like we did at Elkhart," Rahal said, referring to a road race earlier this season at Road America when he ran out of fuel while leading just three laps from the end.

"We ran the car conservatively and decided not to rev it high to save fuel," Rahal said. "I was just watching people blow by me on the straightaways, but I had to have faith in my guys in the pits who told me to lay back and wait."

Fabi appeared to have the 500-kilometer — 313.5-mile — race well in hand when he drove into the pits on lap 74 for what was to be a routine fuel and tire stop.

However, a broken air jack cost Fabi's crew valuable time, keeping him in the pits for a disastrous 55 seconds. That allowed Rahal, driving the Red Roof Inns-sponsored March-

sports car racer back onto the track in just 20 seconds. Fabi, who had won his first major professional victory at Pocono two weeks ago, was further penalized when he was black-flagged into the pits for running over an air hose during his long stop.

Rahal started in the second row and never let the leaders out of sight, but it was Indy-car rookies Fabi and Al Unser Jr., as well as all-time Indy-car road course champion Mario Andretti, who dominated the first half of the grueling race run in 100-degree heat.

Unser was eventually slowed by an ignition problem and Andretti was sidelined by a broken gearbox.

Rahal, the seventh different winner in eight Indy-car races this season, crossed the finish line 29 seconds ahead of Fabi's March-Cosworth.

Another Indy-car rookie, John Paul Jr., was

• **DUTCH GRAND PRIX** at Zandvoort, Netherlands — Frenchmen Rene Arnoux and Patrick Tambay scored a one-two victory, keeping their hopes alive in the 1983 world championship. The championship leaders Alain Prost of France and Nelson Piquet of Brazil crashed within seconds of each other while leading the race.

Piquet's Brabham-BMW ran off the track as the Frenchman tried to pass at the Tarzan hairpin. Prost's Renault turbo went off into the guardrails a few hundred yards further on, with apparent mechanical failure.

Britain's John Watson, fighting to retain his place in the McLaren team next season, placed third from way down the starting grid in his non-turbo car.

• **WARNER HODGDON 200** at Riverside — Greybeard Hershel McGriff outdueled Scott Miller and Bill Schmitt to win the stock car

RICK CORRALES / Los Angeles Times

Bobby Rahal rounds Turn 6 en route to a 28-second victory over Teo Fabi in the Times/Budweiser 500-kilometer race

LORI SHEPLER / Los Angeles Times

Al Unser Jr. has the lead in early stages of the Times/Budweiser 500K race Sunday and was in contention all the way before finishing fourth.

Polesitter Rick Mears said, *"To get around Riverside, you have to be smooth. To survive the race and be around at the finish is even more demanding. We've developed a strategy for coming out of eight and going into nine, because that long straight is the easiest place to pass. After waiting all lap to get to eight, the slightest mistake means you don't get a pass that lap."*

Rahal found winning the race was a bit easier then downing his king-sized victory drink.

Rocky Moran: *"I had tested with Gurney at Riverside but the best (or worst story) was when Dan asked me to fill in for Geoff Brabham, who had a schedule conflict. I was leading, ahead of Mears and Rutherford, when at the last pit stop, the refueling rig malfunctioned and I spilled a load of fuel on pit road and ended up four gallons short. Ran out of fuel on lap 57 of 60 – That was at the Glen, by the way"*

Teo Fabi

Tom Sneva

Danny Ongais

John Paul; Penske Cosworth

Ted Dawson   Bob Flaherty   Tommy Hawkins   Jim Hill   Garry Scott Lee   Andy Leopold

Pamela McInnes   Harry Newman   Bob Steinbrinck   Bruce Wayne

DOMINO PIZZA CELEBRITY CHALLENGE

Continued from First Page

ness News sportscaster who was named Sportscaster of the Year in 1977. Dawson started his career in Utah while a student at the University of Utah and worked in Nevada and Oregon before coming to Los Angeles.

Bob Flaherty, KGIL's "Skywatch" traffic reporter. Flaherty makes 18 daily reports for the San Fernando Valley station, covering six freeway systems with a daily sweep of more than 750 miles in his Cessna 132 aircraft.

Tommy Hawkins, KABC sportscaster and Sportstalk host. Hawkins was a well-known figure nationally before turning to radio. He played basketball at the University of Notre Dame, then spent 10 years in the NBA, the last six with the Los Angeles Lakers.

Jim Hill, Channel 2's sports anchorman and host of the Sunday Sports Final. Hill combined his football career with sportscasting in both San Diego when he was with the Chargers and Green Bay when he played for the Packers.

Gary Scott Lee, ESPN auto race

broadcaster and PA announcer at Indianapolis Motor Speedway. Lee covers the pit action for ESPN's busy motor racing coverage crew. He also is sports anchorman for an Indianapolis TV station.

Andy Leopold, Channel 11's sports anchorman. Leopold has been in the Los Angeles area only since January, but has gained quite a following. He started out giving radio reports on the Miami Dolphins at the age of 14 and became a full-timer at 18.

Pamela McInnes, KMPC's "Airwatch" traffic reporter. McInnes is a native of New Zealand where as a girl she hung around a garage owned by the late Kiwi race driver Bruce McLaren's dad. The only female in the race, she is backed by the Good Morgan Team.

Harry Newman, KLAC midmorning personality. Newman has been nominated five times by the Country Music Assn. as the Country Music Disc Jockey of the Year. An avid golfer and auto race fan, Newman also handles pre and post race interviews for KLAC.

Bob Steinbrinck, KMPC's news director. Steinbrinck has broadcast

races from Riverside Raceway since 1961 and has seen just about every race staged at that facility, the now gone Ontario Motor Speedway and the streets of Long Beach. He has never driven in a race, however.

Bruce Wayne, KFI's "Eye In The Sky" and "Traffic on the KOST" reporter. The senior traffic reporter in Los Angeles, Wayne started his career in Boston. He has flown more than 3 million air miles and has logged 25,000 hours of flying without an accident.

Lightning-quick Indy cars!

TIMES BUDWEISER 500

Warner Hodgdon 200

Sunday, August 28
Riverside
International Raceway

Numbered among the drivers are seven past Indy 500 winners who will be competing for $120,000 in prize money . . . 95 tough laps on Riverside's 3.3-mile road course. This is your only chance this year to see these powerful Indy cars in Southern California. And it's the only time you'll be able to see such racing giants as 1983 Indy Champ Tom Sneva and Rick Mears, defending race and CART/PPG series champ.

The field will also include some hot newcomers like Al Unser Jr., already stamped as a future great, and Teo Fabi, the diminutive Italian who shredded the Indy 500 qualifying record in May en route to Rookie of the Year honors.

The spectacular day of racing gets under way at 11 a.m. with California's version of the "Good Ol' Boys," the Winston West stockers. The Warner Hodgdon 200 is 48 laps of the slam-bang action you expect from drivers like Roy Smith, Bill Schmitt, Jim Reich, Jim Robinson and the legendary Hershel McGriff, winningest driver in Riverside Raceway history.

See celebrities in action!

At noon, sports broadcasters and other personalities test their driving skills Domino's Pizza Celebrity Challenge. See Bob Steinbrinck and Pamela McInnes of KMPC and Andy Leopold of KTTV and others as they tangle in a 10-lap race in the Formula Ford racers.

Get your tickets today!

In Person. Riverside International Raceway Box Office; Times Special Events, 212 W. First St., Los Angeles; Theatre Jewelry Center, 655 S. Hill St., Los Angeles; All Mutual and Ticketron Agencies including Tower Records and most Sears stores. By phone. Use your Visa or MasterCard and call (714) 653-1161, (213) 627-1248 or (213) 972-5775.

Sponsored for charity by the

Los Angeles Times

Les Richter Quits as President of Riverside Raceway

By TRACY DODDS, *Times Staff Writer*

Les Richter, president of Riverside International Raceway for 21 years, has resigned the post but will stay on as Director of Racing, a new position.

The announcement Wednesday was made jointly by Richter and Fritz Duda, a Dallas-based real estate developer and spokesman for the board of directors. Richter's decision to stay on the staff, after earlier saying he would simply resign as president, came after a week of discussions with raceway and board personnel.

"This was my decision," Richter said. "The whole move was initiated by yours truly.

"I had some philosophical differences with the ownership interest in the track about what we were going to do and how to run the track in the future. Initially, I thought that the best thing for an old grey-haired, pot-bellied, out-of-shape guy like me was to have a change of lifestyle, to just go out and do something else. But then I sat down with Fritz Duda and we came to an amicable conclusion. I was asked to reconsider my position.

"This way he can run the raceway the way he sees fit,

Closing Of Riverside Evokes Memories Of Fabled Track

RIVERSIDE, Calif. — No matter who wins today's Budweiser 400, it'll always be remembered as the date they closed ol' Riverside Raceway down.

After the NASCAR Winston Cup Series stock car race is completed at about 7 p.m., no more major events are scheduled on the 2.62-mile road course that dates to the mid-1950s.

Only an off-road scramble remains to be run in August. Then, the bulldozers that already are plowing up the desert terrain along the track's backstretch will move onto the 700 acres of speedway property.

Riverside Raceway eventually will be no more, in time becoming only a blur of a memory buried beneath the condos and office parks of a fast-growing new city called Moreno Valley.

Motorsports

Tom Higgins

Here are some comments and facts about the track:

• Les Richter, now a powerful NASCAR vice president, was president of Riverside Raceway for many years. He helped buy the facility for a group of owners that included comedian Bob Hope in 1959.

"I'll never forget the first time I saw the place," said Richter, then an all-pro linebacker for the Los Angeles Rams. "It was just a strip of asphalt twisting over hilly desert. There were rattlesnakes, coyotes, owls and no telling what else around.

"It took us a while to get started, to be taken seriously. . . . I think that what really enabled the track to take off is when NASCAR's Wood Brothers, Glen and Leonard, came out and Dan Gurney, probably the most respected driver in America at the time, drove their Fords to three 500-mile victories in 1964, '65, and '66. Parnelli Jones won in '67 and Gurney again in '68 to give the Wood boys five straight."

Richter laughed.

"I'd say more types of vehicles and more drivers have raced here than any track in the world," he continued. "The list includes Winston Cup, USAC, CART, Formula One, World Endurance, IMSA, SCCA, Winston West, the Southwest Tour, dragsters, motorcycles, go-karts and off-road machines.

"The place has been the site of dozens of movies and commercials. Also automotive tests."

Richter's most humorous recollection involved one of the tests.

"Ford was matching its pickups against Chevrolet and Dodge," he said. "They were going to run 67,000 miles consecutively in 1967. Naturally, this was boring to the drivers, especially on the night shifts.

"Topless dancing had just come in then. So we had this idea. We hired two or three of these strippers and stationed them around the track. They'd suddenly appear, naked, making like they were hitchhiking. Then they'd dart into the darkness. The trucks were equipped with radios, and you can imagine the conversation and hooting that went on when some driver claimed he'd seen a nude woman beside the track."

Richter's most touching memory?

"It happened in '69," he said. "Al Dean, Sr., a great backer of Indy-car racing, was dying. His last wish was to see his car, with Mario Andretti driving, win the championship.

"We parked him in an ambulance in Turn 9. He was attended by doctors and nurses. Mario came through for him."

• Riverside Raceway always will be revered by today's pole-sitter, Ricky Rudd, Bill Elliott and Tim Richmond. The track gave them their first Winston Cup victories. . . . It will also be remembered as the last place that colorful little Joe Weatherly ever raced. Weatherly, the Winston Cup champion, was killed in a Turn 9 crash in 1964. A Riverside wreck also took the life of Winston West rookie Tim Williamson in 1981. . . . Among others to die in accidents at the track was Rolf Stommelen, the German road racer, killed in an International Motor Sports Association event.

• Perhaps no driver feels more strongly about the closing of Riverside than Darrell Waltrip.

He clinched all three of his Winston Cup titles at the track. He has won five times at Riverside.

Said Waltrip:

"I'm going to miss coming here. We're losing a track with a lot of tradition. It's like it should be on the national register as a historic place they can't tear up. . . ."

Chapter Thirteen - Crooks and Thieves

Racing seemed to be a good way to launder money or in many cases, a way to raise money to go racing. Sometimes bad guys were also racers. Outlined here are a few criminals with a connection to Riverside

Tony Parravano

The earliest crook with connections to Riverside Raceway, L.A. area builder Parravano imported a variety of Ferrari and Maserati racecars. Jack McAfee most often drove them;, Shelby also drove a couple of times. The last appearance of a Parravano car was at the Riverside opener in 1957, a Maserati 450s driven by Skip Hudson. Indicted for tax evasion, Parravano fled to Mexico and attempted to take nine cars with him. Five were seized at the border and later auctioned off, four made it across. He disappeared in 1960, never seen or heard from again, just before his trial was scheduled.

Tax Evasion Case Figure Missing; Foul Play Hinted

LOS ANGELES (AP) — A millionaire building contractor failed to show up in court yesterday in an income tax evasion case against him and his attorney hinted at foul play.

Tony Parravano, 42, of Manhattan Beach, was indicted on 21 counts of tax evasio. and government officials said they have more than 3 million dollars in liens on his operations.

Parravano's attorney, Edwin M. Rosendahl, said the prominent auto racing figure had many business appointments this week he would not cancel normally. His car with three suits in it was found at the rear of his business office.

"I have been his friend and legal adviser for 10 years," said Rosendahl, "and I must presume him to be a victim of foul play."

A federal grand jury indicted Parravano and Henry E. Albachten, 44, charging they set up 43 corporations to build homes in Gardena and Torrance from 1953 to 1955 and failed to pay income taxes while depositing at least $325,000 in foreign banks. Albachten is reported in Guadalajara, Mexico.

ARROW FONTANA VA 2-3614
Mon.-Fri. at 7 — Sat.-Sun. Cont. 2
"Noah's Ark"
— ALSO —
"Battle Flame"
SCOTT BRADY

Suspect in Tax Case Misses U. S. Hearing

LOS ANGELES (UPI) — Wealthy contractor-sportsman Tony Parravano, 42, accused tax evader who allegedly has large amounts of money in foreign banks, was sought today as a possible victim of foul play.

Parravano's disappearance came to light Monday when he failed to appear for arraignment in federal court on charges he evaded payment of more than three million dollars in income tax.

U.S. Assistant Attorney W. Bryan Osborne said investigation showed the two men have sent at least $325,000 in cashiers' checks to Italy, Switzerland and Uruguay between 1953 and 1955. This presumably was a maneuver to put the money beyond the jurisdiction of the government, Osborne said.

Coolidge, Slavkin Highest Bidders

By Special Correspondent

VAN NUYS, Calif.—Spirited bidding marked the public auction of two machines from the Tony Parravano scuderia seized by the U.S. Internal Revenue Service for delinquent taxes recently.

One, a 1955 Ferrari Monza, went for top bid of $3500 to Sidney Coolidge, North Hollywood. He also was high bidder at $275 for an accompanying trailer.

Ben Slavkin, a Los Angeles professional auctioneer, was successful bidder for a 1956 Maserati at $4550. The sale was conducted here by W. D. Roeder, Inglewood district manager of the IRS, with nearly 50 in attendance.

Cal Bailey

A twice convicted felon and Corvette racer, Cal had Dan Gurney driving his much modified Corvette a few times at Riverside, winning the 1957 big bore production race. Though reportedly not a great driver, he raced there himself in a number of club events, But his real claim to fame, after almost incinerating himself in an arson attempt at his failing bowling alley in Kern County (he was charged but not convicted), was the poorly planned attempt to kidnap Firestone heir, Leonard Firestone in 1966. The police were there waiting for him and he died in the subseqent shootout.

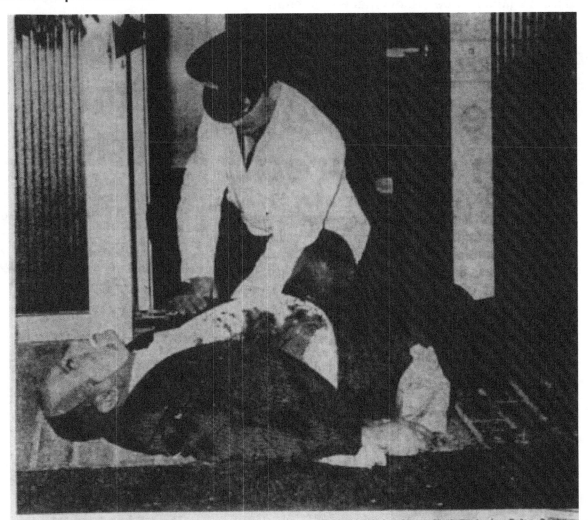

Exclusive Citizen-News Staff Photo by Peter Banks

BLASTED BY POLICE—The body of Cal Bailey, 44, still wearing a face mask and rubber gloves, lies on the doorstep of the home of Leonard Firestone, Beverly Hills, where he and George Skalla, 25, were shot by police as they attempted to force their way into the house. Police said they were waiting for the pair on a tip that Firestone was to be kidnaped. A r r o w points to spot where police gunfire hit door. Bag next to Bailey contains adhesive tape.

Slain Kidnaper Suspected in North Edwards Jet Bowl Fire

Just what led former Kern County bowling alley proprietor and arson suspect William C. Bailey along the path from successful businessman to his present status — one of the two slain, unsuccessful kidnapers of Leonard K. Firestone?

That was the question asked today by relatives and friends of the 44-year-old Bailey, and by police and newsmen.

It was the same Bailey — William Clark Bailey or Cal Bailey to his Kern County acquaintances; William Calvin Bailey to his southland associates—who, wearing a Halloween mask and carrying a cocked automatic, was shot to death Thursday night in the rubber magnate's Beverly Hills mansion.

At the same instant Bailey's companion — 28-year-old George H. Scalla, who police have since identified as their informant and whom, police said, Bailey recruited to perform a role in the doomed kidnap plot — was fatally wounded when he failed to leap from the path of police bullets as previously arranged. He died three hours later.

Bailey was burned severely and his face and body

BH Ransom Plan Aimed At Firestone

BEVERLY HILLS (AP) — Pistols raised, two men crashed into the home of Leonard K. Firestone Thursday night in an apparent attempt to kidnap the wealthy industrialist. Staked-out police killed both with shotgun blasts. Cal Bailey, 44, was killed instantly as he attempted to rush into the living room of the palatial home. George Skalla, 25, fell wounded on the threshold and died three hours later in the prison ward of General Hospital. They held three guns, but never got a chance to fire a shot.

Police said the men may have planned to ask $2 million in ransom.

Police Informed

The deaths ended three weeks of police undercover work, during which the proposed kidnaping was tipped by an undisclosed source. Firestone, 58, was warned to leave the city.

"This has been a very distressing and upsetting thing to have gone through," said the president of the Firestone Tire and Rubber Co. of Calif. at the home of a friend in San Francisco Thursday night. He complimented the police for a "thorough, intelligent, masterful job."

Macabre Story Told

Capt. John E. Hankins, chief of Beverly Hills detectives, told this sequence of events:

First hint of the kidnap came three weeks ago in connection with a burglary that took place in the jurisdiction of the Los Angeles police. Ten days ago, the tipster disclosed that the intended victim was Firestone, the handsome son of rubber empire founder Harvey S. Firestone.

HIDE-OUT

Firestone To Wed Socialite

SAN FRANCISCO (UPI) — The abortive kidnap attempt on Leonard K. Firestone took the headlines today from much happier news regarding the millionaire industrialist.

The San Francisco Chronicle reported that Firestone, 58, was engaged to San Francisco society matron Mrs. Stuart Heatley, 45. The engagement was disclosed shortly after two men who allegedly had hoped to kidnap Firestone were gunned down in a trap by Beverly Hills police, the Chronicle said.

Firestone has spent the past few days in Northern California hiding out from the kidnapers. But friends here said he and Mrs. Heatley would open Firestone's Pebble Beach home within a day or two in preparation for next week's Bing Crosby Golf Tournament and the whirl of society activity that accompanies it.

'Informer' Shot Down In BH Trap

LOS ANGELES—High police officials today revealed that the informer in the Firestone abduction plot was one of the kidnapers killed by police when the kidnapers burst into the wealthy industrialist's home.

Police officials said that George Skalla, 28, of 4938 Hesperia Ave., Tarzana, first informed police on Jan. 3 there was going to be a kidnap attempt in the near future.

Scalla and his partner, William (Cal) Bailey, 44, of 23022 Mosby St., Woodland Hills, were cut down in a hail of police bullets as they burst through the door of Leonard K. Firestone's home at 919 N. Alpine Ave., Beverly Hills, Thursday night.

Police revealed that Skalla feared that Bailey would kill him and dump his body in the desert if he didn't aid him in the plot to kidnap Firestone.

It wasn't until Jan. 6 that Skalla informed the police that Firestone was the intended victim of the kidnap scheme. At that time, police tried to convince Skalla to back out of the plot, but the man was so terrified for his safety that he insisted on carrying out his dual role, officers said.

Skalla told police that Bailey rented a $150-a-month home at 5618 Etiwanda Ave., Tarzana, as a headquarters for the kidnap plot. According to the plan devised by Bailey, Firestone was to be brought to the Etiwanda Ave. hideout after he was abducted.

Skalla told police that Bailey also rented an alternate hideout for $200 a month at 7447 Loma Verde Ave., Canoga Park. The man reportedly told police that the kidnaping of Firestone was originally planned for Wednesday night but that Bailey

Andy Porterfield

In 1960, Andy was convicted of both car theft and burglary while on probation for a 1959 car theft conviction. Sentenced to twenty five years, he apparently got out early as he was racing again in 1966. He drove Art Evan's Devin at the 1959 Times Grand Prix and claimed to have raced every year from 1956 to 2012, omitting the years in prison. He won Southern Pacific Driving Championships and Cal Club Regional Championships numerous times, along with two national championships. Andy competed in 40 Trans Ams and 20 IMSA races. Not concerned about his past, I guess, he was on the Cal Club board for 16 years, Regional Executive for five and on the SCCA Board of Directors, receiving numerous awards, in the SCCA Hall of Fame and was inducted posthumously into the Road Racing Drivers Club

Andy Porterfield Starts Sentence

Former race car driver Andy Porterfield has begun two consecutive prison terms totaling 25 years for burglary and car theft. Porterfield, 28, of 9401 Alverstone Ave., Los

Race Car Driver Gets Prison Term

SANTA MONICA — UPI — Andy Porterfield, 28, who used his race car driving experience to get away from fur and jewelry robberies, started two consecutive prison terms totaling 25 years yesterday.

Superior Judge Edward R. Brand sentenced Porterfield

Racer Arraigned on Stolen Cars

LOS ANGELES (UPI) — Race driver Andy Porterfield, 26, Friday was arraigned in Superior Court on a grand jury indictment charging him with five counts of grand theft involving stolen sports cars.

Judge Lewis Drucker ordered the Los Angeles driver to enter a plea to the charges May 22. Bail was set at $10,000.

Porterfield is accused of stealing three Corvette sports cars and selling parts from two of them.

Rex Ramsey

Rex was a pretty succesful driver; had good connections to the LeGrand factory, racing in Formula A and some rides in the Single Seat Can Am series and in IMSA. He had some issues with stolen cars in 1966 which were dismissed due to an unconstutional search, then a drug conspiracy and cocaine distribution charge in 1984 and a number of later civil issues in Ohio and Hawaii. It was rumored that the fuel cells on his Eagle could be filled with dope on accassion and a dry sump oil pan manufactuer reported building avery deep pan wth no baffles for Rex.

Valley Dope Raids Top $1 Million During Week

Largest of Three Seizures Involves Heroin, Cocaine in Sun Valley Worth $962,400

BY KENNETH HANSEN
Times Staff Writer

Valley narcotics officers have seized more than $1 million worth of drugs in the last week, more than in any week in recent history, it was reported Tuesday.

The latest seizure involved movie stunt man and race driver Rex A. Ramsey, 26, who was booked early Tuesday af-

lieved to have come from the Middle East. He was charged with possession for sale.

Ramsey is scheduled to go to trial on the earlier charge on Dec. 3 in Van Nuys Superior Court. The charge was filed in Van Nuys because the arrest followed a joint investigation by Valley and state narcotics officers, Trotsky

Glen Ellen man jailed on cocaine plot charge

By CLARK MASON

A Glen Ellen man has surrendured in connection with a $2 million cocaine conspiracy case originating in Florida, and about eight ounces of suspected cocaine was seized at his ranch in Sonoma County, sheriff's office spokesmen said.

Rex Andrew Ramsey, 41, was arrested Tuesday and booked into Sonoma County Jail, where he is being held on $5 million bail. The sheriff's office, however, did not announce his arrest until today.

Ramsey, also known as Sterling Brian, is a race car driver who competes in the Camel GT series. He came in third in the prestigious prototype class last July at a Sears Point race.

Internal Revenue Service agents and sheriff's deputies seized various automobiles at the Glen Ellen ranch, including a Maserati estimated by sheriff's sources to cost $150,000.

Sheriff's office officials said they received information from the Marin County Major Crimes Task Force in early February that Ramsey was being sought in Sumpter County, Fla., on a cocaine conspiracy warrant. On Feb. 10, law enforcement personnel from the sheriff's office, U.S. Marshall's Office and Marin County went to Ramsey's ranch at 14037 Highway 12.

persuaded to surrender.

A spokesman for the Sumter County Sheriff's Office in central Florida said the warrant for Ramsey's arrest grew out a December 1982 seizure of 65 pounds of cocaine on a ranch Ramsey owns in that rural, agricultural county. Five Columbians and one American were arrested in a mobile home, which authorities say was being used as a "factory" for purifying the drug. The spokesman said some of the cocaine was as much as 99 percent pure.

Although Florida is well known as an importation center for illicit drugs, the spokesman saidSumter County has had few large drug busts other than for homegrown marijuana.

Ramsey also owns a house in the Fort Lauderdale area, the spokesman said, in addition to several businesses there. She said one of them is a machinery shop specializing in racing engines.

After the arrests at Ramsey's Florida ranch, the Columbians posted cash bonds, reportedly between $50,000 and $100,000. Four then failed to appear for their court dates. The American, James Parillo, is still in Sumter County Jail. Bail for him was set at $1 million.

During the investigation the Internal Revenue Service notified the Sonoma County Sheriff's Office that Ramsey is

J. David Dominelli

He was really Jerry Dominelli from Chicago; a shy, physically nondescript, hard of hearing guy with bad eyesight and a bad temper but a self proclaimed financial genius; according to people who knew him. Considered now to be San Diego's biggest swindler, he was an  investment scammer who spent an estimated $112 million of other San Diegan's money on racing and numerous other things, from 1979 to 1984. Forced into bankruptcy when his claims of 40% return on investments disappeared, he initially fled to Montserrat, then to Antigua in the Caribbean and finally, was arrested upon landing in Miami, leaving drivers like John Fitzpatrick wondering there the allegedly on order Porsche 956's were. The contents of his shop, considered a masterpiece among race car shops, was auctioned off to satisfy creditors. Pleading guilty to mail fraud, bankruptcy fraud and tax evasion, he was sentenced to twenty years, paroled after ten, serving his time as the prison librarian at the federal prison in Boron, about 100 miles north of Riverside. His girlfriend, Nancy Hoover, former mayor of Del Mar, was accused of being a partner in the scam and was paroled after serving thirty months in a federal prison in Spokane.

The rise and fall of J. David
Dominelli's financial empire now in bankruptcy court

By LAURINDA KEYS
Associated Press

SAN DIEGO — Checks bounced, investors lost confidence, bank acounts ran dry, lawsuits were filed. Finally, the financial empire of J. David Dominelli was in bankruptcy court, and he was in jail.

But the whereabouts of $125 million to $150 million that investors had given him to take advantage of the fluctuations of foreign currency markets was a secret known only to Dominelli.

The silver-haired, 43-year-old former broker, who founded his J. David & Co. five years ago, stayed in federal prison for only 10 hours Saturday night on a contempt of court charge.

He was released after he began to cooperate with Earl Cantos, who had been appointed trustee of Dominelli's affairs by a bankruptcy judge on Feb. 17.

Investors — disappointed after being told they could reap up to 50 percent profits by rapid conversion of money on foreign markets —

want J. David to be declared involuntarily bankrupt. The company was closed down last week by Cantos.

U.S. District Judge Lawrence Irving on Saturday ordered that the financier begin turning over his assets and records or sit in jail.

Dominelli's attorney, Charles Goldberg, said Irving's order may compromise Dominelli's constitutional protection against self-incrimination as his client prepares to testify before a federal grand jury on Wednesday.

Dominelli had resisted providing numbers of the foreign bank accounts — in Saipan, Hong Kong, London, Lugano, Switzerland and the Caribbean island of Montserrat — where he indicated that about $125 million in funds lies.

He has been equally protective of his list of clients — as many as 1,500 people whose investments ranged from $16,000 to $10 million.

"I'm telling my clients the money is gone," said Patrick Shea, whose

law firm sued J. David on behalf of investors.

"There are assets," Dominelli said outside a court proceeding in the case attended by FBI agents last Thursday, "if the trustee doesn't . . . continue to deplete them with lawyers and accountants."

He is hoping to have the bankruptcy action made voluntary, allowing him to remain in control of his company and its 30 subsidiaries.

But Dominelli was ordered by bankruptcy Judge Ross Pyle not to engage in transactions, and Irving made him hand over his passport.

Cantos said that in a conversation on Feb. 19, Dominelli said his company made payments of $25 million to investors from Jan. 1 until early this month, leaving $125 million. But Dominelli has denied that he ever said "what was left."

"Only Mr. Dominelli can tell us" how much money there is and where it is, Cantos' lawyer, Ron Orr, said in court.

The trustee's investigators say they have found no records in the

Associated Press

J. DAVID DOMINELLI
... investor leaves jail

company offices of any transactions.

Dominelli and his associate, Nancy Hoover, bought six homes in San Diego County, paid $6 million in bonuses to attract 60 brokers to the company, gave big parties, bought cars for their friends and employees

Please see Dominelli on Page 12

Financier Dominelli pleads guilty, ends empire on fraud rap

By DENNIS GEORGATOS
Associated Press

SAN DIEGO — J. David Dominelli and an associate pleaded guilty yesterday to federal charges stemming from the collapse of Dominelli's investment empire last year.

Dominelli and Parin Columna, a former J. David employee, entered the pleas during a hearing before U.S. District Court Judge William Enright, formalizing a plea bargain agreement reached earlier this month.

Dominelli, 43, pleaded guilty to two counts of mail fraud, one count of bankruptcy fraud and one count of income tax evasion. In entering the plea, Dominelli admitted in a prepared statement that he had carried out a massive scheme to defraud investors.

He faces a maximum prison term of 20 years and $107,000 in fines when he is sentenced June 24.

Columna pleaded guilty to a misdemeanor criminal contempt charge which carries a maximum penalty of six months in jail, a $1,000 fine or both.

Dominelli, jailed for nearly a year and ailing from a stroke suffered last fall, once controlled a sprawling, multimillion-dollar financial network that included La Jolla-based J. David & Co. and 52 affiliates.

He was once regarded as a financial wizard with a knack for making money in the volatile but potentially lucrative international currency exchange market.

"This has been an immense tragedy for many people. It has shattered lives, ruined businesses and crushed dreams of many people across the country," said Assistant U.S. Attorney Bob Rose.

Dominelli's defense attorney, D. Gilbert Athay, left the courtroom without comment.

"Between June 1979 and February 1984, I carried out a scheme to defraud investors by means of my J. David companies," Dominelli said in the statement, which was read in court by Enright. "I did so knowingly and willfully. I used false and fradulent promises, representations and promises to obtain money."

Dominelli's statement said his firm and its affiliates took in $200 million over the 4½-year period between the founding of J. David and its bankruptcy. Dominelli's sprawling financial network was formally declared bankrupt a year ago yesterday by U.S. District Judge J. Lawrence Irving.

Dominelli said about 60 percent of the $200 million was returned to investors before February 1984, when J. David was forced into involuntary bankruptcy proceedings. He said he owed investors "not

DOMINELLI IN DECLINE — J. David Dominelli, right, with attorney Gilbert Athay, in this rendering of court proceedings.

more than $80 million."

On March 21, 1984, Irving formally declared the J. David financial network bankrupt.

Prior to the collapse, the company took in some $60 million from 1,000 investors who had been promised annual returns of 40 percent to 50 percent.

The bankruptcy led to a federal grand jury probe and the subsequent indictment of Dominelli on 25 criminal charges of fraud, conspiracy to commit fraud, contempt and perjury. Columna, 31, was named in nine of the counts.

The contempt allegations against Dominelli, 43, stemmed

from his flight to the Caribbean island of Montserrat last April. The island's government expelled him two weeks later.

Columna, who accompanied Dominelli to Montserrat, had been charged with helping his former employer conceal documents and equipment from the trustee overseeing the liquidation of J. David.

Dominelli, meanwhile, still faces state perjury and conspiracy charges for allegedly plotting with Mayor Roger Hedgecock and two others to finance Hedgecock's 1983 campaign with $357,000 of J. David money. Local election laws limit individual contributions to $250 and prohibit donations from corporations and unions.

Financier Sought By U.S. Taken Into Custody In Miami

Associated Press

MIAMI — Fugitive financier J. David Dominelli, sought by federal officials trying to find $112 million in missing investors' funds, was arrested Saturday at Miami International Airport.

three were ordered held without bond pending an appearance before a federal magistrate Monday.

Dominelli refused to answer reporters' questions as agents took him from the jet and through cus-

John Paul Jr. and Sr.

John Paul Sr. was a Harvard educated mutual fund manager who became a multi million dollar racecar team owner and driver. He won the 1980 World Endurance Championship, 24 Hours of Daytona and Sebring and finished second at both the 1979 and 1981 IMSA Times Grand Prix at Riverside. IMSA, was jokingly known as the "International Marijuana Smuggling Association" in the '80's, the result of some many big dollar cers whith no visioble sponsorship. Paul, a really unpleasant guy, had temper tantrums which prompted one IMSA official to say; "Senior is the most terrifying man I have ever met". After a couple of wives, one who disappeared without a trace, he married Hurley Heywood's sister Hope. First convicted of drug smuggling in 1979, he then skipped bail on a murder charge in 1983 and was caught in Switzerland. Extradited and convicted of tax evasion and drug smuggling, he served eleven years, was paroled and disappeared; never to be seen again.

John Paul Jr. won thirteen IMSA races and a championship, did well at Indy and then spent three years in prison on a racketeering conviction for his involvement in the family business, derailing a promising career. Paul Jr. claimed his father had intimidated him into participating in the drug business. He had a moderately successful driving career after prison until being struck down by Huntington's Disease, inherited from his mother.

John Paul arrested in attempted murder case

ST. AUGUSTINE, Fla. (AP) — A Dutch immigrant who made a killing ... Wall Street and ... on to become ... day, said sheriff's Lt. Ronald J. Bochenek. Bochenek said the sheriff's office ... investigated by U.S. Customs and the Internal Revenue Service. If convicted of the attempted first- ... lands for the United States. He went to college in Indiana, then earned a fellowship to Harvard University.

Fourth fugitive located in drug case

MIAMI — One of eight people indicted in a federal drug case involving racing car entrepreneur John Paul Sr. has been taken into custody by the Coast Guard, a prosecutor says.

Charles Evers, 32, of Miami was picked up Wednesday when Coast Guard officers intercepted his sailboat between Haiti and Cuba, Assistant U.S. Attorney Thomas Morris said.

Evers is one of eight defendants — who include Paul and his son, race car driver John Paul Jr. — indicted on charges of importing more than 200,000 pounds of marijuana from Colombia into Florida and Louisiana.

Evers was scheduled to appear before a federal magistrate in Tampa next week, Morris said Saturday.

Paul Sr., 44, owner of a now defunct competitive-racing company, has been accused of being the chief organizer of the alleged eight-year trafficking operation.

He was arrested in Geneva, Switzerland, where he is awaiting extradition to Florida. Paul Jr. surrendered to federal authorities in January, but remains free on $125,000 bond pending trial on the charges.

Racing fugitive Paul indicted

ATLANTA (AP) — Fugitive racing entrepreneur John L. Paul Sr. was indicted Tuesday on 17 counts involving money laundering, and his father was charged in four of the counts.

Assistant U.S. Attorney Jim Fagan said the indictment alleged Paul was engaged in a conspiracy with his father Lee J. Paul, to launder John Paul's profits from drug trafficking.

John Paul already has been sought by the FBI, the Internal Revenue Service and the Gwinnett (Ga.) County tax office.

The FBI has pursued Paul since Dec. 12 when he failed to appear for trail for attempted murder of a government witness. Shortly after he was declared a fugitive, the IRS filed a lien against him in Gwinnett County, claiming he owes $456,000 in personal income taxes for 1978 and 1979.

Special to the Times — MARY ANN CARTER

"I went out to the garage to feed the dog and found

Getting back in the race

John Paul Jr. restarts his driving career after spending time in prison

■ Sullivan qualifies. 8C

By BRUCE LOWITT
Times Staff Writer

INDIANAPOLIS — His hands were trembling and his eyes were red-rimmed. It would be a while before John Paul Jr. zipped up his firesuit, slipped on his crash helmet and tried to conquer the Indianapolis Motor Speedway. For now, though, he was thinking about Alexandra.

"She's 4," he said, his voice almost inaudible, "and this is the toughest thing I've had to live with — telling her, 'Daddy's in jail.'

"I've been up front with her already about why I was in jail," he said. "She was only 2 years old when I went in. She didn't understand, but I told her...

...father to unload boatloads of marijuana, how he figured that was his only route into auto racing.

John Paul Jr.'s last chance to qualify for the May 28 Indianapolis 500 comes today. He is 29 years old. He and Patricia and their daughter live in West Palm Beach. His chance of making the Indy field is slim, but he already has come a long way since he was released last October from a federal prison after serving 28 months of a five-year sentence.

He said he has grown up a lot since August 1985, when he pleaded guilty to a charge that in 1979 he unloaded Colombian marijuana in Louisiana.

And he said he should have known better.

So did his father.

USAC should just say no to this guy

Driver Paul ought to be banned for past drug offenses

In 1986, John Paul Jr. was indicted, convicted and sentenced to five years in an Alabama prison after pleading guilty to a racketeering charge stemming from a drug-smuggling conspiracy.

Even worse, Paul was incredibly bold enough to transport the drugs in the very car he used in a race just weeks before.

But, wait. That isn't all.

In 1979, the then-18-year-old Paul was busted when he and his father, John Paul Sr., were caught loading marijuana in a Louisiana swamp. The operation was headed by the father, who in 1987 was sentenced to 25 years in prison for marijuana smuggling and other drug-related charges.

Like father, like son.

They both were reputable race car drivers. And they both are 2-time losers.

But somehow, John Paul Jr. has been given a third chance to redeem himself and become something closely resembling a decent citizen. Yet, there are men still behind bars for committing lesser crimes.

If Paul had been a player in

AUTOS

Ralph Paulk

Muncie, Ind., native started 24th and finished 15th.

Paul was officially welcomed back to racing in February.

Paul attempted — and failed — to qualify for Sunday's Indy 500 and the logic in Indianapolis seemed to be that he had paid his debt to society by serving just two years of his sentence.

Officials of the United States Auto Club just lightly slapped his hand before allowing him to attempt to qualify at Indy.

Thanks, USAC.

That's all we need, a major sanctioning body to tell its members that associating themselves with drugs in any way, fashion or form doesn't jeopardize their careers. USAC officials ignored the fact that drugs are a major prob-

such notables as Geoff Brabham, who was more deserving.

If Baker made the move to create some off-the-track controversy, then he succeeded. In teaming Paul with Steve Chassey, who qualified in a Lola-Cosworth, the Baker team invited criticism from other drivers and team owners.

"Personally, if I was running the sanctioning body," said driver Derek Daly, "I would ban for life anybody who is convicted of drug-related offenses because I believe it's such a major problem in the nation."

"I don't think we're sending the right message to young people," said 2-time Indy 500 champion Gordon Johncock. "We talk all the time about the seriousness of the drug problem, and that's why I can't comprehend the decision to allow (Paul) to compete again."

Said rookie driver Steve Saleen: "I believe almost anyone deserves a second chance. But this makes it look as though we're condoning this kind of thing, and we're not."

Perhaps one could sympathize with Paul if he had convinced us that this was all a terrible mistake. And, Paul held a press conference during qualifying at Indy in an attempt to explain himself.

"I just want to forget what happened," he said, "and go on with my life. I've learned a lot in the past three or four years. I've really gone through a lot.

"I don't have any bad feelings about my father and what we got involved in. I still communicate with him."

No one, no matter how self-righteous or right, has any reason to suggest that Paul disassociate himself from his father. Unquestionably, he made some poor decisions in the past, and this one is a judgment call he alone should make — right or wrong.

The fact remains, however, that John Paul Jr. committed an unforgivable crime — not once, but twice. There's nothing wrong with compassion, but let us not get carried away.

SPECIAL

Bill, Don and Dale Whittington

Bill and Don showed up at the 1979 running of the 24 Hours of Le Mans with a duffle bag filled with enough cash to not only buy each of them a seat ($20,000 each) in the Porsche 935 K3 that would win that year, but also to purchase the car itself on a whim; for $200,000 in cash. They also bought the Road Atlanta racetrack, where they allegedly landed planes filled with contraband on the back straight in the middle of the night.

Dale

Don

Bill

The Whittingtons had racing talent; At Riverside, Bill and Don won the 1979 Times Grand Prix; ran fourth in 1980; won again in 1982 and 1984. Both ran in the 1980 Winston Western 500 stock car race, finishing eighth and ninth. All three eventually ran in the Indy 500 and set a record; they were the only three brothers to ever qualify for the Indy 500. In 1986, Bill pleaded guilty to income tax evasion and conspiracy to smuggle marijuana. A year later, Don pleaded guilty to money laundering charges. Bill was sentenced to fifteen years in federal prison in 1986 when he plead guilty to tax evasion and conspiracy charges. Don was sentenced to eighteen months for money laundering in connection with the whole scheme. As part of the plea deal, the brothers had to make a $7 million restitution to the government, which included selling the P-51 Mustangs, the 1979 Le Mans winning 935, other race cars and team equipment. Don was paroled in 1988 and Bill was released in 1990. They somehow got into the aircraft leasing business and were investigated again in 2013 but not charged and then bought a Colorado resort. In 2018, Bill was again convicted of tax evasion, at the age of 68, and sentenced to 18 months and had to pay $1.8 million in restitution. Investigators determined that Dale Whittington, the youngest of the three brothers, was not involved in the operation and he was never charged with any crime. Dale went on to compete in the IMSA American Le Mans Series in 1999 and 2000 before dying of a drug overdose in 2000.

Race drivers charged in drug case

By M. Anthony Lednovich
Staff Writer

Veteran race car drivers Bill and Don Whittington of Fort Lauderdale, who gained international acclaim when they won the prestigious 24 Hours of Le Mans in 1979, have been charged with defrauding the U.S. government of millions of dollars in taxes derived from the profits of a large-scale marijuana-smuggling ring.

Also charged was Gary R. Levitz, 47, of Fort Lauderdale, the son of the founder of the Levitz furniture chain, according to federal information filed Monday in Fort Lauderdale by Assistant U.S. Attorney Lurana S. Snow.

The charges are the culmination of an 18-month investigation by the Internal Revenue Service, the U.S. Drug Enforcement Administration and the Fort Lauderdale Police Department.

All three men have been negotiating plea agreements with authorities since last December and are expected to formally enter guilty pleas Friday to the various counts before U.S. District Judge Jose Gonzalez Jr.

The brothers also are expected to forfeit $7 million in assets, while Levitz will give up $1 million in property.

Snow was sworn in as Broward's new U.S. magistrate, replacing Patricia Kyle, three hours after filing the document and is prohibited from commenting about the case as a judge.

In addition to fraud and income tax evasion, Bill Whittington, 37, was charged with one count of conspiracy to smuggle "multi-ton quantities of marijuana" into the United States from March 1977 to August 1981.

Both brothers are longtime Fort Lauderdale residents who built a $16 million empire that included a 2.8 mile Georgia road racing track, fixed-based aviation operations at Fort Lauderdale Executive Airport and Fort Collins, Colo., a 110-acre Georgia mobile home park, a *Please see DRIVERS, 8A*

No IRS charges for pair in tax case

Women are daughters of race car driver Bill Whittington, who pleaded guilty

BY MARIE C. BACA
JOURNAL STAFF WRITER

The federal government has agreed not to prosecute two prominent Albuquerque businesswomen in an Internal Revenue Service criminal investigation that led to a guilty plea from their father, a former race car driver.

Nerissa Whittington and Keely Whittington are the owners of Albuquerque-based Gulfstream Worldwide Realty and bigbyte.cc, a co-location data center. The pair also own The Springs Resort and Spa in Pagosa Springs, Colo., among other business interests.

Auto-racing brothers get jail terms

They still deny drug charges

By PATTY SHILLINGTON

Whittingtons trying to earn respect

Don (left) and Bill Whittington insist rumors about them are not true. *UPI photo*

By Dave Wieczorek
Staff Writer

INDIANAPOLIS — Take it from Bill Whittington, everything you've heard about him and his brother Don during the last couple of years is probably false. They don't run drugs for a living, they don't drive recklessly at 190 mph and they don't support the slaughter of baby seals.

They haven't had to defend themselves against that last charge yet, but Bill Whittington wouldn't be surprised should that day come. "You're thinking you're a nice guy," said Whittington, "and all of a sudden you're a jerk."

That is the media image the Whittingtons wear like grease spots and find just as difficult to wash away.

Since entering their first Indianapolis 500 in 1980, the Whittingtons have been linked with drug smugglers, questionable driving skills and cockiness that borders on arrogance.

They drive fast with less practice time than any other driver. Don had one of the fastest practice times of the month at 205.8 mph and both drivers qualified for Sunday's race at better than 197. You won't hear many of their fellow drivers criticize them by name, but veterans such as Gordon Johncock and Tom Sneva say drivers with limited experience in Indy-type cars (the Whittingtons have competed in only five such races) don't belong here.

"These guys go out all year and bust their guts, and we show up and go fast," Don Whittington said. "They are flat-out jealous. Nobody likes to be outrun. If you're a nice guy and walk around the pits and go slow, everybody loves you. But when you're up front, they're irritated."

Brother Bill insists the Whittingtons are victims of a bum rap, on and off the track. "If you talk to the horse's mouth rather than the horse's behind," said Bill, "you'll get a different story."

So we take you straight to the horse's mouth.

Charge one: The Whittingtons compete in big-time racing thanks to the millions they've made from running drugs into Florida.

"We have a Lear jet business, a charter business, a [recreational vehicle] business and we develop mobile-home parks," said Bill Whittington, at 33 four years younger than Don. "I've lived in Fort Lauderdale for 15 years and if you don't think people come in to buy an RV with bags of money, you're sick.

"But we put all our money right in the bank. You can check it out. But all of a sudden we're linked with smugglers. Don doesn't even smoke. There's not a straighter guy in Lauderdale than Don. If we've been in Florida that long and been dealing in drugs, how is it we're not in jail yet?"

No one ever proved that the Whittingtons acquired their money by illegal means, though they were under police protection at the Indianapolis Motor Speedway last

Please see WHITTINGTONS, 8C

Randy Lanier

A high school dropout from South Florida, Randy made it big as a major marijuana smuggler in the '80s. At the same time, he took up racing, first in IMSA, winning the Times Grand Prix in 1984 and then at the 1986 Indy 500, where he took Rookie of the Year honors and finished tenth. Along the way, he teamed up with the Whittington brothers to create Blue Thunder Racing and win the 1984 IMSA championship with a March prototype. Indicted, he fled to first to Monte Carlo, then tp Antigua, where he had a house. In 1988, Lanier was convicted of smuggling and distributing 300 tons of Colombian marijuana and sentenced to life without the chance of parole as the kingpin of a continuing criminal enterprise plus he forfeited $60 million in assets. His wife divorced him; his second wife that he married while in prison was convicted of money laundering and deported and after his release in 2014 he got back together with the first wife, During his time at Leavenworth, Lanier took long walks in the prison yard with fellow inmate John Paul Sr., reminiscing about their racing days.

Race car driver fails to appear for court date

By DEBORAH PETIT
Staff Writer

Race car driver Randy Lanier was a no-show in federal court on Wednesday and is considered a fugitive by authorities.

"We have reason to believe he has absconded," said strike force prosecutor Lothar Genge, with the U.S. Justice Department.

Lanier, 32, a Davie resident who in 1986 was named the Indianapolis

was planning to turn himself in Wednesday morning before U.S. Magistrate Lurana Snow in Fort Lauderdale.

He didn't show up, and Genge told Snow he wants to revoke the $100,000 bond Lanier posted in the Florida case. Genge said he didn't think Lanier would show up given the seriousness of the charges he faces and the fact that he is the subject of ongoing investigations.

Action on the revocation motion

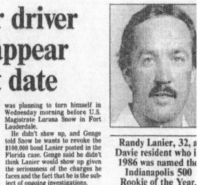

Randy Lanier, 32, a Davie resident who i 1986 was named the Indianapolis 500 Rookie of the Year,

Indianapolis 500 driver among 13 suspects in drug ring

FORT LAUDERDALE (AP) — Federal agents Thursday rounded up three suspects in a $30 million, international drug-trafficking and money-laundering ring that allegedly involves some South Florida attorneys and this year's Indianapolis 500 racing rookie of the year.

Attorney Michael I. Levine, 33, of Miami, surrendered to federal authorities Thursday on charges of conspiracy and possession of drugs with the intent to distribute.

On Wednesday, race driver Randy Lanier, 32, the 1986 Indianapolis 500 Rookie of the Year after his 10th-place finish, was arraigned on the same charges Wednesday. The Davie resident was released on $100,000 bond.

"This is completed a major drug and money-laundering organization," said Paul Teresi of the U.S. Drug Enforcement Administration in Fort Lauderdale. "They were significant importers."

The two were among 13 people who had warrants issued for them after DEA informants reported that ring members were aware of an ongoing seven-month federal grand jury investigation and had made preparations to flee, said Teresi. By mid-afternoon, six suspects were still at large.

The local news media reported that some prominent South Florida attorneys are expected to be indicted by Tuesday at the earliest, but Teresi said he couldn't comment on the grand jury proceedings.

The ring allegedly smuggled 100,000 pounds of marijuana into South Florida between September 1983 and June 1986, said the criminal complaint filed Wednesday.

They then used funds in England, Panama, Hong Kong, the British Virgin Islands and other locations to launder $30 million in profits, the complaint said. Britain's New Scotland Yard and the U.S. Internal Revenue Service aided the investigation, said Teresi.

Earlier this year, Lanier was in the news because he sometimes teamed with Don Whittington in Indy-car racing events.

Whittington pleaded guilty last spring to running an interstate, $73 million marijuana smuggling organization out of Broward County between 1977 and 1981.

Lanier also was a racing buddy of Davie ... race car driver Marty Hinze. Hinze pleaded guilty Wednesday afternoon for his involvement in Whittington's marijuana smuggling operation and faces a possible 10-year prison term.

"We heard rumors for years," Lanier said in the interview. "It's unfortunate, but I don't think time off him as a person. I hope people will take me for my driving skills, not where I associated with."

Race car driver, 12 others charged in smuggling ring

By EMILIA ASKARI
Herald Staff Writer

Race car driver Randy Lanier, ... finish of the Miami at this ...

have surrendered. The latest was Miami lawyer Michael I. Levine, who had no comment for reporters

Michael Little of Fort Lauderdale; Edward Curran of Dania; John Dennis Cason, who lives near

Where have you gone, Randy Lanier?

FBI seeks racer, missing since January, on drug charges

By JEFF SNOOK
Palm Beach Post Staff Writer

INDIANAPOLIS — Dennis McCormack won't forget Halloween night of 1985.

McCormack, a CART/Indy-car racing team manager, and his family were in Miami for the Indy Challenge, which was still more than a week away.

More than a thousand miles from his Indianapolis home, McCormack wouldn't think of taking his 2-year-old daughter Lauren trick-or-treating in foreign territory. But Randy Lanier, a 32-year-old race car driver from Davie, solved his problem.

Lanier was well into his first season as an Indy-car driver for Arciero Wines, McCormack's employer.

"Randy asked me if my family was in town," McCormack said. "He told me to bring my wife and daughter over to his house and he would take them trick-or-treating.

"He loved children. He took his daughter and my daughter around his neighborhood door-to-door that night. That's what I remember about Randy Lanier."

Seven months later, Lanier turned in the fastest qualifying lap (209.964 mph) ever by a rookie for the Indianapolis 500. He finished his first Indy 500 in 10th place and was named the race's Rookie of the Year.

"He drove a good consistent race," McCormack said. "A couple of yellow flags at the wrong time hurt him or he would have finished higher.

"He was real excited that day, I know that. Everybody thought he had a great future."

Little did anyone know that Lanier's future was destined not only to be tarnished but virtually destroyed.

Randy Lanier is not one of 33 drivers entered in next Sunday's Indianapolis 500. Chances are excellent that he will never drive a race car again.

Just where is Lanier as the anniversary of his first Indy 500 rolls around? No one knows. Not even the best of FBI agents trying to learn his whereabouts.

Lanier, indicted Oct. 15, 1986 in Fort Lauderdale on drug-trafficking charges and Jan. 23 in Benton, Ill., on drug-smuggling charges and running a "con-

Please see LANIER/8C

Randy Lanier was Rookie of Year at last Indy 500.

Marty Hinze

Not as big an operator or as good a driver, Marty started racing in 1975; had a number of drives in IMSA GT including the Times Grand Prix in 1981 with Preston Henn. He joined forces with the Whittingtons and Randy Lanier to form Blue Thunder racing and often co-drove with both. He was really in the fence building business in Fort Lauderdale, somewhat over his head in the smuggling business. He plead guilty to conspiracy and smuggling charges in connection with his involvement with the Whittingtons,

Lanier, Hinze implicated in smuggling rings

Indianapolis 500 Rookie of the Year Randy Lanier, of Davie, is among 12 people who have been charged by federal agents with running a major marijuana ring. And, in a separate drug investigation, Fort Lauderdale driver Marty Hinze has admitted to being part of a group which imported tons of marijuana into South Florida in the late 1970s.

Lanier, 32, was named Wednesday in a criminal complaint filed in Fort Lauderdale by the U.S. Drug Enforcement Administration. Paulo Teres of the DEA said he was charged with conspiracy and possession with intent to distribute.

Lanier's bond was set at $100,000.

Hinze was to have gone on trial Wednesday for his role in a smuggling group headed by fellow race driver Bill Whittington, the Fort Lauderdale Sun-Sentinel reported. Hinze instead pleaded guilty before U.S. District Judge William Zloch after working out a last-minute agreement with prosecutors. Zloch set sentencing for Nov. 21. Hinze faces a maximum penalty of 16 years in prison and a $35,000 fine.

Whittington pleaded guilty last spring to running a $73 million marijuana smuggling ring out of Broward County in the late 1970s. His plea agreement called for him to forfeit $7 million and spend at least five years in prison. Whittington has not yet been sentenced.

In the case involving Lanier, several Florida attorneys are charged with helping marijuana smugglers launder at least $33 million in profits through banks in Great Britain, Panama, Hong Kong and the British Virgin Islands.

An informant told a federal grand jury that more than 700,000 pounds of marijuana was brought into

South Florida between September 1982 and June 1983.

"This is considered a major drug and money laundering organization. They were significant importers," said Paul Teres, resident agent in charge of the DEA's office in Fort Lauderdale.

Lanier won Rookie of the Year honors at the Indy 500 this year after finishing 10th an earning $103,437.

He is entered in the Nov. 9 Nissan Indy Challenge at Tamiami, the season finale on the CART circuit. He finished 15th in last year's race.

Driver pleads guilty in drug conspiracy

By DEBORAH PETIT
Staff Writer

Professional race car driver Martin John "Marty" Hinze admitted in federal court Wednesday that he was part of a conspiracy to import multi-ton loads of marijuana between 1977 and 1981 and failed to report smuggling profits on his tax returns.

Hinze, who is president of the family-owned Hinze Fence Co. in Fort Lauderdale, was to have gone to trial Wednesday.

The government would have tried to prove that he was an integral cog in a smuggling group headed by fellow race car driver

Whittington, along with his brother, Don Whittington, pleaded guilty last spring for their roles in the $73 million operation.

Bill Whittington's plea agreement called for him to forfeit $7 million to the government and serve at least five years of a 15-year term in prison. Don Whittington's agreement called for him to spend 18 months in prison.

The Whittingtons have yet to be sentenced, as lawyers apparently still are ironing out details of the agreements.

Hinze was called to testify before the grand jury investigating the Whittington marijuana smug-

Ron O'Dell

Ron was a pretty good amateur race car driver; Mary Ellen, his wife, a hairdresser and world class skeet shooter. Ron had aspirations of racing Ferrari's on a Porsche budget and secured a ride in the 1960 Times Grand Prix in a ex Arciero Ferrari. Married eleven months, they quarreled and she shot him with a .357 magnum. According to the L.A. Times; he reportedly said he didn't love her any more. She said she didn't recall shooting him. She was charged with murder, pleaded innocent because of temporary insanity, convicted of manslaughter and sentenced to one to ten years.

EARLY WINNER—Ron O'Dell, in car number 77E, wins production F race at Riverside Raceway with 77 m.p.h. average over curvaceous course. Starter Jimmy Jackson gives him checkered flag. Classic 200-mile Times Grand Prix is scheduled this afternoon.

Times photo by Art Rogers

Skeet Expert Shoots Mate With Pistol

Wife Held in Slaying; Says Mate Spurned Her

A Huntington Park woman shot and killed her husband Friday morning when he told her he didn't love her, according to police.

Mrs. Mary Ellen O'Dell, 32, was booked on suspicion of murder after the death

O'Dell died at Maywood Hospital with a bullet in his chest. Police quoted Mrs. O'Dell as saying she shot him in anger during a marital quarrel when he assertedly said: "It didn't take me

Eric Haga

Eric Haga had a pretty fair career in racing, competing at Riverside in some USRRC, Can Am and Formula 5000 events. His career had a couple of notable downturns. He critically injured a corner worker in a crash at the Formula 5000 race in Seattle in 1971 (not intentionally, I'm sure) and his wife and daughter were murdered in Seattle in 1966. The crime when unsolved for five years unti he was charged with and convicted of the crime in 1971, accused of using the life insurance money for racing. He received two life sentences and was paroled in 1989 and currently is involved in vintage racing.

A Window On Murder

What a neighbor saw through a sheer curtain was the prelude to a mystery that tantalized the cops for years

By ANN RULE
and KERMIT JAEDIKER

Crack racing-car driver Eric Haga had more than a finish line to cross after he became a suspect in the murders of his pretty wife and baby daughter.

AT 6:45 ONE July morning, on a quiet, middle-class street in Kent, Wash., a suburb of Seattle, Marshall Lewis started his car and let the engine idle. As he did so he looked around and saw something odd.

The drapes of the living-room window of the Haga house across the street had been drawn open. Lewis had never seen those drapes open during the morning.

The big window was slightly obscured by a sheer curtain and through it Marshall could dimly perceive the figure of a stocky man. The man appeared to be wearing a garment bulky around the neck, rather like an overcoat with a heavy collar.

The man behind the curtained window bent forward, but what he was doing was not perceptible. Lewis shrugged, put his car in gear and drove off.

Evidence Slim

This was the prelude to a double-murder mystery whose solution, obvious and yet somehow just out of reach, tantalized police for five long years before they finally decided they had enough evidence to nail their prime suspect.

The murders came to light July 6, 1966. One hour after Marshall Lewis drove away, still wondering about the shadowy figure he had seen, Eric Haga came running out of his home with his 3½-year-old daughter, Paola, in his arms.

The 25-year-old Haga was a draftsman, but he was much better known as a racing-car driver who often competed at Seattle International Raceways. He was 5 feet 10 and on the stocky side, and at the moment he was wearing a plaid bathrobe with a bulky collar.

He ran to the house next door and banged the kitchen window and his neighbors jumped up from breakfast and joined him. "There's something the matter with Judy!" gasped Haga. Judy was his pretty blonde 23-year-old wife.

Haga handed Paola to the woman neighbor and her husband accompanied him back into his home via the patio doorway. Haga pointed a shaking finger at a mound of blankets on the living room floor. "There she is."

The other man pushed aside an overturned coffee table and went to the mound and caught a flash of Judy's hair. She and her husband and their two daughters had just spent the July 4th weekend in Oregon with her family and during the holiday a woman relative bleached Judy's hair a stunning strawberry blonde.

The neighbor pulled back the blankets. Judy lay face down. She had on a quilted shortie robe. Her bikini pants had been tugged down to her thighs. Her wrist was warm but her pulse was imperceptible.

The neighbor went to the phone, but it was dead. "I'll run home and call an ambulance," he said.

A State of Shock

When he returned, Haga appeared to be in a state of shock. He kept muttering, "Her neck. There's something around her neck."

The neighbor lifted the hair away from Judy's neck, and saw a necktie. She had been garroted with it.

Haga suddenly let out a yell. "I forgot. The baby!" With that he dashed to a bedroom down the hall. Then the neighbor heard him cry, "My God. The baby, too!"

The child, Perri Lynn, 7 months, had been strangled with a pink satin ribbon.

The neighbor found a paring knife and cut the ribbon but Perri didn't respond. The necktie, wrapped three times around Judy's neck, was also cut away.

An ambulance arrived. One attendant gave Perri mouth-to-mouth resuscitation while another inserted an airway into Judy's throat and put a respirator into action. But mother and baby were dead and had been dead for hours.

King County homicide detectives arrived, persuaded the upset Haga to take it easy next door and then began examining the house. There were clear-cut signs of struggle. There was the overturned coffee table. A woman's purse, its contents spilled, lay among magazines scattered on the rug.

Struggle in Bathroom

But clearly, the struggle between Judy and her killer began in the bathroom. Its floor was littered with curlers and bobby pins and its rugs had been twisted and pulled halfway into the hallway.

Every room was photographed, with notations stating the time each picture was taken. One photograph in the master bedroom would show an electric clock and, as would become significant later, it was keeping correct time. The bed was rumpled. And tossed on it was a man's plaid bathrobe.

As detectives George Helland and Robert Andrews hunted clues within the house, other investigators fanned out through the neighborhood, knocking on doors and asking questions.

Eric Haga returned to his front door and asked the patrolman posted

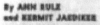

DRIVEN TO KILL

By JOSEPH McNAMARA

MARSHALL LEWIS ALWAYS let his car idle the first thing in the morning. As he did so one summer day, his gaze strayed to the Haga house across the street from his home in Kent, Wash., a quiet suburb of Seattle. Lewis stared. He had never seen the Haga living room window drapes drawn open so early in the day.

Through the sheer curtains partially obscuring his view, Lewis dimly perceived the figure of a stocky man wearing a garment that appeared bulky at the neck. The man bent over, but Lewis could not see what he was doing. Lewis drove off to work. It was 6:45 a.m. July 6, 1966. Somehow, what he had seen did not seem important — then.

An hour later Eric Haga came running out of his house, carrying his daughter Paula, 2. He wore a plaid bathrobe with a bulky collar.

Haga, 23, was a heavyset 5-feet 10, a draftsman who was better known about Seattle as a race car driver. He often drove at Seattle International Raceway, rarely a winner but often second or third place.

Highly agitated, he now rapped on his neighbor's kitchen window, and cried out, "There's something the matter with Judy."

Judy was Eric's pretty, 22-year-old wife, usually a blond but a stunning redhead since a family member did her hair July 4.

Leaving Paula with the neighbor's wife, the two men returned to the Haga living room. With shaking finger Haga pointed to a mound of blankets on the floor.

"There she is," Haga gasped.

The neighbor shoved aside an overturned coffee table and lifted the blankets. Judy lay face down on the floor, clad in a quilted shortie robe. Her bikini pants were tugged down to her thighs. Still warm, she had no pulse.

PHONE WAS DEAD

Finding the phone dead, the neighbor dashed home and called police. He returned to find Haga in shock.

"Her neck. There's something around her neck," Haga suffered.

The neighbor lifted Judy's tresses and saw a necktie she had been garroted with.

"I forgot!" Haga suddenly screamed. "The baby!"

Down the hall he dashed, then cried out, "My God. The baby too!"

Perri Lynn, 7 months old, had been strangled with a pink satin ribbon. The neighbor cut off both instruments of death, but neither victim responded. A coroner was to rule both mother and baby had been dead for hours.

King County homicide men found signs of a fierce struggle that began in the bathroom, where curlers and bobby pins were strewn about and rugs twisted, into the hallway and then the living room, containing Judy's ransacked purse.

In the bedroom a table clock hummed away. A man's plaid bathrobe lay across the bed.

WIRES CUT

As Detectives George Helland and Robert Andrews hunted for clues, Haga buttonholed a patrolman guarding the front door. Leading the cop to an exterior phone connection, Haga explained he had dropped his cigaret lighter and accidentally kicked it against the house. As he bent to retrieve it, Haga said, he saw a sheen of broken wires through the under-part of the phone box.

The cop bent down but was unable to see the wires. He wondered how Haga could. The lawman could feel the wires with his fingers. They had been cut.

At headquarters Haga told this story.

The previous day Judy had been frightened on seeing a "prowler" in his 20s in their backyard. He wore worker's clothes. When Haga came home for lunch, he saw the "prowler's" legs through a patio door and he gave chase — but failed to catch the man.

Because of the prowler and the fact that Judy and the kids had a virus, Haga took the afternoon off from work. They dined out, but that evening he felt himself coming down with the virus. He took a sleeping pill and slept in the master bedroom. Judy slept on the divan so she would not disturb him.

Haga said he awakened at 7:30 a.m. and found the bodies. He said $100 was missing from Judy's purse.

Detective Ted Forrester compared notes with Helland

THE JUSTICE STORY

and Andrews. There was no sign of forced entry. How, they asked, could Haga have slept through a sex attack and the obvious battle? And why would a sex-killer slay an infant that could not implicate him?

NO SEX ASSAULT

Actually, medics found no evidence of sexual assault. Both victims died between midnight and 2 a.m. And when Lewis reported seeing the "stocky man" behind the picture window at 6:45 a.m., the sleuths realized this was almost an hour before the time Haga said he awoke. If it were the killer, why would he hang around for hours?

Also, no neighbor had seen the "prowler."

Haga had said he and Judy enjoyed a perfect marriage. But now probers learned that

IT WAS MURDER:

A necktie was used to strangle Judy Haga (under blanket above) of Kent, Wash., on July 6, 1966, and a pink ribbon was used to do in her 7-month-old, Perri Lynn. A detective's nagging suspicions lead to the arrest and conviction of the slain woman's husband, Eric (l.), in 1971.

in April 1965 Judy took a vacation alone in Oregon and met a handsome guy she liked. She spent the weekend with him, and within weeks left Haga for her new-found lover.

Judy, it turned out, was six weeks pregnant, by Haga, when she met Mr. Nice Guy, who — informed of the pregnancy — decided maybe he would not leave his wife. Judy returned to Haga.

"Did you ever think Perri might not be your child?" Haga was asked.

Haga said he had, but he decided Judy was pregnant by him when she met her heartthrob and she did not know it.

A lie-detector test proved inconclusive. Haga was too emotionally upset. Cops could see a case against Haga, but it was circumstantial, weak. The coroner's finding: "Murder by person unknown."

Haga threw himself headlong into racing while a family member raised Paula. Years passed. Helland made lieutenant, but he could not forget Haga's "X-ray vision" that enabled him to see the cut phone wires.

Also, probers learned that just before the slayings Haga tried to borrow $3,800 but his bank knocked him down. On Judy's and Perri's deaths Haga collected $16,722 in insurance.

Haga told cops he had not worn his bulky collared bathrobe for months before the

slaying. But his neighbor said Haga wore it the morning of the murders, and cops had found it lying on the bed. Haga had said the bedside clock did not work. It did.

The big break came when they finally found Judy's long-missing lover. He said he was logging in Casper, Wyo., the day of the killings.

Authorities figured the time was ripe to tag Haga. On Aug. 30, 1971, he was put in the book for the slayings of his wife and daughter and that December he went on trial. Found guilty with recommendations of mercy, Haga was sentenced to two concurrent life terms.

CONVICTION UPSET

However, the Washington State Court of Appeals reversed the conviction on grounds the testimony of one witness was prejudicial and was not expert testimony. An ambulance attendant had testified that Haga did not seem as grief-stricken as most new widowers would, and that Haga seemed worried when Judy, under artificial respiration, seemed to be breathing.

Haga was retried, in late 1973, and was convicted once more. By this time trial investigators were able to verify, through the statement of a postmaster, that Judy's lover had indeed been logging in Wyoming the day of the murders.

In early 1974 Haga was sentenced once more to two concurrent life terms.

He was paroled in 1989.

Chapter Fourteen - Other than Racing

The Olympic Athlete and Sports Car Relay, billed as a charity event, took place on a hot July Sunday in 1964. Each team had a walker. a sprinter, a bicycle rider, a motorcycle rider and a sports car driver. According to the L.A. Times, nobody showed up and due to some confusion, bicycles and sports cars were on the track at the same time. The event was never held again.

READY TO RIDE—But what? Auto driver Miles Gupton (from left), motorcycler Tony Murphy and bicycler Tim Mountford check strategy for Sunday's mixed-up Olympic Fund relay race at Riverside. Twenty teams will compete in event.

Times photo by Art Rogers

Everything Races In Olympic Event

Just about every means of racing will be included in the Olympic Athletic and Sports Car Relays Sunday, July 19. Runners, bicycles, motorcycles, sports cars, even press photographers will get their chance to compete at the Riverside International Raceway.

Olympics Benefit At Raceway

How can one amateur spor[t] help another?

The sports car crowd ha[s] found a way, by scheduling th[e] Olympic Athletic and Sport[s] Car Relays at Riverside Race[-]way on Sunday, July 19.

Object is to raise money fo[r] the U.S. Olympic Fund, whic[h] finances the American team['s] trip to the Olympics at Toky[o] in October.

In addition, sports car fan[s] will be exposed to two kind[s] of Olympic competition—run[-]ning and bike racing.

Runners will start the action performing what amounts to [a] distance medley relay for on[e] lap of the 2.7-mile Grand Pri[x] course.

At the end of that lap they will pass batons to bicycle[s] racers, who will figure to hi[t] 65 miles per hour on the down[-]hill straightaway. They in tur[n] will pass off to motorcyclists. The motor bike racers will pass batons to sports car drivers who will carry on through [a] series of races.

The Olympic van, filled with mementoes of past U.S. Olym[-]pic performances, will be sta[-]tioned in the raceway infield. Spectators may tour the "Olympic Museum on Wheels" free of charge on both days o[f] racing.

Veteran Monise To Drive In Riverside Olympic Show

Veteran sports car driver Frank Monise, a hero in the South and a villain in the North, will compete tomorrow and Sunday in the unique Olympic Athletic and Sports Car Relays at Riverside International Raceway.

The successful 38-year-old Glendora driver has entered his Lotus 23B in the four-and-a-half-hour speed show Sunday to raise funds for the U.S. Olympic team.

Monise, who operates a foreign car service in Pasadena,

has been nearly unbeatable [on] the California Sports Car Cl[ub] racing circuit and current[ly] ranks third in Pacific Coast Modified divisional point stan[d]ings.

HIS LIST of victories in th[e] past year and the capabiliti[es] of his car have prompted ra[c]ing fans to refer to every ra[ce] track in Southern Californ[ia] as "Frank Monise's course."

However, race enthusias[ts] and officials in Northern Ca[li]fornia rate Monise as bein[g] anything but a mild-manner[ed] and popular sports car drive[r].

In fact, his disputes wit[h] Northern officials have r[e]sulted in hanging on Moni[se] the comic strip nickname [of] the "Terrible Tempered M[r.] Bangs."

Whether it be Mr. Bangs [or] Mr. Monise, he still boasts [a] string of impressive victori[es] over the past year at San[ta] Barbara, Pomona, San L[uis] Obispo and Del Mar.

This weekend's sports c[ar] activities will be a new exp[eri]ence for Monise, as well as t[he] other top entrants. Tomorr[ow] the cars will compete in qua[li]fying races for Sunday's r[e]lays with the positions bas[ed] on fastest overall times a[nd] not classes.

Sunday's Olympic progra[m] will be an honest-to-goodne[ss] relay race complete with bat[on] passes involving runners, bi[ke] racers, motorcylists a[nd] sports car drivers in one co[n]tinuous show.

The weekend races a[re] jointly sponsored by the Ca[li]fornia Sports Car Club a[nd] Riverside International Rac[e]way in cooperation with t[he] U.S. Olympic Committee.

The qualifying portion of t[he] Southern California Sports C[ar] Championship Races will [be] featured on KTTV (Chann[el] 11) from 2 to 4 p.m.

Riverside Schedule

WHAT: Olympic Athletic and Sports Car Relays
WHEN: Sunday. Qualifying tomorrow
WHERE: Riverside International Raceway
PURPOSE: To help raise funds for U.S. Olympic team.
KIND OF RACING: An honest-to-goodness relay race with baton passes, probably the first of its kind in this country, with runners, bike racers, motorcyclists and sports car drivers all competing in one continuous speed show.
TEAMS: There will be 20 teams making up the event, which will consume approximately four and a half hours. Each team will consist of runners, a bike rider, motorcycle riders and sports car drivers.
QUALIFYING: Qualifying will be necessary only for sports cars tomorrow with a series of races. Cars will run according to class but will be grouped in Sunday's relays according to qualifying speeds, regardless of class.
PROCEDURE: The runners and bicycle will start from the start finish line on the track proper while motorcycles and sports cars will be staged on pre-grid positions off the track. As soon as one relay team moves out another is moved in and made ready.
ADMISSION: $2.50 on Sunday and $1.50 tomorrow.
COURSE: Riverside's 2.7-mile Grand Prix course.
OTHER RACE ACTIVITIES: Tonight following qualifying races a barbecue will be held for participants and the public at the Raceway. Admission, $2.50. Following the barbecue, a tree-planting ceremony and footwarming are scheduled. Sunday, the "Fat Fotographers Fifty." A footrace of 50 yards (or less) for news photographers. All entries must be accompanied by $2 donation to Olympic Fund. A one-lap Olympic walking exhibition by top American competitors. The Olympic Van, containing displays of past Olympic Games, will also be on display at the raceway both Saturday and Sunday.
SPONSORS: Jointly sponsored by the California Sports Car Club and Riverside International Raceway in cooperation with the Olympic Committee.

Champion Dragster Favored at Fontana

FONTANA—John Peters of Santa Monica will be favored to win the gas eliminator title in his world record holding dragster tomorrow night at Mickey Thompson's Fontana International Dragway.

Peter's car, named "Freight Train" because of it's size and two big supercharged Chevrolet engines, currently holds the mark with a speed of 185.94 mph.

In fuel eliminator competition, Gary Gabelich driving the Sandoval Bros. dragster from San Fernando is co-favored with San Diego's Jerry Baltis to win top money.

Both Gabelich and Baltis

Beach topped world record holder Frank Cannon of Compton in two straight heats of their scheduled two out of three match race last Saturday night at the Dragway.

Tom McEwen, also of Long Beach, later defeated Southerland to win top eliminator honors, but had to set a strip record of 7.88 seconds to do so. It was Southerland's first loss in more than three months of competition.

Gas eliminator went to John Peters of Santa Monica with Olen McDowell of San Diego middle eliminator and Jack Bayer of Fontana stock eliminator.

Local Driver Set For 'Relay Races'

Floyd Shannon, a Montclair school teacher with a flair for sports car racing, will test his skills in the unique Olympic Athletic and Sports Car Relays Saturday and Sunday at Riverside Raceway.

motorcycle riders. The motor bike riders, divided into smal[l] and large bore classes, wil[l] complete two separate relay legs before passing the bato[n] to the first of several sports car classes.

Proceeds of the foot-whee[l]

In 1967, Ford ran a test, comparing their trucks to Chevys and Dodges; driving 24 hours a day for 67,000 miles. Les Richter hired some strippers to appear out of nowhere in the dark, just to keep drivers from getting bored.

Les Richter tried a variety of ways; attempting to make the track solvent; one of which was leasing out the facility for a sorts of vehicle testing. In the 70's, cars, trucks, busses and motorhomes drove around twenty four hours a day, producing revenue but severely damaging the track. This produced a washboard section at eight and the notorious turn one bump.

The Ford test program included a number of twenty four seven programs with Pinto's, F100 pickups, Mavericks and even Continentals. They used the "Ford Road', a little cut at the entry to turn six,

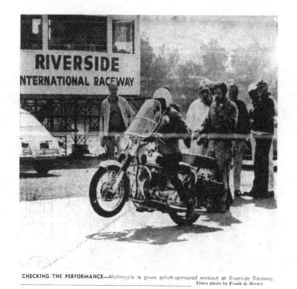

CHECKING THE PERFORMANCE—Motorcycle is given police-sponsored workout at Riverside Raceway.
Times photo by Frank Q. Brown

State Patrol to Test Vehicles on Raceway

RIVERSIDE, Dec. 4—The new International Speedway, at the foot of Box Springs Mountain just off Highway 60, is expected to serve the California Highway Patrol as a testing ground.

Besides providing thrills for race fans, the raceway this week also became a testing ground to help the CHP determine what make of automobile will stand the grueling pace in the field to the best advantage.

To determine what make of car best fits the need the CHP has previously resorted to roping off sections of highways, or made arrange-

ments to use private property for testing of new cars.

All the features of the raceway fit into the exact testing pattern of the Highway Patrol.

It not only duplicates actual road conditions but it also has facilities such as electronic timing devices in operation.

In addition to the tests, the CHP purchases cars on the basis of cubic centimeter displacement of the piston, price, top speed and past performance.

Testing is accomplished in two or three days where it used to take about a week to 10 days.

On a cold wet November day in 1961, Petersen Publishing put on a Corvair test, billed as a 24 hour economy run. Under the aegis of Carroll Shelby, two cars, one stock, one modified, were prepared by Chevy expert Bill Thomas (of Cheetah fame). Drivers named Shelby, Gurney and Unser were joined by NHRA head Wally Parks and Sports Car Graphic editor John Christy. Things didn't go as planned for the modified car which broke in the first hour but the stocker clocked 1549 miles at an average speed of 66 mph and got 16.6 mpg, in spite of clocking 105 mph down the long back straight. Quoting from Hot Rod Magazine, *"contestants and observers agreed this was one of the most demanding controlled endurance tests ever encountered by an American stock car"*

444

Motor Trend spent a lot of time at Riverside

Motor Trend tested a Berkeley in 1959 and a Fiat 1200 in 1960

A Tempest and a Falcon

A Dodge wagon and a GT-35

Volkswagens on the drag strip

446

A Borgward Isabella

1966 Dodge and 427 Cobra

Charley Budenz: *"Over a considerable span of years from the 60's to 70's General Motors conducted engineering and certification tests at Riverside. Convenient to the University of California, Riverside campus and the state emission testing laboratory there, Riverside raceway became a standard testing location for, among others, the General Motors 4-6-8 powerplants, another means of generating income for the generally cash starved facility. They even tested some hydrogen powered cars once.*

Sequentially timed traffic lights would be setup between the pits and turn one, then again after turn six for stop and go testing, then highway speeds down the straight and around turn nine. There were a few incidents of cars, trucks and even buses having rear end collisions at the stop lights but none required my services as volunteer tow truck driver".

Motor Trend and Sports Car Graphic Testing

Ford Antipollution Tests in Riverside Area

By LEE HARRIS

Sun-Telegram Staff Writer

RIVERSIDE — Following Monday's announcement that the Ford Motor Co. may face temporary plant shutdowns because of improper exhaust emission testing, it was learned that many Ford automobiles are undergoing pollution tests at Riverside International Raceway.

(Related story on Page A-6)

The cars, trucks and vans have been tested at the raceway and on a number of back roads in Riverside County since early March, sources said.

A raceway spokesman referred queries to Herman Spur, in charge of the emission project at Ford's Pico Rivera plant.

Spur could not be reached for comment. However, a spokesman at the plant confirmed the project's existence. The spokesman, an employee of the pro-

Ruckelshaus, disclosed Monday that unauthorized maintenance had been performed on 1973 cars being tested for pollution reduction by Ford.

It could not be learned if these tests were conducted at the raceway.

There was a possibility that Ford could be shut down for at least three months because the engines would not be certified as meeting the tougher emission standards for '73.

Ruckelshaus told a Senate subcommittee that Ford withdrew its application for EPA certification when it was discovered by the company that unauthorized maintenance had been performed on its test fleet.

Residents in the Pigeon Pass area said anywhere from 10 to 20 vehicles, driven by men and women, have been observed by night and day seven days a week

is required on the smog devices.

It could not be learned if Monday's EPA announcement affected the testing program at the raceway.

Hydrogen Powers Clean Car

RIVERSIDE — A hydrogen-powered car ranked as the cleanest vehicle in the First Annual Clean Fuel competition held at the recent Riverside International Raceway according to results just released by Clark Taylor, president of the University of California, Riverside, (UCR) Sports Racing Club which sponsored the day-long event.

Twelve automobiles using special low-polluting fuels underwent tests for emissions and performance as part of the competition, intended to measure the effectiveness of various fuels as alternatives to gasoline, Taylor said.

"All 13 cars we tested — including two gasoline-powered vehicles used as a comparison — were below the emissions standards set by the Federal Government," he added.

"I think the low emissions, coupled with the high driving performances for all the cars, shows that today's technology can be used to build cars which are not only low-polluting but which give good performance," Taylor emphasized.

Various cars burned hydrogen, methanol, propane, butane, natural gas, and even diesel fuel in the competition which was also co-sponsored by the Riverside Chamber of Commerce, the city of Riverside

proximating the various speeds of normal highway driving by using a device called a dynamometer furnished by Auto Lab, a local automobile testing company.

The finishing order was based on scoring in four categories — emissions, acceleration, top speed, and general driveability.

Receiving the trophy for first place was a 1971 Plymouth Road Runner using propane gas and entered by John Wiskirchen of Cal-Gas in Riverside, a propane marketer.

The cleanest vehicle, a 1973 Chevrolet Monte Carlo — built for the city of Riverside by the Energy Research Corporation in Provo, Utah — took second place in the overall competition.

A methanol-powered Gremlin, entered by the University of Santa Clara, was second lowest in pollution but fell to eighth position when its transmission burned out during the acceleration testing.

Finishing with the most pollution and also ranking in the last two positions were two propane vehicles. "This illustrates that even using relatively clean propane, the engines must be kept in good tune," Taylor said.

Equally significant, he pointed out, is that a gasoline-pow-

fuels, and after a careful scrutiny, all the auto makers should decide on a new standard fuel and build cars to run on it."

He also noted that both hydrogen and methanol fuels can be burned in present engines when the carburetors are replaced with specially-designed units. "Hydrogen is also a safer fuel than gasoline because when spilled out, it simply evaporates quickly into the air and doesn't remain in combustible puddles."

"At today's prices for gasoline, both hydrogen and methanol give about the same driving costs per mile as gasoline," he noted.

"Obviously, there are a lot of factors which must be taken into account when comparing low-polluting fuels. For example, both hydrogen and methanol give fewer miles per gallon than gasoline," he explained.

"While two diesel powered cars came in third cleanest, we were measuring for oxides of nitrogen, hydrocarbons and carbon monoxide emissions, and the relatively large amounts of smoke diesel fuel emits didn't show up in our tests," Taylor added.

"Although the strengths and weaknesses of various fuels

will have to be carefully weighed," he concluded. "This competition showed what can be done. I hope Detroit will take notice."

In 1966, Honda conducted the first tests of their Formula One car at Riverside, driven by Richie Ginther and Ronnie Bucknum. The car was hauled on a rented trailer from Honda in Gardena to the track.

Bus Driver Swings, Takes Hot Lap at Riverside's Raceway

RIVERSIDE, Calif. — Well, you haven't lived until you've taken a hot lap at the raceway here in a Greyhound bus. Some 50 motor sports correspondents can testify that it's quite a thrill.

The group were attending a demonstration of new Shelby competition cars at the track, and part of the program called for an orientation tour of the famous circuit. Pete Brock was along as guide, and was giving a running description of the course on the bus PA system.

"We're approaching turn 7," said Pete, "and right about here, you want to complete your braking, shift down, and get set for the hard left-hander just over the crest of the hill."

Everyone was paying rapt attention, except the bus driver, who apparently thought Pete was kidding. It felt like the bus was airborne over the rise, and 50 right feet jammed down on 50 nonexistent brake pedals, as a great cry went up to "cool it!!!"

Well, the driver made it — to everyone's amazement — and the color of 50 white faces gradually returned to normal. Later, the driver remarked, "that was fun," but nobody seemed ready to agree with him.

Driving Schools

John Morton: *In 1962, I drove out from Waukegan, Illinois to attend Shelby's school. The school car was CSX2000, the first Cobra built. Got there a week early; Pete Brock, the instructor, said, "What are you doing here, stick around ?" What a week !! Reventlow was testing a rear engine Scarab, went to lunch with him and Brock. Shelby came out to test a Cobra with Bill Krause. Asked him for a job - then worked at Shelby's for three years !!*

Jim Russell's British School of Motor Racing

Bob Butte: *"I moved with the Jim Russell School from Mont Tremblant to Riverside to run the west coast branch of the school and ran it until 1988. We wanted to use Riverside but due to Les Richter's substantial vehicle testing programs, we couldn't get enough track time and shifted our operation to nearby Ontario Motor Speedway. Les seemed to have connections there also. Space and time became available in 1980 and we moved across town to Riverside. A Separate story – Les Richter housed us in this shaky A-frame. The story behind it; apparently it was being trucked somewhere, wouldn't fit under the Highway 60 bridge so Les bought it and made it our office – No AC, no heat etc."*

BEHIND THE WHEEL — Actress Cybill Shepherd adjusts her helmet while listening to instructor Jacques Couture at Jim Russell's British School of Racing at Riverside International Raceway. Ms. Shepherd said her three-day course improved her driving skills.

Students of British School of Motor Racing at Riverside work their way through a turn.

This School a Blacktop Jungle

By JOHN SCHEIBE, *Times Staff Writer*

Mark Mitchell of Beverly Hills is a tow-truck driver who dreams of the day he can drive a different kind of vehicle professionally.

Mitchell is a product of a race-driving school that helps promising pupils try to become pro drivers by (1) teaching them an expert's skills and (2) loaning them a car and equipment and (3) putting them on an amateur circuit that ends with a series offering $30,000 in prizes.

Mitchell, 22, hooked up with the British School of Motor Racing at Riverside Raceway after competing in clandestine late-night competition along Mulholland Drive, which winds along the top of the Santa Monica Mountains.

"I used to race my Camaro Z-28 and Pontiac Trans Am up there every night," he said. "It gave me a lot of experience at handling corners and prepared me for a lot of the maneuvers taught at the school.

"I started with a Mercury Cougar. It was nice to look at, but it was all potatoes and no meat. The cops caught me all the time and I got cited for speeding or something illegal, like no bumpers.

"Then I got my Camaro and they couldn't catch me. Of course, I had 300 more horsepower than those black-and-whites, so they just sat back and watched. But I needed to go a step further, so I signed up for the school."

★

Jacques Couture, a former Canadian national champion who has raced formula cars, sports cars and Can-Am racers, is the instructor at BSMR, which opened at Ontario Motor Speedway in 1977 and moved to Riverside in January after the Ontario Speedway closed.

Couture has started other schools at Le Circuit

Aspiring Drivers Learn About Racing by Readin', Writin' and Shiftin' Gears

St. Jovite, Quebec; Bridgehampton on Long Island, and Laguna Seca near Monterey.

On a recent morning at Riverside, Couture stood at the top of Turn 6 and watched seven drivers take their cars one at a time through the turn and accelerate down a hill to Turn 7.

"Some of our students have the attitude that they are quite familiar with race cars and need only a few pointers to help them become another Emerson Fittipaldi or Gilles Villeneuve," said Couture.

"Others are almost frightened to get behind the wheel of a Formula car. Our first step is to get everyone in a car right away so they can decide that the car is not all that complicated after all, or that perhaps there is more to racing than they first realized."

Couture, who was a senior instructor for the Canadian Automobile Sports Clubs' Quebec Region and a student at the Taruffi School in Italy, has modeled his schools after the Jim Russell Racing School at Snetterton Circuit in Great Britain.

Russell's school is one of the oldest and most successful in England.

"The most important function is when we sit down with the driver and talk things over," Couture said. "I find that my students learn very quickly how to develop a relationship with the car, and when we mention weight transfer

Please see SCHOOL, Page 16

Mark Mitchell: *"I was a Mulholland racer, totally illegal and dangerous. Some of the guys were crazy; some went on to real racing. I went to three day Russell school, liked it, did well and went to work for them as a mechanic, which meant I got to drive for free. Lived in a nearby fleabag motel with some other guys and managed to win the BSMR Ford Festival. Manager Bob Butte must've liked me, promoted me to any of the press guys who turned up as "tow truck driver who wanted to be a racer".* **Compiler's Note** – Mark went on to a successful career in the Escort and Firehawk series and is still competing today in a variety of endurance races.

The British School of Motor Racing often invited journalists and celebrities to attend the school as a promotion. Doug Stokes claimed he won the press and journalists race at the school and is seen here giving advice to Chips TV show star Larry Wilcox.

Racing cars attract actress wanting to 'improve driving'

RIVERSIDE (AP) — You're not likely to see a grimy-faced Cybill Shepherd take the checkered flag at next year's Riverside 500 automobile race, but racing actor Paul Newman might want to keep an eye on his rearview mirror for the newest entry on the celebrity-driver circuit.

Miss Shepherd, 33, took the first step toward big-time car-jockeying recently when she completed a three-day course in formula race driving at Jim Russell's British School of Motor Racing at Riverside International Raceway.

In completing the $950 course on Riverside's twisting, 2.6-mile Grand Prix-style raceway, Miss Shepherd joined the ranks of such celebrity drivers as actor Burt Reynolds, San Francisco 49ers quarterback Joe Montana and 49ers linebacker Jack Reynolds, said Bob Butte, the school's managing director.

And although she admitted that she's always been interested in cars, Miss Shepherd said Wednesday that the main benefit of the course was that it improved her overall driving ability.

"It makes you a much better driver on the streets," said the star of such films as "The Last Picture Show," "Taxi Driver" and "The Lady Vanishes."

Getting a start in racing is thorny task for woman

By TRACY DODDS
The Los Angeles Times

RIVERSIDE. — On a weekday morning, the only cars on the track at Riverside Raceway are the little Formula Fords of the Jim Russell British School of Motor Racing. The only mechanics in the pit and garage areas are the young mechanics who work for the school, maintaining the cars used for the weekday classes and the more powerful Formula Russells used for weekend racing. Which is to say, it's not a real glamorous setting. Just a lot of noisy engines, grease and dust. Literally the nuts and bolts of racing, attractive only to the hard-core engine enthusiast.

No star drivers swaggering around in fireproof racing suits. No fans, no groupies. No TV cameras.

Except for a couple of instructors and head mechanics, the people in and around the Jim Russell School garage are amateurs. Young hopefuls.

The mechanics are learning on the job, trading their labor for their training and for — the big incentive — racing time.

How many times has Kenny Cesare engineered the program? Well, at least once a week. Every time a new group of students arrives. Not that it was her job to explain the program. Her job was to...

...becoming another of the few pioneers in the world of racing.

Nobody said it would be easy. In fact, Bob Bulle, who runs the school at Riverside, tried and tried to talk her out of it. But she insisted that she could stick it out in the program, which runs from March to November, because she was that serious about getting in those 11 races.

"I was hesitant at first," Bulle said. "I could envision all sorts of problems. I think there were a couple of little personality problems along the way with a couple of the guys.... But it worked out. She worked as hard as anybody did and she stuck it out."

Toward the end of the program, they made her an assistant instructor and put her in charge of parts, and she seemed more comfortable than she had been in the garage. "She started to realize that she didn't have much of an aptitude for mechanics," Bulle said. "But then, a lot of men don't have a lot of aptitude for mechanics. A lot of drivers don't. She was learning. In fact, she couldn't have handled the parts job if she hadn't known what she was doing with the cars."

It was important to Cesare that she learn about the workings of a race car.

"Of course my goal is to get some good sponsorship so that I can go race..."

...for a woman to suddenly take on that lifestyle.

"It was a big decision to do this," Cesare said. "I've made some sacrifices. It was a big change in my life, and there was no going back. I had just gone through a divorce and I felt like I wanted to start over. I had always wanted to move to California, and since I had been going racing with friends, I knew I'd love racing. But I didn't really have the money to finance my own racing.

"To come out here I sold everything I owned in Florida. Everything. I've been living off that for months. It's just about gone."

Now she is looking for sponsorship for her racing, or for a racing-related job that will allow her to keep at it.

Cesare is attractive enough and personable enough to be an asset to any number of racing organizations, especially given her knowledge of the business. She is hoping that this, along with her driving ability, will start to pay off soon. As she says: "Racing is a business, and it's a lot like the advertising business. Sponsors need someone who can represent their product well, who can get them exposure, and who can do it tastefully. I think I will get the sponsorship if I can just make the right contacts."

She has even ordered a pink driving...

Raceway Amateurs Have Lots of Guts, No Glory

By PAUL DEAN, *Times Staff Writer*

RIVERSIDE— These drivers race with the smell of the greasepaint . . . , yet far from the roar of the crowds. Their cars are rented. Each fee includes mechanics, gas, maintenance, tires, pit crew, course marshals, soft advice, hard criticism, and ambulance and towing services as required.

And the grandstands always are deserted when the 10 Formula Fords, flattened down, flat out and reaching beyond 120 m.p.h., scram past the pits.

No Champagne Shampoos

For losers, there's no consolation of appreciative fans wishing better luck next time. Win and there are no champagne shampoos or publicity kisses from Miss Anywhere Grand Prix.

There is the tradition of a victory lap to the quickest driver, but the checkered flag he carries isn't much more than black-and-white shreds taped around a stick and the circuit is empty, silent, lonely and out of context for any racing man's moment of glory.

"But that doesn't matter because I do this (race) for me," explained Charles Wilson, here from Charlotte, N.C. He's 44 and single, financially satisfied, a former Air Force pilot, and his wedding-white Simpson driving suit is fresh out of the box because this is Wilson's first race weekend. "All the audience I want is in the car. So what if there's nobody to see me win? I'll know I've won and the people I've raced against will know I've won."

Wilson's expression is common to this high-speed playground that on other, fully public weekends is recognized as Riverside International Raceway.

But on these Fantasy Island weekends, on the Saturdays and Sundays and midweek warmup days when the 2.7-mile track is closed for private parties of the Jim Russell British School of Motor Racing (BSMR) . . . .

An attorney finishes a 10-lap practice session, wriggles out of his car and heads for the public telephones near Gasoline Alley. It is time to demonstrate concern for a client. After all, the man is on trial for rape and the jury could return to the courtroom anytime.

He Isn't Satisfied

A television producer frets about a different time slot. One minute and 48 seconds isn't exactly dawdling around the nine-turn track. But where is he slowing? Is he at full throttle coming off the banking and leaving turn nine? He clearly isn't satisfied with an average lap speed of 90 m.p.h., even if that does translate to more than 110 m.p.h. through Riverside's wriggling esses.

An investment counselor says he has organized his entire business year so he can drive BSMR's annual schedule of private racing spread over 32 weekends and four tracks in two countries. Caught with his realities down, a 29-year-old liquor-store owner from San Francis-

Please see DRIVERS, Page 20

Racer takes time for moment of contemplation before start of race.

For the Thrill of the Moment or Dreaming of Indy

Driving School Teaches ABC's of Racing

By TRACY DODDS, *Times Staff Writer*

Within an hour of arriving at The Jim Russell British School of Motor Racing in the infield at Riverside International Raceway, the newcomers are wearing driving suits and helmets and learning their way around a short loop of track in Formula Ford race cars.

It's great fun.

The school keeps the classes small. There were nine in the group I was in. Three young guys were sure they

the school and can teach the first installment of how to brake in a straight line, turn the car and find the apex of a corner.

It was to Wolocatiuk that I confessed that I had never driven a car with a clutch, although someone did show me how when I was in high school. He was patient. He didn't even laugh.

On Tuesday morning we met Spenard, a former

December 1988 Ad - L.A. Times

Bob Butte: *"I had connected with Skip Barber and put together, with track manager Dan Greenwood, a school using a shortened version of the track. We ran a number of schools in 1989 and 1990, the very last, with bulldozers looming in the distance, in May 1990"*

Ray Crampton: *"A three day weekend school- I'm with Bob Swenson and our usual 15 Sports Renaults. We were finishing up after Saturday practice and had actually got out the chairs to watch the world go by before dinner. A guy with a Formula Ford had parked across from us in Turn Nie, yelling at his obviously volunteer crew about how to put the car in the trailer, lock stuff up, etc. The kicker was the trailer had no skin!! It was just the steel frame on basically a flat trailer. Shouting about putting the car in forwards, and do this this way, and don't do this, the driver was a real asset. Bob waited till that whole group left, then walked over to the skeleton of a trailer, picked the lock, and motioned us over. We opened the door and rolled the car out and rolled it back in backwards, and relocked the door. We went to dinner, raced all day Sunday, knowing this driver wouldn't be back until Monday for the driver school. Monday comes, we are absorbed getting ready for our first session, and the crew shows up. They are all scratching their heads about how the car had reversed itself. Then their driver arrives, screaming about how stupid the crew is, " I gave you instructions on how I wanted the car loaded, etc". Two of his crew left in disgust, leaving the driver and his wife and one lone crew man to continue to receive the verbal abuse. We had to go hide on the backside of the PBS semi trailer we were laughing so hard. I don't think the driver even finished the school that day, and left early, skinless trailer and all."*

The lines weren't long at the Giant Country Spring Festival in Riverside

Staff photo by Juan Garcia

'Giant' country festival was good but not a giant

By MARK LUNDAHL
Special to the Sun-Telegram
RIVERSIDE — Big things...

Though it does not hit the universal chord that "Shove It" did, "Stick It" is finally come into her own...

...the past as Loretta Lynne's little sister, Crystal has were very ordinary and lackluster...

...plause, but often her songs Gayle was worthy of her acclaim, but when she...

Gilley prodded the best dancing action of the day with his motivated blend of...

BOB HARRINGTON
Chaplain of Bourbon Street
New Orleans

CRUSADE
8 NIGHTS

Beginning
SUNDAY, SEPT. 16
thru
SUNDAY SEPT. 23

7:30 p.m.
nightly

National TV Appearances
with
Merv Griffin • Art Linkletter
Hee Haw • Phil Donahue
Rex Humbard • Jerry Falwell

*Bob Harrington
has his own syndicated
TV Program
has written 4 books
and has recorded
14 albums — including
1 gold record.*

Riverside International Raceway
Turn six

FREE ADMISSION
AND PARKING
9,000 Seats

For Further Information

JACK PRICE
Crusade
Music Director

Invites
Local Christian
Talent
to join in our
600 voice
choir.

CALL
The Harrington Crusade
Riverside Office
TELEPHONE
682-2144

Riverside Bike Races

By RYAN REES
Sun-Telegram Motor Sports Writer

Riverside Raceway is going to the dogs. But not in the normal sense of that statement. Riverside Raceway is hosting the Sportsman Racing Assn. scrambler bike riders this Sunday in a special one-day racing program.

Featured rider for the day will be "Cookie", a 5-year-old mutt who rides in these rough and tumble affairs.

"Cookie" was featured in a short segment of Bruce Brown's "On Any Sunday". The canny canine rides on a special seat built just behind the handle bars and in front of his master, Jack McGowan of Los Angeles.

The odd couple have been competing together the past two years and are great favorites of the cross country racing fans.

Sunday's program at Riverside will be on the asphalt track and dirt. The bikes will start from the normal pit area but then go through the esses out in the dirt. They will cut across turn six at the top of the track and go straight for turn eight where they will leave the road course and take off into the bushes behind the track. The course will tie back in at eight and use the long back straight before taking off into the dirt inside turn nine.

Races for Novice, Beginners

The racing program is open mainly to novice and beginner riders of the association. Racing gets underway at 8:30 with the first of seven races for various bike classes and rider divisions.

Entry fee is $7 for the riders who may sign up Saturday or Sunday morning before the racing begins.

General admission is $2.50 with children under 12 free. All grandstands are open and will be in good positions for viewing most of the track.

There will be a special two-hour practice session Saturday from 3-5 p.m.

"Cookie" doesn't need much practice. He rode with McGown two weeks ago in a 170-mile race from Indio to Parker, Ariz. and was ready for more at the finish.

Air Circus to be held at Riverside raceway

The first annual Memorial Day Air Circus, a two-day carnival of aerobatic acts, will be held May 30-31 at Riverside International Raceway, Raceway President Les Richter announced.

Riverside Raceway, one of the best known automobile racing facilities in the world,

Helms names two girls for honors

LOS ANGELES (UPI)—Two young Southern California girls who participated in the 1968 Olympics were named today by the Helms Athletic Foundation as co-athletes of the month for April for prowess in swimming and gymnastics.

Susie Atwood, 17, a Millikan High School student, won eight individual swimming events in the National AAU and International events during April and set a new American 100-yard backstroke record.

Cathy Rigby, 18, of Los Alamitos, who became America's first gold medal winner in international gymnastics competition, won four medals in Africa last month and took the

will be turned over Memorial Day weekend to World Air Shows, Inc., which will conduct the first major air show in Southern California this year.

Identical three-hour, 17-act shows will be performed both Sunday and Monday, May 30-31, beginning at noon. Among the performers will be Art Scholl, America's top aerobatic pilot, Mira Slovak and para-kite pilot Carolyn Salisbury.

Other acts include a skydiving demonstration by the U.S. Free Fall Exhibition Team, stuntman John Kazian who performs from the wing of Joe Hughes' Super Stearman airplane, gyrocopter pilot Ken Brock and Bill Bennett the Australian Birdman.

There will also be an antique plane fly-by and display, radio control model planes and hot air balloons.

The show will be conducted over the Raceway's 400-acre infield with spectator areas located at the north end of the track. Free grandstand seating for up to 8,000 spectators will also be available.

Admission each day is $3.50 per adult, $1.50 for persons under the age of 16 and children under six will be admitted free.

Riverside Raceway

Memorial Day air show set

Wingwalkers, open-cock-pit aerobatics and aerial clowns will recreate the barnstorming atmosphere of the early days of aviation Sunday and Monday in the Memorial Day Air Circus at Riverside International Raceway.

The show starting at noon both days is the first event scheduled by World Air Shows, a company formed by combining the talents of the two leading West Coast aerial extravaganza organizations, headed by Art Scholl and Gerry Curtis.

Besides veteran pilot-performer Scholl, the show features Mira Slovak, Czech refugee who became the world's first skyjacker by stealing a plane to escape the Iron Curtain 20 years ago, and Carolyn Salisbury, one of the world's top female aerobatic pilots.

Joe Hughes will do loops, stalls, figure eights and rolls with his highly-modified Stearman biplane, converted to an aerobatic machine by replacing its original 225 horsepower engine with a 650 horsepower supercharged engine.

The Stearman will also be the platform for John Kazian's wingwalking act.

A former circus trapeze artist, Kazian will perform many of his daring stunts without benefit of safety belt or braces.

Other acts include Roy Sprague and his portrayal of a tipsy pilot, Ken Brock's gyrocopter demonstration, Australian Birdman Bill Bennett, a sky-diving competition by the U.S. Free Fall Exhibition Team and an antique aircraft display and flyby.

Tickets for the 17 individual performances in each days show go on sale at the Raceway gate at 8 a.m. Sunday and Monday. Prices are $3.50 for adults, $1.50 for children six to 16 years of age, with children under six admitted free.

Riverside Raceway is located at the junction of Highways 60 and 395, eight miles east of Riverside.

Legislation killed

SACRAMENTO (P) — Legislation to extend the fair housing law to prevent discrimination in renting on basis of sex was killed by the Assembly Ways and Means Committee Wednesday.

In 1966, Sports Illustrated recruited Steve McQueen to test a variety of sports cars at Riverside - Read the entire article on the attached DVD

Doug Stokes: *"In what must have been one of the last events held at the track, I attended the Audi Quattro Performance Driving School in December, 1988. Much of the track had been removed and, on a terrible rainy day, I was the ONLY attendee. This was marketed to lifestyle writers rather than the racing crowd and I guess lifestyle people didn't go out in the rain. Instructors Kathy Rude and Ludwig Heimrath Jr. had a good time showing me the driving techniques required in a Quattro in the rain"*

AP LaserPhoto

"That poor thing just crumbled," said track employee Betze Snead as the Goodyear Tower came down.

Mall leaves Riverside race tower in the dust

MORENO VALLEY (AP) — The big blue observation tower at Riverside International Raceway has fallen for the last time as the track is torn down to make way for a new shopping mall.

The 72-foot steel and glass structure originally was built in 1951 as the traffic control tower at Los Angeles International Airport. A decade later, it was dismantled and trucked in sections 70 miles to the raceway, where it was reassembled.

From the top of the tower, track officials spent more than 25 years gazing down on every conceivable type of racing, from go-carts to international grand prix events to NASCAR stock cars.

Then suburban sprawl took the lead in this fast-growing community and on Tuesday, the tower fell a second time, crumbling in a heap as a wrecker pulled it down to make way for the Moreno Valley Mall at TownGate.

By afternoon, workmen were cutting sections of the tower with blowtorches to be sold for scrap metal.

Some who watched the tower's plunge were moved to tears.

"That poor thing just crumbled," said 24-year track employee Betze Snead as the structure, known as the "Goodyear Tower," slammed into the ground.

"That's sad. It makes me feel bad. I didn't think it would bother me but it has," Snead said.

"There will be a lot of history lost," said Les Richter, a former Los Angeles Rams offensive lineman and linebacker who took over track operations in 1962 and bought the tower for $1.

"It was something that made Riverside a famous racing facility. It was an identifying spot at the track. It was a landmark known throughout the world," Richter said.

Chapter Fifteen - The Actual Legends of Riverside

One of the greatest gatherings in Riverside Raceway history; with drivers from 1958 (Bill Krause, George Keck, Pete Lovely, Bruce Kessler, Bob Bondurant, Dick Guldstrand, Davey Jordan, Scooter Patrick, Tommy Meehan, Ralph Ormsbee, Carroll Shelby, Parnelli Jones and Dan Gurney) to 1988 (Rick Knoop, Bobby Allison, Herschel McGriff, Elliott Forbes Robinson and John Morton) and hundreds in between. Don't know who these people are ? Google them; they are the creators of California motorsport !!

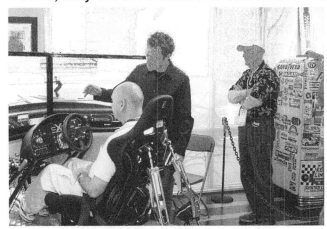

George Follmer, being instructed by Chris Considine, while EFR watches

Scooter Patrick, Doug Stokes, Tommy Meehan and Ralph Ormsbee

Doug Stokes and Lew Spencer

Mike Savin and Bill Peacock

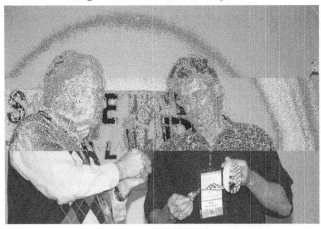

Doug Stokes and Bob Kovaleski

Ginny Dixon and Doug Stokes

Bobby Allison and George Follmer

Bruce Flanders and Bob Bondurant

Bruce Kessler

Davey Jordan and Chet Knox

Lew Spencer and John Wilson

Dean Case, Dusty Brandel and Friends

Albert Wong and Dave Friedman

Richard Medoff and Alice Hanks

Tim Considine, Doug Stokes and Dave Wolin

Bruce Kessler, Tim Considine and Dave Wolin

Joe Playan, Pete Brock, Andy Porterfield, Tony Settember and Dave Wolin

Paula Murphy, Mary Davis, Carroll Shelby and Ginny Sims

Dave Wolin and Arlene Sidaris

Bret Ginther and Pete Lyons

Joe Aves, Bondurant and Arthur Newman

Bobby Allison and Bill Losee

Bobby Unser, Hia Sweet and Ed Justice Jr.

Bob Schilling, John Morton and Scooter

Bob Schilling

Sherry MacDonald

Bruce Flanders

Bob Tronolone

Denise McLuggage and Dave Nicholas

Ormsbee, Keck and Meehan

Dick Guldstrand, Bret Lunger and EFR

Casey Annis, Damon and Alma Hill

Gayle and Pete Brock, EFR and A2Z

Dick Guldstrand, Chic and Chris Vandegriff

Parnelli Jones and Dan Gurney

Dusty Brandel, Mary McGee and Bobbie Colgrove

Jerry Entin and Jim Dittemore

Gary Gove

Casey Annis, EFR and Bret Ginther

Tim Considine and John Dixon

Linda Vaughn and Rick Knoop

Bob Bondurant and Dan Gurney

Arthur Newman

Dave Wolin

Danny McKeever

Jerry Entin

John Wilson, Allen Kuhn, Dave Friedman and Jim Gessner

Bill Losee, Hia Sweet, Dick Woodland and Bobby Unser

Peter Bryant and Jane Wolin

Dave Wolin and Bob Bondurant

Wolin, Stokes and Considine

Vince Howlett and Jerry Entin

Toly Arutunoff and EFR

Alice Hanks and Hila Sweet

Scooter Patrick

Davey Jordan

Howden Ganley

Lothar Motschenbacher

Doug Stokes, Howden Ganley,
Allen Grant and Eric Haga

Dick Guldstrand, Davey Jordan
and John Morton

Jerry Grant and Parnelli Jones

Fitzpatrick, Grant and Follmer

Howden Ganley and John Fitzpatrick

EFR and Jim Jeffords

Jim Jeffords, Lothar Motschenbacher and Tony Adamowicz

Joe Playan, Pete Brock, Andy Porterfield, Tony Settember and Dave Wolin

Tony Settember and Scooter Patrick

Rod Campbell

Oscar Kovaleski and Michael Lynch

Frank Lance, Remington and Ike Smith

Carroll Shelby and Parnelli Jones

Sherry MacDonald and Bob Bondurant

Parnelli and Linda

Dick Guldstrand and Bill Krause

Rick Knoop, Linda Vaughn and John Morton

Dan Gurney and Bobby Allison

John Morton and Jerry Grant

Doug Stokes and Chuck Jones

Gary Schroeder and Phil Remington

Jerry Grant, Eric Haga and A2Z

John Morton and George Keck

Pete Lyons and George Follmer

Jane Wolin and Oscar Kovaleski

Doug Magnon and Dick Messer

Oscar Kovaleski and Michael Lynch

Carroll Shelby

**Harvey Lassiter and
Tony Adamowicz**

**Philippe DeLespinay
and Reeves Callaway**

Chapter Sixteen - The End

Everything came to an end in 1989. The last race, an SCCA regional, took place in July (There were a number of last races as the track was being fug up but paving a section from turn seven across to the back straight kept things going

Linda Haneline provided this photo of the workers at the last race

Closing Of Riverside Evokes Memories Of Fabled Track

RIVERSIDE, Calif. — No matter who wins today's Budweiser 400, it'll always be remembered as the date they closed ol' Riverside Raceway down.

After the NASCAR Winston Cup Series stock car race is completed at about 7 p.m., no more major events are scheduled on the 2.62-mile road course that dates to the mid-1950s.

Only an off-road scramble remains to be run in August. Then, the bulldozers that already are plowing up the desert terrain along the track's backstretch will move onto the 700 acres of speedway property.

Riverside Raceway eventually will be no more, in time becoming only a blur of a memory buried beneath the condos and office parks of a fast-growing new city called Moreno Valley.

Here are some comments and facts about the track:

Motorsports

Tom Higgins

• Les Richter, now a powerful NASCAR vice president, was president of Riverside Raceway for many years. He helped buy the facility for a group of owners that included comedian Bob Hope in 1959.

"I'll never forget the first time I saw the place," said Richter, then an all-pro linebacker for the Los Angeles Rams. "It was just a strip of asphalt twisting over hilly desert. There were rattlesnakes, coyotes, owls and no telling what else around.

"It took us a while to get started, to be taken seriously. . . . I think that what really enabled the track to take off is when NASCAR's Wood Brothers, Glen and Leonard, came out and Dan Gurney, probably the most respected driver in America at the time, drove their Fords to three 500-mile victories in 1964, '65, and '66. Parnelli Jones won in '67 and Gurney again in '68 to give the Wood boys five straight."

Richter laughed.

"I'd say more types of vehicles and more drivers have raced here than any track in the world," he continued. "The list includes Winston Cup, USAC, CART, Formula One, World Endurance, IMSA, SCCA, Winston West, the Southwest Tour, dragsters, motorcycles, go-karts and off-road machines.

"The place has been the site of dozens of movies and commercials. Also automotive tests."

Richter's most humorous recollection involved one of the tests.

"Ford was matching its pickups against Chevrolet and Dodge," he said. "They were going to run 67,000 miles consecutively in 1967. Naturally, this was boring to the drivers, especially on the night shifts.

"Topless dancing had just come in then. So we had this idea. We hired two or three of these strippers and stationed them around the track. They'd suddenly appear, naked, making like they were hitchhiking. Then they'd dart into the darkness. The trucks were equipped with radios, and you can imagine the conversation and hooting that went on when some driver claimed he'd seen a nude woman beside the track."

Richter's most touching memory?

"It happened in '69," he said. "Al Dean, Sr., a great backer of Indy-car racing, was dying. His last wish was to see his car, with Mario Andretti driving, win the championship.

"We parked him in an ambulance in Turn 9. He was attended by doctors and nurses. Mario came through for him."

• Riverside Raceway always will be revered by today's pole-sitter, Ricky Rudd, Bill Elliott and Tim Richmond. The track gave them their first Winston Cup victories. . . . It will also be remembered as the last place that colorful little Joe Weatherly ever raced. Weatherly, the Winston Cup champion, was killed in a Turn 9 crash in 1964. A Riverside wreck also took the life of Winston West rookie Tim Williamson in 1981. . . . Among others to die in accidents at the track was Rolf Stommelen, the German road racer, killed in an International Motor Sports Association event.

• Perhaps no driver feels more strongly about the closing of Riverside than Darrell Waltrip.

He clinched all three of his Winston Cup titles at the track. He has won five times at Riverside.

Said Waltrip:

"I'm going to miss coming here. We're losing a track with a lot of tradition. It's like it should be on the national register as a historic place they can't tear up. . . ."

Riverside: Cut down in its prime

By NATE RYAN
Sun Sports Writer

The way Les Richter sees it, the demise of Riverside International Raceway wasn't so much a case of bad timing as bad luck.

While Ontario Motor Speedway closed because it couldn't draw big crowds in the days before motor racing boomed, Riverside was shut down in 1988, when NASCAR was on the verge of entering its golden age.

Unfortunately, Southern California's real estate market also was hitting its stride, and the Riverside track had the unfortunate distinction of being owned by Fritz Duda, a developer. Duda sold the track, which was razed to make room for a shopping mall.

Richter, the president of RIR from 1963-83, believes the road course was cut down in its prime.

"The person who owned Riverside felt that his property had a higher value as a mall," said Richter, now executive vice president of the California Speedway in Fontana. "I don't know if he'd agree with that now."

Many NASCAR drivers still on the circuit agree with Richter that Riverside's twisting and turning road course had become one of the favorites on the circuit.

"It broke my heart when they closed Riverside," 18-year Winston Cup veteran Geoff Bodine said during a test session at the California Speedway. "It used to be the perfect road course for racing."

Said 30-year Winston Cup veteran Dave Marcis: "I always enjoyed Riverside. We had a lot of race fans out here, and they always seemed to have sellout crowds."

And it had a long time to develop that reputation. Unlike OMS, which flamed out after 10 years, Riverside had a rich history. Home to some of the biggest names in racing dating back to the '50s, RIR opened with a sportscar race on Sept. 21, 1957 and played host to its first NASCAR race the following year.

During the 31 years that followed, RIR's diverse racing schedule drew drivers from nearly every racing discipline — from off-road to Indy Car to NASCAR to Formula One. A partial list of drivers who took on Riverside reads like a who's who in motor racing:

SUN PHOTO

Riverside International Raceway, a twisting, eight-turn road course, was open for 31 years. It closed in 1988 to make room for a shopping mall.

Jimmy Clark, Jackie Stewart, Parnelli Jones, Dan Gurney, Kyle Petty, A.J. Foyt, Darrell Waltrip.

Even a brash young driver named Roger Penske captured the Riverside Grand Prix in 1963, defeating such luminaries as Jones and Gurney.

Penske, of course, built the California Speedway, the track that will bring NASCAR back to Southern California.

The last Winston Cup race at Riverside took place before a record crowd of more than 75,000 on June 13, 1988, when Rusty Wallace won the Budweiser 400.

"I'm sorry to see this track go," Wallace said after holding off Terry Labonte, Ricky Rudd and Dale Earnhardt. "It's a happy time down here."

AutoWeek

July 25, 1988
$1.25 USA $1.75 Canada

RIVERSIDE REQUIEM

The west's best racetrack fades into the sunset

Read Pete Lyon's Article in Autoweek on the Attached DVD

490

Bibliography and Info

And for more racing history about some of the people mentioned in the book, we recommend these - Most can be bought at Autobooks in Burbank - www.autobooks-aerobooks.com or on Amazon:

David Hobbs • Brian Redman • Howden Ganley • Parnelli Jones

Toly Arutunoff • George Follmer • Jackie Stewart • Carroll Shelby

Hurley Haywood • Bruce McLaren • Peter Bryant • Bill Pollack

John Morton • John Fitzpatrick • Jim Clark • Dan Gurney

John Zimmerman • Linda Vaughn • Sam Posey • A.J. Foyt

Photo Credits: Will Edgar, Pete Lyons, Frank Sheffield, Tam McPartland, Dave Friedman, Getty Images, Bob D'Olivo, Brent Martin, Martin Hill, Pat Brollier, Bob Tronolone, Woodand Ato Display, Abert Wong, Henry Ford Museum, Petersen Museum, IMMRC, Michael Keyser, Allen Kuhn, Kurt Oblinger and Don Hodgdon among others,

On The DVD

Video Interviews

Dan Gurney	Dick Guldstrand	Sam Hanks	Phil Hill
Davey Jordan	Bruce Kessler	Ruth Levy	Jack McAfee
John Morton	Bill Murphy	Warren Olsen	Joe Playan
Bill Pollack	Carroll Shelby	Cy Yedor	Bill Watkins

Racing Movies

Sound of Speed

The Racing Scene

Racing Videos

1957 Sports Car Races	1960 Lap of Riverside
1962 Grand Prix for Sportscars	1963 Times Grand Prix
1964 Champion Spark Plug Commercial	1964 Times Grand Prix
1965 Can Am	1966 Compilation
1968 Rex Mays 300	1971 Hobbs Can Am
1984 IMSA Times Grand Prix	1985 Onboard With Jim Busby
1985 IMSA Times Grand Prix	1986 IMSA Times Grand Prix
	1988 Riverside History

Made in the USA
Las Vegas, NV
01 March 2025

18902835R00273